THE COMPLETE GUIDE to
HOME
INSPECTION

ROGER C. ROBINSON & MICHAEL LITCHFIELD

The Taunton Press

The Taunton Press, Inc.
63 South Main Street
PO Box 5506
Newtown, CT 06470-5506
e-mail: tp@taunton.com

Editor: CHRISTINA GLENNON
Technical Editors: SCOTT GIBSON, GLENN MATHEWSON, DOUGLAS HANSEN
Copy editor: CANDACE B. LEVY
Indexer: JAY KREIDER
Cover & interior design: CAROL SINGER | NOTICE DESIGN
Layout: CAROL SINGER | NOTICE DESIGN
Illustrator: VINCENT BABAK
Photographer: ROGER ROBINSON except where noted

The following names/manufacturers appearing in *The Complete Guide to Home Inspection* are trademarks
Basement Systems®, Benjamin Moore®, B-I-N®, Cedar Breather®, COPALUM®, Corian®, Dumpster®,
DuPont®, eBay®, Fujitsu®, GLULAM®, Google™, HardieShingle®, International Residential Code®, LeadCheck®,
Medex®, Medite®II, National Electrical Code®, Natura®, NFPA 70E®, Phillips®, Q-LON®, R-Wrap®, Safecoat®,
Sheetrock®, SierraPine™, Simpson®, Strong-Tie®, Stylistio®, Surveymaster®, The Nest®, Transite™, Tyvek®,
Vycor®, Watco®, Watts®, Wi-Fi®, Windows®

Library of Congress Cataloging-in-Publication Data
Litchfield, Michael W.
  The complete guide to home inspection / Michael Litchfield and Roger C. Robinson.
      pages cm
  Includes index.
  ISBN 978-1-62710-480-7
  1. Dwellings--Inspection--Handbooks, manuals, etc. I. Robinson, Roger (Roger C.) II. Title.
  TH4817.5.L58 2015
  643'.12--dc23
                    2014047561

Printed in the United States of America
10 9 8 7 6 5 4 3 2 1

ACKNOWLEDGMENTS

Shortly before this book went into production in fall 2014 its principal author, Roger Robinson, passed away, so it falls to me as his co-author to say a few words about him.

By any measure, Roger was an amazing man. For starters, he inspected both residential and commercial properties in the San Francisco Bay Area for more than 35 years, and once estimated that he had personally inspected six or seven thousand homes. As Roger was 6 ft. 5 in., just entering all those crawl spaces and cramped attics boggles the mind. And he was famous for the care he took with every inspection.

His reach extended far. He trained many prominent Bay Area home inspectors and held classes and seminars nationwide and in Canada. The consummate pro, he helped found several professional chapters for CREIA (California Real Estate Inspection Association) and ASHI (American Society of Home Inspectors) and over the years he was president of CREIA and served on national and state committees to raise inspection standards. Roger's many awards include the Monahan Award (the highest national award) and the John Daly Award (the highest state award).

Roger was a lucid writer and one of the most persistent photographers I've ever met. He hauled his lanky frame and his cameras pretty much everywhere and managed to get shots in some of the darkest, dankest places on earth. He wrote many training manuals and articles for home inspectors, and he and I first collaborated on *House Check: Finding and Fixing Common House Problems* (Taunton Press, 2003).

His friends will remember him best as a warm, generous, kind soul who would go to any length to ease your load or share his knowledge. We may be the poorer for his passing, but we are immensely richer for his having lived—and lived so well.

Roger's generosity and passion for detail are echoed by the many talented people who helped create this book, several of whom Roger trained. Thanks to Brian Cogley, who is depicted in the book's introduction; to Douglas Hansen, who knew Roger for 35 years and is a co-author of the widely praised *Code Check* series; to the Bay Area members of ASHI, who were helpful in many ways; to Scott Gibson and Glenn Mathewson for closely reading and improving the manuscript; and to Christina Glennon, Peter Chapman, and all the Taunton Press crew for working so hard to achieve excellence.

Roger would be proud of all of you.

Mike Litchfield
Point Reyes, California

CONTENTS

INTRODUCTION

PEOPLE INTERESTED IN BUYING A HOUSE have always wanted to take a good look at it first, the same way that someone buying a horse would look at its teeth. It's just not wise to buy blind. Likewise, someone selling a house would naturally wonder what it was really worth. So in the old days, a seller might ask a trusted friend who knew houses—a master builder—to have a look and fix, or at least report on, what needed fixing. That done, one side or the other would suggest a price and there would be a bit of back and forth—horse trading—till finally they agreed on the terms and shook on the deal.

Times have changed, but that's still basically how it's done. There's much more pressure now, of course. Houses have gotten quite pricey, and especially when the housing market is hot, transactions have become complex and fast paced. Now there are real estate agents and mortgage brokers and title companies. But in the middle are still two parties trying to come to an agreement. And somewhere at the heart of it all, poking around the attic or peering into a crawl space, is a home inspector trying to create an objective report about the house.

The Complete Guide to Home Inspection walks you through the inspection process in a logical, orderly way, from first impressions to final conclusions. To make this complex body of information about houses more accessible to readers, *The Complete Guide to Home Inspection* chapters present each house system in sequence, more or less in the order that a home inspector might examine it.

If you hope to buy a house, this book's information should give you a more realistic idea of what that house's ultimate cost will be, including repairs. If you are a seller, this information will help you figure what the house's true value is, what a realistic sales price would be, and what deficiencies should be fixed before putting a house on the market. Whether you are a buyer or a seller, *The Complete Guide to Home Inspection* will help demystify inspections and shed light on reports. If you are a building professional who is thinking about becoming a home inspector—many inspectors were builders first—this book will provide rich insights into the practice.

Last, *The Complete Guide to Home Inspection*'s principal author, Roger C. Robinson, has personally inspected thousands of houses, so his decades of experience will give you a feel for the close scrutiny and creative thinking that go into every comprehensive home inspection report.

A Home Inspection in Real Time

Before we explore the many systems of a house, let's follow the steps of an actual inspection. In the sequence to follow, veteran San Francisco Bay area home inspector Brian Cogley does a preinspection for a homeowner who is thinking of selling. What follows is not an inspection report but, rather, Brian's firsthand reactions to what he is seeing in his own words. Later, when he goes home, he'll compile his findings in a detailed inspection report that typically runs 30 or 40 pages.

STEP 1: DO A WALK-AROUND

"When I approach a house, I often have a gut feeling. Say, whether someone has lived there for 30 years or whether someone has just purchased the house and is trying to flip it. Sometimes if I go inside and see additional signs, I change my mind. Generally I'm right. But whatever my first impression is, facts are facts. And that's what I'm here to gather.

"You might assume this house's fresh paint means it's being flipped. Not so. Here, it's more of a sign that the housing market is hot and the long-time owner is working hard to get it on the market. I've been told the family has lived here for over 20 years. Fresh paint isn't always a red flag. What gets my attention is the debris that is scattered over the yard—old lumber, old insulation, paint cans, paint scrapings. Again, it's just a clue, not a conclusion, but debris like this suggests that the work is not being done by profes-

Start your inspection with a walk-around. Get the big picture. What's the lay of the land, the house's overall condition, the level of craftsmanship?

sionals. Pros would rent a Dumpster® first thing and probably clean up at the end of each day to keep the client happy.

"Note, too, the paint chips on the ground. Old house, so it's probably lead-based paint. Since 2010, contractors working on houses with lead-based paint have to follow certain work practices to limit dispersing contaminated materials.

"During the walk-around, I get a preview of the systems I'll investigate later.

"The foundation looks typical for a house this age on a relatively level lot. There's been some movement. That gap between the siding and the foundation—where the foundation has rotated—will be super visible when we go into the basement and the sun backlights it (see p. 6).

"There's a three-wire service entry, so the electrical service is delivering 120 volts/240 volts. Opening the door to the service panel, I see it is an outdated brand that's difficult to get replacement parts for, so it probably needs to be replaced.

"And I see a lot of nonstandard plumbing connections on the exterior. Again, that's common for older houses in the area, but it has me curious about what I'll find inside."

STEP 2: EXTERIOR

"Another thing you see with houses of this vintage in this area is horizontal redwood siding nailed directly to studs, meaning the siding is the sheathing. And, of course, no building paper behind it, which has its pros and cons. Air blows through it like a sieve, but it also dries any excess moisture so you rarely get rot in living-space walls.

"The basement and the foundation perimeter tell another story, especially if siding is too close to the soil. I'll know more when I go under the house, but you can see new paint along the bottom that's already starting to peel. The siding's probably wicking moisture.

"Up above, the eaves look worn. Some of the trim is splitting, and those beams that stick out beyond the roof line always get a lot of weather. They'll last

longer if you keep them painted or flashed. Houses built in the good old days were pretty good, but they weren't perfect."

STEP 3: ROOF

"I usually don't take notes on a roof. I would rather be paying attention to where I'm going and have my hands available in case something happens. You'll notice I'm wearing gloves because it's summertime and things can get hot, which you don't think about till you touch the roof from the ladder.

"The composition shingles on this roof show moderate wear. There are some mossy areas, a handful of exposed nail heads that need to be sealed or covered, and several rows of shingles spaced too far apart and overexposed to the weather. But the big news about this roof is its slope: It's too low for composition shingles. Built-up or modified bitumen roofing (see p. 62) would have been a better choice, especially on the roof section in front.

"That said, composition shingles on a low-slope roof better have all its details right. Which is not the case here. The shingles along its valleys are lifting and water can get under them. When you've got

In older houses, siding is frequently nailed directly to studs. Here, the siding is also too close to grade, which may mean rotted framing behind it.

If it's safe to get up on the roof, be sure to examine details that aren't visible from the ground, such as the louvered vent under this overhang.

Be sure to wear eye protection as you open an attic access hatch. If it hasn't been opened in a while, dust and debris may rain down on you.

center-cut valleys (see p. 66), you've got to offset overlapping shingles by a couple of inches so the cut line doesn't run down the middle of the valley. That wasn't done. Metal flashing runs on the outside of the roof edges rather than being overlapped by shingles above. So water will dam up. The gutters are shot and need to be replaced, and the downspouts empty too close to the foundation. Well, you get the idea.

"Faulty details like this probably account for the goop (mastic cement) that's smeared all over. Too much goop is always a sign that things aren't right, that there's a leak, or that shingles aren't staying down. That's the big picture. The roof sags, but that's normal in an older house with undersize rafters. When I'm in the attic I'll look for cracking rafters and leaks. Chances are, though, that the roof framing is still serviceable after a century, sags and all."

STEP 4: ATTIC

So what are you seeing up there?

"The usual. Old, outdated framing. No ridge board, but no broken rafters, either. Before they reroof, a contractor should check out the framing. Knob-and-tube wiring. Exposed electrical connections, which should be in a box. Blown-in fiberglass insulation. Some fiberglass batts. Bunch of newspapers, which

is a fire hazard. Unscreened attic vents, which will let all sorts of critters and insects in. Water stains, but it's not clear if they are active. This attic needs more ventilation, lots more ventilation."

STEP 5: FOUNDATION, BASEMENT, AND SUBSTRUCTURE

"Under the house is where the 'money stuff' is: drainage, foundation, HVAC, plumbing systems— big-ticket items. Over here is that gap above the foundation we saw outside (see the photo on p. 6 and on the facing page). That's the back of the siding, without a scrap of building paper in sight.

"A lot of times, when people see basements in older homes with tall ceilings, they think, 'Free living space, let's Sheetrock® it.' But you can't always do it. It's relatively dry in here now but there's no building paper (that is, no moisture barrier). If water gets behind the siding, there's plenty of air to dry it out. But if you 'rock the framing as it is, moisture will get trapped in the walls and soon you'll have a mold factory.

"Foundations this old rarely have steel in them. Adobe soil expands in the wet months and shallow foundations like this rise and fall with it. So you're going to have cracks. If you look back into the corner

Backlit by the sun, a gap between the siding and the mudsill is easy to see. Foundations of this vintage usually are not reinforced with steel.

The old service panel is a Zinsco, an outdated brand that's difficult to get replacement parts for. It should be replaced by a licensed electrician.

of the crawl space, which still has its original foundation, you see a big crack, an inch across. Plus, the foundation is obviously rotating and will need to be replaced. This lot doesn't slope much, but that corner is the high side. So chances are, surface water has collected there over the years and exerted pressure on the foundation.

"Originally, there were shallow footings and a crawl space under the whole house. Later, they dug out this section to create enough headroom for a laundry area and a place for the water heater. So this retaining wall between the crawl space and the laundry room is interesting. It's hard to say exactly how far down the concrete goes because the bottom half of the wall is parged with mortar. How do you put a retaining wall directly under an existing footing? Well, you usually can't in a situation like this. Or at least not without a lot of engineering and expense. So though this wall above feels solid (he raps the wall panel with his fist), a structural engineer needs to have a look."

STEP 6: ELECTRICAL

"The house is wired with three types of wiring: Romex®, flexible metal cable, and knob-and-tube wiring. Especially in attics and at ceiling-mounted fixtures, knob-and-tube's insulation becomes brittle and breaks down. So it's not surprising that a lot of insurers won't write you a policy if there's knob-and-tube still in use.

"This mixture of wiring types is pretty typical in older houses with electrical systems that haven't been overhauled. That and it's not uncommon to see a lot of extension cords because there aren't enough outlets. That's something that should be addressed because it's a fire hazard, not to mention very inconvenient.

"Grounding is the other big issue. In this house most of the receptacles are the three-hole type. But my tester showed that a number of them were not, in fact, grounded, so an electrician needs to examine and upgrade them. There are several GFCI-protected outlets but more need to be added, especially in the basement laundry area. Given the age and condition of the service panel, a housewide electrical upgrade would be a good idea soon."

This gas-fired water heater has several issues that need to be corrected, including a pad that leans, supply pipes that are not electrically bonded, and a flue pipe that slopes downward.

STEP 7: PLUMBING

"The plate on the 40-gal., gas-fired water heater gives an ANSI (American National Standards Institute) date of 2006. I usually add 2 years to give me a ballpark date of when it was installed. So this one was installed around 2008, which puts it at about half of its useful life. Nationally, water heaters average about 11 years. Out here we get about 15 years out of them because the water quality is good.

"This water heater has a number of issues, starting with a ½-in. water supply pipe that will restrict flow. The larger problem, though, is that the supply main (or house service main) leading to the building is ½-in.-dia. galvanized steel pipe. The minimum standard for modern construction is ¾-in. copper. So we've got undersize supply pipes throughout the house and water flow that has been further constricted by deposit buildup inside the galvanized pipe. When I tested the water pressure outside it was 70 psi, which is within a normal range. But with supply piping this small, you can bank on a significant drop in water flow when you open several faucets at the same time.

"Back to the water heater. It leans. A new pad would bring it to a vertical position. The water pipes above the water heater are not bonded for electrical safety (see p. 139). The flue pipe venting the unit slopes downward before it slopes up, which can leak flue gases and corrode the flue prematurely. The single-wall vent pipe is penetrating a wooden wall, which is a code violation. Single-wall vents need at least 6 in. clearance from combustibles. The tank has only one seismic strap, there should be two. There's a TPR (temperature and pressure relief) valve, but it uses flexible pipe for a discharge valve, which isn't allowed because it could obstruct the discharge flow.

"The waste piping consists of cast-iron, galvanized-steel, copper, and ABS piping. Pretty typical to have a little bit of everything in an older house. The old cast-iron pipes are rusty from previous leaks and should be replaced."

STEP 8: HEATING AND COOLING SYSTEM

"There's a gas-fired furnace in the subfloor area (crawl space). It has a fan-powered, induced-draft venting system that draws exhaust fumes through a heat exchanger for better efficiency. Furnaces like

This furnace did not respond to its controls and its heat exchanger was not accessible to visual inspection, so it should be examined by an HVAC specialist.

this are often called 'plus-80 systems' because their efficiency is typically rated at 80% or better. The data plate on the furnace indicates that the unit was manufactured in 2002, which means it's about half-way through its life.

"This furnace did not respond to its controls and its heat exchanger was not accessible to visual inspection (for cracks), so the furnace should be examined by an HVAC specialist and repaired as necessary to operate properly. This is a good recommendation for any type of heating/cooling system; they have become so complex and high-tech.

"Two other things I noticed. The service-disconnect fuse is too large for the rating listed on the unit; it should be replaced with a properly sized fuse. And the furnace has aluminum vent piping, which is not an approved gas appliance venting material. Most jurisdictions now require the use of double-wall, Type B vent piping, which is cooler, more efficient, and requires only 1-in. clearance to combustibles."

STEP 9: CHIMNEYS, FLUES, AND FIREPLACES

"This house doesn't have a masonry chimney. Whatever the material of a chimney or flue pipe, it must be intact to prevent superheated gases from escaping and setting fire to combustible materials, such as wood framing. Inspectors should also note clearance distances from chimneys or flues to combustibles, which are specified by building codes."

STEP 10: INTERIOR

"Closets tell a lot of secrets. Nobody paints them, so that's where you're going to see cracks or stains from roof leaks. Little cracks may not mean anything, but bigger cracks can telegraph shifting foundations. Normally, painters come in and patch or fix up everything so an inspector is at somewhat of a disadvantage. Since owners don't usually want to pay to paint closets, these areas can be the key to figuring out what's going on."

Faced with an existing switch box that was troublesome to move, a homeowner got creative with the jamb trim instead.

Old windows and doors lend a lot of charm; they can also leak a lot of energy.

STEP 11: DOORS AND WINDOWS

"Inspections aren't just about solving mysteries. Sometimes nonconforming conditions are right out in the open. The bedroom casement window (not shown), for example, is too small for egress if there were a fire. And it swings open out onto a deck, which is a safety issue because someone could walk into it and get hurt. No code says you can't have a window opening onto a deck, but there's no point in asking for trouble.

"Regarding egress, if they are the house's original windows, they don't have to be changed. But if they were added later and are too small to allow egress—and permits were not pulled when they were installed—that could become a big issue. At some point building codes were violated and may have to be set right. A lot of the houses I inspect are older so many of them don't meet code requirements for egress. Houses built in the 1950s, for example, often have a lot of smaller modern windows high up so there's no way you could crawl in or out of them. In my reports I have to point out these issues so buyers know what they are getting into. If such windows are in a bedroom, they may need to be upgraded."

STEP 12: KITCHEN AND BATHROOMS

"This kitchen's in the middle of a major overhaul so there are things that, obviously, the owner knows about, like the cabinet pulls that haven't been installed yet and the uncapped gas valve that will connect to the stove. Inspectors can't make assumptions about the future. If a detail is unsafe or doesn't meet code when I make my inspection, it goes into the report.

"There are openings in the wall of the cabinet below the sink that need to be repaired. Sink edges need caulking to keep water from entering between the sink and the countertop. There is some moisture damage to the cabinet beneath the sink, which may be caused by the trap arm's negative slope or the drain outflow being too high. In any event, the sink drainpipes need to be reconfigured.

"On a positive note, there are several GFCI-protected receptacles in the kitchen, which is a good safety feature. There are also GFCIs in the bathrooms.

"The house has two bathrooms, with fixtures that are worn but serviceable. Tub tile joints and the like need caulking. Notably, the toilets in both bathrooms are cramped. According to modern practice in California, there should be at least 21 in. of clear space in front of the toilet and at least 30 in. of space side to side, including the width of the toilet (see "Bath Fixture Clearances" on p. 261).

The area under the kitchen sink is a prime hunting ground for inspectors. Even little leaks from faucet washers can, in time, soak the cabinet and cause it to deteriorate.

"When several faucets are opened at the same time, the water flow drops dramatically, not surprising since we know that the main supply pipe is only $\frac{1}{2}$-in.-dia. galvanized steel. Bathroom drains are pretty slow, particularly the tub's, so they should probably be unclogged. Replacing both supply and DWV (drain, waste, and vent) pipes may not be too far off.

"Both bath fans vent into the attic, so both need extension ducts to vent moisture to the building exterior. Venting moist air into the attic is never a good idea. Excess moisture trapped in a house is a recipe for mold and rot."

STEP 13: GARAGE AND ATTACHED STRUCTURES

"There is a detached garage at the back of the lot that I did not inspect, as requested. From what I know about garages of this era, its construction is outdated with a shallow foundation. Often times the mudsills are in contact with the ground. So lots of rot. No drainage to speak of and a concrete floor that's cracked and uneven because there's no steel in it.

This deck's posts rest on precast concrete pier blocks sitting on top of the ground. If an earthquake or hurricane struck, the blocks could move, causing the deck to settle or collapse.

"The most common attached structures are decks. Seen from underneath, the joists of this deck are spaced too widely. Presently there are only undersize galvanized screws securing the deck ledger to the house framing. Screws this small could shear off if the deck became overloaded, the ledgers would fall and the whole thing would collapse. At a minimum, the ledger should be attached with structural screws designed for this purpose along with lateral load connectors. Metal connectors should reinforce all connections, whether joists to ledger, stair treads to deck, or treads to stringers. There is no diagonal bracing so if there were any movement—whether seismic or a crowd of people horsing around on the deck—the structure could collapse. Added to which, the deck posts rest on precast concrete pier blocks just sitting on top of the ground. In a shake-up they'd 'walk.' Posts should be anchored to solid footings.

"Railings are another critical point. The railing height may be OK, but railings now are supposed to be able to resist 200 lb. of force, 42 in. up from the deck, which translates to a lot of torque. So railing post-to-deck connections also need tension ties."

Clothes for a crawl space: hat, heavy-duty leather boots, sturdy coveralls, kneepads, a tight-fitting mask with a HEPA filter, and heavy-duty leather gloves over a pair of rubber ones.

STEP 14: HAZARDOUS MATERIALS

"The hazards of lead paint and asbestos are pretty well documented. They are generally not a problem unless they become airborne. So if a renovation is likely to disturb them, it's best to hire an abatement specialist trained to minimize contamination and dispose of materials safely.

"Because of their importance, hazardous materials get a separate section in my reports. As real as hazardous materials are to homeowners, they're of even more concern to me. I frequently crawl through hazmats during an inspection, so I take dressing the part very seriously.

"When it's time to explore a crawl space—usually the last part of an inspection—I suit up. Hat, heavy-duty leather boots, sturdy coveralls, kneepads, a tight-fitting mask with a HEPA filter, and heavy-duty leather gloves over a pair of rubber ones. The rubber gloves protect you from toxic chemicals such as copper naphthenate, a wood preservative that cut-rate contractors sometimes apply improperly and indiscriminately when doing mudsill and subfloor repairs. The few times I have touched chemical-fouled areas when *not* wearing rubberized gloves, I felt sick for days.

"Sometimes you also find naturally occurring conditions under a house that are almost as noxious as the illegal chemicals you may find. Such as raccoon latrines. They actually dig a trench for communal use. Whew! When it's time to go home, I remove the coveralls and put them into a plastic storage bin immediately. I don't want that stuff wafting around my van."

"There's less than 18 in. of headroom in there, but I confirmed some hunches I had about the foundation."

POSTSCRIPT

After Brian emerges from the crawl space. "It was pretty tight in there, less than 18 in. of headroom in places. But I confirmed some hunches I had about the perimeter foundation in front. The dirt floor of the crawl space was already 1 ft. below grade and the top of the mudsill was buried 3 in. *under* the dirt of the floor. (A mudsill is supposed to be at least 6 in. above grade.) So if anything, the foundation and subfloor framing of the porch were even worse than I suspected. But that's why you try to go everywhere you can."

Safety

Keeping safe mostly takes using common sense and trusting your gut. Above all, don't go anyplace or perform any inspection task that doesn't feel safe to you.

STAY OFF ROOFS that are wet or too steep, aren't easily accessed, or are covered with slick roofing materials such as slate, tile, or metal. Some inspectors simply refuse to get on a roof as part of their inspection. If a roof is relatively low pitch or flat and is easily accessed—such as the roof shown at right—inspecting it seems straightforward.

If you are not comfortable making a rooftop inspection, don't. If you ascend a ladder, make sure it is securely footed and keep your hips between the ladder's side rails.

RESPECT ELECTRICITY. For starters, keep your distance from electrical service cables if you do inspect a roof (see p. 124). If it's raining or misty, however, stay away: Electricity can arc (jump) to nearby objects, such as a person on a metal ladder. Likewise, if an electrical panel is in a damp basement, stay out. Licensed electricians routinely refuse to enter such locations.

If you're not sure if an object is energized with electrical current, test it with a voltage tester. The voltage tester shown in the photo on the facing page doesn't need to touch a conductor directly. It can also detect current when its tip is touched to a service panel cover, to the plastic sheathing of a wire, or to a suspect metal duct. *Always test a tester first*, to be sure it's working correctly.

Chapter 6 has more on electrical safety, including panel inspections. National Electrical Code requirements for inspecting an energized panel are listed (and shown) on p. 123.

GIVE YOURSELF ROOM. Older houses frequently have small access openings to attics and crawl spaces. As noted on p. 77, attic hatches should be at least 22 in. by 30 in., with 30 in. of headroom. In crawl spaces, 2 ft. of headroom is minimal; 18 in. of headroom is really tight. Keep in mind that you may need to get out of confined spaces in a hurry. So if, for example, you see animal droppings in a crawl space or an attic, staying out may be the wiser course.

SHED LIGHT ON THE SUBJECT. Inspectors are paid to see things, so don't scrimp on flashlights. For about $100 you can get a powerful, rechargeable light. Headlamps free up your hands but a flashlight is easier to focus and aim at something you want to see well.

DRESS FOR WORK. You can wear street clothes for most of an inspection. But when it's time to inspect an attic, an unfinished basement, or a roof, protect yourself by wearing soft-rubber-soled shoes that won't slip, eye protection, and heavy gloves. If

LADDER SAFETY

FOR THE GREATEST SAFETY AND DURABILITY, buy a Type IA ladder, which is a construction-grade ladder rated for 300 lb. For most home inspectors, the choice will be between aluminum and fiberglass.

Fiberglass ladders are sturdy, nonconductive, and more expensive than aluminum. Aluminum ladders are a reasonable compromise in price and weight but are electrically conductive. Note, however, that all ladder materials can conduct electricity if they're wet.

As you work, always keep your hips within the ladder's sides.

Safe working lengths of ladders are less than their nominal lengths. When using an 8-ft. stepladder, for example, stand no higher than 6 ft. on it, and don't stand on the top step. Likewise, a 32-ft. extension ladder is only 26 ft. to 28 ft. long when extended. Ladder sections overlap about one-quarter, and a ladder leaning against a building should be set away from the wall about one-quarter of the ladder's extended length.

Ladders must be solidly footed to be safe, especially extension ladders. After setting up the ladder so that its sides are as plumb as possible, stand on the bottom rungs to seat the feet. Adjustable leg levelers are available for leveling ladders on slopes. If you're at all unsure about the ladder's footing, stake its bottom to prevent "creeping."

Never place ladder feet on a section of sloping roof to inspect a higher roof. The feet might slip, especially if the roofing has a granular surface or wood shingles could tear out. Instead of inspecting the roof, you might suddenly be seeing stars. Play it safe.

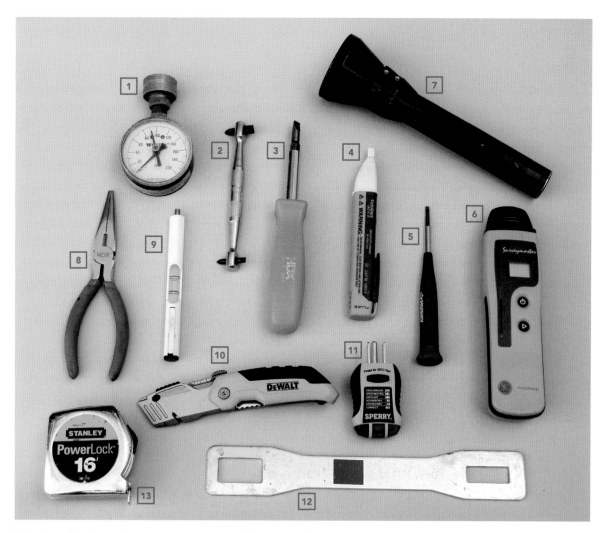

Brian's tool belt: **1**, water pressure gauge; **2**, offset screwdriver; **3**, six-in-one screwdriver; **4**, voltage tester (non-contact tester); **5**, jeweler's screwdriver; **6**, moisture meter; **7**, rechargeable flashlight; **8**, needle-nose pliers; **9**, pocket level; **10**, utility knife; **11**, three-prong tester; **12**, gas meter wrench; **13**, tape measure.

you'll be crawling through hazmat territory, suit up in coveralls, kneepads, boots, a respirator mask, eye protection, and nitrile rubber gloves inside heavy leather gloves, as shown in the right photo on p. 10.

Brian's Tool Belt

Some inspectors' tool belts are so crammed with stuff that they look like walking hardware stores. In comparison, the contents of Brian's Cogley's tool belt are pretty minimal. Typically, he doesn't wear it; he sets it by the front door when he arrives and takes out tools as he needs them. Here are Brian's most-used tools, with a typical task or two in his own words for each.

"**Pressure gauges** check water pressure as part of ASHI standards. Typical pressure is 40 lb. to 80 lb. If the pressure is over 100 lb., I tell the homeowner to get a pressure regulator; if it's under 40 lb., I say, 'See how it works for you, you may need to get a pressurizing system.'

"My **regular screwdriver** is a six in one. It's got two different sizes of flat heads and Phillips®, and if you take the screwdriver bits out, you have sockets with two different hex sizes, both of which are pretty standard for HVAC panels and for electrical panels. A six in one is useful because you need only one to handle most situations. The cheapest one is about $2.50; it's orange so you can see it in a crawl space, but if you lose it, no big deal.

"An **offset screwdriver** is useful in tight areas, such as in an older house where panel access is obstructed by framing. In other words, places where a straight screwdriver won't fit.

"A **voltage detector** is probably the single most important electrical tool an inspector has. The type I use, also called a noncontact voltage detector, can tell if a panel is energized without removing the panel cover or if a wire in a crawl space is energized by holding the tester's point to the wire sheathing. Mine beeps or flashes when it detects voltage. It also beeps when it shuts itself off to save battery life.

"My **rechargeable flashlight** can cast a focused beam 100 ft. With run-of-the-mill battery-powered flashlights, you can't really see anything. A super-bright flashlight is one of the most important tools you can have. This one cost about $100. Our job is to see things, so anything that helps you see is worth the extra money.

"I also carry a tiny **jeweler's screwdriver** because I like to show homeowners how to reset the seismic shut-off valve on a gas line. (Most of the devices are tripped by mechanical action or motion and have a tiny little reset screw.) I don't actually reset the valve, but I think it's important for people to know how.

"I don't use a **moisture meter** all that much, most often I bring it out to prove or disprove something. In fact, I generally don't let people know I have one because they sometimes get carried away and want to test every last stain. If it's raining, say, and a client is freaking out that their vinyl windows are leaking, I might use the meter to show them, 'Look, it's bone dry' and put their mind at ease. My Surveymaster meter has both probes and a deep-scan sensor so it can distinguish between subsurface and surface moisture. Very useful if, say, there is wetness around the base of a toilet and you want to see if there is moisture *under* the toilet as well.

"**Needle-nose pliers** are handy for a couple of inspection tasks. I use them to pull up a corner of carpet in a closet, for example, to see if there are hardwood floors underneath. Sometimes I use pliers to bypass thermostats that are not working. If I can turn on the furnace by touching the two sides of the pliers to thermostat terminals, I know the thermostat is bad.

"A little **pocket level** is handy to see if furnace ducts are sloped in the right direction. If the flue of a high-efficiency, induced-draft furnace is improperly sloped, the unit can rust out in 2 years or 3 years instead of the 20-some years that they are supposed to last.

"I use a **tape measure** to check railing heights, stair treads, and openings between railings. I also use it to measure ceiling heights because in older houses there are a lot of nonconforming spaces. If a listing says 'three bedrooms' and a bedroom ceiling must be 7 ft. 6 in. to satisfy local codes and a couple bedrooms are actually 7 ft. 5 in., I need to let my clients know.

"My primary use for a **utility knife** is to score around the edges of electrical subpanels that have been painted over. (Happens all the time.) I don't want to cop out and say 'I wasn't able to look at the panel because somebody painted over it' and I don't want to damage the walls. With a nice sharp razor you can score the paint around the edges and get the panel cover off cleanly without ripping off the paper facing of the drywall.

"**Three-prong testers** tell you if a receptacle is properly wired or, if not, what's incorrect. The model shown on p. 13 has a little GFCI button that tells you if a receptacle is GFCI protected.

"The **gas meter wrench** is another tool I use to educate clients—in this case, to show them how to physically turn off the gas. It's important to know. I also show them how to turn off the water and the electrical. Folks appreciate that you're looking out for them."

Taking Notes on Site

"I use a Fujitsu® Stylistic® tablet to take notes; I buy them used on eBay®. I own three now and have killed two in the last 10 years. Stuff happens. Job sites are hard on computers.

A tablet computer with a stylus is a handy way to record inspection notes on site.

"I don't use special inspection software, just a Word doc that I've modified and a Windows® Journal for handwritten notes, using the tablet stylus. I dump everything—along with photos—into my desktop computer when I get home and try to make some sense out of it that night. Then I send it to my editor who inserts the photos, formats the report, and otherwise makes me look like I understand grammar. After he sends it back to me, I reread his edited version, turn it into a PDF, and send it to the client.

"The onsite inspection is the easy part. Creating a useful and accurate report is what takes the time. Some inspectors use a checklist-style report system, but I don't think those can do justice to the diverse and unique housing stock we have around here."

Taking Care of Clients

Buying and selling a house is stressful for everyone involved, whether buyer, seller, or real estate agent. House prices and closing fees are huge and home inspections aren't cheap either. Every closing has myriad details to get right and, especially when the housing market is hot, everything seems to happen at breakneck speeds. So a little TLC goes a long way.

A seasoned home inspector who has been through it all before can be a calming presence and keep things moving. Rather than playing everything by the book, he knows that a personal touch is often a better way to proceed. For example, most clients are curious about what's going on with a house so, if it feels right, why not invite them along for the adventure?

EXPLORING DOWN UNDER

"When clients want to go under the house with me, I say, 'Sure, let's go check it out.' I loan them coveralls and a powerful flashlight, and have them put on nitrile gloves, then leather gloves, and a respirator.

Living the dream. Most homeowners are curious about what's going on with their house. A brave few are willing to suit up and crawl under the house with the inspector.

And it is a respirator, by the way, not just a cheap dust mask. I buy respirators in boxes of 25 and three-packs of gloves.

"It's *great* when they go under the house because it makes things way easier to explain. When you're trying to explain a seismic retrofit for example, you can say, 'Right here is where a piece of plywood has to go, right here is where an anchor bolt needs to be,

Sometimes an inspector needs to gain access to do a thorough inspection. *Left,* a lopper to cut back bushes; *right,* a bolt cutter to snip padlocks. Of course, get permission before you cut.

Being thoughtful doesn't cost much. Replace locks you must cut; provide gloves, a respirator mask, and coveralls if a client wants to join you under the house; and sweep up any mess you make.

and over here, a hold-down.' Clients usually won't want to go everywhere you go because you have to go *everywhere,* so for some tasks they will just sit and watch you at a distance.

"But when they see the lengths you're willing to go to thoroughly inspect their place, some kind of bonding takes place and you're much less likely to have hassles about small things. They may never go under the house again, but if they have retrofit work done there later, they can visualize to a degree what is going on. A lot of time I will take a picture of them under the house, all dirty with the mask on, and send it to them or clip it to the report."

SAVING TIME, SOLVING PROBLEMS

"I always have extra locks on hand for when the main electrical panel in a garage, or a storage room is padlocked. Rather than take a hard line and say, 'It's inaccessible, I can't inspect it, and if I come back it's going to be 150 bucks,' I can just say, 'Look, call the listing agent and ask if it's OK with the homeowner if I cut the lock, I've got another lock, and I'll leave the keys.' It's a nice way to build your reputation as a problem solver rather than some hard-nose with his hand out for a check. It just makes the transaction go smoothly for everyone and keeps things moving forward."

PUTTING COMMON COURTESY TO WORK

"If I open an attic hatch and a bunch of crud falls on the floor, a little whisk broom and dustpan are perfect. It's just common courtesy to sweep it up. If I came home and someone left me a mess, I'd be peeved. So I clean it up as soon as I'm finished with that inspection point. Or if the attic access in an old house is through a closet where clothes are stored, I'll cover them up with an old sheet before I go up. If you do things right, homeowners will hardly know you've been there."

CHAPTER 1

The WALK-AROUND

THERE ARE MANY VARIABLES that make a property desirable, including lot size, views, vegetation, and proximity to services. But when evaluating a lot's suitability as a house site, the three most important criteria are slope, drainage, and soil composition.

A level lot is generally the easiest to build on. Yet as towns and cities become built up, the only lots available are often those once thought to be marginal—too steep or too wet to build on. Such conditions can be overcome to a degree by technology: by properly engineered foundations, effective drainage systems, careful grading, retaining walls, sidewalks, and driveways that disperse water rather than concentrate it—in other words, elements that complement a site rather than fight it.

From a builder's perspective, soil composition is largely a matter of how well water moves through it. Sandier soils drain better, whereas clay soils are less permeable and more likely to become saturated. So saturated, in fact, that as some clay soils expand and contract, they raise and lower the houses built atop them! Soil stability, in turn, can be impacted by slope, as water flows toward and collects against the uphill side of a foundation, exerts lateral pressure on foundation walls, and, in extreme cases, causes foundation failure.

It's difficult to generalize about the cost of remedying site conditions. Keeping gutters and downspouts clear, for example, costs little but does much to keep water from collecting next to a foundation. On the other hand, solutions such as retrofitting perimeter drains can be big-ticket items. First you need to find out what the underlying conditions are. So a thorough inspection will generally start with an observant walk around the site.

Drainage and Grading

Over the eons, Nature has devised an elaborate drainage system to accommodate the movement of water. Rain soaks into the ground, ground water flows in underground runnels and filters into aquifers, or surfaces as streams and rivers. Low-lying areas become marshes, bogs, ponds, and lakes. Periodically, heavy storms cause water to overflow these natural channels and basins, and flooding occurs. The areas along rivers that periodically flood are called floodplains.

In the old days, floodplains seemed like good places to build (especially during dry years). Such land was flat, fertile, and accessible to river transport. As long as farms were small and spread out, flooding affected relatively few people. During the boom years that followed World War II, however, the shortage of flat building lots led to the unwise and widespread practice of developing floodplains. Millions of homes were built on them. In most years, such sites were dry, but rare as floods might be, they came as a nasty shock to homeowners who had no idea their homes were on a floodplain.

If a year-round creek is located on a low-lying part of a lot, it may be channeling runoff or underground springs. It does not necessarily indicate that the water table is high.

In response, governmental agencies began identifying areas subject to flooding, and the mapping continues to this day. In 2004, the Federal Emergency Management Agency (FEMA) began a massive project to update and digitize floodplain maps across the United States. To see if a property is in a floodplain go to www.floodsmart.gov. Enter the state, county, and town to learn the risk of flooding in your area. City and county planning departments should also have detailed maps.

With the rising seas and storm surges associated with global warming, building in coastal floodplains has also become a concern. The National Oceanic and Atmospheric Administration (NOAA) estimates that 16.4 million people (5% of the U.S. population) resided in a coastal floodplain in 2010 (see stateofthecoast.noaa.gov/pop100yr).

Presently, federal flood insurance is available to homeowners in communities that flood periodically. But whether such federal assistance will survive the current rage for budget cutting and fiscal austerity is anyone's guess.

WATER TABLES

GROUNDWATER WILL FLOW DOWNWARD until it hits an impervious layer, typically dense clay or rock. At that point it will run more or less horizontally or pond up because the earth beneath it is saturated. This level is called the *water table*. Water tables often rise in response to heavy rains and surface runoff. Sites with high water tables are ill-suited to septic systems and full basements because water may penetrate both. Connecting to a municipal sewer system and building a house on a slab or a crawl space are better strategies where seasonal water tables are only a few feet below the surface.

CONTROLLING SITE RUNOFF

Surface runoff can occur any time there are heavy or sustained rains. If a building site is on a slope or surrounded by hills, the concentration of runoff can be considerable. If the soil is exposed, runoff will hasten erosion, which is particularly a problem if there has been excavation recently and new plantings are not yet established. In low-lying properties, runoff may pond up unless it is diverted into a storm drain.

There are several ways to reduce erosion, keep runoff away from a house foundation, and prevent water from seeping into a basement or crawl space. Please note that grading and drainage solutions can be quite complex; this list is just a cursory overview.

PLANTING VEGETATION, whether ground cover, grasses, or bushes, is the most effective way to stop erosion. But plantings need to be skillfully done and watered and maintained for several months to allow the plants to establish roots. Mulching a bare site will reduce erosion as long as rains are not too heavy but is at best a stopgap measure. We'll say more about landscaping later.

GRADING (reshaping) the site can slow runoff by intercepting it with terraces, mounds, or swales (depressions) perpendicular to a steep slope. There's the same amount of water, of course, it's just diverted so that the runoff isn't as concentrated or, in the case of surface rivulets, doesn't run as fast or erode as much.

Grading takes skill, however. On a steep site, excavating a huge hole can hasten underground runoff (and erosion) because water is no longer slowed by soil in its path. This is evident when you see a foundation excavation quickly fill with water or massive erosion around a foundation perimeter.

SITE DRAINAGE can be an expensive way to remove excess water but is sometimes the only strategy that works on a chronically wet site. Complex drainage solutions are typically reviewed by a soils engineer: Most involve excavating a trench, filling the trench bottom with gravel, installing a network of perforated drainpipes, and carefully backfilling. Swale drains (also called curtain drains) typically intercept water flow some distance above a house and reroute it.

Unsupported hillside soil can be a real problem in wet weather. A landscaping contractor can suggest native or low-maintenance plants to support the soil and reduce erosion.

At a low point in the land, runoff needs to go somewhere. If a property is large enough, the water may pond up or be absorbed into the ground. If the water collects over a septic system leeching field or tank, however, that's potentially a health problem. The septic tank may fill with water and back up, or effluvia may rise toward the surface rather than draining down into the soil. A strong septic smell may result.

Where natural dispersal is not an option, runoff should be directed into a catch basin. (Catch basins typically consist of a porous concrete or concrete-block basin, with perforated pipes radiating out from it. Gravel around the basin and pipes aids dispersal.) In suburban and urban areas, runoff is usually directed into a city storm drain.

WHAT TO LOOK FOR

- Is there standing water on the property? If there is, is it long-standing (algae on surface, lush vegetation, and so on) or does it seem to be the temporary runoff of a recent storm?

- When walking the lot, can you see springs, rivulets, streams, or the like? Are any of the low-lying areas damp? If so, note them on a quick sketch of the lot.

- What is the general lay of the land: flat, gently sloping, steeply inclined? Are any of the hillsides eroded? Are there adjacent lots above or below the one you're inspecting?

- Where on the lot is the house located? If there were a downpour, would runoff head toward the house or away from it?

- Has any portion of the lot been recently excavated—say, within the last 5 years? Has vegetation grown over the excavated areas or is bare soil visible?

- Is there evidence of grading such as swales running perpendicular to a slope? If local codes require permits for grading that affects adjacent properties, were permits pulled?

- Are there surface drains on the lot? Are there other signs of a high water table?

- As you walk the lot, are there septic smells, especially in low-lying or damp ground?

- If the property is near a large river or a seacoast, is it in a floodplain?

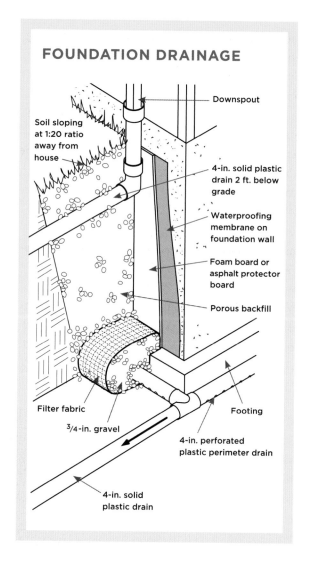

FOUNDATION DRAINAGE

Soil sloping at 1:20 ratio away from house

Downspout

4-in. solid plastic drain 2 ft. below grade

Waterproofing membrane on foundation wall

Foam board or asphalt protector board

Porous backfill

Filter fabric

¾-in. gravel

Footing

4-in. perforated plastic perimeter drain

4-in. solid plastic drain

DIRECTING WATER AWAY FROM THE HOUSE

The soil around the house should also be graded properly. For starters, the bottom of the siding should be at least 6 in. to 8 in. above grade (soil level). Around the perimeter, the soil should slope downward away from the house at a rate of at least 6 in. within the first 10 ft. Because foot traffic will compact the soil, it may be necessary to regrade the soil around the house from time to time. Inspectors should take note of any soil near the house that slopes downward *toward* the house.

Even with proper grading, however, a certain amount of water is going to accumulate near the house, whether from surface or roof runoff. Keeping gutters and downspouts clear is essential. Equally important is foundation drainage that's properly installed.

As shown in the drawing on the facing page, foundation drainage can be complicated. It is typically installed after foundation walls are poured but before the excavation is backfilled. (Not surprisingly, retrofitting such drainage is expensive and disruptive.) A bed of gravel is poured around the perimeter, just below the level of the footings. Perforated footing drains are placed—holes down—in the bed and carefully topped with additional gravel. (The gravel bed may also be wrapped with a fabric filter to keep soil from clogging pipe openings.) Details vary, but foundation walls are usually sealed with a water-resistant coating or membrane, insulated, and then backfilled with a porous mixture of sandy soil and small gravel.

Seeing a downspout terminate in a subsurface drain does not mean the system is functional. This system's subsurface drains are badly clogged. Test all subsurface drains periodically.

NOTE: Downspouts should not connect to footing drains; rather they should terminate in solid drainpipes buried roughly 2 ft. below the surface.

WHAT TO LOOK FOR

- Are gutters and downspouts complete, connected, and clear of debris? (Flush them with a garden hose to be sure.)
- Do downspouts terminate into subsurface drainpipes, pipes running above ground, onto a splash block, or just empty out onto the lawn? (Subsurface drains are preferred.)
- Are there any signs of erosion or wet ground at the base of the downspout?
- Are there surface drains or sump pump enclosures near the foundation? (They indicate a high water table or persistent drainage issues.) Are both in working order?
- Do discharge pipes stick out of a foundation wall—say, for a basement sump pump?
- Does the ground consistently slope down and away from the house or do portions slope toward the house? Are there sunken areas within 10 ft. of the foundation?
- Is vegetation growing against the house? Plants retain water and can contribute to basement dampness. If there is a sprinkler system, turn it on: Do jets wet the house?

Retaining Walls

Correctly built, retaining walls employ both grading and drainage. The grading part is obvious: a sloping lot is reshaped to create level terraces, with walls holding back (retaining) the soil of the terrace above. Retaining walls are usually classified as wet (stones, blocks, or bricks are laid up with mortar) or dry (built without mortar). In addition to laid-up masonry units, retaining walls may also be built from poured concrete, timbers, railroad ties, recycled concrete walkways, and so on.

Less apparent is the need to provide adequate drainage behind a retaining wall, so the soil doesn't become saturated. Without drainage, hydrostatic pressure can crack mortared joints or, in time, push a wall over. At the very least, the back (uphill) side of a

Dry-stack retaining walls are not mortared, but the bottom course of blocks must be placed on an adequate footing. A screwdriver can be used to check for concrete or gravel footings, neither of which was found here.

WHAT TO LOOK FOR

- Does the retaining wall have weep holes and, if so, are they filled with dirt or open? (Water running out of the weep holes is a good sign.)

- Are stones loose or bulging out from the face? If it has been built without mortar, it can be repaired by tearing down the wall till you get to the loose section and then rebuilt.

- Is the wall cracked or heaving outward? Surface cracks are generally not a problem, but through cracks wider than ½ in., in which one side has moved farther than the other, should be inspected by a soils engineer.

- In cold regions, if the base of a wall has heaved and become dislodged, with soil and water oozing out from underneath, you are probably looking at frost heaving.

- If wood retaining walls are slumping, probe their back face to see if the wood is rotting.

- What are other retaining walls in the neighborhood doing? If most are leaning in the same direction, the property may be in a slide zone. In which case, sidewalk slabs may also tilt in the same direction. In earthquake-prone regions, check city records to see if the house is in a slide area or a fault zone.

retaining wall should have a bed of gravel backfilled along its base. Concrete and concrete block walls need weep holes placed every 4 ft. to 8 ft. to allow water to drain out. Retaining walls in especially wet slopes or slide zones may also require drainpipe systems.

Where a hillside is unstable, such as in a slide zone, retaining walls may also need anchors that tie them to the hills. Anchors vary according to the wall material used, but most are T-shaped elements that run perpendicular to the face of the wall. The foot of each T-anchor is spliced to the face of the retaining wall; the body of each T runs back into the hillside and is held in place by the weight of soil backfilled on top of it.

In actual practice, most retaining walls are done quickly, without drains, gravel backfill, or anchors. Consequently, though walls ideally should be vertical, or perhaps lean into the hillside, most lean away from the hillside and have been pushed outward by lateral pressures. Finally, if a retaining wall is taller than 4 ft., most building codes require that it be designed by an engineer.

The higher a retaining wall, the more soil and soil pressure it must withstand. This wall is failing. Generally, new walls higher than 4 ft. must be designed by a qualified engineer.

The parallel cracks in this asphalt roadway suggest that we are looking at a slide area. Have a geotechnical or soils engineer review the site and search for previous slippage in the area.

Cracked, lifted, or uneven sidewalks represent a tripping hazard and should be repaired. In most towns this is the homeowner's responsibility.

Sidewalks

During the site walk-around, inspect the condition of sidewalks, driveways, paved areas such as patios, and incidental objects such as in-ground trash bins. These objects are rarely a cause for concern, but if they are in poor repair they may look bad, present a tripping hazard, or when sloped improperly, may direct runoff toward the house.

Sidewalks are typically concrete, though they may also be constructed from brick, stone, asphalt, or precast blocks. Cracked, lifted, or uneven sections represent a tripping hazard, so they should be repaired. Interestingly, though sections of sidewalk running between the front of a house and the street curb are often on municipal land, homeowners are often responsible for their repair and upkeep. That is, if someone trips on a faulty section and breaks a hip, the homeowner can be sued.

Most cities and towns inspect sidewalks periodically, inform homeowners of defects, and offer to repair flawed sections for a nominal amount. It's usually a good deal, especially if tree roots have lifted the sidewalk, because the city also secures the permissions needed to make repairs. (A homeowner can't just go in and chop offending roots: Trees lining the streets are generally considered city property, and trees deemed historic enjoy additional protections.) Homeowners can wait till the city inspects sidewalks, but given the liability involved, it's in homeowners' interest to be proactive by alerting the city to failed walks or by repairing the sidewalks themselves.

SIDEWALKS AND PATHS around the house should be inspected for the same defects. Paths fashioned from precast blocks or stepping-stones tend to settle unevenly, so note path steps that are markedly higher, lower, or tilting. In addition, check the slope of sidewalks near the house. If they slope *toward* the house, they may direct rain runoff toward the foundation.

If there are other pathways around the property, look out for sudden changes in elevation. Gradual rises are not generally a problem, but unexpected single steps can send someone tumbling. Better to remove that orphan step, regrade the soil, and replace the step with an evenly sloping walkway. Alternately, paint an orphan step's riser to make it more visible.

Mortared brick walkways are difficult to repair in a way that looks good. The raised edge creates a real trip hazard. The best long-term solution may be to install a new walkway made of a material that won't crack as it settles.

Wood steps or timbers that divide raised areas typically rest on the earth, which makes them problematic in at least two respects: Wood on soil is likely to retain water and rot. And vegetation is likely to grow over them. Such vegetation obscures exactly where the wood step is, becomes slick when wet, and may have roots that trip walkers.

NOTE: All sidewalks and paths on the property should be lit by low-voltage trail lights. They are simple to install and solar-powered models won't raise house electricity bills.

STEPS TO THE STREET AND DRIVEWAY are usually concrete; they typically match adjacent walks or paths. Make note of cracked or broken steps because they are trip hazards. Whatever material was used, it should be in good repair and free of vegetation or any surface that could become slippery when wet.

If there are more than two steps, there must be a sturdy railing on at least one side. Tug on the railing to test its solidness and inspect its base to be sure it is securely attached to the stair platform.

NOTE: The single most important safety consideration is that step risers (the vertical distance from one tread to the next) be uniformly spaced. Uneven step heights can cause a fall. Write up steps with uneven rise or whose treads tilt—a trip hazard that is compounded in regions with freezing temperatures.

Stairs that lead to porches or entry doors are discussed in Chapter 13.

WHAT TO LOOK FOR

- Are any sections of sidewalk broken, tilted, or otherwise a trip hazard?
- Is vegetation overgrowing sidewalks, paths, or sidewalk steps?
- Do all paths and walks have trail lights?
- Are steps leading up from the street evenly spaced and level?
- Are any steps crumbling or cracked?
- Are steps painted? In general, painted steps tend to become slick when wet, except for sand-impregnated paints, which offer greater traction.
- If there are more than two steps, is there a sturdy handrail?

Driveways

Driveways are typically made of gravel, asphalt, concrete, or paver blocks that allow rain to soak into the ground. (Occasionally you see brick driveways but, on the whole, they are not very durable.) A rutted or eroded gravel driveway can be repaired by grading it flat, adding new gravel, and rolling the gravel so it seats well in the substrate. Asphalt drives can be patch repaired or resurfaced, and uneven paver blocks can be removed and resituated. Of all driveway materials, concrete is the most difficult to repair because it cures into a monolithic slab; faulty sections can be repaired but patches will be obvious.

Hairline surface cracks are generally not a problem, whereas wider cracks ($\frac{1}{2}$+ in.) with crumbling materials and low spots suggest improper base preparation. Crumbling edges are another indication of a poorly constructed drive. If the edges of the drive are eroding or low points have standing water, it's likely that drainage is subpar as well.

If a garage door opening doesn't look square, have an engineer review it. Because the driveway slopes into the garage, a slot drain across the opening would be better than the small square drain presently there.

Driveways that drain down toward the house are particularly problematic because of the potential for flooding a garage or basement. A channel drain (trench drain) in front of a garage entrance can intercept a substantial amount of runoff, but only if it connects to a properly installed drainage system that is rigorously maintained to prevent clogs. Such systems are expensive. Yet even the best of them can be overwhelmed by a heavy downpour. A driveway, like a roof, concentrates a prodigious amount of water.

If the house is below the street, there should be a slight ridge at the top of the driveway, running parallel to the street, where the driveway meets the curb cutout. This ridge will direct runoff toward storm drains in the street, rather than down the driveway. Finally, an inspector should note how functional a driveway is: How easy it would be to enter and exit? A driveway should be at least 8 ft. wide, with 10 ft. desirable if there is a walk along one side. Is there room to walk by a car sitting in the driveway? (Imagine your arms loaded with groceries.) How steep is the drive? Would it be a

problem getting up and down it in snowy or icy conditions? Must one back out into traffic or is there room to turn around in the drive? And how is visibility at the end of the drive—could you safely enter traffic?

WHAT TO LOOK FOR

- Is the driveway surface intact or is it cracked and crumbling?
- Are driveway edges deteriorating?
- Are there low spots or standing water in the driveway?
- If the driveway slopes downward toward the garage or house, is there a channel drain to intercept runoff? Is the channel drain clogged or clear?
- If the driveway slopes toward the garage, are garage floors wet or dry? Any evidence of water stains from previous storms?
- How steep is the driveway? In freezing weather, would it be difficult to exit?

Fences, Gates, and Trellises

Outdoor objects such as fences, gates, garden walls, and trellises are constructed with varying degrees of skill. Some are simply constructed, modestly maintained, and rarely a serious concern for home buyers or sellers; whereas others (particularly masonry structures) are massive, dangerous when decrepit, and expensive to repair or replace. An inspector should note any outdoor structures that are in bad repair and represent a safety hazard.

Most fences and trellises are built out of wood, which rots out eventually, even if it is pressure treated. Typically, wood posts are sunk in the ground, with one-quarter to one-third of their length buried. Gravel packed around the base of the posts will aid drainage and longevity. A better way to support a post is to bolt it to a metal post base in a poured concrete pier; also called a standoff, the metal base elevates the bottom of the post several inches above the ground to avoid wood–soil contact. So post bottoms are *the* crucial detail to inspect.

This trellis is heavily damaged and could cause serious injury when it falls. It needs to be removed.

Vegetation is the other bugbear of outdoor structures because it retains moisture and hastens rot. Once an old wood fence gets completely overrun by berry bushes, the bushes may be all that are holding up the fence. Most folks just enjoy the foliage, eat the berries, and let the fence lean a little. Garden walls built of brick or other masonry materials are theoretically a greater hazard if they lean but, again, if they're not high, don't lean much, or are greatly overgrown, they're probably not going anywhere.

WHAT TO LOOK FOR

- Is rot present where there is wood–soil contact?
- Was the wood used treated with preservatives? (Preservatives can prolong wood life but some have been banned, or their use proscribed, because they are extremely toxic.)
- Are the posts and superstructures of trellises or arbors solid or do they sway to the touch? Is bracing needed? Is there any rot at wood-to-wood junctures?
- If there are brick, block, or stone structures in the yard, is the mortar intact? Are sections leaning or dislodged?

Landscaping

Carefully planned, planted, and maintained yards lend charm, increase the value of a property, and help control erosion. Green landscaping can also conserve water and provide shade, reduce home energy consumption, and provide food and habitat for local creatures.

As an inspector walks around a property, he or she should note low spots that need filling, walks or paths that present a trip hazard, structures that are leaning or in bad repair, and keep an eye out for signs of tunneling pests such as gophers or moles. Made of freshly dug earth, tunnels are soft and easy to collapse when you step on them. Local nurseries or home centers can describe your options for getting rid of such pests.

Note too if there are bushes, climbing vines, or other vegetation in contact with the house foundation or siding. Plants retain water, which leads to mossy siding and damp basement walls. Ivy is particularly a problem. Ivy's tendrils can lift paint and siding, crush gutters and downspouts, and, if a main stem is large

Seen up close, ivy doesn't look charming. Here, ivy tendrils have breached the topcoat of this stucco siding, allowing water to enter and do more damage.

enough, create a gap where walls meet the underside of a roof. Ivy holds moisture, which can rot out wood trim. It houses numerous insects and provides rodents, raccoons, and opossums with easy access to eaves and the attic.

If homeowners are sentimental about keeping their ivy, they should at least cut it back periodically to limit the damage it does. Homeowners who like the look of wisteria, bougainvillea, and other flowering vines can limit the damage they do by supporting vines with a hinged trellis that can periodically be pivoted away from the house (for painting, maintenance, etc.) without killing the plant.

The inspector may also turn on any irrigation system, especially lawn sprinklers, and note if water is spraying directly onto siding. It's easy to adjust sprinkler trajectories. As an alternative to sprinklers, drip-irrigation is inexpensive, easy to install, and water conserving.

Finally, inspectors should note the health of trees on the property, especially those close to the house. A licensed arborist should take down dead trees or limbs. If the inspection takes place after deciduous trees have lost their leaves, branches without bark, insect holes, and woodpecker drillings can help identify dead limbs or trees. Speaking of insects, dead trees too close to a house may lead to an infestation of wood-boring insects inside.

In general, branches that overhang a roof should be cut back: at the least, they'll clog gutters with leaves and at the worst, they could fall, damage the roof, and perhaps injure the people inside. In arid regions, trees too near or touching a house are often a fire code violation. (And, on occasion, a reason for insurance companies to deny claims.)

WHAT TO LOOK FOR

- Is vegetation in contact with the foundation or siding? Is the siding mossy?
- Do lawn sprinklers spray onto the house?
- Are climbing vines attached to the house? Is there damage to siding or trim?
- Do tree branches overhang the roof or touch any part of the house? Are there large leaning trees that could lose branches or fall on the house in a storm?
- Do tree branches come in contact with electrical service wires (see p. 123)?

Periodically, a licensed arborist should take down dead trees or limbs. Large trees that lean toward buildings should also be assessed and, as necessary, pruned as needed or removed.

POOLS AND POOL SAFETY

APPROXIMATELY 4,200 CHILDREN A YEAR are treated in hospital emergency rooms after being submerged in a pool or spa (hot tub). Each year, more than 300 children under the age of 5 years drown. To reduce the number of such tragedies, in 2007, the Pool and Spa Safety Act (PSSA) became law. You can read the law in its entirety and get other common-sense safety suggestions at www.poolsafely.gov.

Homeowners (and home inspectors) should familiarize themselves with the publication Safety Barrier Guidelines for Residential Pools, which is available at poolsafely.gov/wp-content/uploads/362.pdf.

An inspection should note the presence (or absence) of these safety features:

- Every pool or spa should be completely surrounded by a fence with a self-closing gate. Fences should be at least 4 ft. high, though some states and municipalities mandate a 5-ft. height. Fences should not have horizontal elements that a child could climb up.
- If the home serves as one side of the barrier, every door leading to the pool or spa area should have a loud door alarm that sounds for at least 30 seconds.
- Pool and spa covers must be in good working order. Local authorities typically require that such covers have locks or latches that a child cannot open.
- Any pool or spa must have an anti-entrapment safety drain cover. Drain entrapments typically occur when a swimmer's body, hair, limbs, or clothing becomes entangled in a faulty or flat drain or grate.
- Annually, a trained pool and spa professional should evaluate water quality and inspect the physical condition of all pool and spa surfaces as well as mechanical equipment such as pumps, electrical devices, and safety equipment.

NOTE: Unused and empty pools and spas can also be safety hazards.

Pool surfaces are hard and frequently slippery when wet. Someone falling into an empty pool could easily break bones. In addition to the points above, an inspection should note the following:

- Are surfaces around a pool in good repair or could loose tiles or crumbling masonry cause someone to trip?
- Are surfaces around or in the pool slick with algae or other vegetative growth?
- If there is a pool cover, is it sufficiently sturdy (and attached) to break someone's fall—that is, to keep them from hitting the bottom of the pool?
- Is there standing water in the bottom of a pool or spa? Mosquitoes can breed in as little as ½ in. of still water, so local vector control should be notified about derelict pools.

Last, if pool surfaces have deteriorated and perimeter walkways are cracked and uneven, the pool lining may have failed and in-ground leaks may have compromised the soil around the pool. Depending on the sources and extent of the failure, it may be more cost-effective to fill in the pool than repair it. Have a pool professional make the call.

This site is a serious hazard. The retaining wall above the pool has failed and the masonry decking around it is in poor condition. This pool may not be repairable and should probably be removed or replaced. It should be drained to prevent mosquitoes from breeding, and a fence or barrier needs to be installed to prevent access.

CHAPTER 2

EXTERIORS

AFTER YOU HAVE WALKED THE SITE, inspecting the house begins in earnest as you scrutinize its exterior. This is both a detailed look at exterior elements—siding, trim, windows, doors, eaves—and an overview of the house's general health. Has the house been well maintained? Is the siding in good shape overall? Are walls plumb? Are window and door corners square? Do site concerns such as, say, surface runoff recur as you look closer at the building? Are patterns starting to emerge in what you observe? Keep looking and take notes.

The visible elements of a house's exterior—which include eaves, gutter systems, trim, siding, doors, and windows—combine to protect the wall sheathing and framing behind.

How Walls Shed Water

The exterior walls of a house are multilayered membranes that weatherproof a house in much the same way that a roof does. In addition to protecting underlying elements from damage by sun and wind, the exterior intercepts water and keeps it away from sheathing and wood framing. (We'll touch on masonry houses later on.)

The visible exterior layer consists primarily of siding and trim. Beneath the siding, ideally, is a water-resistive barrier (WRB), typically building paper or plastic housewrap. (Houses more than 100 years old usually don't have a WRB layer.) In addition, flashing seals transitions from one material to another and directs water around potential obstructions such as window and door trim, vent hoods, and outdoor outlets. If it sticks out of a wall, it can dam up water. Finally, caulks and sealants fill gaps, bond materials together, or cut air infiltration.

During an inspection, you are limited to what you can see, obviously. For the most part you will not be able to see things such as felt building paper under the siding. But it's important to understand how those hidden components work.

No matter how well siding or trim is installed, sooner or later water will work its way behind it. Typically, this happens when storms drive rain into

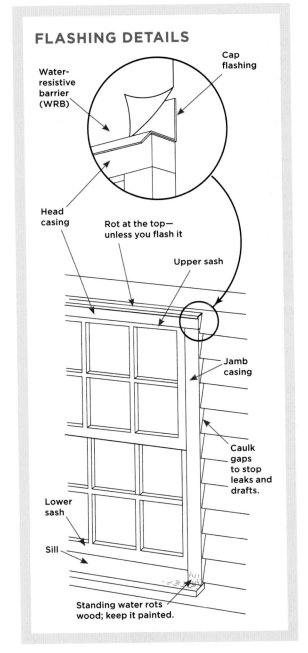

FLASHING DETAILS

Cap flashing

Water-resistive barrier (WRB)

Head casing

Rot at the top—unless you flash it

Upper sash

Jamb casing

Caulk gaps to stop leaks and drafts.

Lower sash

Sill

Standing water rots wood; keep it painted.

building seams or gaps around doors or windows. Water can also be drawn inward and upward by capillary action. For these reasons, builders cover exterior sheathing with a water-resistive barrier. In older houses, the most common barrier is 15-lb. asphalt-impregnated building paper—also called felt paper—and in newer houses, semipermeable plastic housewraps such as Tyvek® or R-Wrap®.

A crucial detail: WRB and flashing must be installed so that they divert water away from the sheathing and the framing behind it. Because water flows downhill, materials above should always overlap those below.

In new construction, water-resistive barriers are usually installed before windows and doors have been inserted into rough openings. Windows and doors are then installed and their perimeters weatherproofed with flashing strips. As shown in "Flashing Details" on the facing page, the uppermost WRB layer overlays cap flashing. Cap flashing, also called head flashing, redirects water that might otherwise dam up behind door or window head casing, leading to stains and mold on interior surfaces, swollen sashes, peeling paint, and rot. All flashing is important, but flashing the head of a window or door is *the* critical detail to get right.

An aside: In addition to keeping rain out, both building paper and plastic housewrap must be permeable enough to allow excessive moisture inside the house to escape. Cooking, bathing, and showering put an extraordinary amount of water vapor into the air, which would become trapped in the walls if it couldn't escape. Moldy drywall, soggy insulation, and even rotted studs can result. Vent fans (p. 260) also help expel moisture.

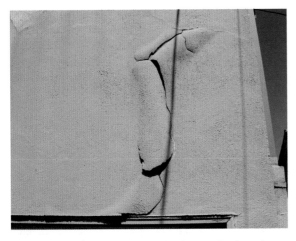

Paint failures like this are usually the result of applying a nonpermeable paint over a damp wall or one that excessive interior moisture was migrating through.

Painted and Stained Exteriors

Most types of siding and trim are painted or stained to better resist the damaging effects of the sun's UV rays and variations in temperature, to shed rain and snow, and to prolong the useful life of exterior materials. Although paint and stain colors are chosen primarily for their aesthetic appeal, these thin layers are also a first line of defense against the elements. So while faded or cracked paint may be only a cosmetic issue, widespread paint failure sometimes telegraphs more serious concerns.

A lot goes into a lasting paint job. (Hereafter, we'll use *paint* as the generic term.)

The substrate (the surface being painted) must be clean and dry, and carefully prepped beforehand. All gaps must be caulked, nails set flush or nail holes filled, and rough surfaces sanded and then wiped clean again. (Note, however, that the lower edge of window trim is often left uncaulked to provide an escape route for any trapped water.) All exposed trim edges must also be primed and painted. Any adverse environmental conditions, such as excessive interior moisture, must also be corrected before the surface is primed and painted.

LEARNING ABOUT LEAD PAINT

LEAD-BASED PAINT ADHERES TO ALMOST ANY surface and weathers well, so it's not surprising that it can be found in 90% of houses built before 1940. However, as lead's health hazards became known in the 1950s, paint manufacturers began to phase it out. It was banned altogether in 1978 by the U.S. government.

Because lead is a neurological toxin, it is particularly damaging to children aged 6 and younger, who seem drawn to it because it's slightly sweet. Breathing or eating it can cause mental retardation in children. In people of all ages, lead can cause headaches, anemia, lethargy, kidney damage, high blood pressure, and other ailments.

Because of its durability, lead paint was commonly used on exteriors, on glossy kitchen and bathroom walls, in closets (which rarely get repainted), and as an enamel on interior doors, windows, stair treads, and woodwork. So each time a swollen window or sticking door was forced open, it ground lead paint into flakes and dust. Roof leaks, drainage problems, and inadequate ventilation added to the problem because excessive moisture causes paint to degrade and detach sooner.

If you have an older home, the presence of lead may not be a dire problem if your home is well maintained and old paint is well adhered. However, lead becomes most dangerous when it becomes airborne, especially during sanding or heat stripping, for then it can be inhaled and easily absorbed into the bloodstream. Therefore, if you are thinking about renovating an old house, be methodical. Postpone any demolition or paint removal until you test to see if lead paint is present.

A number of kits that test for lead are available at home centers. However, at this writing only one satisfies U.S. Environmental Protection Agency (EPA) criteria for false positives and false negatives: LeadCheck®.

Testing is pretty straightforward. Using a utility knife, cut away a small amount of surface paint to get at earlier layers underneath. Rub the test swab on the exposed area: The brighter the swabbed area, the greater the concentration of lead. Test several areas, such as door and window trim and siding. A Lead-Check kit contains 16 swabs and costs less than $50.

For more information about lead-related questions, contact the National Lead Information Center at www.epa.gov/lead.

Lead paint exists in 90% of houses built before 1940. Lead paints were eventually banned by the federal government in 1978.

Testing for lead paint. A small chunk of surface paint is cut out to expose older paint layers, which are rubbed with a test swab. The bright red reading indicates a high level of lead.

The application must be skilled. In addition to careful prep, the painter must choose a paint that is suited to the substrate, keep painting equipment (especially spray-painting rigs) in good working order, apply paint when both day and night temperatures and humidity are optimal, and "follow the sun" as painting proceeds so that the substrate is never too hot.

Maintenance must be ongoing. A quality paint job can last for many years without repainting but a homeowner must keep an eye on conditions that could shorten the life of a paint job. Shrubs and trees should be cut back; gaps that open up, caulked; sprinkler systems calibrated so they don't spray the house; and paint that gets damaged should be touched up. Stain should be reapplied every 3 years to 5 years so it continues to repel water and resist weathering.

Wooden shingles and siding are often protected by a stain instead of paint. Its primary purpose is to protect the wood from the sun's damaging rays, so the more pigment in the stain the better. The advantage of staining is that it is easy to apply. Its downside is that it gets thinner every year and needs to be reapplied more often than paint. Paint lasts longer but requires more surface prep: scraping, sanding, and so on.

WHAT TO LOOK FOR

- Is there bubbling paint, especially on south or west walls? Chances are, the paint was applied when the siding was too hot (especially a problem on south and west walls) or a second coat was applied before the first was dry.
- Are there large areas of peeling paint on the exterior wall(s) of a kitchen or bathroom? Excessive interior moisture is the most likely cause, along with poor ventilation. Fortunately, the fix may be as simple as adding a vent fan.
- Do unheated garages and outbuildings experience chronic paint failure? If so, the cause is most likely exterior. Perhaps the sheathing or siding got rained on and was not dry when painted.

- If paint comes off in large pieces and there is little pigment on the wood siding, chances are that the wood was not primed properly.
- Do the painted surfaces of an older building have a texture like alligator skin? There were too many layers of paint on the building when a new coat was added.
- Widespread paint failure on all sides of a house that was painted within the last year or two is likely caused by inadequate surface prep or low-quality paint.
- Are there widespread rust stains? Someone used common steel nails—not galvanized—to install the siding.
- When you rub a painted surface, is there a chalky residue on the palm of your hand? Relax, that's normal weathering—aka chalking.
- Are there gray stains and mildew on painted surfaces, especially on north and shady sides of the house? For some reason, the siding is not drying completely after it rains and/or the paint used did not contain a mildew inhibitor.
- When stained wood surfaces fade to gray, either the stain used did not contain a UV-blocking agent or the stain was not reapplied soon enough. In general, stains with more pigment will fade more slowly.
- Is there both peeling paint and open gaps where wood siding boards butt to trim or to each other? The boards absorbed moisture and swelled before they were installed and then shrunk as they dried. Or they were milled from green wood and not sufficiently dried at the mill.

Wood Siding

Wood is easy to harvest, mill, and install, so it's no surprise that it comes in so many forms, including clapboards and lap siding, which are installed horizontally; board-and-batten, which is installed vertically; shingles and shakes; plywood with various textures; and hardboard siding, usually a wood-fiber composite mixed with resins to stabilize it. The downside of wood as a building material is that you must fight its natural tendency (as a tree) to absorb water, rot, and replenish the earth. To keep water out, all surfaces of wood siding must be sealed with

The large fungus growing at the bottom of this jamb trim is a dramatic example of how unmaintained wood will absorb moisture and decompose.

paint or stain. When wood clapboards are installed, for example, both faces and all edges must be primed and painted.

Because wood cells are designed to transport water up the trunk of a tree—from its roots to its crown—the end grain of boards is particular porous and inclined to absorb water. So sealing the end grain is especially important, as is caulking board ends when gaps open up. As it dries, wood shrinks in all dimensions, but especially along its length;

so gaps most often occur where siding boards butt together or where boards abut window, door, or corner trim.

Gaps also open up where different siding materials meet, such as wood siding and stucco, because different materials expand and contract at different rates. There again, it's important to keep gaps caulked so water doesn't get behind and soak sheathing or framing.

On heavily shaded sections of north-facing walls it's common for mildew to grow on siding if there is sufficient moisture present. On painted siding mildew spores initially look like a black or brown rash, which can spread till a whole wall is discolored and dirty looking. As long as the paint is intact, washing the siding with a household cleaner will usually suffice to remove the mildew.

If the paint membrane is cracked or peeling, however, mildew spores will feed on the wood siding (molds feed on organic matter) and discolor it. That black or brown streaking is the beginning of rot. Caught early enough, the siding can be scraped, sanded, primed, and repainted. The process is the same for unpainted wood siding or for stained siding whose stain has weathered so much that it no longer offers much protection. Here again, if the mildew is caught early enough, the siding can be sanded and restained. Paints and stains are available with mildew inhibitors.

Redwood and cedar siding contain oils that resist water and help the wood weather more slowly than other woods, so they are frequently left natural (unfinished). A combination of UV rays, wind, and water turns cedar and redwood siding a uniform gray, which traditionalists like the look of. As long as the siding is intact, free from splits, cupping, and the like, it will remain an effective exterior membrane. Gaps that develop on natural siding are usually caulked with a clear caulk or with a caulk whose color closely matches the weathered wood hue.

One final detail: Siding should be attached with galvanized, color-matched, or stainless-steel siding nails. Uncoated steel nails will rust and streak down

Wood clapboard siding is especially vulnerable where it abuts window and door trim. If there are gaps along the joint, water can soak clapboard ends, causing them to swell and split.

CLAPBOARD DETAILS

1×6 clapboards (actual width 5¼ in.)

Stud center

6-in.-wide building paper splines behind joints

Nails barely above top of clapboard below

4-in. exposure

Nails long enough to penetrate siding

Sheathing

Position clapboard joints over stud centers. For the most weathertight joints, bevel-cut ends. Note: For clarity in this drawing, building paper between clapboards and sheathing isn't shown.

the face of the siding. On painted siding, rust can bleed through the paint. Of all types, annular ring shank nails hold the best and offer the greatest resistance to pullout and cupping boards.

HORIZONTAL WOOD SIDING

Horizontal wood siding includes clapboards and lap siding. Clapboards are a beveled wood siding milled from redwood, red cedar, or spruce; for best results, builders specify Grade A or better. Inferior grades are likely to have knots or holes.

Lap siding is milled from 1-in.-thick stock to resemble two courses of clapboard. Wider boards are also somewhat more likely to cup. Horizontal wood siding is less likely to cup if it is nailed to stud centers, instead of being nailed only to sheathing. This is especially true of siding joints, where the end of one board butts against another.

WHAT TO LOOK FOR

- What is the general condition of the siding? Are any boards rotted? Are knots visible? If so, are knots bleeding through the paint—or missing? Is paint adhering well?
- Are clapboards or lap siding cracked and splitting? Is there any rot around cracks and splits?
- Are there any signs of cupping? Are there nail pops? Do you see rusty nails?
- Have gaps opened up between board ends or where boards abut exterior trim?
- Are clapboard or lap siding ends lifting from the sheathing?
- Is siding discolored due to persistent moisture, especially around the bottoms of walls? Is the bottom course of siding at least 8 in. above grade?

WOOD SHINGLES AND SHAKES

No. 2 grade shingles and shakes, milled from cedar or redwood, are fine for an exterior siding. (Shakes are thicker and split rather than sawn for a rougher look. We'll use *shingles* as the generic term for both.) Shingles should be knot-free and reasonably straight grained.

These wood shingles on a south-facing wall are so weathered that they are falling off. The lower courses are much grayer because of splashback from the shed roof below.

Shingles are able to shed water because they overlap several courses. Thus the amount that each course is exposed and the distance that shingle joints are offset (staggered) is crucial. Shingle joints must be offset 1½ in. for three courses; in other words, shingle joints can line up only every fourth course. As with any siding, shingles must also fit tightly against trim. Some contractors will place a bead of caulk on the underlayment behind the shingles as a waterproofing measure.

In general, shingle nails should not be exposed; they should be covered by overlapping shingles. An excessive number of visible nails indicates an installation problem.

An inspection should also note any shingle defects that could admit water, including cracks, splits, open knots, cupping, and loose or missing shingles. Not surprisingly, most defects will occur on south-facing walls, where the sun is strongest and weathering is accelerated.

WHAT TO LOOK FOR

- What is the general condition of the shingles? Are any split, loose, or missing?

- Are shingle joints correctly offset for three courses? If not, are there signs of water damage or wear between shingles?

- Do shingles butt tightly to vertical trim pieces or are there gaps? If there are gaps, are they caulked to keep water out?

- Are shingles cupping? How widespread is the problem? Is building paper or sheathing visible at any point?

- Were shingles skillfully nailed or are nail heads visible throughout the exterior? Are there any signs of shingles splitting because of excessive nailing?

PLYWOOD AND HARDBOARD SIDING

Plywood and hardboard siding are economical siding choices that, on the whole, are not as durable as the types described to this point. Both are engineered products in which wood fibers are bonded with waterproof glues under heat and pressure.

PLYWOOD PANELS have face plies that are textured or grooved to lend visual interest. Panels are 4 ft. wide by 8 ft., 9 ft., or 10 ft. long; with thicknesses ranging from ⅜ in. to ⅝ in. They are installed vertically to minimize the number of horizontal joints, because such joints are the most vulnerable to water

Plywood siding was popular in many areas in the 1970s and 1980s. Left unpainted, its surface veneer will wear away to expose the interior plies.

This hardboard siding has absorbed a substantial amount of water and swelled; the nails show the siding's original thickness. Siding this damaged should be replaced.

Minor visible damage on the surface of hardboard siding may conceal substantial interior wall damage. Sometimes the only way to know is to remove a few boards.

intrusion as it runs down exterior walls. Consequently panels' horizontal joints are shiplapped (upper panel edges overlap those below) or flashed with metal Z-flashing. Inspectors should scrutinize panel edges for splits, delamination, and rot.

The standard spacing for plywood siding nails is 6 in. around the perimeter of each sheet and 10 in. in the field (center areas of the panel). Insufficient nailing, a common defect, can allow plywood siding to buckle and pull away from the framing. Some wrongly assume that a single nail will secure two sheets along the vertical edges. You should see two nails, one for each panel, 6 in. apart along the vertical seams.

To save money, plywood panels are sometimes installed directly to studs (without sheathing) on garages and other outbuildings. In these cases there should be building paper or plastic housewrap between studs and siding to forestall rot.

HARDBOARD SIDING is available in 4-ft.-wide panels and 9-in.- to 12-in.-wide planks. There are wide variations in the longevity of such siding and an ongoing controversy (since the 1990s) over whether product defects or faulty installation are the primary cause of hardboard siding failures on hundreds of thousands of homes.

The central issue seems to be that hardboard siding's wood fibers, compacted under great pressure, "relax" and swell when moisture enters. Not painting plank backs is a common cause of failure. Bottom edges are particularly susceptible to damage and rot. Because wood fibers are oriented in a random manner, planks expand along their length to a greater degree than solid wood does, so buckling occurs. Such exterior symptoms are often accompanied by mildew and structural rot behind the siding.

WHAT TO LOOK FOR

- Are plywood panel edges delaminating, especially along the bottom of a wall or at the horizontal joints where panels meet?

- Was metal flashing used to weatherproof the horizontal joints between panels? Or are the joints shiplapped? Are there gaps between any panels?

- Are plywood panels buckling or pulling away from the framing? Are panels adequately nailed, especially around the edges?

- Are the face plies of plywood paneling so weathered that you can see interior plies? (Such siding is near the end of its useful life and needs to be replaced.)

- Have plywood panels been installed directly to studs, without benefit of sheathing in between? If so, are wall studs diagonally braced to resist shear forces?
- Is hardboard siding swelling around nail holes?
- Are hardboard plank edges, especially bottom edges, swollen or deteriorating? Are there loose or broken sections?
- As you sight along hardboard edges, do they appear wavy or are they straight? (Wavy lines indicate planks that are buckling.)
- Is there dark discoloration or fungus growing on the siding?

Stucco

Stucco consists of a cement-and-sand plaster applied in several layers to a wire-lath base over wood-frame construction or to a masonry surface such as brick, block, or structural tile. Stucco is usually applied in three coats: (1) a base (or scratch) coat approximately ½ in. thick, scored horizontally to help the next coat adhere; (2) a brown coat about ¾ in. thick; and (3) a finish coat (called a dash coat by old-timers) ⅛ in. to ¼ in. thick. For repair work and masonry-substrate work, two-coat stucco is common.

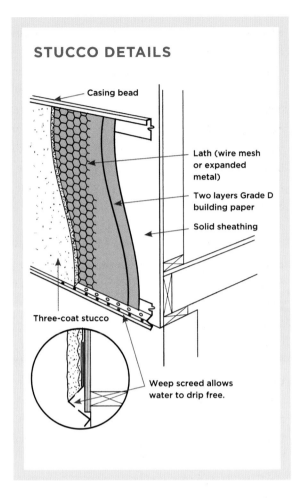

STUCCO DETAILS

Casing bead

Lath (wire mesh or expanded metal)

Two layers Grade D building paper

Solid sheathing

Three-coat stucco

Weep screed allows water to drip free.

Lacking a weep screed, the stucco wicked moisture and cracked. The concrete sidewalk may have pulled the stucco down and away from the concrete foundation behind.

Stucco is not waterproof. In fact, unpainted stucco will absorb moisture and wick it to the sheathing underneath. So before wire lath is attached, a waterproof layer of building paper must be installed over the sheathing. This waterproof layer is not always present in older homes or, if present, the paper may be fragile, so stucco repairs frequently involve replacing at least some of the waterproofing membrane.

Relatively newer stucco homes (say, 1940s on) have weep screed, a metal strip nailed to the base of exterior walls. Weep screeds are an easy way to make the bottom edge of stucco look crisp and clean. And because the weight of the stucco flattens the screed down against the top of a foundation, the screed creates a positive seal against termites and other pests. Stucco's tendency to retain moisture makes rot and insect infestation particular problems. So the bottom edge of the weep screed also allows water penetrating the stucco to drip free.

The bottom of stucco walls should stop at least 6 in. above grade or 2 in. above nearby paved surfaces. In older buildings, however, the bottom of stucco often extends below soil level and may conceal moisture or termite entry. So an inspector should gently probe the base of old walls to see if the stucco is crumbling or sheathing is rotting and then—when inspecting the basement or crawl space—look for corresponding signs of water damage or infestation inside.

FROM AN INSPECTION STANDPOINT, stucco condition can tell you a lot about a house. Stucco cracking, for example, is common and may be caused by movement in the wall framing, foundation settling, seismic activity, or stucco shrinkage. Minor cracks usually do not need repair and are normally fixed when the stucco is painted. Cracks large enough to allow water entry should be caulked or patched.

Diagonal cracks running out from the upper corners of windows or doors may telegraph big trouble. Building loads often concentrate on a header—a load-bearing member over a door or window opening—and diagonal cracking may be a sign that the header is not adequately supported. That is, the house's framing or foundation may be shifting. A structural engineer should have a look and suggest a solution.

Old stucco that is bulging from the wall or detached is another symptom that merits a closer look. It suggests that stucco has separated from the lath or that sustained dampness has rusted out lath nails. A possible suspect is water rising up through the foundation. Where that is the cause, the base of the wall is frequently crumbling as well. Rainwater penetration at a failed window flashing is another common cause.

WHAT TO LOOK FOR

- Is there widespread cracking? How wide are the cracks?
- Do any of the cracks run diagonally from the corner of a window or door?
- Does the stucco move when you press on it with the palm of your hand?

EIFS: SYNTHETIC STUCCO

AN EXTERIOR INSULATION AND FINISH SYSTEM (EIFS) is not stucco, but it looks like it. So it's usually referred to as "synthetic stucco." In a typical EIFS job, (1) rigid foam panels are installed over exterior wall sheathing, (2) a base coat is spread over the foam, in which (3) fiberglass mesh is bedded, and (4) a finish coat is applied over the mesh.

Whatever the theoretical merits of an EIFS exterior, presumably good R-values, the system has been plagued by widespread failures. Unlike real stucco, which has a waterproof layer between the sheathing and the stucco, EIFS has no such protection. So when water gets between the EIFS membrane and the sheathing, it gets trapped there, soaking and eventually rotting the sheathing and framing in as little as 2 years or 3 years.

Water typically enters where the EIFS material meets window or door frames, exterior trim, and building joints such as corners, wall-roof junctures, deck attachment points, wall penetrations for pipes, and so on. Presumably, caulking cracks and gaps help keep water out, but there are simply too many places where EIFS fails for caulking to do any good.

The EIFS industry eventually added drainage channels that allowed trapped water to escape, but by then the technology's reputation was in tatters. To learn the extent of moisture damage, an EIFS inspection specialist should be called in after the general inspection is complete.

EIFS (synthetic stucco) features rigid foam panels over sheathing. The foam can be easily damaged, exposing layers beneath to water damage.

Building loads often concentrate on a header—a load-bearing member over a door or window opening—and diagonal cracking may be a sign that the header is not adequately supported.

- Is the bottom of the stucco 6 in. above grade or does it run all the way to the ground? Is stucco crumbling at the bottom?

- Does the stucco terminate at least 2 in. above a concrete or paver surface?

- Are there gaps around windows or door trim or where stucco meets a dissimilar material?

- Has the stucco been patched repeatedly? If so, try to get a record of repairs. Patched sections typically have slightly different textures than surrounding areas.

Masonry Walls and Veneers

Masonry walls—usually brick—provide both structural support and an exterior facade. Brick and stone houses are handsome and prized by traditionalists

for their solidness and durability. However, because masonry is extremely dense, it is poor at retaining heat. Consequently, as energy conservation becomes ever more important, fewer and fewer masonry homes are being constructed. (Wood-frame homes have significantly higher R-values.) So most of the brick homes that an inspector is likely to encounter will be older. Masonry-veneer homes—in which a wood-frame house is faced with brick or stone—are somewhat more common.

Another shortcoming of masonry is its rigidness. In response to differential foundation settlement, seasonal changes in temperature or ground saturation, and seismic shifting, masonry walls crack. Not all cracks are significant, though all should be sealed to keep water out. Fine cracks in mortar joints are common and usually cosmetic, though deeper cracks, especially those that continue *across* several courses of bricks, should be inspected by a structural engineer experienced with masonry buildings.

Door and window openings are particularly vulnerable in masonry buildings. The perimeters of win-

Window and door openings in brick-clad buildings often use steel headers to support bricks above the openings. Unpainted, the steel may rust over time, causing it to expand and crack the adjacent brickwork.

dows and doors are susceptible to air and moisture infiltration. Gaps often open up because these units expand at different rates from the masonry surrounding them. Gaps should be monitored and caulked as needed.

The large openings required for doors and windows are also problematic in a structural sense: Loads above must be transferred across openings, typically by a steel lintel (header). Steel is strong, but it expands at a different rate from masonry, which encourages cracking. And exposed steel headers rust and often expand, causing cracks to occur in the adjacent brickwork. The steel headers in these areas should be painted with a rust-inhibiting coating and monitored periodically for any future rust damage. So inspectors must pay close attention to the perimeters of windows and doors in masonry walls.

Deep cracks running from corners can indicate structural problems, including different settling and foundation failure. These cracks may run diagonally across bricks or may step-crack along mortar joints. Where cracking sections are also bowing or bulging outward, the masonry wall may be close to failure; have a masonry specialist assess their soundness.

The condition of the mortar is often telling. Some erosion is to be expected, but any erosion deeper than 1 in. below the surface of the facade should be considered serious. Likewise, missing mortar should be replaced to keep water out. Mortar that crumbles when scraped by a screwdriver or pocketknife is also in poor shape; it should be scraped out and new mortar added and repointed—shaped and compacted with a pointing tool.

Efflorescence, a powdery white substance on the surface of masonry walls and foundations, is common where sustained moisture has leached salts through brick or concrete. Over time, the concrete or masonry will deteriorate as the salt crystals form deeper; surfaces can be wire-brushed clean and sealed. But persistent damp can cause a host of other problems, from mold to rot, and should be addressed.

BRICK-VENEER WALLS

Brick-veneer walls are freestanding (they stand on a portion of the foundation) but employ galvanized ties to attach them to the wood-frame walls behind. Brick-veneer walls work well enough as long as (1) the ties don't rust out, (2) water doesn't leak down behind the brick facade, (3) the brick wall has weep holes at the base that allow moisture to escape, (4) there is sufficient clearance (at least 8 in.) between the bottom of the brick and the ground to keep moisture from wicking upward, and (5) the brick is rated for exterior use.

There are other details to get right, but you get the idea: It's a complicated way to construct an exterior wall, with much opportunity for moisture to get behind the facade, soak the sheathing, and cause a lot of mischief.

Accordingly, inspectors should scrutinize mortar joints and bricks for cracks, splits, and loose materials, giving special attention to the top of the veneer wall(s), where brick meets siding or wood sheathing. All gaps must be caulked. Here again, door and window frames are especially vulnerable because they can shrink back from the masonry and leave gaps that water can leak into. Note also any large cracks in veneer bricks.

Brick-veneer siding often separates from the wall behind it after galvanized ties rust out. The gap can be caulked to prevent water entry and framing decay, but the veneer should eventually be removed.

In moist, shady areas, mold will grow on aluminum siding. This is primarily a cosmetic condition that can be scrubbed off periodically.

WHAT TO LOOK FOR

- Do masonry walls run all the way to the ground?
- Are there signs of moisture wicking up into the masonry? Use a moisture meter (p. 14) to determine the ambient moisture of the bottom of the wall.
- Is cracking widespread? Are cracks shallow or deep? Do cracks follow mortar joints or do the cracks run across bricks as well?
- Do any cracks run diagonally from the corners of door or window frames?
- Are door or window frames reinforced by a steel lintel at the top? Is the lintel rusted? Is there cracking in the bricks around the lintel?
- Have gaps opened up around window or door frames? Are those gaps caulked?
- Do any wall sections bulge?
- Are mortar joints crumbling or eroded? How deeply are they eroded?
- Are there bricks or sections of mortar missing?
- Is there efflorescence on the bottom of masonry walls? Are walls often damp?
- Is there a gap between the top of a low brick-veneer and the wall behind? Is it caulked to prevent water entry?
- Are veneer walls plumb or do their tops lean away from the building?

Aluminum and Vinyl Siding

Aluminum siding was among the first nonwood sidings, touted as a no-maintenance alternative to painted wood siding. It does require some maintenance, notably washing it periodically to remove grime. Aluminum siding's enamel paint is quite durable because it is applied and baked on at the factory. Though metal siding does not respond to changes in humidity, as wood siding does, it does contract and expand with temperature shifts. Thus metal siding will need to be repainted every 10 years or so.

Aluminum, a lightweight metal, flexes, scratches, and dents. To prevent corrosion, scratches that expose bare metal should be touched up with a compatible paint. Dents are usually left alone unless they compromise the exterior's weathertightness. However, loose and missing sections should be replaced and open joints must be closed.

Butt joints (where siding planks butt together) should be covered by H-molding; there are also end caps and specialty pieces to resolve corners and siding-trim joints. Such accessories are colored matched to the planks. If an inexpert installation resulted in widespread gaps around door and window trim, have an aluminum siding specialist do repairs. (Siding manufacturers generally recommend *against* caulking gaps because it is a temporary fix that can limit the metal's ability to expand and contract.)

The knock on standard aluminum siding is that its R-value is low and it does almost nothing to cut air leaks. In response, siding makers now offer an insulated aluminum siding which, when installed with a plastic housewrap, cuts air infiltration and helps older houses retain conditioned air. The insulation, usually a rigid foam, isn't very thick (⅜ in.) but it helps. As always, there are tradeoffs, with the downside being moisture retention behind the insulation. (Rap on the siding with a knuckle to see if it's insulated; uninsulated siding rings hollow.)

A code quirk: Check with local building code authorities to see if aluminum siding must be grounded to prevent shocks. If that's the case, a ground wire should be bonded to the siding, with the ground wire attaching to a ground rod or an approved water-pipe clamp. The code will specify how the grounding is to be done; to be effective, the metal siding has to be in continuous contact and the grounding device must be connected to bare metal, not painted metal.

WHAT TO LOOK FOR

- Does the siding gap where it joins trim, turns corners, or butts other siding boards? (Especially note where siding planks butt to window and door trim.)
- Are there dented or missing sections of siding that need replacing?
- Is the aluminum siding insulated?
- If siding is discolored, will washing remove the stains or is it time to repaint?
- If local codes require that aluminum siding be electrically grounded, are connections to the siding and to the grounding device mechanically solid?

VINYL SIDING

From a distance, vinyl siding looks like aluminum siding—it has end caps and H-molding, for example—but it has a slightly oily texture and its color is infused throughout the plastic. It is typically installed with a rigid foam insulation backer board that lends rigidness and boosts R-value. Also like aluminum siding, the critical points of a vinyl siding

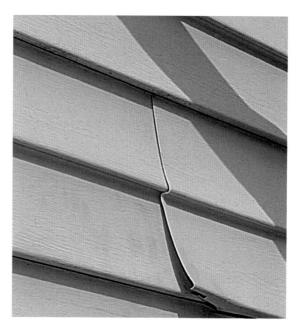

Aluminum siding can be low maintenance, but a sharp impact from, say, a car bumper, can crush the soft metal. This damaged siding and corner trim should be replaced.

Vinyl siding panels should clip together at the horizontal joints. If not installed correctly, the panels may buckle, causing joints to open. Siding should be checked periodically.

installation are at corners, where boards butt each other, and where siding abuts window and door trim. Look for gaps at those points.

Vinyl expands and contracts more than aluminum, so it's particularly important that installers get the nailing right. When it is incorrectly nailed, the material can't move freely and so buckles and looks wavy. In moderate temperatures vinyl stays flexible, but it becomes brittle in extreme cold. Consequently, though it rarely dents, it can crack or shatter if it's struck when very cold. Inspectors should note such damage.

WHAT TO LOOK FOR

- Are there gaps at building joints where siding boards meet trim?
- Do any sections of the vinyl siding look wavy or bulge out?
- Are any siding boards missing, split, cracked, or loose?

Cement-Based Siding

Cementitious siding is tough but relatively brittle, durable but inclined to crack or break if it gets a hard knock. Consequently, cement-based siding is typically reinforced with fibrous materials to make it more flexible.

ASBESTOS-CEMENT SHINGLES

Asbestos is well established as a carcinogen when its dust or fibers become airborne. But asbestos in a rigid form such as asbestos-cement siding is not considered to be particularly hazardous by many specialists. This type of siding is no longer manufactured, but because it is durable, rot- and insect-resistant, stable, and fireproof, it can still be found on many older homes.

If struck by a hard object, asbestos-cement shingles can crack or shatter. So nailing asbestos shingles can be tricky. Because these shingles are no longer made, it's common to see replacement shingles that don't match the color or texture of others on the wall. Large numbers of loose or missing shingles suggest

Asbestos-cement shingles are durable and can last many years if undamaged. Asbestos siding is not considered friable and will not easily enter the air. Only an experienced asbestos abatement contractor should dispose of it.

that siding nails are rusting through, and it's probably time to remove the cement-asbestos shingles and replace them with a more up-to-date material. Only a qualified asbestos abatement contractor should remove or dispose of such shingles, to minimize (and contain) the hazardous dust that will be created.

Inspectors should note cracked, loose, broken, or missing shingles.

FIBER-CEMENT SIDING

Fiber-cement (FC) siding is asbestos-free, consisting of reinforcing fibers, sand, and portland cement. Available in a wide range of sizes and textures, FC products now include trim boards, clapboard siding, and panels manufactured to simulate wood-shingle courses. HardiePlank® lap siding and HardieShingle® are two popular brands.

Fiber-cement siding paints like a dream, is impervious to insects and rot, and won't burn. Once installed, it is stable, durable, and virtually maintenance free. The trick is handling and installing it without damaging it. Unlike wood clapboards, which are lightweight and springy, fiber-cement siding is heavy, short-fibered, and brittle. Carried incorrectly, it can flex too much and crack across its face. Siding nails driven too deep will crack it, and errant hammer blows can chip or break it. Inspectors should note damaged or missing sections.

Exterior Trim

Exterior trim includes fascia, soffit, and frieze trim along a building's eaves; rake trim along its gable ends; corner boards; window and door molding and sills; and water-table trim that runs around the base of a building, below the siding. Exterior trim's basic function is to cover critical building joints, keeping water out and reducing air infiltration.

Exterior trim is installed in many different ways, depending on the design of the house and the type of siding. For wood shingles or clapboards, trim boards are typically thicker than the siding and nailed to the sheathing before the siding is installed. On older houses with shiplap or board-and-batten sidings, trim boards are frequently installed over the siding at corners, around windows and doors, and so on.

As is true with siding, there should be at least 6 in. of clearance between the bottom of trim boards and the ground below and 2 in. above masonry walks or driveways. Ideally, siding or trim that makes contact with the ground or a concrete sidewalk should be

Wood trim and siding should stop 6 in. above soil and 2 in. above walking surfaces. It should never be embedded into concrete because it will absorb moisture. The faulty detail shown here is common around garage door openings.

repaired to prevent rot damage or insect infestation. In protected areas where repair is not practical, however, a lesser clearance is acceptable, as long as the trim shows no sign of damage.

WOOD TRIM CHOICES

Traditionally, exterior trim has been milled from solid, rot-resistant woods such as redwood, cedar, or hard pine—sufficiently dry to avoid shrinkage, cupping, and checking. For those reasons, builders generally avoided softer, less stable species such as sugar pine, knotty pine, hemlock, and fir.

As mature, old-growth timber became scarce, the industry began fabricating finger-jointed trim stock from shorter lengths of high-grade wood. It also fashioned hardboard, fiberboard, and wood-fiber composites from wood chips that were steamed, pressed, and glued. Today, such engineered wood products are widely used as trim. Though more dimensionally stable than solid wood, they still have wood's tendency to absorb water, to swell, and in time, to rot.

When inspecting exterior trim, start by getting an overall impression of the wood quality. Knotholes, knots bleeding through, splits, and widespread cupping suggest an inferior grade of wood was used. (Cupping may also be caused by not priming the back faces of trim boards.) Painted trim that is peeling needs to be repainted. Gaps between trim boards should be caulked; boards may also need to be re-nailed (or screwed).

PRIMING AND PAINTING

Primer must be applied to all faces and edges of exterior wood (and engineered wood) siding, and trim, including the back faces. Although an inspector cannot, of course, see if siding is back primed, wood that is not back primed will cup (edges will curl up) when the sun dries out the exposed front face if the back retains moisture. The greater the moisture differential between front and back faces, the more likely the cupping. Equally important, as trim boards are cut and fitted to the exterior, cut edges must be

All edges and board ends must be painted to seal out moisture, unlike this example where the underside of the trim was left unpainted. Inspectors should look at as many of these surfaces as possible to be sure all are properly painted.

spot-painted to seal out moisture. End grain is especially thirsty. If you see swelling around nail holes, chances are you're looking at hardboard trim: If nails are driven too deep, they may compromise its waterproof surface and admit moisture.

OTHER TRIM CHOICES

As noted earlier, aluminum and vinyl siding have matching trim pieces made of the same material. Metal and vinyl trim pieces are durable and expand only slightly, so gapping is a problem only if the

siding system is incorrectly installed. Fiber-cement siding also has companion trim pieces, milled in thicknesses from 7/16 in. to 1 in. Last, cellular PVC plastic is a rapidly growing category of exterior trim. In some respects, PVC trim is easier to work than wood, but it tends to expand and contract along its length, so when joining long boards, carpenters must bevel-cut ends so they overlap. Otherwise, PVC trim will buckle as it expands.

ATTACHING TRIM SECURELY

As a rule, exterior trim should be nailed to framing. In those rare instances where installers have only sheathing to nail to, they must angle the nail so that it will be less likely to pull out. If you see trim boards lifting, they were likely nailed only to sheathing. As is true with siding, trim should not be attached with uncoated, non-stainless-steel nails: They will rust and stain the exterior.

WHAT TO LOOK FOR

- Do any trim boards make contact with the ground or with a concrete sidewalk? Is the bottom of the trim rotting?
- Are corner trim and siding discolored and degraded at the corners of the house? Look for a missing or leaking downspout.
- Are there gaps between trim board edges? Open joints should be caulked and edges should be drawn together with screws or nails driven in at an angle.
- Are there gaps where siding butts to siding? Gaps should be caulked with an elastomeric caulk that will accommodate the expansion and contraction of siding boards.
- *All* trim faces and edges must be painted to seal out moisture. Do you see any bare wood? (Use a mirror to look under the bottoms of corner boards.)
- Are trim boards cupping? Most likely, the back faces of boards were not primed.
- Are nail pops common? Trim boards were probably nailed to sheathing, not to framing.
- Can you see widespread rust stains?

KEEPING FIREWOOD AT A DISTANCE

FIREWOOD SHOULD BE STORED WELL AWAY from a house for fire safety and to prevent infestation by termites or other wood-destroying insects that are often present in firewood. Also, areas obscured by firewood cannot be accessed and inspected.

- Are trim boards at the eaves badly deteriorated or detaching from rafter ends? The cause is probably a roof leak or missing drip edges (discussed at right).

- Is the trim at eaves and roof excessively weathered or splitting? If it is on south- or west-facing walls, you're seeing water and sun damage. The trim should be replaced.

- Do vinyl, PVC, or aluminum trim boards buckle? Individual boards may have been butt joined too tightly to allow for expansion.

- Do trim boards swell or crack around nail holes? Moisture has entered hardboard trim because it was incorrectly nailed.

INSPECTING THE EAVES

Eaves are the area where roof framing meets or overhangs exterior walls. The eaves get a lot of weather, so carefully inspect trim at the eaves and rakes (sloping boards along gable ends).

Three more terms: Exterior *soffits* are the enclosed areas under eaves or other horizontal projections. *Fascia* is a flat board fastened along the eave ends of roof rafters. *Frieze* is a traditional trim board between the top of the siding and the soffit. These three types of trim are not always present.

A gap behind this rain gutter allowed water to flow over the rafter tails and eaves boards and rot them in several places. Chances are, the roof's drip edge was installed incorrectly or not at all.

DRIP EDGE FLASHING

The single most important detail to get right at these critical horizontal roof–wall junctures is installing metal drip edge flashing. Drip edge is discussed at length in the next chapter (see p. 65), but here we'll note that it is a metal edge that projects along roof edges and causes water to drip free of eaves trim. (Drip edge is installed under roofing and over the sheathing or fascia, so the flashing also covers and protects sheathing edges from gutter splashback and ice dams.) Otherwise, water would travel, by capillary action, behind the exterior trim and siding.

As you inspect eaves trim, try to see if proper flashing protects all roof edges. (Along gable edges, look for rake edge flashings.) Drip edge doesn't stick out much so you may need binoculars to see the farthest reaches. In addition, look for signs of water damage such as splitting, lifting, or rotting trim boards. Also note gaps between trim where individual board ends meet. Ideally, board ends should be beveled so there's not an open seam due to shrinkage, but that doesn't always happen.

Look also for leaking or poorly attached gutters (more on p. 73) and stains or water damage on trim or siding behind them. Also note the condition of painted trim. Badly peeling paint may be an indication that trim boards are retaining moisture. In the Snow Belt, trim is often badly weathered or loosened by ice dams (p. 67). Such trim should be routinely checked, reattached if necessary, and repainted at the end of each winter.

Scrutinize the tops of exterior walls: If water is getting behind trim and siding, you may see peeling paint, discoloration, and lifting boards. If rafter tails or roof beams are exposed, look for rot. It is important that the upper surfaces of such exposed framing be kept painted to prevent water damage. (Upper surfaces are typically not visible from the ground, so examine them when you inspect the roof.) Exposed rafter or beam ends are often covered with sheet-metal caps to prevent water damage.

If the house has enclosed soffits, they will often contain ventilation ports or slots to allow air to circulate under the roof, thus reducing excess heat and moisture. The edges of vent ports and slots should be kept painted to resist rot and covered with screen to keep insects and animals out of the attic. If there are vent screens, however, they should not be painted over, which would block the flow of air.

WHAT TO LOOK FOR

- Are all roof edges protected with metal drip edge flashing?
- What is the general condition of eaves and rake edge trim? Are any trim boards lifting, split, or cupping? Are board joints tight or are there gaps?
- Are gutters in good condition or are they rusty and leaking? Behind damaged or rusting gutters, is trim discolored or rotting?
- Is painted trim in good condition or is peeling widespread?
- Are overhead service drops well anchored to the house or are porcelain insulators pulling trim boards away from the house?
- Are exposed rafter tails or roof beams sealed with paint? Or are they peeling or bare wood? Are rotted ends visible?
- Are soffits ventilated? Are soffit vents covered with screen? Are screens painted over?
- At the tops of exterior walls, is there peeling paint, water damage, missing siding, or signs of rot?

BAD CONNECTIONS

OVERHEAD ELECTRICAL SERVICE CABLES— also called a service drop—must be securely anchored to a house. Ideally, drops should run to a weatherhead (p. 125) atop a length of rigid conduit. On many older houses, however, service cables run to a porcelain insulator screwed into eaves trim. If an insulator screw attaches *only* to trim, in time the weight and tension of the cables will pull the trim board away from the house. This is dangerous and should be corrected by the utility company or a licensed electrician.

Windowsills get a lot of splashback and standing water, so sills and the lower corners of wooden window sashes are vulnerable to rot. Commonly, sash rails and stiles will split.

Windows and Doors

Windows and doors have to put up with a lot: extremes of hot and cold, UV damage from the sun, water soaking and swelling their frames and sashes, and all manner of abuse from people trying to force them open when they are swollen or painted shut. When you inspect the exterior, get an overview of the windows' and doors' condition. When you go inside, you can check to see if they are operating correctly, as explained in Chapter 11.

WINDOW TYPES

In your inspection report, note (1) what types of windows are present; (2) what materials window frames and sashes are made of, if apparent; and (3) their overall condition. When you go inside, you'll also wanted to note if windows are single, double, or triple panes. Here's a quick summary of window types and materials.

Double-hung windows are by far the most common in older construction; both upper and lower sashes slide up and down to admit fresh air. Single-hung windows have a fixed upper sash; the lower sash slides. Casement windows are side hinged and swing outward, usually operated by a crank. Awning windows are hinged at the top, the bottom swings outward. Hopper windows, which tilt from the bottom, are like upside-down awning windows. Tilt-and-turn windows are hybrids that tilt like a casement or bottom tilt like a hopper. Horizontal slider windows are like miniature patio doors; sashes slide in tracks. Jalousie windows are typically a series of pivoting glass louvers (slats) in a metal frame. Fixed windows don't open.

WINDOW FRAME AND SASH MATERIALS

Window materials are trade-offs of durability, insulating level, maintenance, and of course, cost. Color may also be a consideration because not all materials can be painted. Wood windows require the most maintenance because they can absorb moisture, swell, and in time rot if paint is not maintained. Clad wood windows, on the other hand, require less maintenance, can be painted, and are the most expensive type listed here. Metal windows (aluminum or steel) have poor insulating levels, are cold to the touch in winter, and are prone to condensation; more expensive models come with thermal barriers. Vinyl windows are economically priced and are rated fair in durability, maintenance, and R-value; color selection is limited. Solid fiberglass window frames and sashes are ranked good in all characteristics and are almost as expensive as clad wood; they are paintable.

When inspecting windows, pay close attention to the corners of sashes where horizontal rails meet vertical stiles. They should fit tightly, without gaps. Note how sashes fit into frames. Both frames and sashes should be square and so should the window casing (trim) around them. Scrutinize the perimeter of window casings, where siding butts against them. There should be no gaps where water could enter or if there are, they should be well caulked. Finally, note the presence or absence of flashings where needed, especially head flashings above windows.

FLASHING WIDOWS AND DOORS

To rain running down a building exterior, door and window trim must look like the Hoover Dam, especially the head casing that runs across the top. When this film of water encounters obstacles in its path, it will flow into gaps between the head casing and the sheathing or into gaps along the sides of a window or door. Unless, that is, such gaps are correctly flashed—particularly with head flashing—to direct water outward and keep it running harmlessly down the siding till it drips free.

The cap flashing, correctly installed over this header trim, will keep runoff from getting behind the trim. Now if only the painter had painted the end of the trim!

WHAT TO LOOK FOR

- What window types are present? Based on your observations and the type of siding used, what do windows appear to be made of? (Your inspection inside will give you a closer look.)

- What is the general condition of windows? Do any have peeling or missing paint? Do any appear to be painted shut? Do window frames appear to be square?

- Are any frames or sashes badly weathered or cracking? Are sash corners tight or gapping?

- Are there gaps between siding and window casing (trim)? If there are gaps, are they caulked or could water enter?

- Do all windows have head flashing? (Use binoculars to examine upper-story windows.)

- Are any glass panes cracked or missing? Is window putty cracked or missing?

- What is the overall condition of windowsills and bottom sash rails? Are any badly weathered, cracked, or rotted?

- Are metal windows corroded or rusted?

- If the house is in a cold region, are there storm windows? If the inspection takes place during warm months and storm sashes have been removed, ask the homeowner where they are stored and examine them.

EXTERIOR DOOR TYPES

The drill for exterior doors is the same as that for inspecting windows: Start with an overview of the doors' condition. If you see missing flashing and badly weathered sills outside, when you go inside, look for corresponding water damage, drafts, and so on, as explained in Chapter 11.

Most exterior doors are hinged, though sliding doors are common where a deck or a patio adjoins the house. There are also sleek pivot doors that turn on a single shaft within the door spine, but they tend to be architect-specified, custom-made, and very pricey. Doors may also be classified according to whether they are stile-and-rail, a traditional design whose panels float within a solid-wood frame; or flush, a more modern look whose flat faces are laminated to a solid core that is augmented to improve its thermal efficiency. In general, exterior doors with glass lites tend to have a lower cumulative R-value than those without glass.

DOOR MATERIALS

Apart from the glass that makes up most of a sliding door, the principal materials used for exterior doors are wood, steel, and fiberglass. As with windows, door materials are a trade-off of durability, maintenance, price, and energy efficiency.

FIBERGLASS DOORS offer the best bang for the buck overall, with R-values of 8 or higher. They are typically fiberglass skins applied over a wood-composite, laminated veneer lumber (LVL), or steel frame; the core is filled with foam insulation. Fiberglass expands and contracts at the same rate as glass, so glazing seals are especially stable. Such doors require the least maintenance.

WOOD DOORS are the traditional favorite, but they are the least durable and require the most maintenance; if they don't get it, wood doors will absorb moisture, swell, and in time rot. Protected by an overhang or a porch, they'll weather more slowly. Their energy profile is so-so. On average they have an R-2 value, although more efficient ones achieve R-5.

STEEL DOORS are economical but unexciting. They are also durable, easy to maintain, and, when filled with foam, almost as energy-efficient as fiberglass. (Cold goes right through them, when uninsulated.) Steel doors need repainting every 3 years to 5 years, otherwise they will rust. Once the steel skin starts to rust, it can go fast. Steel-framed windows and doors were common in the 1940s, and many homeowners want to preserve them to maintain the home's original architectural style.

This metal sweep protects the bottom of the door and keeps driving rains out. However, the wood sill is worn and needs to be refinished and rot is visible where jamb trim meets the sill.

WEATHERPROOFING DETAILS

Because doors are relatively large areas with low R-values, it's important to reduce air infiltration and energy loss as much as possible. From an inspection point of view, weatherproofing doors is not an expensive item, but it's a good indicator of the general level of care given to the house.

WEATHER STRIPPING can be sophisticated, with compressible stripping that slides into kerfs (slots) between the door and the doorstop as well as flexible sweeps or shoes that seat securely to sill/threshold units. Open and shut each exterior door to see how tightly it fits into its frame; it should open and close easily, but with a slight resistance as the stripping compresses.

DOORSILLS get a lot of abuse from rain, snow, grit, and foot traffic. Examine them closely to see if they are badly worn, cracked, or rotted. Step on them to see if they move; if so, the framing underneath may be damaged. In areas with driving rains, an all-weather doorsill system will reduce drafts and resist water seeping or blowing in under the door.

Storm doors reduce air infiltration and retain heat. Most houses have metal or wood frames with removable storm and screen panels. Check the condition of doors, particularly noting the corners. Lightweight metal storm doors tend to separate at the corners as they near the end of their useful life.

WHAT TO LOOK FOR

- What type and material is each exterior door?
- Are exterior doors protected by overhangs or porches?
- Are door frames and casing square? Wracked frames with diagonal cracks at the corners may indicate structural problems.
- Do exterior doors open and shut easily or do they stick? Is there weather stripping? Are there gaps between the door and the frame?
- Does siding butt tightly against the door casing or are there gaps? Are gaps caulked?
- What is the condition of the doorsill? Is its surface abraded, split, or rotted? Are there signs of water damage? How high above the stoop or deck is the doorsill?
- Are the bottoms of any doors damaged or delaminating? Is there peeling paint? In snow country, could snow pile up against the base of the door?
- Are metal doors rusting or dented?
- Do all exterior doors exposed to the weather have storm doors?

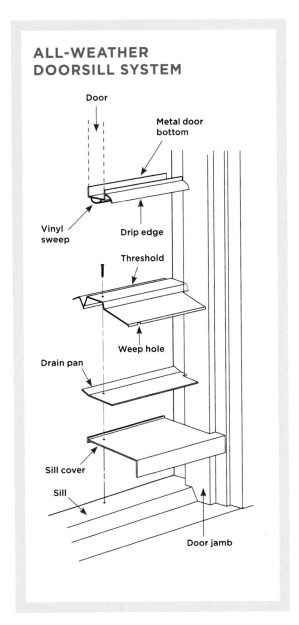

ALL-WEATHER DOORSILL SYSTEM

Door
Metal door bottom
Vinyl sweep
Drip edge
Threshold
Weep hole
Drain pan
Sill cover
Sill
Door jamb

CHAPTER 3

ROOFS

A ROOF IS A BUILDING'S MOST IMPORTANT LAYER of defense against water, wind, and sun. Properly constructed and maintained, a roof system will deflect rain and snowmelt and route water away from the building. Properly insulated and ventilated, the roof system will also moderate moisture and temperature in the living spaces below, ultimately leading to a house that's more healthful, comfortable, and energy efficient.

Roofing Basics

Reduced to its simplest elements, a roof system consists of (1) wood framing, typically an array of rafters or ceiling joists; (2) roof sheathing (or decking), usually plywood or oriented-strand board (OSB) panels or boards nailed to framing; and (3) roofing materials that cover the sheathing.

WATER SHEDDING OR WATERPROOF

There are two basic roof types: steep slope and low slope. Steep-slope roofing sheds water and needs a downward slope of at least 4 in 12. Slopes down to 2 in 12 are allowed if special double underlayments (water-resistant sheet materials under the roofing) are used. Lower slope, or low-slope, roofing is designed to be relatively waterproof. All low-slope roofs, including so-called flat roofs, should be designed to slope to drain properly. Minor standing water is permitted on low-slope roofing as long as it dries within 48 hours.

Historically, roofs were sloped to shed water, as most still are. Sloped-roof materials traditionally included clay tile, wood shingles and shakes, metal, and slate. Although all of these materials are still used, composition shingles, commonly called asphalt shingles, are by far the most common type. Used with felt paper underlayment, these roofing materials will shed water but, it must be noted, they are *not* waterproof. Rather, they allow water to flow over them, unimpeded, down and away from the building. If roofing is incorrectly installed or becomes worn, water can get underneath it.

Flat roofs have quite a bit of history too, and hot asphalt (also known as bitumen) was applied to roofs in the Middle East as early as the fifth century B.C.E. *Flat* is something of a misnomer: Every roof should slope somewhat so water doesn't pond up. Roofing materials for flat and low-slope roofs include built-up roofing, single-ply membranes, roll roofing, and spray polyurethane foams (SPFs) that both insulate and waterproof.

Know your limits. Many home inspectors won't get onto a roof. If you go topside, do so only in dry weather and stay alert.

FLASHING AND DRAINAGE

Today's roofs have protruding vent pipes, chimneys, skylights, and dormers—all potential dams that need to be flashed (see p. 64) to direct water around them. As runoff approaches the lower reaches of the roof, it must be directed away from the building by means of overhangs, drip edges, gutters, downspouts, and other drainage elements (see p. 73).

Steep-Slope Roofs

Steep-slope roofing must shed water, so your inspection should focus on how well it's doing that. From the ground, sight along the roof ridge to see if it's straight. If the ridge sags in the middle, suspect too many layers of roofing or undersize rafters. Older houses in regions with temperate climates were often framed with 2×4s, sometimes 24 in. on-center. Over time, such rafters may sag, especially under several layers of roofing. If the sagging has stabilized, no repairs may be needed, however.

SAFELY INSPECTING ROOFS

INSPECTING A ROOF CAN BE DANGEROUS.
The higher the roof and steeper its pitch (and the more difficult it is to access), the greater the danger. Consequently, some authorities suggest that you inspect a roof solely from the ground, using binoculars as you walk around the house. Indeed, if the roof is very steep or roofed with a slippery material such as slate, tile, or metal, it's probably a good idea to survey it from the ground.

In most regions, inspectors routinely get up onto the roof for a closer look, especially on single-family houses built in the last half-century. In drier regions, many houses of this vintage have low-slope (a pitch of 4-in-12 or less) or flat roofs, good access, and asphalt shingles that offer soft-soled shoes a decent grip. If you do go up, play it safe:

1. Make sure there's a second person within earshot in case you fall or need help. (Having a real estate agent on site during an inspection can be helpful.)

2. Don't venture up when the roof is wet or near freezing or extremely warm. When wet, most roofing materials are slippery. Cold asphalt shingles are brittle; warm asphalt can stretch and tear. Always wear shoes with soft nonslip soles.

3. Ladder safety is essential. Position ladder feet securely away from the building. Ideally, the top of the ladder should stick up at least 2 ft. or 3 ft. above the roof surface. Whether ascending or descending, always face the ladder.

4. When on a roof, try to walk directly over rafters, to which the sheathing is nailed. Roofs tend to be less springy over rafters, and you'll be less likely to break through rotted sheathing on an old or poorly maintained house.

5. Be thorough and stay alert: Walk around as much of the roof perimeter as is safe to do. And always walk forward as you inspect—never backward.

Going topside enables you to examine the roof and its ancillary structures closely. Be thorough, but stay alert. Move forward as you scan the roof perimeter. And minimize multitasking: Record your observations when you're back on the ground.

Note any rooftop sagging on your report and later, when you inspect the attic, look for cracked rafters and signs of active leaks, which may indicate distressed framing that needs structural reinforcement (such as adding braces or purlins beneath the rafters) or, possibly, requires roof stripping and rafter replacement. (It's almost always best to wait until reroofing to do any framing reinforcements.)

If the roof sags and its low areas run parallel to rafters, the sheathing may be too thin and needs to be replaced during reroofing. Isolated low spots are more likely caused by rot or, where skip sheathing (see p. 58) was used beneath an old shingle roof, individual boards have failed.

A roof surface that is wavy and uneven probably has too many layers of roofing—anything more than two layers is too many. It will need to be stripped when a new roof is installed.

When scanning a roof, you can also get a quick read on how well it's been maintained. Do trees

This roof surface is very lumpy, probably due to too many layers. The roof-to-wall flashings are not visible and are therefore suspect.

overhang the roof or branches touch it? Branches can abrade roofing and leaves can clog gutters and downspouts. Are shingles mossy? Are there widespread patches of roofing cement? Chances are, each tried to stop a leak. Note where these conditions occur, then look for leak stains when you go inside. If you're diligent, you'll start to see patterns.

COMPOSITION OR ASPHALT SHINGLES

Asphalt shingles are fabricated by infusing a fiberglass/felt mat (base) with asphalt to resist water and then coating the weather face of the shingle with mineral granules. The granules deflect sunlight and its damaging UV rays, helping prolong the life of the mat. Consequently, granule loss is a key indicator of a shingle roof's age and condition.

The three-tab shingle, shown in "Shingle Lingo" on p. 56, is the most common type. Slots cut into the exposed part of the shingle add visual interest and allow heat expansion. But slots tend to erode and shed granules faster than the body of the shingle. Thus correct installation is critical. To minimize leaks, installers use only four nails per full-width shingle, and those nails must be covered by the shingle course above. The bottom 5 in. of each shingle course is left exposed to the weather; most shingles today also

have a self-seal strip that melts and adheres to the shingles above to prevent uplift.

Shingle weight and dimensions vary; the most commonly installed are 12 in. by 36 in. Common three-tab shingles weigh about 200 lb. per square. Shingle weight is a rough indicator of longevity: standard 200-lb. shingles last 15 years to 20 years, depending on maintenance and sun exposure. Architectural-grade laminated shingles can last 30 years to 35 years, and some 450-lb. luxury shingles come with 50-year warranties.

The lines of black glue spots are self-seal strips. Correctly installed beneath a row of shingles above, the adhesive melts and secures the shingle tabs above. Here, an inept roofer badly overexposed two rows so the seal strips aren't even covered. This job should be redone.

SHINGLE LINGO

THESE DEFINITIONS WILL HELP YOU MAKE sense of roofing terms.

- **Course:** a horizontal row of shingles.
- **Butt edge:** the bottom edge of a shingle.
- **Exposure:** typically, the bottom 5 in. of the shingle, left exposed to weather. Shingles with metric dimensions are usually exposed $5\frac{5}{8}$ in.
- **Cutouts:** slots cut into the exposed part of a three-tab shingle, to add visual interest and allow heat expansion.
- **Offset:** the distance that shingle slots or ends are staggered from course to course.
- **Self-seal strip:** the adhesive on the shingle face that, when heated by the sun, fuses to shingles above and prevents uplift.
- **Fastener line:** on shingles with a 5-in. exposure, a line roughly $5\frac{5}{8}$ in. up from the butt edge. Nails along this line will be covered by the shingles above. (If shingles don't have such lines marked, nail just below the self-seal strip.)
- **Control lines:** chalklines snapped onto underlayment to help align courses and cutout lines.
- **Underlayment:** a water-resistive sheet material—usually building paper—that covers the roof sheathing.

THREE-TAB SHINGLES

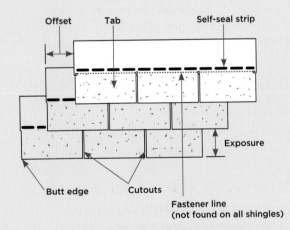

COMMON ASPHALT SHINGLE FAILINGS

Asphalt shingles are quite durable but occasionally they fail prematurely. Look for the following signs of failure.

WIDESPREAD CUPPING, eroded edges, curling, and loss of granular surfaces—and gutters filled with granules—suggest that it's time for a new roof. Estimating how many years an asphalt shingle roof has left is an inexact science, so as a rule of thumb, reroof when a third of an asphalt shingle roof looks worn out.

ROOFING CEMENT PATCHES suggest a homeowner who has found leaks and is trying to buy a few more years by patching obvious cracks. Aside from looking shabby, this approach may lead to sustained water damage.

LUMPY, UNEVEN ROOFING probably has three or more layers of shingles that will need to be removed before reroofing. Sometimes you can count roofing layers along the rakes, where the shingle edges are visible.

ODD-COLORED SHINGLES here and there are probably patches over old leaks. However, if the roof is relatively new and shingles are worn in only one

Composition shingles with ragged edges and pitted surfaces, cracked cap shingles along the ridge, and a roof vent slathered with roofing cement to stop leaks are all clear signs that it's time to reroof.

The best place to count shingle layers is along roof edges. As you count, keep in mind that roofers often double shingles along the edges to stiffen the overhang. In most locales, you must now strip the roof before reroofing if there are two or more layers on it. Note the popped roofing nail: It can't even reach the sheathing.

These asphalt shingles are worn out and will soon need replacement. The darker shingles have prematurely aged because of a poor factory coating. The shingles' protective mineral granules have worn off, exposing the bituminous base beneath.

area, perhaps one or more bundles of shingles were defective.

WIDESPREAD WEAR AND CUPPING on a relatively new roof (5 years to 10 years old) suggests a product defect. The shingles should be stripped before reroofing.

MANY MISSING OR LOOSE SHINGLES indicate that shingle nailing was improper, possibly because the installer's power nailer was set too deep and drove the roofing nails through the shingles. Have a licensed roofing contractor survey the roof— it may need to be stripped and replaced. A few shingles missing on an otherwise sound roof may have been caused by wind damage.

MOSSY SHINGLES are common to north-facing roof slopes and sections overhung by trees. The best fix is prevention: Cutting back branches and periodically clearing debris off the roof will help.

ERODED GRANULES alongside roof dormers and below dormer downspouts have been washed away by concentrated runoff. Extending dormer downspouts so they empty directly into main gutters is one fix. Roof drainage is discussed further on p. 73.

WHAT TO LOOK FOR

- Has the roof been well maintained? Are gutters free of leaves? Are shingles mossy?
- Does the roof have any appreciable sagging? Is the ridge straight?
- Are there widespread patches of roofing cement?
- Is there widespread shingle cupping, eroded edges, curling, or loss of granular surfaces?
- If the roofing surface is wavy and lumpy, there may be too many layers of shingles on the roof. If roof edges are visible, try to count the layers.
- If there are odd-colored shingles, are they isolated (patches) or widespread (defective)?
- If there are a lot of missing or loose shingles, suspect faulty power nailing.
- Is widespread wear visible although the roof shingles are relatively new?

WOOD SHINGLES AND SHAKES

Wood shingles and shakes are milled from water-resistant woods such as red or white cedar or cypress. Wood shingles are sawn; shakes are split and tend to be somewhat thicker and more irregular. Only No. 1 (blue label) shingles should be used on roofs because

Debris trapped behind chimneys and other obstructions will collect leaves that restrict water flow. Install V-shaped sheet metal flashing or a cricket above such obstructions. Periodic cleaning of such areas is also advised.

they are free of sapwood and knots. (Lesser grades are fine for siding but may leak on a roof.)

Wood shingles are manufactured in lengths of 16 in., 18 in., and 24 in., for recommended exposures of 5 in., 5½ in., and 7½ in., respectively, on roofs with a 4-in-12 pitch. Ultimately, roof pitch determines exposure: Greater shingle exposure is possible on steeper roofs because they shed water faster.

Wood shingle and shake roofs can last 30 years or more if they are correctly installed. There should be ¼-in. space between shingles or shakes to allow for expansion when they become wet. Because joints are vulnerable, they should be offset at least 1½ in. from joints in the course above; joints should line up no more than every fourth course.

Even rot-resistant wood will rot eventually if it stays moist for too long; wood roofing needs to dry periodically. Consequently, wood shingles were traditionally installed over skip sheathing, widely spaced 1-in. boards that allow air to circulate under shingles and dry them.

Today, most sheathing is plywood panel, so wood roofs require a ¼-in.-thick synthetic mesh (Cedar

Breather® is one brand) between the building paper and the shingles. The mesh has enough loft to allow air circulation. Periodically clearing debris will also help prolong the life of wood roofs, because debris holds moisture.

COMMON WOOD-ROOF FAILURES

Wood shingles and shakes are more susceptible to natural forces—especially water, sunlight, and temperature shifts—than asphalt ones.

MOSSY SHINGLES on a north-facing roof slope are common, especially if it's shady. Moss retains water, which degrades wood in time. Moreover, if moss builds up, it will raise shingle butt ends, which driving rains can get under. Wire-brushing or hand-scraping will remove moss. To keep moss off, staple a length of 10-gauge or 12-gauge bare copper wire to a course of shingle butts all the way across the roof. Run one wire along the ridge and another about halfway down. During rains, a dilute copper solution will wash down the shingles, which acts as a fungicide. It's a nice alternative to toxic chemical treatments.

This wood shake roof is completely worn out, and should not be walked on. The wood roofing should be removed; and solid decking, plywood, or OSB, should be applied before reroofing.

Sliding new wood shingles below gaps in old shake or shingle roofing is a good short-term repair technique. This roof will need to be removed and replaced soon.

DAMAGED OR DECAYED SHINGLES along rake edges or eaves have usually absorbed water for too long. Replacing individual shingles is not difficult, but it's often best to simply slide new wood shingles over the old damaged ones and tap them into place because it requires no shingle removal or nailing.

AN OLD ROOF (30 years or more) with cupping, splitting, and missing shingles has come to the end of its life. Strip and replace the shingles.

A RELATIVELY NEW ROOF (10 years or less) with cupping, splitting, and rotted shingles was probably installed directly over solid sheathing, trapping moisture on the underside of the shingles or shakes. It needs to be stripped. If the sheathing is in decent shape, consider reroofing with asphalt shingles.

MANY SHINGLES WITH HOLES are most likely caused by the installer using an inferior grade of shingles intended for walls. If you see water stains on the underside of the sheathing, the roof is leaking. Strip the shingles and reroof.

WOOD SHINGLES IN HOT, DRY AREAS may violate local fire codes; check local codes to see what roofing materials are approved. When it's time to reroof, you may need to install a Class A, fire-rated roofing material.

WHAT TO LOOK FOR

- Are shingles (or shakes) around the roof perimeter rotted?
- Are most of the shingles on the roof cupping, splitting, or rotted? It's time to reroof.
- A new roof with shingles that are cupping or splitting was probably not installed correctly.
- Do a lot of the roof shingles have holes? If there are leaks in the attic, suspect those holes.
- If the house is in a local fire zone, a wood shingle roof is probably not allowed.

SLATE, SYNTHETIC SLATE, AND CLAY TILES

Slate and tile are relatively brittle, expensive, and easily damaged if you don't know what you're doing. And they're slippery when wet. In most cases it's best to hire a roofer experienced with these materials to make repairs.

Tile and slate are so durable that they often outlast underlayment (roofing felt) and the fasteners used to secure them. Consequently, if the roof condition warrants removing all slates or tiles, installing new plywood sheathing and reinstalling them, don't scrimp on replacement materials. Use heavy underlayment

This clay tile roof has seen repairs—note the irregular courses—but it's still leak free. Any damaged tiles that can't be reached from a roof edge should be replaced by a pro. There's an art to getting onto a tile roof without causing more damage.

The aftermath of a falling tree limb. Several of these tiles are broken and others are missing. The felt underlayment should be checked for damage and repaired or replaced as needed. New or reused tiles can then be installed to complete the repair.

(30-lb. building paper or a self-adhering bituminous membrane), copper attachers, and copper flashing.

COMMON SLATE AND TILE FAILINGS

Slate and tiles are relatively fragile. Synthetic versions of slate and tile are less expensive than the originals but are still prone to chipping and cracking.

CHIPPED OR ROUND EDGES and flaking surfaces on slate are common and rarely a problem. In regions with hard winters, however, excessive flaking and splitting may be caused by freeze–thaw cycles when moisture has been trapped, such as in a leaf-filled valley or in debris behind a chimney.

CLUSTERS OF BROKEN TILES or cracked slates along roof edges have probably been damaged by falling branches. If you can reach the damage without walking on the roof, replacing a few tiles or slates is not difficult. But for damage that is extensive or far back from the edges, have a professional make repairs.

SLATE THAT SPLITS along surface striations is probably ribbon slate, an inferior grade with softer material running through it. Such failure occurs when the slate roof is relatively new, say, 15 years or less. Strip the roof and start over.

LOOSE TILES AND RUST STAINS are usually caused by steel nails that are rusting away. (Copper nails are recommended for slate and tile roofs.) If the roofing is in decent shape, it can be removed and renailed, but that repair will be expensive. Reroofing with an alternate material would probably be more cost-effective.

RUST STAINS ON SLATE ROOFS are typically caused by original drip edge flashing that has worn out. If there's no evidence of leaking, live with it. Otherwise, replace flashing when reroofing.

CONCRETE ROOF TILES were frequently installed without felt underlayment in the 1970s and 1980s. This is no longer approved because of the greater potential for leaks. Leave tiles alone if the roof isn't leaking; otherwise, remove all tiles, install plywood sheathing, cover the sheathing with felt paper, and then reinstall the tiles.

VALLEYS SLATHERED WITH ROOFING CEMENT have likely been leaking. Such patches will soon dry, crack, and leak again. The roof should be looked at by a licensed roofing contractor before the next rainy season.

The metal apron flashing on the downslope side of this brick chimney is missing and the mortar is crumbling and should be repointed. The slate is in pretty good shape, however.

These outdated synthetic (fiber cement) shakes break easily when walked on. This type of shake is no longer manufactured and is not considered repairable.

WHAT TO LOOK FOR

- Is the roof well maintained? Is flashing intact and are gutters free of leaves?

- Although rounded or chipped edges are common on slate, excessive flaking is a problem, especially in regions with freezing temperatures.

- Do tree limbs overhang the roof? Clusters of broken slates or tiles were probably caused by falling limbs.

- Are there rust stains or loose tiles or slates? Steel nails may have rusted through.

- Are valleys debris free? If the valleys are open (visible), is the flashing in good condition? If roofing cement is slathered in the valleys, they may be leaking.

METAL ROOFS

Metal shingles and panels are increasingly popular because they are cost-effective, durable, and relatively maintenance free. They shed water well. Older metal roofs will typically be bare galvanized steel; surface rust is not a concern unless the roof leaks. Newer metal roofing has a galvanized steel core clad with a factory-painted enamel. In time, painted metal roofing will fade or chalk, but it's cosmetic. Not a concern.

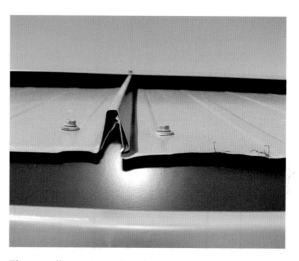

The standing seams of modern metal roofing panels are self-flashing; they cover the exposed edges of adjacent panels. Washered bolts keep water from getting under the bolt heads.

Never get up on a metal roof to inspect it: it's too slippery, even in dry weather. Using binoculars, scan metal roofs for popped nails, lifted panels or shingles, and tight panel joints. Shingles or panels should always overlap those below. Look also for evidence of galvanic action, corrosion caused by combining dissimilar metals.

- Can you see popped nails or lifted roof panels?
- Is there any evidence of galvanic action on the metal roofing?

Flat Roofs

First of all, no roof should be completely flat or it won't shed water. Even flat roofs must slope slightly toward perimeter openings and interior drains. Flat roofs can be safely inspected by walking on them. When inspecting a flat roof, use a tape measure to pinpoint badly worn or damaged areas, so that when you continue your inspection inside, you can correlate rooftop damage to leaks you may find.

Speaking of which, inspectors must be sleuths to match interior water stains to roof leaks. Water is very opportunistic and follows a path of least resistance. It may, for example, run some distance along a rafter before it finally drips free onto the back of a drywall panel. Flat roof leaks are somewhat easier to trace, but on steeply sloped roofs . . . good luck.

Flat roof materials must be waterproof. In addition to correctly installing an impervious membrane, the roofer must also take pains to get the details

Because water can pond up on so-called flat roofs, their seams must be tight. Seams along the eaves are especially prone to lift, so inspect them closely.

right, especially flashing that membrane to vertical elements such as parapets, skylights, and vent pipes. Drainage is also essential to roof health, as is regular maintenance.

BUILT-UP ROOFS

Built-up roofs (BURs) once represented half of all flat roof coverings. BURs consist of three to five alternating layers of heavy roofing felt and hot asphalt. Small-dimension gravel was embedded in the top layer to reflect sunlight and decrease UV damage. Today, modified bitumin (MB) is the king of the BURs; they have torched-on cap membranes that fuse them to fiberglass-reinforced interplies, or base coats.

SINGLE-PLY COVERINGS

Single-ply coverings include membranes of EPDM rubber, PVC or TPO plastic, and modified bitumin. Methods of attachment and seam sealing tend to be propriety for each system. Some feature cold-sealed joints in which a chemical bond fuses sheets together. Some membranes are adhered directly to the roof deck, and others are laid loose and held in place by the weight of gravel. Others employ a combination of chemical adhesives and mechanical fasteners. Although a general home inspection can identify suspect areas, if the roof is in poor shape a roofing installer specialized in single-ply systems should assess the roof.

SPRAY-POLYURETHANE FOAMS

Spray-polyurethane foams (SPFs) are relatively new, but gaining popularity in Sun Belt states, particularly as retrofits on mid-century houses with flat roofs. SPFs' appeal is that they can be applied over an existing flat roof, once it has been adequately prepared, which saves the considerable mess and expense of stripping the old roof. The foam is also an excellent way to upgrade the roof's insulation, without losing headroom inside. Once dried, the foam is strong enough to walk on and, when sprayed with a top coating that protects against UV degradation, an SPF roof is quite durable.

ROLL ROOFING

Roll roofing is not very waterproof and so it's not advisable for use as a primary membrane. Nonetheless, it's economical, easily installed, and widely used on porch and shed roofs.

COMMON FLAT ROOF FAILINGS

To avoid failure, the hot mop coating between the layers of felt on a flat roof must be complete. Any voids will contain some air with moisture that will expand, creating blisters. In time, the blister is likely to split.

IF BLISTERING IS WIDESPREAD, the roof will need to be replaced; whereas isolated, individual blisters can be lanced, drained, and patched easily enough. Avoid stepping on blisters, which could drive water under the membrane and soak framing or finish surfaces below.

OLDER BUR SURFACES that are cracked, wrinkled, alligatored or that have exposed felt paper are showing UV damage. The oil in the surface coats has likely evaporated. Depending on the age of the roof and the extent of the damage, worn areas should be coated with aluminized asphalt emulsion every 2 years or 3 years or reroofed. If repairs look piecemeal or there are just too many, the whole roof should be recoated.

BARE PLACES ON A GRAVEL-TOPPED ROOF are probably not serious: the gravel has migrated because of water movement or foot traffic. If the membrane is intact, uncovered areas can be spotcoated with fresh asphalt emulsion or roofing cement and recovered with gravel.

CRITICAL JUNCTURES between a roof's steep- and low-sloping portions should be carefully examined. Flat roof membranes should run at least 10 in. up the sloping section. The top edge of that membrane should then be overlapped by the underlayment of the sloping section and its roofing materials so that water can run downhill unimpeded. Because of the high volume of water coming off a sloping area, the juncture is vulnerable to leaks if not properly detailed.

Gravel-surfaced built-up roofing (tar and gravel) requires a covering of gravel for solar protection. About 50% of the gravel should be embedded in the final layer of hot asphalt. If the asphalt cools too soon, good embedment doesn't happen and some of the gravel washes away. Recoat such areas and add gravel as needed.

YOUR PLACE IN THE SUN

REPEATEDLY WALKING ON A FLAT ROOF will abrade its membrane. If inhabitants want to use the roof for *al fresco* dining and sunning themselves, a rooftop deck should be installed, secured to rafters (through the sheathing) so it cannot move, with its supporting posts correctly flashed so the roof membrane is not compromised.

WATER PONDING is caused by clogged drains, drains that are too small, or insufficient slope toward drains. The rule of thumb is that minor standing water is OK as long as it dries within 48 hours. Drains should be checked periodically and cleared as needed; of course, areas below should be monitored for leaks.

Drains that are too small clog easily. This drain was cut through spray polyurethane foam (SPF) roofing. It should be made larger and additional scuppers (perimeter drain openings) should be added by a qualified roofer.

Single-ply plastic PVC membrane is typically quite durable and waterproof. The single drain in the parapet wall is probably large enough. The slope nearby is a bit shallow, which has caused some minor ponding. In general, minor standing water is OK if it dries within 48 hours.

SINGLE-PLY ROOFS ARE VULNERABLE at parapets, skylights, and other vertical elements. Examine those joints to make sure the membrane is continuous—that is, that there are no gaps. If mechanical fasteners are present, check for stretching and wear at attachment points.

FOAM SHRINKAGE. On SPF roofs, look for gaps around vertical elements such as chimneys, skylight curbs, and vent pipes; they may be signs of foam shrinkage. Foam that has been properly sealed with a UV-resistant acrylic coating should not shrink.

DAMAGED FOAM. If you see damage by a tree limb, filler foam and a top coating may need to be reapplied. A certified roofing foam specialist should inspect an SPF roof.

ROLL ROOFING SEAMS and joints where they abut walls are the most likely to leak, so make sure they are tight. Raised nail heads are also problematic. If there's any question, a dab of urethane caulk or roofing cement should be put under nail heads before they are driven down; likewise, roofing cement should be spread along suspect joints. If the roll roofing's surface is cracking or its granules are worn off, it should be replaced.

Roll roofing is not very durable even when correctly installed, and this low-slope roof was not done well. Exposed rusty nails along the edges have popped up, inviting leaks, and the gutter was poorly secured. The roof should be replaced.

WHAT TO LOOK FOR

- If the flat roof shows widespread blistering, it probably needs to be replaced.

- An older BUR roof that is cracked, wrinkled, or alligatored or has exposed felt paper is showing UV damage. If it can't be recoated, it should be replaced.

- Where sloping and flat roof sections meet, are flat roof membranes overlapped?

Open valleys clear water well. The standing seam (crimp) down the middle of metal valley flashing prevents cross-valley runoff from running under the shingles on the other roof plane.

The edge of this roof sheathing is not protected by a metal drip edge, which would direct water into the gutter. Consequently, the sheathing has absorbed water over the years and is delaminating. To avoid clogs, keep gutters clear.

- Does water pond up on the roof? Are roof drains clear?
- Check single-ply roof membranes for gaps at parapets, skylights, and stacks.
- On SPF roofs, gaps around vertical elements such as chimneys, skylight curbs, and vent pipes may be signs of foam shrinkage.
- Are roll roof seams and joints tight? Are any nails popped up? If roll roof surfaces are cracking or worn, they should be replaced.

Roof Flashings

If roofs were only sloping planes, making them weathertight would be relatively easy. But today's roofs have protruding vent pipes, chimneys, skylights, and dormers—all potential dams that need to be flashed to direct water around them. Consequently, the condition (or absence) of roof flashings is of vital concern in home inspections.

DRIP EDGE OR RAKE EDGE FLASHING

Drip edge flashing diverts water away from roof edges, rather than allowing the water to be drawn by capillary action back up under shingles or sheathing. The drip edge also covers and protects sheathing edges from gutter splashback and ice dams along the eaves. The crimped edge of drip edge flashing also resists bending and thus supports overhanging shingles.

In new construction, drip edge along the eaves is nailed directly to sheathing and then overlapped by building-paper underlayment, which also covers the roofing nails that secure the drip edge to the sheathing. Along gable ends, rake edge flashing is installed.

If the shingle ends along the eaves are deteriorating and the eaves and rake trim are splitting, chances are that flashing was not installed correctly or at all. If possible, lift the shingle edges to see if roof sheathing is delaminating or damaged. This soaking may also be caused by clogged gutters (see p. 73). When it's time to reroof, unsound sheathing should be replaced and drip edge installed around the perimeter of the roof.

Rust or light scaling on metal drip edge is not a problem if there's no sign of leaks. Rusty flashing should be scraped or sanded clean and coated with rust-inhibiting paint. However, metal drip edge with corroded nail heads is probably a result of galvanic action, typically when steel nails were used to fasten aluminum flashing. Caulk holes or cover them with roofing cement to prevent leaks; replace the flashing when reroofing.

One way to reduce leakage is to use roofing cement to glue shingle layers along the valley line. The inspector should lift a few shingles to see if they're secure. The minimal patch in this photo has failed and will need resealing.

VALLEY FLASHING

The greater the water flow over an area, the greater the likelihood of (and damage from) leaks. Roof valleys are particularly vulnerable because they channel runoff from two roof planes. Basically, there are two valley types: open, in which metal valley flashing is exposed, and closed, in which flashing (if any) is covered by shingles.

NOTE: Ideally, there should be no roofing nails within 6 in. of a valley center.

Either valley treatment can shed water well, but the slick metal flashing of an open valley clears water faster, especially during a heavy downpour. The standing seam in the middle of the flashing also prevents water from running across a valley and flowing under shingles on the other side.

There are two common ways to shingle closed valleys: Woven valleys, in which shingles from both roof planes overlap the valley, so that the valley center is two shingles thick. The other type, closed-cut valleys,

is more vulnerable because there is only one shingle layer in the middle of the valley: shingles from only one roof plane cover the valley. Roofers often trim the overlapping shingle down the valley center, which could allow rainwater from one side to flow under adjacent shingles. Cut shingles (the shingles that do not overlap the valley) should be placed about 2 in. above the valley center. (To keep shingles in place, roofers often apply roofing cement or urethane caulk under closed-cut shingles edges.)

When inspecting valleys, look for (1) debris that could dam up water, (2) composition shingle (aka asphalt shingle) surfaces that are worn or damaged, (3) shingle edges that have curled up or eroded, (4) nails or patched nail holes within 6 in. of a valley, and (5) roofing cement slathered down the center of a valley—a common sign of leaks. Open valley flashing that has light rust or scaling is unsightly but generally not a source of leaks.

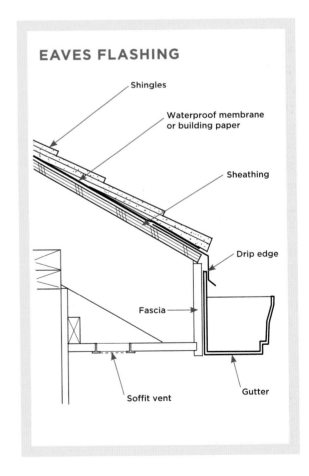

EAVES FLASHING

Shingles

Waterproof membrane or building paper

Sheathing

Drip edge

Fascia

Soffit vent

Gutter

RAKE AND EAVES FLASHING

You should also inspect a sloping roof's rake edges (along gable ends) and eaves (the lowest parts of a sloped roof). There you can best see how many layers of shingles are on the roof; if there are more than two, the old layers must be stripped before reroofing. In high-wind areas, you are most likely to see lifted or damaged shingles along rakes and eaves. There should also be metal flashings beneath the roofing along the perimeter. Make a note if flashings are missing or in poor condition.

In regions with long winters and a lot of snow, examine eaves closely. If you see lifted or damaged shingles, gouged or bent-up drip edges, weathered or splitting eaves trim, or loose and deformed gutters, you may be looking at the aftermath of an ice dam. Inside, you may find discolored insulation in the attic or water stains where walls meet ceilings. Such damage can occur even on new and well-built houses.

Ice dams typically occur when snow on the roof melts, flows over the shingles, collects at the eaves, and refreezes there. The sun melts some of the snow, but the real culprit is heated air from living spaces that rises into the attic and escapes through the roof deck. As those picturesque icicles build along the eaves, the ice blocks new snowmelt and water starts backing up under the shingles, soaking roof sheathing and framing. Water stains on finished surfaces and mold in the walls can follow.

WHAT TO LOOK FOR

- If the metal gleam of drip edge or rake edge flashing is not apparent, lift shingles along the edges of eaves or gable ends for a better look.
- What's the condition of shingles along the roof perimeter and, if accessible, the condition of roof sheathing? Have shingles along the roof perimeter been lifted by wind?
- Are any sections of metal drip edge or rake edge flashing corroded?
- If the roof has multiple planes, what type of valleys are present? Can water run freely down them or are they clogged with leaves or debris?

Ice dams form when snow on the roof melts, collects at the eaves, and refreezes. That ice will block new snowmelt, forcing water back up under shingles, where it can leak and stain interior surfaces.

- If roof valleys are open or have cut-edge shingles, look for curled or eroded shingles.
- Are nail holes visible in valleys, or are valleys smeared with roofing cement?
- In cold regions, has flashing along the eaves been damaged by ice dams or by homeowners chopping ice free?
- Where there is evidence of ice dams, look for water stains or damage on interior surfaces.

VENT STACK FLASHING

Vent stacks, also called drain, waste, vent (DWV) pipes, vent sewer gases. Vent stack flashing (or jack flashing) is usually an integral unit with a neoprene collar atop a metal base flange. If the rubber collar of the vent stack is cracked or deteriorated, it is showing normal UV damage. Collars are cheap and easy to replace; do so before leaks occur. Some pros prefer all-metal units because UV light won't degrade them, but metal collars must be snipped and spread to receive the stack, before being caulked with urethane to prevent leaks, whereas neoprene collars slide easily down stacks.

With either type, roofing courses above overlap the top of the base flange, covering the two nails that secure it to the sheathing. The bottom of the base flange, which overlaps shingles below, is secured by a bead of polyurethane caulk underneath.

If the base flange of the vent stack flashing sits atop roof shingles, it has been installed incorrectly. It should be reinstalled so that its upper edge is covered by the course of shingles above. Caulk the underside of its lower edge with polyurethane or apply roofing cement to seal it to roofing.

NOTE: Vent stacks vent sewer gases, so they must be at least 3 ft. from operable windows.

Stacks that are less than 3 ft. from an operable window or a ventilator opening are a code violation. Sewer gases could enter living spaces. Pipe extensions can be added to increase stack height or the stack will need to be relocated, which can be expensive.

VENT STACKS THAT TERMINATE UNDER the roof—that is, in the attic—are a serious code violation and health risk. In winter, moist air rising from the stack may condense, damaging sheathing and framing. Sewer gases can also be highly combustible, creating explosions when sufficiently concentrated. The stack should be extended above the roof. Alternatively, a new solution to the problems caused by too many roof penetrations is to use air-admittance valves (see p. 173): They allow air to flow into fixture vents, facilitating waste water flow at fixtures, but close automatically to prevent the escape of sewer gases.

WHAT TO LOOK FOR

- Do flashing collars fit tight to vent stacks or are there gaps that water could enter?
- Are rubberized collars cracked and deteriorated? They should be replaced.
- Do shingles above overlap flashing base flanges, and do flanges overlap shingles below?
- Are any vent stacks less than 3 ft. from an operable window or a ventilator opening?
- Do any vent stacks terminate under the roof—that is, indoors?

CHIMNEY FLASHING. Chimneys are complex structures, so we'll divide their inspection into two parts: Here, we'll focus on chimney flashing as it

Plumbing vents typically extend above the roof to allow air flow into DWV pipes. Such vents should be flashed to prevent leaks. Rusty steel vent flashing can be coated with a rust-inhibiting paint to prolong its life, but this whole roof is shot and needs replacing.

There are at least a half dozen bad building details here, but we'll focus on just one. The black vent pipe should technically terminate above the upper roof to vent properly. Instead, it is next to a louver, which could allow sewer gases into the house. The vent pipe is old and short, which suggests that the green-trimmed building section (at left) was an unpermitted and uncompleted addition.

SUPPORTING STACKS AND VENTS

THIS UNSUPPORTED METAL GAS APPLIANCE vent/flue needs bracing. Though ABS plastic plumbing stacks stick up only 1 ft. or 2 ft. above the roof, they don't need additional support. But vent flues, TV antennas, and electrical service pipes need adequate bracing and flashing. Flash where flues exit the roof and where braces attach to it.

This unsupported metal gas appliance vent/flue should be checked to see that it extends above the upper roof line. The strict rule (rarely observed) is that gas appliance vent/flues closer than 8 ft. to an adjacent wall must extend at least 24 in. above the upper roof surface.

relates to roof integrity. We'll cover the safety and structural aspects of the chimney as part of the heating system (see Chapter 8).

Chimneys must be counterflashed. The upper pieces of counterflashing are usually tucked into chimney mortar joints and made to overhang various pieces of base flashing, which are nailed to the roof deck. Counterflashing and base pieces aren't physically joined, so they can move independently yet still repel water. This independence is necessary because house foundations and chimney footings often settle at different rates, which would cause single-piece flashing to tear and leak.

BASE FLASHING has several components. As shingles butt against the chimney's downslope face, a metal apron is placed over them. Then, as shingles ascend both sides of the chimney, they overlap the bottoms of L-shaped step flashing. When shingle

The black roofing cement around the base of this chimney was probably applied to repair leaks, so the interiors below should be checked for stains. A silver-colored final coating over the patch would look better and last longer.

CHIMNEY FLASHING

Base Flashing

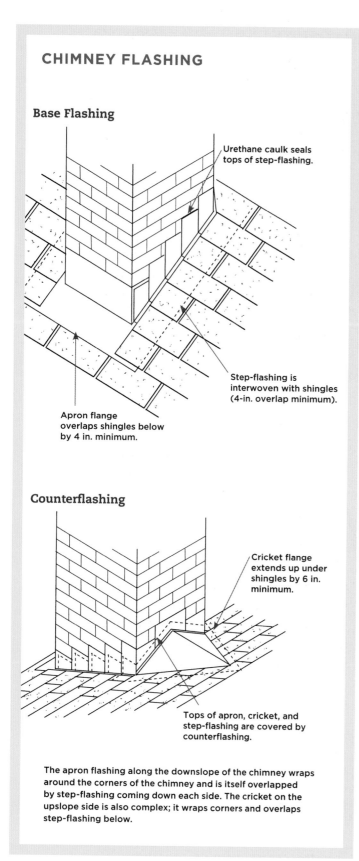

Urethane caulk seals tops of step-flashing.

Step-flashing is interwoven with shingles (4-in. overlap minimum).

Apron flange overlaps shingles below by 4 in. minimum.

Counterflashing

Cricket flange extends up under shingles by 6 in. minimum.

Tops of apron, cricket, and step-flashing are covered by counterflashing.

The apron flashing along the downslope of the chimney wraps around the corners of the chimney and is itself overlapped by step-flashing coming down each side. The cricket on the upslope side is also complex; it wraps corners and overlaps step-flashing below.

courses along both sides of the chimney reach the back (upslope) face of the chimney, the lower flanges of a cricket overlap them. A cricket, also called a chimney saddle, is a sloping mini-roof whose slope(s) divert water around the chimney.

COUNTERFLASHING should overlap base flashing by 4 in. Traditionally, shallow slots were cut into chimney mortar joints to receive the barbed (folded) lips of counterflashing. After jamming the lip of counterflashing into the joint, the mason packed strips of lead to hold the flashing in place, followed by fresh mortar. These days, the joint is then filled with a bead of urethane caulk to seal out moisture.

WHAT TO LOOK FOR

- Is the chimney correctly counterflashed, with upper flashing overlapping base pieces?
- Look for loose or uplifted chimney flashing, which should be reseated so there are no gaps.
- Roofing cement slathered along the base of a chimney is a short-term solution for leaks. Though unsightly, it will usually stop leaks if it is reapplied periodically.
- If there is no cricket on the upslope face of a chimney, debris, snow, and runoff can collect there. Any chimney more than 2 ft. wide should have a cricket.
- Is chimney mortar intact? Chimneys with eroded mortar joints are more likely to admit water leaks, allow combustion gases to escape, and fail structurally.
- Rusty joints or pinholes on metal chimneys (flue pipe) can allow superheated gases to escape and set fire to combustible materials nearby. Damaged flue pipe should be replaced.

SKYLIGHT FLASHING

Skylight flashing on sloped roofs is similar to chimney flashing, with an apron on the downslope side of the skylight frame, L-shaped pieces of step flashing along both sides, and a large piece of head flashing along the upslope side of the skylight frame. Cladding or curb caps cover (counterflash) the tops of base flashing. Flashing kits tend to be proprietary to each skylight manufacturer.

Water runs downhill, so the roofing cement spread beneath this skylight is a fair indication that the perimeter of the skylight was not properly flashed and thus leaked.

These asbestos-cement ridge shingles have been repaired in the past and need a little work. This type of shingle can be very long lasting, but when it needs to be replaced, it should be done only by a certified asbestos removal specialist.

Skylights on older flat roofs were typically flashed by running membrane materials up the sides of the skylight curb, which were then sealed with several layers of molten bitumen. Metal caps covered and sealed the exposed membrane edges. The whole assembly was coated with an aluminized emulsion to reflect sunlight. It was a serviceable if somewhat unsightly assembly and durable as long as the emulsion didn't dry out and the membrane remained intact.

DRIPS, LEAKS, AND RATTLES

If a skylight drips and there is condensation between its doubled panes, chances are the seal around the panes has failed. The unit should be reglazed when weather permits or replaced. If the skylight leaks and, roof side, the flashing is corroded, it's likely that nails incompatible with the flashing were used. The flashing should be caulked to stop leaks and replaced as soon as possible. This will mean disturbing roofing around the unit. If skylight flashing is intact but the unit leaks on its upslope side, the head flashing of the skylight may have been incorrectly installed.

Persistent ice dams around the skylight, with concomitant leaking, are probably caused by heat escaping around the perimeter of the unit. In other words, there is inadequate insulation in the ceiling around the skylight lightwell. The insulation should be upgraded. A skylight frequently covered by snow may be mounted too low to the roof. Skylight curbs typically rise 6 in. above the roof deck.

Skylights that rattle during storms may not be adequately secured to the sheathing. The problem may be fixed with additional fasteners, which should be caulked.

RIDGE FLASHING

Traditionally, ridges were flashed with a continuous strip of building paper folded lengthwise, which straddled the ridge and overlapped the top courses of shingles. The paper was then covered with a shingle saddle or overlapped ridge boards. Metal flashing was sometimes used instead of building paper. These days, ridges are often covered with ridge vents that allow hot air to escape.

WHAT TO LOOK FOR

- Are all pieces of skylight flashing securely attached or have some worked loose?
- Can you see corrosion on any sections of metal skylight flashing?
- Is double-pane skylight glazing cloudy? Chances are the seal between panes has failed.

- Are there signs of water stains or damage inside, below the skylight?
- If possible, ask the homeowner if the skylight is frequently covered with snow.
- Is the roof ridge vented to allow hot air to escape, or is it unvented?

FLASHING ADJOINING STRUCTURES

Where dormers rise from sloping roofs or shed roofs abut sidewalls, there will be a greater concentration of water and thus a greater potential for leaks. Correct flashing is the key to preventing such leaks.

NOTE: In both cases, there should also be at least 1 in. of clearance between the bottom of the siding and the roof surface beneath it. Otherwise wood siding will wick moisture, stay damp, and perhaps rot the sheathing and framing behind it. In snow country, builders often leave 2 in. or 3 in. of clearance.

Where a shed roof abuts a wall, the upper leg of an L-shaped flashing should run up at least 4 in., under both underlayment and siding—8 in. in snow country. (Obviously, an inspector will not be able to tell how high up the flashing runs under the siding.) The lower leg of the L-shaped flashing goes over and is caulked to the top course of shingles on the shed roof.

Where a gable-end addition abuts a sidewall or a sloping roof meets a dormer wall, step flashing should protect those junctures. This step flashing is similar to the L-shaped base flashing used along the sides of a chimney, but there is no counterflashing in this case. The upper legs of the step flashing are nailed to wall sheathing and overlapped by underlayment and siding. The lower legs of the step flashing are interwoven with shingle courses.

When the sidewall–roof juncture leaks, homeowners often try to seal it with fibered roofing

FLASHING A SHED ROOF THAT ABUTS A WALL

Siding

Sheathing

Underlayment

4 in. minimum

Flashing

1-in. clearance above roof

Flashing seated in roofing cement or urethane caulk

Wood shingles should terminate 1 in. to 2 in. above the roof surface, and the shingle–roof joint should be flashed with L-shaped metal flashing whose upper legs are covered by siding. Here, wood shingles rest right on the roofing. This is not the sort of rooftop garden you want.

cement, which tends to be black and ugly. As the cement ages it turns gray, dries out, cracks, and fails.

WHAT TO LOOK FOR

- Does the bottom of sidewall or dormer siding come in direct contact with roofing?
- Do you see discoloration and rot on the bottom of the siding where it meets the roofing below? Is that juncture clogged with leaves, moss, or debris?
- Is the sidewall–dormer roof juncture smeared with roofing cement?
- Does the roofing cement look freshly applied or is it old and cracked?

Roof Drainage

In a heavy rain, a roof sheds an enormous amount of water, so gutters and downspouts are needed to carry runoff away from the house and its foundation. To clear water adequately, gutters must be sized properly and cleared of leaves and debris at least twice a year—in spring and in fall.

GUTTERS

Building supply centers have elaborate gutter-sizing charts based on regional rainfall, roof square footage, and pitch. In general, 5-in.-wide gutters are standard: 6-in. gutters are indicated for high-rain areas. Downspouts should be sized to match gutters and made of the same material.

GUTTER MATERIALS. Aluminum is by far the most popular gutter material because it is durable, resists corrosion, is easily worked, and is reasonably priced. Galvanized steel is stronger, heavier, and harder to dent, but it rusts if its paint wears off. PVC plastic and vinyl are economical but the most prone to cracking if struck or splitting if standing water in a clogged gutter or downspout freezes. Copper is handsome, malleable, durable, and, thanks to soaring global prices, far more expensive than aluminum.

On sloping roofs, most gutters are surface mounted because they are easier to install; built-in gutters, an extension of roof framing, are typically wood.

The hole in this wall at the gutter end is a very likely point for rainwater entry and moisture-related damage.

Downspouts often come loose, especially when unfastened. Homeowners should review all rain gutters and downspouts periodically during rainy weather for obvious failures.

Regular maintenance is especially critical to built-in gutters, "landlocked" as they are by materials that rot. The two most common gutter profiles are half round and K-style, in which the gutter has a squared-off back and an ogee front. (K-styles are also called fascia or box gutters.)

GUTTER SUPPORTS. Gutter sections should be supported by hangers (support straps) at least every 32 in.; closer if there's a heavy snow or ice load. Gutter hangers can be grouped into two general types: roof mounted, which employ a strap nailed to roof sheathing, and fascia mounted, which screw or nail directly to fascia boards or rafter tails. Gutters should slope at least 1 in. over 12 ft. toward a gutter outlet (drop outlet).

Every gutter outlet must empty into a downspout. As obvious as this fact is, it's easy to overlook missing downspouts unless you make a point of looking for them during an inspection. Downspouts should discharge water at least 6 ft. away from the house or into *solid* subsurface drainpipes. Downspouts should not empty directly into perforated pipe because water will immediately drain out, close to the house.

CLOGS, LEAKS, AND RATTLES. If you observe water stains or leaks behind gutters, most likely gutters or downspouts are clogged. How bad the conditions are depends on how long the clog(s) has existed. The remedy may be as simple as removing the clog, but cleaning up the damage may require stripping siding or finish surfaces to uncover rot and mold. The absence of drip edge flashing may contribute to stains and leaks behind gutters. If clogs have been cleared and gutters still overflow, they may be undersize for the amount of runoff.

Galvanized gutters that are leaking or stained have likely rusted through. Patching rusted areas with polyurethane or mastic can prolong a gutter's usable life for a season or two, but the gutters will need to be replaced soon. If gutters have collapsed sections, there are several possible causes, including ladders leaned against gutters or tree limbs banging into them. In snow country, ice dams can also crush gutters.

Gutters and downspouts that bang in the wind are not adequately attached to the house. Similarly, gutters that sag or overflow from an end without a downspout are insufficiently sloped or the support straps have pulled loose. Gutters should slope at least 1 in. for every 12 ft.; a gutter mount every 32 in. is recommended if rafters are spaced 16 in. on-center. If water shoots out the end of a gutter, it's probably missing its end cap.

Built-in wood gutters that leak haven't been maintained. Check for stains and damage to interior surfaces. Once the gutters have dried thoroughly, survey them for rot. Scrape off rot and line damaged areas with rubberized self-adhering flashing tape. Replacing built-in gutters will be expensive.

DOWNSPOUTS

As noted, downspouts should be the same size and material as gutters.

Leaky joints on new downspouts are usually caused by an incorrect installation in which downspout sections have been installed upside down. In other words, the tapered ends of upper sections should fit *into* lower sections to correctly channel water. If you see upper sections overlapping lower sections, they

Note the rotted eaves trim. The absence of drip edge flashing may contribute to stains and leaks behind gutters.

Sheet-metal rain gutters can be very rusty inside, so they should be checked annually and resealed as needed. The exposed wood sheathing above and at the end of this gutter lack metal flashings.

Part of a thorough inspection is noting what's not there. Judging from the rotted fascia boards at right, this gutter's end cap has been missing for a long time.

Flexible corrugated piping is a poor choice for downspouts connected to subsurface drain lines. It is easily damaged by foot traffic and difficult to run a snake through when clogged. This piping is especially egregious because it is perforated (has holes) and should be used only to collect subsurface water, never to transport it.

Stained stucco behind a downspout seam indicates that the downspout split. It should be removed from the building, repaired, and remounted. Stucco is somewhat porous, so it's wise to move fast on a leak like this.

WHAT TO LOOK FOR

- What are gutters and downspouts made of? What's their general condition?

- Are gutters continuous and without gaps or missing sections? Have any sections been crushed or collapsed? Does every gutter outlet empty into a downspout?

- Are gutters adequately supported or are there loose or sagging sections?

- Use a garden hose to flush gutters. Are gutters open or clogged? Does water leak out of the gutters and run down the siding? Are there water stains or discoloration on the siding?

- Are galvanized gutters streaked with rust or rusted through? Have they been patched with roofing cement or mastic to stop leaks?

- Have wood gutters been maintained? Are there any signs of rot or leakage? Is adjacent trim or siding water stained or rotting?

- Do upper sections of downspouts fit into lower ones? Are all downspouts securely attached to the house?

- Do downspouts discharge at least 6 ft. away from the house or into subsurface drains?

- When you flush gutters and downspouts with a garden hose, does the water disappear into subsurface drains or gush out of the bottom of the downspout—a sign of clogged drains?

- If downspouts empty into perforated drainpipes, write them up; drainpipe should be solid.

need to be reversed. If you see stained siding behind a downspout, look first for an incorrect installation and next for rusted-out or split seams.

If a downspout discharges too close to the house, the ground next to it may be soggy and sunken, and basement walls may be damp. Downspouts that discharge directly onto the ground (rather than into subsurface drains) should discharge at least 6 ft. away from the house. Grading soil away from the house will also help.

If soil near the house is damp when downspouts feed into subsurface drainpipes, the drains may be clogged or damaged. A pipe inspection service can determine the cause. If you see downspouts empty directly into perforated drainpipes, write it up in your report. Perforated pipes should not be used as subsurface drains; solid drainpipe is required.

CHAPTER 4

ATTICS

THERE IS NO ONE RIGHT SEQUENCE for inspecting a house. After examining a house's exterior, however, many pros resume the inspection in the attic. Flaws you noted atop the roof will be fresh in mind as you look for leaks on its underside. Plus, if you start at the top and systematically work down, you'll be less likely to miss things.

Before you enter an attic, reconnoiter. Are there floorboards? Can you move freely about the attic or should you do your inspection from the access opening?

Attic Safety

You're likely to find just about anything in an attic, from an airy, light-filled suite of rooms to a suffocatingly hot, dark, dusty crawl space. Access to attics is similarly diverse, from a flight of stairs to a pull-down ladder to a hatch tucked away in a hall or closet stuffed with clothes. Prepare for the worst and you'll be ready for anything.

Let's assume that you'll be inspecting an unfinished attic in which the underside of the sheathing and the framing will be visible. For starters, if your attic access is a ceiling hatch, wear eye protection in case dust and debris rains down on you when you open things up. Wear a dust mask and heavy gloves, too. You'll need a light source, preferably a flashlight strong enough to illuminate the perimeter of the attic, where the roof meets the walls.

Reconnoiter before you enter. Is there enough height for you to move around or should you make your observations from the hatch opening? Is the attic so jammed with boxes and stored items that there's little room to move? Are there floorboards? If not, you could bring up a few boards or scraps of plywood to span attic floor joists and create a walkway. But as a rule, professional inspectors won't bring walkway boards up into an attic. Stepping from joist to joist is risky—you could step through the ceiling—and likely to distract you from inspecting. If roofing nails stick down through the sheathing, wear a hard hat to spare your head. Last, is your tetanus shot up to date?

Note anything else that might impede your progress or impair your safety. From the hatch, can you see exposed wiring splices, not in an electrical box, that may pose a shock hazard? Is the attic cool enough for you to spend the time you need to inspect it carefully? Unvented attics can reach 140°F in the summer, so it's best to inspect them early in the morning before things heat up.

Framing and Sheathing

"Roof Support Elements," on p. 78, contains most of the framing elements you'll find in an unfinished attic, though all may not be present. Most terms are obvious enough, but a few may be unfamiliar. Collar ties connect opposite rafters and keep them from spreading; purlins are horizontal beams that support rafters and keep them from sagging. Around the perimeter of the attic, rafters rest on the walls' top plates, which are often doubled. Typically, attic floor joists are also ceiling joists for the rooms immediately below.

INSPECTING THE FRAMING

In older homes, a certain amount of sagging is normal. In regions that don't get snow, old rafters

---

CLOSE CALL

FOR ATTIC EGRESS IN NEW CONSTRUCTION, the International Residential Code® specifies a minimum opening of 22 in. by 30 in., with 30 in. of headroom. When home inspectors encounter access openings smaller than that, they must make a judgment call about how tight an opening they are willing to worm through. In some cases, it's a close call.

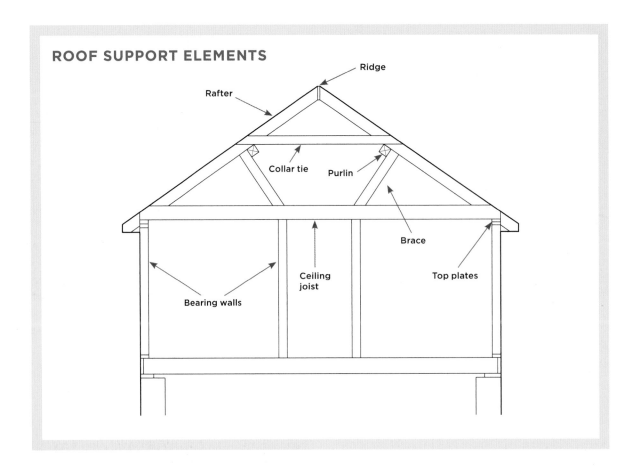

ROOF SUPPORT ELEMENTS

Ridge

Rafter

Collar tie

Purlin

Brace

Ceiling joist

Top plates

Bearing walls

The most common cause of rafter and purlin failure is excessive loading during reroofing or, over time, too many layers of roofing. This broken purlin should be supported till it can be replaced.

are often undersize by today's standards, commonly 2×4s spaced 16 in. or 24 in. on-center. In time they sag, especially if weighed down by several layers of roofing. After the old roofing has been stripped and a new roof applied, rafters may still sag because they have deformed into that shape. It's generally not something to worry about. (Installing new sheathing will usually stiffen the roof up.)

Of greater concern is framing that has cracked due to stress, such as the purlin shown in the photo at left. A structural engineer should inspect such failures and prescribe a fix. (A cracked rafter or rafter support may need to be bolstered from below, reinforced with lumber sistered to it, or replaced.) Note any framing members that are failing because an inept renovator cut into them, perhaps to install a skylight, vent an exhaust fan, or run a plumbing vent stack.

When examining framing in the attic, don't forget ceiling joists. In older houses joists are often undersize for the distances they span or the weight of the stuff stored on them. This situation may be exacerbated if walls below have been removed. In addition, homeowners sometimes cut or notch ceiling joists, which lessens the distance they can span. Use a level to see if attic joists are sagging and, roughly, by how much. Note too if joists seem especially springy as you shift your weight on them. In older houses with plaster ceilings, some inspectors won't traverse attic joists because they don't want to risk damaging the plaster.

Occasionally, an inspector will find framing charred by a fire. Charred lumber is typically wire-brushed to determine the extent of damage. Many building departments require that significantly damaged framing be replaced, whereas minor damage may be painted to seal in smoke odors. If there's any doubt about the integrity of the framing that remains, replace *all* fire-damaged lumber before installing new roofing.

INSPECTING THE SHEATHING

The primary reason to inspect the underside of the roof sheathing is to look for active leaks. Occasionally, an inspection will turn up plywood sheathing that is delaminating or sagging between rafters because the plywood used was too thin. Sagging sheathing should be replaced or supplemented the next time the roof is stripped, but otherwise it's rarely a problem that needs to be attended to right now.

In older houses, the original skip sheathing is sometimes still on the roof. Skip sheathing (or spaced sheathing) consists of 1-in. boards nailed to rafters, with spaces between boards to allow circulating air to dry wood shingles between rains. Often, the skip sheathing was covered with plywood or OSB sheathing the first time the roof was stripped and composition shingles were installed. But if the roof was never stripped, you may see the original wood shingles from underneath, buried under one or more layers of roofing.

The underside of roof sheathing or framing is often discolored and water stained, but that doesn't mean

ROOF TRUSSES

IN HOUSES BUILT FROM THE 1950S ON, you may find roof trusses, an engineered framing system whose many diagonal braces make it difficult to move through an attic. You can, of course, limit your inspection to what you can see from the attic opening. But two triggers should encourage you to brave the braces and inspect as many trusses as possible:

1. If roof sags are visible from the exterior, the truss system may have failed.
2. If you see any indications that the original truss framing was improperly modified, say, to add an attic furnace, a skylight, or an addition.

Any modifications to the original truss framing should be approved by an engineer.

Wood shingles are designed to fit tightly and become waterproof as they get wet and swell. This kind of water staining is common and doesn't indicate active leaks. The best way to check for active leaks is to shine a bright flashlight through the attic when it's raining.

there are *active* leaks. The only way to be sure of that is to be under the roof when it's raining. Beyond that, look for water pooled on attic floors or insulation, or note wood that is damp or spongy with rot. The most probable places to find active leaks are where chimneys, skylights, vent stacks, exhaust fans, and flue pipes exit through the roof. As you saw in Chapter 3, correct flashing is the key to avoiding leaks. So use the notes from your roof inspection to inform your inspection under the roof. (We will say more about chimneys, vents, and flues at the end of this chapter.)

In snow country, especially look for water stains, water damage, and other evidence of leaks along roof–wall joints, where rafters rest on the top plates. This is the area where heat escapes, melts snow, and causes ice dams (see p. 67). These junctures are often narrow triangular spaces, but do your best to shine a flashlight beam into them. As you will see in the following sections, sometimes water damage is not caused by leaks from above but from water vapor rising up from living spaces.

So even if you are not 100% sure what is causing all the stains or moisture problems in the attic, note *where* you see them. By comparing the careful observations you make throughout the house, you should soon be able to pinpoint problems and identify probable causes.

The framing near this brick chimney was weak and had to be bolstered when a new roof was installed. Examine the chimney flashings to be sure they are correctly installed.

- After a rain, can you see isolated stains running down rafters or sheathing? Is any wood damp to the touch?
- Are there water stains or discoloration where chimneys, flues, pipes, or vents pass through the roof? Are there stains around skylights?
- Are there water stains or signs of pooling on the attic floor or in insulation?
- If winters are severe, can you see water stains or damage where the roof meets the walls?
- Do rafters sag? Are there gaps where rafters meet at the ridge?
- Are any rafters or other structural members cracked or broken? Have any been cut into?
- Do structural supports (such as collar ties) appear to be missing?
- Are there signs (or smells) of earlier fire damage?
- If the roof is supported by trusses, have any been cut through or notched? When you inspected this (trussed) roof from the outside, did it sag?
- What kind of sheathing is visible from the underside of the roof? Does the roof appear to have many layers of roofing?
- Is sheathing discolored, delaminating, or sagging between rafters?
- Do attic floor joists seem excessively springy? Have any floor joists been cut through or notched? In which direction do floor joists slope?

Ventilation

Adequate ventilation is essential to the comfort and health of the people who live in a house and to the health of the building itself. By getting rid of excess heat trapped under the roof, ventilation lowers ambient temperatures and thus lowers energy costs (for air-conditioning). Roofing manufacturers argue that a cooler attic extends the life of the roofing as well. But perhaps the most compelling reason to improve ventilation is getting rid of excess moisture.

The average household generates a prodigious amount of water vapor, principally by cooking and showering. Exhaust fans in kitchens and bathrooms can help reduce interior moisture. But because warm

ATTIC VENTS

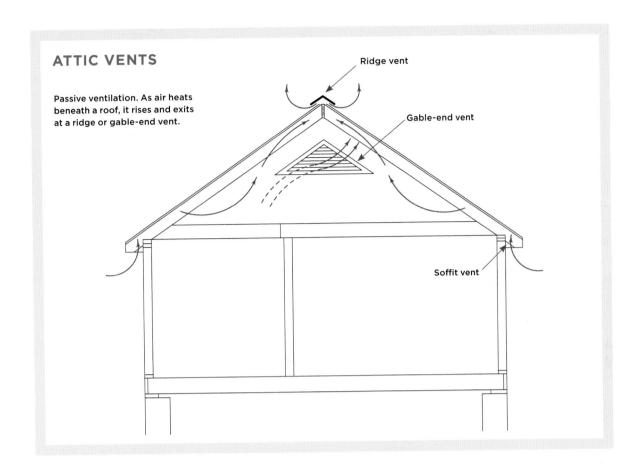

Passive ventilation. As air heats beneath a roof, it rises and exits at a ridge or gable-end vent.

Ridge vent

Gable-end vent

Soffit vent

air rises, a large portion of that water vapor will collect near the ceiling, where it will migrate into the attic through air leaks in recessed ceiling light cans, seams between wall and ceiling drywall, and uninsulated air shafts and attic floors.

When warm, moist air gets to the attic, it will stay there unless circulating air (ventilation) allows moisture to exit the building through roof vents, gable-end louvers, and the like. In time, excess moisture can soak insulation and delaminate sheathing. It starts as water stains, progresses to mold, and can end as rotted framing. When it's cold outside, warm, moist interior air condenses when it gets to unheated attics. It may be visible as frost on the underside of the sheathing or on roofing nails. And if there's snow on the roof, that warm, rising air will melt it, causing water to run down the roof and then refreeze at the eaves, producing spectacular and highly destructive ice jams. All totally avoidable with adequate attic ventilation.

PASSIVE AND MECHANICAL VENTILATION

There are two ways to ventilate an attic, one of which costs nothing to operate. Passive ventilation is based on the natural phenomenon that warm air rises. Typically, exterior air enters the attic through soffit vents; is warmed as the sun heats the roof; and exits through a ridge vent, a gable-end vent, or some intermediate vent such as a roof turbine. Codes typically require a minimum of 1 sq. ft. of vents per 300 sq. ft. of attic space, more or less equally divided between eave and ridge vents.

If moist interior air has migrated into the attic, it will mix with incoming exterior air and escape harmlessly. For passive ventilation to work, however, air must flow unimpeded. If soffit vent screens are painted shut or insulation blocks incoming air, passive ventilation won't occur. Exit vents must also be

KEEPING CRITTERS OUT

VENT OPENINGS SHOULD BE SCREENED WITH
mesh fine enough to keep out wasps, mice, and other
pests that would also enjoy a roof over their heads. In
addition to building (and fouling) nests in your insulation, they are fond of chewing things. The sheathing
on electrical cables and telephone wires is a particular favorite.

Bathroom and kitchen fan ducts must extend to the
building exterior, especially in cold weather climates.
In this example the fan duct ends inside the house
where moisture will condense in the attic, possibly
leading to mold and wood decay.

Old-style attic louvered vents have large openings
that can allow rodents and other animals to enter.
Installing ¼-in. metal screening on the inside is usually
the best fix.

clear. In short, inspect all vents to see that they are
open and that the screens are not damaged.

Mechanical ventilation is provided by electric fans.
Ideally, moisture should be exhausted where it is
created by a range hood over the stove or a bath fan
over a shower. Attic fans can be controlled by a
thermostat that turns on when a preset temperature
is reached, or by a humidistat that is triggered by the
level of humidity, regardless of temperature. If the

inspection takes place on a hot day, the attic fan
should cycle during the hour or two that the inspector is there. Otherwise, the inspector can flip the
manual override on–off switch or lower the thermostat till the fan turns on.

If neither of those methods turns the fan on, the
unit is not working and should be inspected by an
HVAC specialist. Assessing why a fan is not working
or assessing its efficiency is not the responsibility of
an inspector doing a general home inspection.

Whole-house fans are typically mounted in an attic,
either on the attic floor or high on an exterior attic wall
(in a house with a sloping roof, on a gable-end wall).
Whole-house fans are usually controlled by a thermostat, though combination thermostat/humidistat
controls are available on more expensive models.

For mechanical ventilation to work correctly,
intake vents must be adequately sized. Otherwise,
powerful fans can create negative pressurization—
also called back pressure—within the house. Back
pressure can suck gas furnace exhaust fumes back
into a house rather than allowing them to rise and
exit out the flue pipe. This is a dangerous situation. If
there is insufficient intake air when the whole-house

fan is running, you can feel air being drawn through electrical outlets or you may notice flames on a gas stove flicker or lean when you turn on the fan. An energy audit with a blower-door test can measure the degree of the back pressure created; an HVAC specialist can also analyze the fan's performance.

Conversely, attic exhaust vents must also be large enough so the overheated air can get out. Otherwise the fan will run and run, with little appreciable change in house temperatures.

WHAT TO LOOK FOR

- Is the attic excessively hot in the summer? During the winter, do ice dams form along eaves?
- Are there soffit vents along the eaves? Are they screened? Are there ridge, gable-end vents, turbines, or other vents high on the roof to allow hot air to escape?
- Are screened soffit vents painted shut? Is attic insulation tucked into the roof–wall joint blocking air coming up from soffit vents?
- Can you see widespread staining, delaminating sheathing, or rusty roofing nails?
- Are ceilings below the attic moldy or water stained?
- Does the attic meet minimum standards for venting: 1 sq. ft. of vents per 300 sq. ft. of attic?
- Are attic fans operational?
- With the palm of your hand held over electrical outlets, can you feel exterior air being sucked into the house when a whole-house fan is running?
- Does the house remain excessively hot even after a whole-house fan has run for hours?

Insulation

Attics should be insulated to conserve conditioned air in the living spaces below. In frigid northern regions, conserving heat is the goal; in sunny southern climes, insulation keeps hot exterior air outside so that air-conditioned living spaces keep cool. If attic spaces are to be finished and used as living spaces, insulation will be installed between rafters. In unfinished attics, however, it is most cost-effective to insulate between ceiling joists.

Insulation batts in unheated attics must be installed so that their vapor retarder—paper or foil facing—faces down, toward living spaces. This batt is installed correctly, but many codes do not allow insulation to cover exposed wires, such as the knob-and-tube wiring shown.

Follow Department of Energy regional recommendations for how much insulation to put in your roof; for more temperate parts of the U.S., the standard for new construction is R-30 or R-35. Precut fiberglass batts are the type most widely installed. Alternately cotton batts treated with borate to inhibit mold are gaining popularity among the green minded. Mineral wool batts, spun from natural stone or metal oxides, are the most fire resistant insulation of any type.

Loose-fill insulation, usually cellulose or fiberglass, is frequently used to retrofit unfinished attics. Loose cellulose, made from recycled newspapers treated with borate, is considered very green and highly efficient. While rodent activity is common in attics with loose fiberglass it is rare or nonexistent with cellulose insulation.

Rigid foam panels have great R-values but they are rarely used to insulate attic floors because joists are frequently irregularly sized or spaced. Even with a lot of cutting and fitting of panels, there would be a lot of gaps.

VAPOR RETARDERS

Excess moisture inside a house can lead to big problems. Thus insulation materials are chosen, in part, on how permeable or impermeable they are to water vapor. Unfaced insulation batts allow moisture to move freely through them; whereas batts that are paper faced or foil faced will retard the movement of water vapor. Hence vapor retarders. (Vapor barriers are materials such as sheet plastic, which completely block water vapor.)

Vapor retarders are especially important in cold winter climates because the temperature differential can cause condensation to form. Vapor retarders are not typically installed in uninsulated floor framing or when attic insulation is added in moderate climates.

NOTE: Insulation should always be installed so that its foil or paper facing is adjacent to the conditioned surface, typically down and against the ceiling in an attic. If you see insulation whose paper or foil facing faces up in an unfinished attic, write it up; it's wrong. Moist air rising from living spaces below will condense on the back of that cool facing and, in time, soak the insulation.

Accordingly, if a homeowner has added new batts atop existing insulation, the new batts should *not* be paper or foil faced. Condensation problems will occur. If there are two layers of insulation with vapor retarders, the paper or foil facing of the top layer should be slit with a razor knife to allow moisture to pass through.

DON'T INSULATE HERE!

In general, insulation should not touch masonry chimneys or old-style light fixtures because that could lead to excessive heat buildup. Nor should insulation cover exposed wire splices (electrical connections not in a junction box) or ceiling-light cans that are not IC rated. These and other fire hazards are explained at greater length later in this chapter. Knob-and-tube wiring, common in older houses, is generally not covered by insulation either, though local code specifics vary.

BIG HEAT LOSERS

Home inspectors should be on the lookout for the items in the following list. They are big air leakers and thus heat losers as well as expressways for warm, moist air rising into the attic.

Insulation should not be placed over or next to ceiling-mounted light cans (fixtures) that are not insulation contact (IC) rated—they may overheat and start a fire. Ideally, such cans should be replaced with safer IC-rated fixtures.

The vertical walls around a skylight well should be insulated; otherwise heated interior air will escape through these walls in cold weather.

1. Uninsulated attic hatch covers and skylight wells. Fortunately, both can be insulated easily with fiberglass batts or rigid foam panels.

2. The 2-in. gap between a masonry chimney and wood framing is required by fire codes in the event that a failed chimney flue allowed super-heated gases to escape. To reduce heat loss through that gap, it should be packed with a noncombustible material such as rock wool and covered with strips of sheet metal.

3. Open framing above chases and soffits can be a freeway for drafts, so large openings should be closed with drywall panels or rigid-foam panels.

4. Old bath fan boxes' flanges and seams can leak moisture-laden air into an attic. Leaks should be caulked. And as noted on p. 80, if any fan exhausts into the attic, rather than to the outside, it needs a vent pipe that exits through the roof or an exterior wall.

5. Recessed ceiling lights (ceiling cans) are big leakers, especially old, non-IC-rated cans that can't be covered with insulation. They should be replaced with IC-rated cans, some of which are airtight; otherwise, they can be covered with special mineral wool covers. An alternative is fire-rated recessed light covers, which are compatible with blown-in or lain-in insulation, mineral wool, fiber glass, blown-in cellulose, and spray foam.

6. Oversize openings for plumbing vent pipes, water supply pipes, and electrical boxes can be sealed with expanding foam, if you can find those openings under the insulation.

7. Heating and air-conditioning ducts without insulation are big energy wasters. Sometimes the insulation is on the inside of the ducts, however, so rap them with a knuckle to see. Insulated duct-raps sound dull; uninsulated ducts sound high and hollow when rapped.

8. The perimeter of an attic with sloping roofs can, with patience, be insulated, but baffles should be installed first to keep insulation from blocking air flow up from the eaves.

WHAT TO LOOK FOR

- Is attic insulation evenly distributed? Does insulation cover hard-to-reach spots?
- What type of insulation is there? If batts, are they unfaced or faced with paper or foil?
- Does paper or foil facing on fiberglass batts face up in an unfinished attic?
- If a second layer of insulation batts has been installed over an original layer, are batts in the second layer faced or unfaced?
- Is attic insulation damp or discolored? Are the undersides of insulation batts moldy?
- Does insulation touch a masonry chimney or cover old-style ceiling light cans?
- Are attic hatches or skylight wells uninsulated?
- Are there large gaps in the attic framing that might leak moist, heated air from living spaces below?
- Are heating and air-conditioning ducts insulated?
- Do any exhaust fan ducts terminate in the attic?

Health and Safety Concerns

As noted throughout this chapter, excessive interior moisture can lead to delaminated sheathing and rotted framing. But long before those dramatic symptoms manifest, mold may be growing on drywall ceilings and walls and circulating throughout the house. Mold can make some individuals very sick, so excess moisture is a health concern as well.

RANGE HOODS AND BATH FANS

Range hoods and bath fans can do much to reduce interior moisture, but only if they are vented correctly through the roof or an exterior wall. This is especially important in cold weather climates where attic ventilation is critical to prevent condensation or ice dams. All too frequently, however, inspectors will find fan ducts that terminate in the attic. This is worse than no fan at all because moisture from bathing or cooking will condense in a cold attic space, near the vent opening, creating conditions conducive to mold growth and worse. Such ducts must be extended outside to vent correctly.

This ABS vent stack's support failed and the stack has fallen into the attic, leaving a hole in the roofing through which rain can enter.

A rodent nest in loose fiberglass insulation. A rodent-abatement specialist should remove the damaged insulation, deal with the infestation, and seal probable entry points.

PLUMBING VENTS

Plumbing vents sometimes fall short, too, and terminate in the attic. In addition to dumping moist air into a closed space, such stacks are a plumbing code violation that should be corrected immediately by extending them through the roof and properly flashing them to prevent roof leaks. Plumbing vents equipped with special air-admittance valves are now being used more frequently because they do not penetrate the roof.

Vent stacks perform two critical functions: (1) They admit air into waste pipes so that when, say, a toilet is flushed, falling wastes do not suck the water out of the fixture trap. Water traps keep sewer gases from entering living spaces. (2) Vent stacks also direct sewer gases out of the house, so that they disperse harmlessly in the air. Sewer gases released in high concentrations in confined spaces can be toxic.

Inspectors should also note plumbing vents that are inadequately supported, such as the vent shown in the left photo above. Even if the vent is intact at the time of the inspection, it could subsequently fail, cracking or slipping down into the attic, creating an unfilled vent hole in the roof.

RODENT NESTS

Rodent nests in insulation are both a smelly nuisance and a health hazard. Rats and mice infected with a hantavirus can transmit it via their saliva, urine, and feces. Should their leavings be disturbed they can become airborne; humans inhaling those airborne particles can become quite ill. For this reason, nests should be removed by a pest eradication specialist.

FIRE HAZARDS

Fire hazards in the attic include the following issues.

FURNACE OR APPLIANCE VENT (FLUE) PIPES that are too close to combustible surfaces or that lack appropriate double-wall roof adaptors are a fire hazard. Safe clearance distances are usually embossed on the flue pipe or on a sticker affixed to it. Single-wall metal flue pipes typically require a 6-in. clearance from combustibles, though many codes forbid using single-wall flues in unfinished spaces. Type B double-wall metal flue pipes require a 1-in. clearance from combustibles. An HVAC specialist should check the flue and roof adaptor; he or she will know local code requirements.

DIRTY, CLUTTERED ATTICS can exacerbate almost every problem mentioned in this chapter.

Here, an unsafe single-wall cap and flue pipe have been used to vent a furnace. This is a fire hazard and superheated flue gases have charred nearby plywood sheathing. Before the furnace is used again, a heating contractor should replace this flue pipe and cap with appropriate double-wall equipment.

When a roof is stripped, it's important that the roofing contractor remove debris that falls into the attic. Otherwise, combustible debris can create a potential fire hazard.

Even if an appliance flue pipe is correctly installed, for example, it becomes a fire hazard if debris generated by a roof stripping is not cleaned up and it lodges next to that flue pipe. Likewise, too much stuff stored in an attic on undersize ceiling joists isn't helping anything.

MASONRY CHIMNEYS are discussed at greater length on p. 208. To summarize, there must be a minimum 2-in. separation between masonry chimneys and combustibles such as framing. Insulation should not come in direct contact with a chimney, with the exception of mineral wool, which is fire resistant. Masonry chimneys must be lined with flue tile, which must be intact (no cracks) and continuous to safely contain superheated gases. The chimney must be correctly flashed to prevent roof leaks, and its concrete cap must be solid and uncracked. In the attic, an inspector should note crumbling mortar joints and cracks, which may denote a chimney that is settling. Take particular note of creosote stains leaking out of mortar joints, which often indicate a failed flue liner, perhaps cracked during a chimney fire.

ELECTRICAL HAZARDS

Electrical hazards in the attic include the following issues.

EXPOSED WIRE SPLICES, a violation of electrical codes, have the potential to shock people who come in contact with them and to set fire to combustibles. All electrical connections must take place in covered boxes. Wires can work loose and electricity can arc (jump) between conductors, especially when connections are exposed. Because arcs are extremely hot—they can approach 2000°F—they can easily ignite combustibles nearby. Insulation coming in contact with exposed splices is very serious and should be corrected immediately. If you see exposed wire splices anywhere, have a qualified electrician perform a detailed inspection.

UNPROTECTED WIRES could be damaged. Electrical wires, whether knob-and-tube or Romex (nonmetallic sheathed cable), should never be run on horizontal surfaces in the attic where residents are likely to store boxes and other items; nor should electrical cables be installed on top of framing within 6 ft. of an attic access opening. Such wiring is typically installed behind finish surfaces, where it cannot be disturbed. Where wiring must be surface mounted, it must be protected by metal conduit or armored cable. Nailing a board next to wires can also provide needed protection.

All electrical connections must be housed in a covered box. Splices like these can separate, arc, and create both shock and fire hazards. Insulation should not cover exposed splices.

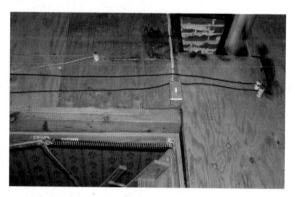

Electrical wires—whether knob-and-tube or plastic-sheathed Romex—should not be installed on horizontal surfaces where residents or stored items are likely to touch or disturb wires.

KNOB-AND-TUBE (KT) WIRING is not inherently unsafe, and most electrical codes allow its continued use if it is properly installed. Because the air that flows around KT wiring is included in its load-carrying capacity these wires need to be kept cool. Thus some areas do not allow covering KT with insulation. In particular, the facing on insulation batts should never touch KT connections: Foil facing is an electrical conductor and paper facing is combustible.

NON-IC-RATED CEILING LIGHT CANS should never come in contact with, nor be covered by, insulation. The standard clearance requirement is 3 in. between non-IC-rated cans and insulation. It can be difficult to determine if a fixture, even if IC labeled, is actually IC rated because the manufacturer's specs

may require special trim, lamp type, and wattage. If in doubt, recommend review by a qualified electrician. Installing special attic covers over them is not a bad plan.

RODENTS chew electrical wires. Another reason to rid the attic of them. Write up any signs of nesting or wire sheathing that appears to be chewed, cracked, or otherwise damaged.

WHAT TO LOOK FOR

- Do bath-fan or range-hood ducts terminate in the attic? Is there condensation or water stains at the end of the duct(s)?

- Are plumbing vents adequately supported? Have any stacks cracked or slipped down from their openings in the roof? Do stacks terminate inside the attic? Any sewer smells?

- Are there any signs of scorched wood near metal flue pipes? Do flue pipes exit the roof through a double-wall roof adaptor?

- Are combustible materials such as framing, roofing debris, or insulation in contact with metal flue pipe?

- What is the general condition of the masonry chimney? Are mortar joints crumbling or cracked? Are any portions of the chimney discolored with creosote stains?

- Does insulation or wood framing come in contact with the masonry chimney or is there a 2-in. clearance all around the chimney?

- Are there any signs of rodents nesting in attic insulation? Has the sheathing of electrical wires been chewed?

- Are electrical cables stapled near the attic access opening? Do unprotected cables run along horizontal surfaces where cables could be damaged or inhabitants could be shocked?

- Are exposed wire splices visible—not protected in covered boxes? Does insulation make contact or cover exposed electrical splices?

- Are old-style (non-IC-rated) ceiling light cans in contact with insulation or covered by it?

- Is knob-and-tube wiring visible in the attic? Is wire insulation in good condition or is it cracked, frayed, or damaged? Does insulation cover or come in contact with KT wiring?

CHAPTER 5

FOUNDATIONS, BASEMENTS, *and* CRAWL SPACES

AS A SEASONED INSPECTOR ONCE SAID, "Under the house is where the 'money stuff' is." Big problems in basements or crawl spaces, such as inadequate foundations, deteriorated substructure framing, or persistent water penetration, can be very expensive to correct.

As a home inspector you must, of course, call it as you see it, but in this area be doubly sure you are seeing it correctly. In other words, consider the simplest, most obvious explanations first. If you see wet foundation walls, for example, make sure that gutters and downspouts are clear and working and that the soil is graded away from the house before assuming that the foundation must be excavated and that an expensive perimeter drain system is the remedy.

Basement stairs are often marginally strong, do not have proper handrails for safe use, and have low overhead clearances.

Access and Safety

Access to basements and crawl spaces varies widely, especially in older houses, where access was often an afterthought. Basements may be accessed by outside stairs, which you should first inspect to be sure they will bear your weight. As outside doors are often locked, have a spare padlock on hand if there's no key for the existing lock. Inside access is typically through interior stairs, although, there again, check their condition before you descend. Crawl space access can be through a hatch in a closet floor, through a basement wall, or through a small door outside near the soil level.

Potential shock hazard: If you see standing water or wet soil *and* improper wiring, don't enter the basement or crawl space. Water or dampness alone is no reason to stay out, but exposed wire splices (not inside a covered box), improperly supported wire runs, or other evidence of substandard practices are signs that there may be shock hazards as well. Add the presence of water and shocks could be fatal. Most licensed electricians won't enter such spaces either, unless they turn off all power to the building first.

If you do inspect under the house, it's a wise precaution to touch a voltage tester (such as the inductance tester shown on p. 119) to metal water supply pipes, metal ducts, the water heater housing, and any other metal surfaces that could become energized by a ground fault. A correctly grounded electrical system (p. 137) should protect you against ground faults, but, again, you should not assume that a system is correctly wired. (That's one of the things you will learn in the course of your inspection.) If your voltage tester indicates electrical current in things that shouldn't be energized, leave the space.

Gas odor: If you smell gas or fuel oil upon opening a basement door or crawl space hatch, stay out till the source of the smell can be ascertained and corrected. Some inspectors limit their risk by turning off the main gas valve, opening up windows to ventilate the space while they perform other tasks, and return later to inspect the space if the smell has abated enough.

Some crawl spaces with barely accessible hatches (18 in. by 18 in.) don't have enough room inside to get around, even though they meet Federal Housing Administration (FHA) minimum standards. Those standards were probably designed with ventilation, not

If you see wet soil *and* improper wiring under the house, stay out. Here, water from a plumbing leak cascades off a heating duct. A plumber should fix the leak and a portable sump pump should be brought in to remove standing water.

home inspectors, in mind. Typically, FHA-minimum headroom is 18 in. from the ground level to the bottom of floor joists, with 12 in. allowable from the ground to the underside of a girder. In newer construction access openings should be at least 16 in. by 24 in. It's wise to recommend a proper access opening be installed. Areas that are inaccessible are much more likely to have problems because they are not available for routine maintenance.

In some areas with poor drainage the crawl space soils are often damp. For any basement or crawl space you choose not to enter, do your best to make your inspection from the doorway or access hatch. A strong flashlight will help. It's not ideal, but it's the best you can do. On your report, note that you could not gain access.

Other obstructions: Access may also be obstructed by ducting, pipes, stored items, finished wall surfaces, furnaces or water heaters, and creatures under the house. If the homeowner is willing to move stored objects, you can resume the basement inspection after that is done. In short, do what's reasonable to access as much of the basement as you can. The report should describe those locations that were inaccessible and recommend further inspection when access can be provided.

Foundation Basics

A foundation is a mediator between the loads of the house and the soil on which the foundation rests. A well-designed foundation keeps a house's wood underpinning above the soil so it doesn't rot or get eaten by insects. And it should be sturdy enough to keep walls plumb and floors level despite wind, water, soil movement, and earthquakes.

FOUNDATION TYPES

Foundations should be appropriate to the site. For example, on sandy well-drained soil, unmortared stone foundations can last for centuries. But an unstable clay hillside may dictate an engineered foundation on piers extending down to bedrock.

Where the ground freezes, foundation footings need to be dug below the frost line, as stipulated by local codes. Below the frost line, footings aren't susceptible to the potentially tremendous lifting and sinking forces of freeze–thaw cycles in moist soil. (Thus, most houses in cold climates often have full basements, sort of a bonus for having to sink footings so deep.)

THE T, OR SPREAD, FOUNDATION is perhaps the most commonly used type, so named because its cross section looks like an inverted T. It's remarkably adaptable. On a flat site in temperate regions, a shallow T foundation is usually enough to support a house, while creating a crawl space that allows joist access and ventilation. When T foundations fail, they often do so because they're unreinforced or have too small or too shallow a footprint.

SLAB ON GRADE is a giant pad of reinforced concrete, poured simultaneously with a slightly thicker perimeter footing that increases its load-bearing capabilities. Beneath the slab, there's typically a layer of crushed gravel covered by sheet plastic to prevent moisture from wicking up from the soil. Slabs are generally installed on flat lots where the ground doesn't freeze because, being above frost line, shallow slabs are vulnerable to frost heaves.

Some slabs are poured over perimeter T foundations and will show the joint between these two sections along the exterior ground level.

POST-TENSION SLABS are a newer type of slab that has steel cables running through tubes inside the concrete. The nuts at the cable ends are tightened after the concrete hardens. Post-tension slabs use less concrete and are considered lighter and stronger than older types. The main rule with these foundations is never to cut into the slab without an engineer telling you where the cables are located.

Although shallow, the large footprint of a slab sometimes makes it the only feasible foundation on soils with weak load-bearing capacity. Because slabs sit on grade (at ground level), their drainage systems must be meticulously detailed.

FOUNDATION TYPES

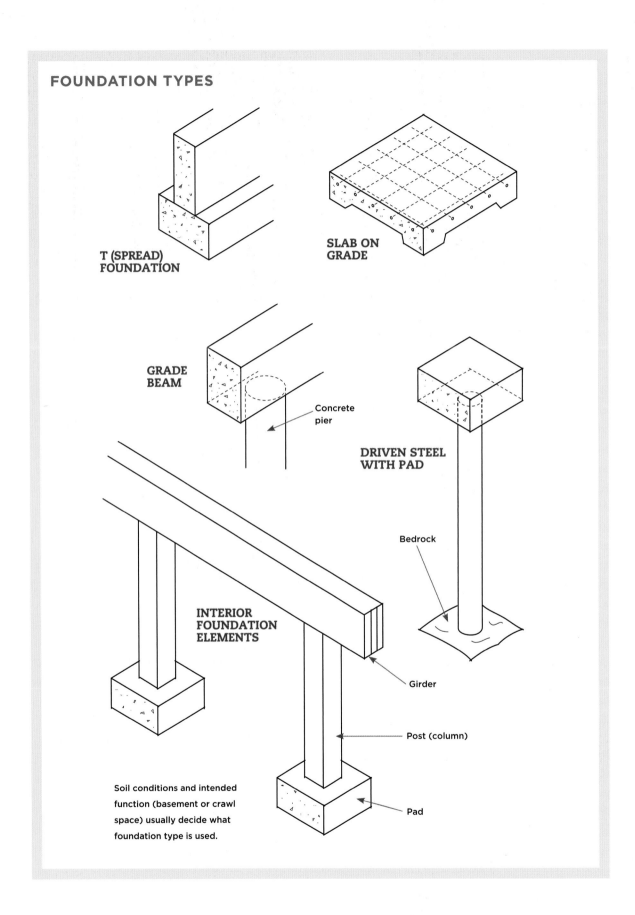

T (SPREAD) FOUNDATION

SLAB ON GRADE

GRADE BEAM

Concrete pier

DRIVEN STEEL WITH PAD

Bedrock

INTERIOR FOUNDATION ELEMENTS

Girder

Post (column)

Pad

Soil conditions and intended function (basement or crawl space) usually decide what foundation type is used.

GRADE BEAMS with drilled concrete piers are the premier foundation for most foundations built on steep slopes. These foundations get their name because pier holes are typically drilled to bearing strata (bedrock). This foundation type is unsurpassed for lateral stability. Also, concrete piers have a greater cross section than driven steel piers and hence greater skin friction against the soil, so they're much less likely to migrate. The stability of concrete piers is enhanced by steel-reinforced concrete-grade beams, placed slightly below grade, connecting the tops of the piers together structurally. Some older 1970s-era pier foundations did not have grade beams, and the piers in some cases moved independently.

DRIVEN STEEL PILINGS are used to anchor foundations on steep or unstable soils. Driven to stable soils or bedrock and capped, steel pilings can support heavy vertical loads. There are various types of steel pilings, including helical piers, which look like giant auger bits and are screwed in with hydraulic motors, and push piers, which are hollow and can be pushed in, strengthened with reinforcing bar, and filled with concrete or epoxy.

INTERIOR FOUNDATION ELEMENTS include girders, posts or columns, and pads. These elements are most often used in conjunction with T foundations. Girders typically shorten the distances joists must span, support load-bearing walls above, and reduce some of the loading on perimeter foundations. Posts or columns, in turn, provide support beneath a girder. Adjustable steel floor jacks or nonadjustable Lally columns are common in some areas with basements. They are strong and can be adjusted periodically as needed. Like perimeter foundations, interior elements must be sized for the loads they bear.

STRUCTURAL SETTLEMENT

All house foundations settle somewhat. The degree of settlement depends on the type of soil, how much the lot slopes, the amount of surface or subsurface water, erosion in a neighboring lot, seismic activity, and so on. As a foundation settles, it will crack. If the settlement is slight or even—all parts of the founda-

Differential settlement has caused part of this foundation to fail, creating a large crack that runs through the foundation wall and the stucco exterior. Have a structural engineer identify the cause(s) of the failure and design a replacement.

tion settle roughly the same amount—cracks will be superficial and nothing to worry about.

When the settlement is uneven—some parts of the foundation sink more than others—the ensuing cracks tend to be larger and the sides of the cracks don't line up. In addition, floors may slope, window and door openings may go out of square, and in extreme cases, walls may go out of plumb. This differential settlement can be a cause for concern and should be assessed by a structural engineer, and perhaps a soils engineer.

It is not unusual to see floors that are higher at the center and lower around the building perimeter. This is typically caused by damp expansive soils in the center or soft wet perimeter soils. It is almost never a good plan to try and level such a house, as that would cause major damage to the interiors.

Floors sloping less than 1/8 in. per 1 ft. are usually not noticeable, whereas everyone can see floors that slope more than 1/4 in. per 1 ft. Eventually with long-term settlement it may become necessary to resupport the foundation and level the floors.

In Chapter 1, the first step of the inspection focused on soil and site conditions. Some soil types are more stable and drain better than others and, in general, the soil of a level lot will exert less lateral (side) pressure on foundation walls than soil on a sloping lot.

Foundations whose footings rest on bedrock will settle least. Footings on sandy soil tend to settle evenly and quickly because sand particles are relatively large compared to the voids (open spaces) between them. Water drains well through sandy soil, in part because sand doesn't absorb it.

Clay soil, on the other hand, absorbs water dramatically, expanding as much as 50% in volume during wet seasons, contracting a similar amount during dry months. Consequently, foundations on predominantly clay soil settle over many years, with cracks in finish surfaces spreading and shrinking seasonally. Sometimes called adobe soil, it has a distinctive alligator pattern when dry (see the photo on p. 105).

Soil with a large percentage of organic matter will also absorb moisture, but if it is otherwise sandy, the organic portion will decompose and the site will eventually stabilize.

The U.S. Department of Agriculture (USDA) has detailed soil maps for most locales. In addition,

U.S. Geological Survey (USGS) topographical maps show streams, lakes, floodplains, and other natural features that could have an impact on a site. Local building and land-use departments also have maps indicating watersheds, slide zones, contaminated soil, and seismic hazard zones.

Sloped building lots tend to magnify the problems of unstable soil types. If there is a subsurface layer of clay, for example, prolonged rain may saturate it and cause it to slip. Because it is almost impossible to design a foundation massive enough to withstand the lateral forces of a hillside of sodden, sliding dirt, some sites just shouldn't be built on.

The good news in this otherwise sobering review is that if a house is older (at least 30 years or 40 years old), it has probably done most of the settling it's going to do. Have an engineer who knows the area assess the house's cracks and out-of-square trim to make sure the site is stable and the foundation is sound.

WHAT TO LOOK FOR

- What is the soil composition of the lot? Is the lot flat or sloping?
- What type of foundation(s) does the house have? (Homeowners may need to consult the original construction document or building-department records to find out.)
- How old is the foundation? Have foundation sections been added to the original footprint?
- Are there signs of settlement such as cracked foundation walls, eroded footings, out-of-plumb walls, or out-of-square windows and doors?

Dampness and Seepage

Damp basements and crawl spaces can have numerous causes, so let's start with seasonal condensation, move on to excess interior moisture, then to common and easily correctable exterior causes, and conclude with seepage, in which water migrates through foundation walls and slabs because of saturated soil or high subsurface water.

In this basement, wetness is caused by seepage along wall-floor joints and leaky plumbing connections. The efflorescence on the walls suggests persistent seepage through the walls as well.

CONDENSATION

Cool air can't hold as much water vapor as warm air, so any time warm, moist air comes in contact with cooler surfaces, water vapor will condense into a liquid. Because the earth has a year-round average temperature of 55°F, subterranean spaces such as basements and crawl spaces are generally cooler than outside air temperatures in the spring and summer. So that's when condensation is at its peak.

The hotter the outside air (and hence the more moisture it can hold) and the cooler the surface, the greater the condensation. Cold water pipes, toilet tanks, A/C coils, and uninsulated foundation walls will be slick with condensation on really hot days.

Opening windows to increase ventilation, and evaporation, can carry away some of the dampness. And many homeowners favor opening windows at night to admit cooler air and then shutting windows and pulling shades at dawn to conserve the cool during the day. Whole-house fans and attic vents (p. 80) are also helpful, to a degree.

But in hot, humid climates—say, Louisiana in August—there's so much moisture in the air that opening windows only admits more water. Shutting all the windows and cranking up the air-conditioner is the preferred way to deal with sultry weather. Air-conditioners also dehumidify interior air somewhat

as water vapor condenses on the A/C unit's evaporator coils, drips into a drain pan, and runs outside. If interior surfaces are still too damp, the air smells musty, or mold is visible, adding a dedicated dehumidifier or two is frequently the next step.

When you see water coursing down a concrete foundation wall it's hard to believe that it's not seepage from underground streams or the first stages of Noah's flood. One test of where the water is coming from is to duct-tape a 6-in.-sq. of aluminum foil to the foundation wall and leave it there for a day. If the front of the foil is dry and the back is wet, supposedly that proves that water is seeping through the wall. On a hot, humid day, however, more likely you'll find that both sides are wet.

To learn more about reducing dampness in crawl spaces, see p. 106.

EXCESS INTERIOR MOISTURE

Cooking and bathing generate an enormous amount of water vapor inside a house. The simple and not very expensive solution to excess interior moisture is adding range hoods or bath exhaust fans over the appliance or fixture generating the moisture. In bathrooms, vent fans should be located as close to the shower as is practicable.

Warm, moist air tends to rise, so excess interior moisture often migrates into the attic, where it can cause mold, rot, and in cold climates, ice dams. But a certain amount of water vapor will find its way to a basement or a crawl space. Exhaust fans can help throughout the house.

HVAC ducts that come apart or split can also dump moisture under the house, in addition to wasting energy. This is true for both insulated and uninsulated ducts. While it's possible to see disconnected sections during a general inspection, it usually takes pressurized duct testing—as part of a complete energy audit—to locate all duct leaks comprehensively.

COMMON EXTERIOR CAUSES

Basement and crawl space dampness is often caused by water collecting next to the foundation because of

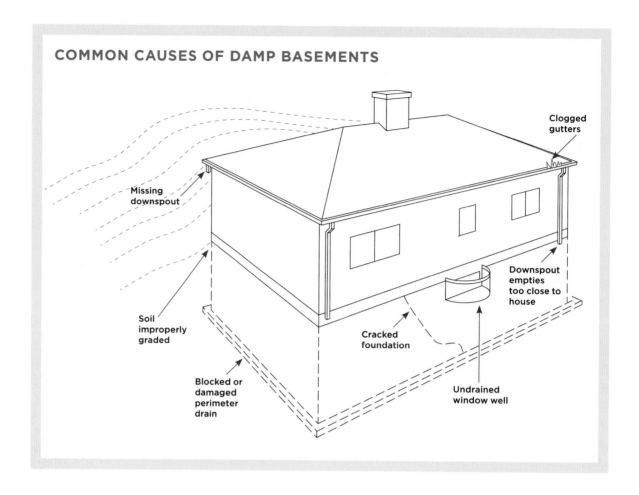

COMMON CAUSES OF DAMP BASEMENTS

Clogged gutters

Missing downspout

Downspout empties too close to house

Soil improperly graded

Cracked foundation

Blocked or damaged perimeter drain

Undrained window well

causes that can easily be detected and corrected by homeowners. These common exterior causes include the following:

- **Gutters and downspouts** that are clogged, damaged, deteriorated, or missing. Instead of directing roof runoff away from the house, they dump it right next to the foundation.

- **Blocked perimeter drains.** If downspouts terminate into a subsurface perimeter drainage system, it should be flushed with water to be sure it is working.

- **Improper grading** that slopes toward the house. Soil next to the house should be graded so that it slopes away from the structure and then regraded, as needed, if that soil subsides or becomes leveled by foot traffic.

- **Walkways or patios** that slope incorrectly toward the house have often settled unevenly and will funnel large amounts of water toward the foundation.

- **Lawn sprinklers** aimed at the house can soak the siding and the soil. Leaky outdoor spigots can, in a month, dump hundreds of gallons of water next to the foundation.

- **Basement window wells** will collect water if they lack drains or rain deflectors.

WATER SEEPAGE

Seepage refers to water that enters through floors or foundation walls. It may rise up through the crawl space soil or a concrete basement floor or seep through joints where walls meet floors. Seepage tends to follows a path of least resistance. If a concrete foundation has oversize holes for sewer pipes or electrical conduits, water may seep through those holes first; similarly, concrete form ties that rust out may provide seepage points. As you inspect foundation walls, note water stains or rust stains.

Two strikes and you're wet. This downspout is dumping roof runoff next to the foundation and a sidewalk tilting toward the house is helping to keep it there.

Basement floors below ground level are very susceptible to water entry. Hydrostatic pressure underneath is forcing water up through cracks in the concrete slab.

If differential settlement causes portions of a foundation to crack, water may seep through those cracks, especially if they run through the foundation. How much seepage occurs also depends on the hydrostatic pressure—the pressure that water exerts—on slabs and foundation walls. This pressure may come from a high water table, subterranean runoff on a sloping lot, soil saturated by prolonged rains, or some combination of these causes.

One home inspector's task is to observe obvious seepage points. Note discolored surfaces (wet concrete will be darker), puddles, wet areas where walls meet floor, and larger areas of standing water. Note if wetness is localized along one wall (likely adjacent to an uphill slope) or if wetness is widespread. Floor drains with standing water or sump pumps are other obvious symptoms. Note too where sump pumps discharge: Is it well away from the house?

Signs of past wetness may be more elusive. In addition to rust stains or water stains, look for chalky efflorescence where water has leeched mineral salts from the concrete. Around the base of foundation walls, look for silt residue. Look for deterioration around the base of wood posts or rust at the bottom of metal columns. (Frequently, the floor around column pads is cracked, which can also admit water.) If there is a water heater or furnace in the basement,

Seepage is quite obvious along the base of these walls. If you inspect during a dry period and suspect periodic seepage, remove a furnace access panel and look for rust inside the housing.

remove the access panel at the bottom and, using your flashlight, look for rust inside the appliance, which may indicate periodic flooding.

The most cost-effective way to correct seepage problems is to start with the simplest, least expensive remedy, see if that works, and then, if it doesn't, move on to the next. Such a progression might be (1) fill foundation holes and cracks with hydraulic cement, injection epoxy gel, or polyurethane foam, (2) seal the entire interior surface of foundation walls with a cement-based or epoxy sealing, (3) excavate the soil around the outside of the building and install waterproofing to the exterior of foundation walls, (4) install perimeter drains around the foundation if none presently exist, and (5) install swale drains uphill to intercept runoff before it gets to the foundation. The first two steps can be attempted by a diligent homeowner; if hydrostatic pressures are not too great, those fixes may suffice. The last three steps will be very costly and typically require input from structural and soil engineers.

An alternative is to dig a trench in the basement floor at the base of the leaky wall, install perforated drainage piping in gravel, and run the piping downhill to the exterior or to a sump. This method can create a relatively dry floor at lower cost. Basement rooms that are used for storage can be kept much dryer by adding a dehumidifier appliance.

WHAT TO LOOK FOR

- Does excessive wetness occur most often on hot, humid days and does it seem limited to cold water pipes and cool concrete foundation walls? (It's probably normal condensation.)

- Does the area under the house smell musty or do you see mold? Are there doors and windows that can be opened to increase ventilation?

- Are there vent fans in all bathrooms and a range hood in the kitchen?

WATERPROOFING MEMBRANES

BECAUSE CONCRETE IS POROUS, PROLONGED hydrostatic pressure can cause water to permeate undamaged concrete slabs and walls whose exterior surfaces have not been waterproofed. Because waterproofing membranes terminate near grade, they may be visible as a tar-like substance or as elastomeric sheets near the top of the foundation. If a membrane is not visible, you can dig down 6 in. to 12 in. to unearth its upper edge or ask to see foundation details on construction documents.

- If basement walls are wet to the touch, is the ground adjacent to the house saturated? (See "Common Exterior Causes" on p. 95.)

- Is there standing water in floor drains and exterior stairwells? (Flush the drains to see if they are merely clogged.)

- Is there efflorescence or a silty residue where floor slabs meet foundation walls?

- When you remove water heater or furnace access panels, can you see rust along the bottom of the appliance housing?

- Is water seeping through foundation walls, especially on the uphill wall of a sloping lot?

- Is water seeping from horizontal cracks in foundation walls that are bowing inward? (See "Reading Foundation Cracks," below.)

- Is the area subject to periodic flooding? (The house may be in a floodplain.)

Concrete Foundations

Concrete is a mixture of portland cement, water, and aggregate (sand and gravel). When water is added to cement, a chemical reaction, called hydration, takes place, and the mixture hardens around the aggregate, binding it fast. Water makes concrete workable, and cement makes it strong. The lower the water to cement ratio, the stronger the concrete.

In addition to getting the right mix and consistency, it's essential that the concrete be correctly consolidated as it is poured into forms, specifically, that the concrete be vibrated to drive out air bubbles and voids before it has hardened. If this is not done, finish surfaces will be more likely to crack and spall (flake), steel reinforcing bars in the concrete will be more likely to corrode, and water seepage will be more likely to penetrate foundation walls.

READING FOUNDATION CRACKS

As noted earlier, all buildings settle. If the settlement is more or less uniform, the stresses on the foundation will be distributed evenly. When the settlement is differential, the stresses will be uneven, sometimes causing minor annoyances such as sticking windows and doors or sloping floors. Over time, such

A crash course in cracks. The rough horizontal bands of this foundation were caused by not vibrating the wet concrete to drive out voids and air bubbles. Shallow cracks throughout the surface are cosmetic and nothing to worry about. The large vertical crack, however, runs through the foundation and may indicate a failed footing. It should be filled and monitored to see if it is active.

STEEL REINFORCEMENT AND FASTENERS

STEEL REINFORCING BAR (REBAR) CARRIES and distributes loads within a concrete foundation, transferring the loads from high-pressure areas to lower-pressure areas. It thereby lessens the likelihood of point failure, either from point loading (concentrated weight) above or from lateral soil and water pressures. Anchor bolts or threaded rods, tied to rebar, bolt down mudsills and thus attach the overlying structure to the foundation. There also are a number of metal connectors—such as Simpson® Strong-Tie®—that tie joists to girders; keep support posts from drifting; and hold down mudsills, sole plates, and the like. These connectors are particularly important in high-wind and earthquake areas.

settlement usually stabilizes, and though the floors will still slant or the windows stick, those conditions probably won't get any worse.

Similarly, all foundations crack, due to settlement or shrinkage. Most cracks are short, superficial, and not anything to worry about. Moderate (¼-in.-wide) or larger cracks that run through the foundation *may* indicate ongoing differential settlement and may need to be repaired later on. But there is no way to determine in one inspection if the settlement is active or if a crack will grow. The best way to predict future movement is to monitor the number and size of cracks over time.

As you review the following descriptions, keep in mind that the larger, more dramatic cracks are relatively rare.

- Short, meandering cracks are usually caused by slight shrinkage as concrete sets. This is a common condition, nothing to worry about.
- Surface cracks or welts (slight ridges) running horizontally the length of a wall, often with aggregate exposed along the edges, are cold joints caused by separate concrete pours. Walls with cold joints are marginally weaker than concrete placed in one continuous pour but are rarely a structural problem.
- Narrow vertical or diagonal surface cracks that are roughly parallel are likely caused by foundation settlement or soil movement but are probably not serious. If water runs from cracks after a storm, they can be filled with an epoxy cement, then coated with a sealant.
- Wide cracks in foundations less than 2 ft. tall indicate little or no steel reinforcement, a common failing of older homes in temperate climates. Unreinforced foundations are more likely to crack.
- Large (½-in. or wider) vertical cracks through the foundation that are wider at the top usually mean that one end of the foundation is sinking—typically at a corner with poor drainage or a missing downspout.
- Large vertical cracks through the foundation that are wider at the bottom are usually caused by footings that are too small for the load. It's common to replace or reinforce sections that have failed.

Wide cracks in foundations typically indicate little or no steel reinforcement, a common failing of older homes in temperate climates.

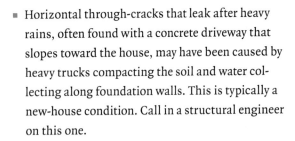

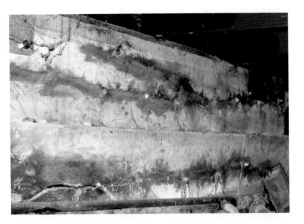

Horizontal cracking and inward bowing suggest saturated soil pressure and possibly ground movement. Because these cracks have been filled and the bottom filling is cracking again, the foundation wall may be failing.

- Horizontal through-cracks that leak after heavy rains, often found with a concrete driveway that slopes toward the house, may have been caused by heavy trucks compacting the soil and water collecting along foundation walls. This is typically a new-house condition. Call in a structural engineer on this one.

- Horizontal cracks though a concrete foundation midway up the wall, *with the wall bowing in*, are most often caused by lateral pressure from water-soaked soil. This condition is most commonly seen on uphill walls on sloping lots. **VERY SERIOUS:** The bowing may indicate that the foundation is failing. Consult a structural engineer at once.

- In cold climates, horizontal cracks through the foundation, often accompanied by a concrete floor that is crowning and cracking, are usually caused by frost heaving when footings are not below the frost line. Consult a structural engineer.

- An older concrete foundation that is rotating probably lacks reinforcing steel or footings that are deep enough. The weight of the building on the outside edge of the foundation wall is causing it to lean. Poor drainage can exacerbate the leaning. A structural engineer will assess the condition and recommend reinforcing or replacing the foundation.

OTHER CONCRETE CONCERNS

In addition to cracking, you may observe the following issues.

EFFLORESCENCE is a white powdery deposit on masonry or concrete that has been in place for a while. Efflorescence is, essentially, mineral salts in the concrete that have been brought to the surface by water migrating through and drying on foundation walls. Minor efflorescence is common even in new construction, but substantial efflorescence indicates defective drainage. Adequate exterior waterproofing is one way to prevent efflorescence.

Another approach is to apply a waterproof coating on the inside of the wall to prevent the salt crystals from forming. Older homes often used parging (applying a plaster coating) on the inside of concrete walls to reduce or eliminate efflorescence. Over time, this parging eventually tends to come loose and fall off.

SPALLING OR FLAKING SURFACES on relatively new foundations are usually caused by incorrectly installed concrete, especially a failure to vibrate the concrete and drive out air bubbles and voids before the concrete sets. If wall forms were not coated with a release agent, the concrete may stick to the forms, creating surface imperfections when the forms are removed. In some cases, aggregate in the

Efflorescence deposits are mineral salts driven to the surface by water. Strong, dense concrete is not damaged by such deposits, though they can cause porous old concrete to crumble.

This anchor bolt retrofitted to secure a mudsill would not do much good in an earthquake because the old concrete foundation would crumble. This retrofit is not very effective.

concrete mixture will be visible. Voids should be filled, surfaces troweled smooth and allowed to dry, and then sealed to prevent water entry.

RUSTY BARS VISIBLE in foundation walls may be caused by a concrete mix that was too dry to flow around the rebar, insufficient vibration to drive out voids, rebar placed too close to the surface, surface spalling, or moisture and mineral salts that corroded the rebar. If the damage is extensive, a foundation specialist should assess the foundation; otherwise, loose rust should be removed and the void filled with an epoxy cement patch.

CRUMBLING OLDER FOUNDATIONS may have been weakened by prolonged moisture penetration. What began as efflorescence developed into widespread mineral salt crystals that expanded and caused surface crumbling. With continued moisture penetration over many years, the concrete may deteriorate to the point where replacement becomes necessary.

POOR-QUALITY CONCRETE is found in many older foundations where too much aggregate was used, which makes concrete porous and weak. In some coastal areas, round beach sand was used instead of sharp sand from a quarry; cement adheres better to sharp edges. Poor-quality concrete is par-

ticularly susceptible to moisture entry and will often crumble and deteriorate with age.

NOTE: Some building departments do not permit the installation of earthquake bolts into poor-quality concrete; to seismically reinforce such buildings, it may be necessary to install new concrete foundation walls.

WHAT TO LOOK FOR

- Is efflorescence present on concrete foundation walls? How widespread is it?
- Are cracks, if any, mostly short and superficial?
- Are concrete surfaces flaking or spalling? Do voids need to be filled and sealed?
- Do any cracks run through the wall (through-cracks)? Are their sides more or less parallel? Or do their sides not line up, indicating different settlement of the foundation?
- If there are vertical through-cracks, are cracks wider at the top or the bottom?
- Are there horizontal through-cracks in the foundation? If so, do foundation walls bow inward along those cracks?
- Are older foundation walls rotating? Are walls above rotating foundations out of plumb?
- Are older foundation walls crumbling? Is rusty reinforcing steel visible?

This concrete block wall does not have a lintel across its opening. The cracking appears relatively minor but its size should be monitored to determine if the stresses are active.

Portions of this brick foundation have been parged to protect its mortar joints and reduce seepage through the walls. Minor wetness aside, it's in decent shape.

Concrete Block and Brick Foundations

Concrete has been around for thousands of years—it was used for the Roman aqueducts, for example—but using concrete in residential foundations didn't become widespread in eastern states till there were pumper trucks to deliver the stuff. Foundations in western states were often poured from wheelbarrows before 1900. Consequently, many houses before the 1940s had concrete block, brick, or stone foundations.

LITTLE RESISTANCE TO LATERAL PRESSURES

Concrete block and brick foundations have decent load-bearing strength but little resistance to lateral pressures. The mortar joints are their weak points and the most likely place for water to enter. So when you inspect these foundations, pay close attention to mortar joints.

Concrete block and brick foundations do best on flat lots with good drainage. It is extremely unusual to see block or brick foundations on sloping lots for the simple reason that they don't work very well. Where block and brick foundations have been installed on clay soil that becomes saturated, they often develop efflorescence, zigzag cracks along mortar joints, widespread seepage, and, in time, walls that bulge inward.

It is possible to improve the lateral strength of concrete block by inserting rebar through block cores and then filling those cores with concrete, but such assemblies never get close to the lateral strength of poured concrete. As is true with poured concrete foundations, concrete block walls with horizontal cracks that bulge inward are particularly at risk, especially if block walls are not reinforced with steel. If walls bulge more than 1 in. from vertical and there's a chronic water problem, foundation failure may be imminent.

CAPPING FOUNDATIONS

Concrete caps are sometimes installed on top of an existing foundation wall by pest-control companies to prevent moisture entry and damage in the wood framing above the foundation. This usually happens when an old mudsill has rotted out because it was too close to the soil. The substructure is temporarily supported by shoring, the rotted framing is cut back, a cap is poured over the old foundation, and a new sill is installed, at least 8 in. above grade.

Modern foundation caps are typically steel reinforced and should improve the strength of the foundation system. They should not, however, be considered as strong as a new foundation. In many cases, the old foundation is a shallow one, made of brick or unreinforced concrete.

Because the old foundation is often in bad shape, it will often be parged with stucco or mortar, which provides some protection and helps keep insects out. If you are able to inspect the old foundation, chances are you will find mortar joints that are soft and crumbling. With a little more digging, you will likely find that the foundation walls have no footing underneath.

(Too small or missing footings are a prime cause of zigzag cracks, as the foundation settles unevenly.) Most capped, shallow foundation should be replaced soon. Till that happens, homeowners should maintain gutters and downspouts so that the ground around the house stays as dry as possible.

WHAT TO LOOK FOR

- Is there efflorescence on concrete block or brick foundation walls? Is the area under the house damp? Is the ground next to the foundation damp?
- Are there zigzag cracks along mortar joints?
- Do cracks run across block faces and walls bulge inward?
- Do walls bulge more than 1 in. from plumb (vertical)? Are there signs of chronic wetness?
- If the foundation has been capped, try to determine the material of the original foundation underneath. In what condition are its mortar joints? Are footings present?

Concrete Floors

Concrete floors will manifest many of the same symptoms as concrete walls, although, of course, floors are not stressed by tons of saturated earth pressing against them. That noted, start your inspection by recording the general condition of the floors: flaking, spalling, efflorescence, and, of course, cracks. Shallow cracks are typically shrinkage and no concern.

Although building codes now require that concrete floors contain steel reinforcement, typically a heavy wire mesh, many older floors are unreinforced. Concrete floors without reinforcement often crack in response to settlement, water pressure beneath the slab, and, in cold regions, frost heaves. If the water pressure is great, concrete floors can buckle upward. So in addition to noting cracks, an inspector should look for signs of chronic moisture.

Cracks that show vertical displacement, where one side of the crack is higher than the other, indicate the absence of steel reinforcing. Concrete with steel mesh or bars inside will bend at any cracks.

READING CRACKS, LOOKING FOR WATER

Concrete floors frequently crack and leak where they meet foundation walls. The joint is inherently weak because it is a cold joint between two different pours. And if the walls are experiencing hydrostatic pressure, the wall–floor joint is typically a path of least resistance. Look there for water stains, efflorescence, and silt residue. Caulking the joint with polyurethane will stop water to a degree, while allowing expansion around floor edges.

Concrete floors frequently crack around concrete pads or pier blocks that support wooden posts or

The soil below this unreinforced slab may be an expansive type whose upward pressure made the concrete lift and crack. Such cracks can be ground smooth to eliminate the trip hazard, but in time this condition will likely reoccur. Replacement is the only sure cure.

metal columns. Pads should be poured independently of floors, but that doesn't always happen. When the pads become point loaded by a load-bearing post or column, the pads sink and cracking occurs. This is usually just a cosmetic issue unless it becomes a water entry point, in which case it should be filled with an epoxy cement patch.

Older concrete floors without a vapor barrier underneath will wick moisture if the soil is persistently damp. Concrete is porous, so this is normal. If you are inspecting under the house after a period of dry weather, look for rust at the bottom of metal columns or rot at the base of wood posts. Remove the access panel of a water heater or furnace to see if there is rust inside the appliance housing. And if you entered the basement by wooden stairs, look behind the stair stringers and the bottom tread for water stains, mold, rot, and the like. Wood that rests directly on concrete will almost always wick moisture if it is present.

SUMP PUMPS

Sump pumps are a good way to remove water once it gets into a basement. Sump pumps are usually installed at a low point in the floor where water collects, though the pump should not be located in a trafficked area where someone could trip over it. Sump pits should be lined with a permeable liner that allows water to seep in while keeping soil out. Though pits are usually 18 in. to 24 in. across, their depth varies according to the type of pump used.

There are two types of pumps. Pedestal sump pumps stand upright in the pit. They are water-cooled and have ball floats that turn the pump on and off. Submersible sump pumps, on the other hand, have sealed, oil-cooled motors, so they tend to be quieter, more durable, and more expensive. And because they are submerged, they can be covered so nothing falls in.

The type of discharge pipe depends on whether the pump is permanent or temporary. Permanent pumps should have 1½-in. rigid PVC discharge pipes with a check valve near the bottom to prevent expelled water from siphoning back down into the pit. If the water

problem is seasonal, many people simply attach a 50-ft. garden hose and run it out a basement window. In either case, the pipe should discharge the water at least 20 ft. from the house, preferably downhill and not directly into a neighbor's property. Moisture-sensing alarms can be installed to warn of pump failure.

Sump pumps need not raise red flags for inspectors. If the pump works, it may be removing seasonal seepage just fine. If there is no water in the sump pit when you inspect the house, use a garden hose to fill it. (Never run a sump pump without water in the pit.) Activate the pump and see if it empties the pit. You should also note where the discharged water goes. It's smart for homeowners to keep a spare pump on hand.

FLOOR DRAINS AND TRAPS. Most basement floors have drains at low points to facilitate normal cleaning and to drain seasonal seepage.

As you inspect floor drains, sniff them at a distance to see if there is a sewer smell. If a floor drain emits an odor of sewer gas, it may be connected to plumbing drains and the drain trap may have dried out. The drain trap can be primed by pouring water into the

Running a garden hose into a floor drain can be a good test to ensure the drain is functional and to locate the drain outflow location.

drain; pouring a small amount of mineral oil into the trap on top of the water will reduce evaporation.

One way to check and see if a floor drain has been improperly connected to the sewer system is to run water in a nearby sink, or ask someone to flush a toilet while you watch or listen closely for any water flow in the drain.

Next, flush the drain for a minute or two to make sure it is not clogged. If you inspect after dry weather, there is no way to know if the drain is adequately removing seasonal flooding, except to look for water stains, residual silt, mold, or rotted wood, as described earlier.

Some basements have a cleanout fitting to provide access to the house's main drain. When this cleanout is in the floor, it is typically in a pit below the floor slab. The cleanout should be plugged with a cap and no sewer smells should be present. The pit should be dry. A wet pit indicates a high water table or a cracked drainpipe, in which case you probably will smell sewer gas. If the cleanout cap is missing, note it in your report. Now and then homeowners remove cleanout caps to alleviate basement flooding (or so they think!), but doing so violates the plumbing code and creates a potential health hazard.

WHAT TO LOOK FOR

- What's the overall condition of the concrete floor? Are there wet spots, efflorescence, flaking, or cracking?
- Is the concrete floor cracking and crumbling throughout? Can you see the earth through some of the larger cracks? (The concrete is probably not reinforced with steel.)
- Is there cracking where concrete floors meet foundation walls? Do you also see water stains, efflorescence, silt residue, or seepage along that joint?
- Are there any signs of prolonged wetness such as water-stained stairs or wood posts or rust at the bottom of metal columns, water heaters, or furnace housings?

- If there is a sump pump, is it functioning? Where does the discharge pipe empty?
- Are there sewer smells in any part of the basement floor?
- Do floor drains empty when you flush them with water?
- If there is a waste cleanout in a pit, is the pit wet? Is the cleanout capped?

Crawl Spaces

Crawl spaces are well named. They tend to be dark, dank, dirt-covered areas only a few feet high—if that. Minimum FHA standards for crawl spaces are 18 in. from the bottom of floor joists to the ground, and 12 in. from the underside of girders. If there is not enough headroom to crawl around the perimeter, use your flashlight to inspect it from the access opening.

Suit up before you go in, as you may encounter critters and toxic chemical preservatives such as copper naphthenate. Your gear should include a hat, heavy-duty leather boots, sturdy coveralls, kneepads, a tight-fitting mask with a HEPA filter, and heavy-duty leather gloves over a pair of rubber ones (see the photo on p. 10). This is another area where it's important to have had a tetanus shot.

You wouldn't know it in the summer, but this adobe soil can absorb so much water that it can raise a building. In most areas its movement is relatively minor, though cracked basement floors are common.

DEALING WITH DAMP

Crawl spaces are often damp. The main causes of that dampness are moisture rising from the soil; warm, moist air condensing on the cool surfaces under the house; not enough ventilation; vegetation too close to the house; and improper surface drainage, such as clogged, damaged, or missing gutters and downspouts. Less often, leaking water supply pipes or split HVAC ducts may add moisture as well; note leaky pipes or split ducts in your report.

In such a dark, moist environment, mold and rot flourish and insects thrive. As you inspect the crawl space, scrutinize wood framing and probe any areas that look suspect. Mudsills, pony-wall studs, and wood posts are particularly prone to rot if they make contact with the earth. Note signs of insect infestation, discussed at greater length on p. 112.

Also note if crawl space walls or floor joists above are insulated. Insulation batts may have foil or paper facing or may be unfaced. If faced batts are installed, the paper facing or foil facing must be placed up, toward the living spaces. If the foil or paper facing faces down (toward the ground), it is incorrectly installed. Finally, note unsupported electrical wires, exposed wiring, and inadequately supported plumbing pipes and sagging heating ducts.

VENTILATING CRAWL SPACES . . . OR NOT

Though an inspector's job is to describe conditions rather than prescribe remedies, you may want to share building scientists' latest thinking on reducing crawl space moisture.

To disperse moisture, building codes typically prescribe 1 sq. ft. of screened vents for each 150 sq. ft. of dirt floor, or 1 sq. ft. of vents for every 1,500 sq. ft. of floors covered with a soil vapor barrier. To achieve cross-ventilation, vent openings are distributed equally along the length of at least two opposite sides; openings should be covered with ¼-in. wire mesh.

The problem with that approach is that open crawl spaces mean cold floors and heat loss in winter; and in summer, warm moist air entering through vents invariably condenses on the cooler surfaces of the crawl space, leading to mold and worse.

Many building scientists (see www.buildingscience .com, for example) now recommend that the crawl space become conditioned space. In other words, close the vents, cover the ground with a sturdy vapor barrier, insulate crawl space walls, seal air leaks, and install a dehumidifier.

SEALING CRAWL SPACES

To seal crawl spaces, advocates suggest first raking the floor to remove debris and sharp rocks, which could puncture a 6-mil plastic vapor barrier. Heavy sheeting will last longer: commercial waterproofing firms, such as Basement Systems®, use 20-mil polyester cord–reinforced sheeting, which can withstand workers crawling and objects stored on it. Then 2-in.-thick EPS foam panels are glued over vent openings, using a spray foam or a polyurethane sealant that adheres well to masonry.

In a 1,000-sq.-ft. rectangular crawl space without jogs, it typically takes five large sheets of polyethylene to isolate the space: a single floor sheet that runs about 1 ft. up onto walls; and four wall pieces that overlap at the corners and the floor by 1 ft. and run up the walls to a height 2 in. to 3 in. below the mudsills. (Mudsills are left exposed so they can be inspected periodically.) Polyurethane caulk attaches the tops of sheets to crawl space walls; if the walls are dirty, they should be wire-brushed first to ensure a good seal.

WHAT TO LOOK FOR

- Before you enter, can you see damp or wet ground and substandard electrical wiring? If so, do *not* enter the crawl space.

- Is the crawl space vented or closed? If vented, do vent screens cover all openings?

- If there is a dirt floor, is it covered with a plastic vapor barrier?

- Inspect the crawl space for wetness and signs of seepage.

FOUNDATION AND SUBSTRUCTURE FRAMING

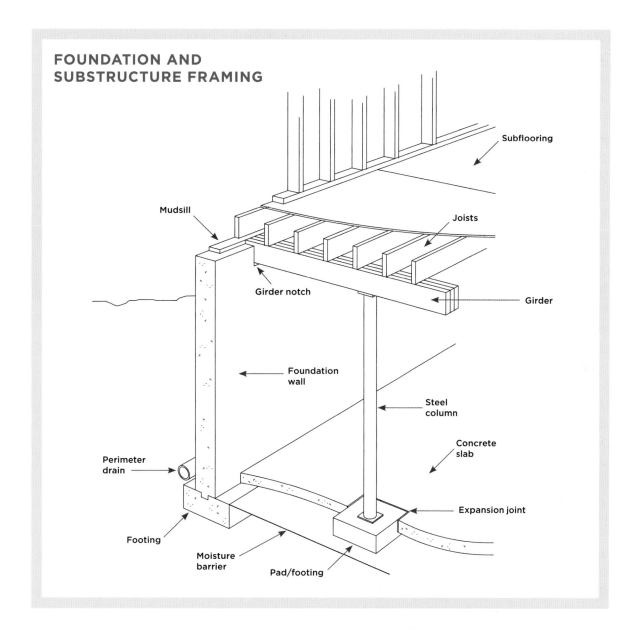

Mudsill

Subflooring

Joists

Girder notch

Girder

Foundation wall

Steel column

Concrete slab

Perimeter drain

Expansion joint

Footing

Moisture barrier

Pad/footing

- Scan all wood framing for rot and insect damage and use a screwdriver point to probe suspect areas. Pay close attention to the mudsills and the bottoms of wood posts.
- Note inadequately supported electrical wires, plumbing pipes, and HVAC ducts.
- Are animals living in the crawl space? Look for rodent droppings and stained insulation.
- Is the crawl space insulated? Are faced insulation batts correctly installed?

Substructure Framing

The structural elements visible under a house are called the substructure framing. In addition to the elements shown in "Foundation and Substructure Framing" above, you might also see pony walls, shortened stud walls that run between the mudsill and the first-floor platform, and the sheathing that covers the pony walls. (Old houses in temperate climates sometimes don't have sheathing; there, wood siding is nailed directly to pony-wall studs, as shown in the left photo on p. 6.)

Most framing members are wood, so your substructure inspection should focus on conditions that affect wood, including excess moisture, wood–soil contact, and insect infestation. Where you see discolored or deteriorated framing, probe it with a screwdriver. If the wood is water-stained but sound, the point of your probe won't sink much below the surface. A common technique is to shove a narrow screwdriver into suspected wood, bend it over, and see if a splinter is created. Decayed wood doesn't splinter, it crumbles.

INITIAL IMPRESSIONS

Start by noting the size and spacing of floor joists, girders, and posts or columns. Though modern floor framing typically spaces floor joists 16 in. on-center, in older houses you may see rough-cut joists spaced 24 in. on-center. Some floors are framed with 4×6 beams supporting 2×6 tongue-and-groove decking; such beams are typically supported on 4×4 posts placed on concrete piers with footings. The true test, though, is how well the joists perform. Are joists stout or do they sag? Are any joists splitting or twisting? Are posts plumb or bowed under stress?

LEVEL OF CRAFTSMANSHIP AND CARE

In a long glance, you can usually get a sense of how skillfully the substructure was framed. Was blocking or diagonal bracing installed between joists to stiffen them and reduce flexion? If diagonal braces were used, were they nailed completely at top and bottom? Unnailed bracing such as that shown in the photo at right is all too common.

On sloping foundation walls, are the bottoms of vertical studs blocked to keep them from drifting downward? Or were metal clips used to secure studs? Details such as these speak volumes about the care and skill of the builder.

Of course, a house may have had many builders and rebuilders over the years, not all of them skilled. Within certain limits, it is acceptable to drill or notch joists or studs to run plumbing pipes and electrical wires. One may, for example, drill holes at any point

Old-style bridging installed to stiffen the floor framing was often prenailed, with the upper ends nailed to joists before the subflooring was laid down. The carpenters often forgot to go down into the crawl space and complete the nailing job.

in the span of a joist provided the holes are at least 2 in. from the joist's edge and don't exceed one-third of the joist's depth. Notches are not allowed in the middle third of a joist span. Otherwise, notches are allowed as long as they don't exceed one-sixth of the joist's depth.

Write up wood butchery such as that shown in the photo on the facing page, where a tub drain and a toilet bend were added. With several joists cut through, it's not surprising that there are widespread water stains on the bathroom subfloor. An inspection of the floor above would almost certainly find springy floors, cracked floor tiles, and water damage.

Often, basements with botched carpentry also contain exposed electrical connections, sagging wires and plumbing pipes, and inadequately supported ducts. That same lack of care is probably reflected in a lack of maintenance, too. If you see wood debris scattered under the house, write it up. Wood scraps, plant materials, and other debris containing cellulose may attract and support termite activity beneath the house and should be removed.

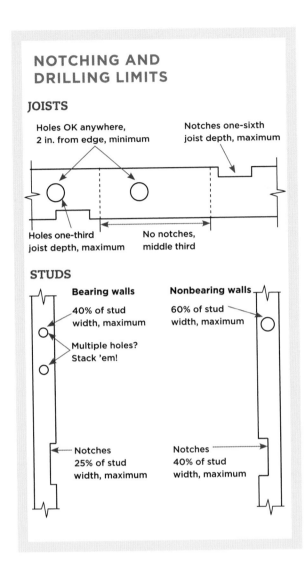

NOTCHING AND DRILLING LIMITS

JOISTS

Holes OK anywhere, 2 in. from edge, minimum

Notches one-sixth joist depth, maximum

Holes one-third joist depth, maximum

No notches, middle third

STUDS

Bearing walls

40% of stud width, maximum

Multiple holes? Stack 'em!

Notches 25% of stud width, maximum

Nonbearing walls

60% of stud width, maximum

Notches 40% of stud width, maximum

Framing seriously weakened by cutouts for waste and supply pipes. This area should be reframed with headers and perhaps structural steel to support the bathroom floor adequately.

ENGINEERED LUMBER

Newer houses are frequently framed with some combination of solid lumber and engineered lumber, such as GLULAM®, laminated veneer lumber (LVL), truss joists with open webs, and I-joists. Engineered lumber is often specified because it can bear greater loads than solid lumber of comparable size and is dimensionally stable. It is also lighter and easier to handle.

But like any lumber, engineered members must be protected from excessive moisture and installed according to manufacturer's specifications. Just as blocking or diagonal bracing must be used to keep solid-lumber joists from twisting, web stiffeners must be installed between I-joist flanges (the thicker portions at top and bottom) to prevent joists buckling out of plane. When a floor platform is framed with I-joists, its rim joists must also be engineered lumber because solid-lumber rim joists could absorb too much moisture, shrink, and shift wall loads onto the I-joists.

Last, I-joist flanges must never be notched or cut into, and holes drilled in I-joists must not exceed the manufacturer's recommendations. Typically, holes $1\frac{1}{2}$ in. in diameter or less are allowable in I-joist webs (plywood or OSB portion between the flanges). An inspector should note visible deterioration on any part of an I-joist or other floor framing.

NOTE: Modern codes require that all exposed I-joist floor members in basements be protected with a fire-rated surface such as $\frac{1}{2}$-in. gypsum board.

WOOD-SOIL AND WOOD-CONCRETE CONTACT

Framing members that come in *direct* contact with soil or concrete should be scrutinized for water damage, rot, and, as we'll see in the next section, insect infestation. It may surprise some people that wood–concrete contact is discouraged because it so regularly occurs. If the concrete is always dry, true,

Over time, thick wood pads will become weakened by wicked moisture and crushed by the heavy loads above. This pier obviously needs to be replaced, ideally with a concrete pier.

there's not much of a problem. Both soil and concrete wick moisture, however, and sustained contact with any moist medium will eventually rot wood.

MUDSILLS sit atop foundations, so when the top of the foundation is less than 8 in. above grade, mudsills routinely rot out in older houses. In general, the closer the mudsill is to grade, the more likely it is to absorb water and rot. Mudsills made of rot-resistant or pressure-treated wood last longer but, in time, wood cells will break down if they stay damp.

GIRDER ENDS may sit in notches at opposite ends of a foundation and are often supported by wood posts or metal columns along their span. In addition, the notches should be at least 1 in. wider than the girder so that there is a minimum ½ in. of clearance on both sides and the end of the girder so that air can circulate and dry the ends of the girder. This is an important detail to inspect. Whenever you find girder ends in direct contact with masonry foundation walls, whether concrete, concrete block, brick, or stone, probe girder ends thoroughly for rot. Rotted or cracked girder ends won't be able to support the loads they did when new, so reinforcement or replacement may be needed.

OLD WOODEN POSTS often sit on precast concrete piers without footings or on pads without steel reinforcement. Consequently, post bottoms are frequently rotten if a basement or crawl space has moisture problems. Typically, the rotted post bottom compresses and the loads supported by the post sink as well. Rotted posts can cause floors to sag and they should probably be replaced. The faulty drainage conditions that caused the decay will need to be corrected.

ANCHOR BOLTS AND BRACING PANELS
Anchor bolts, which secure house framing to a foundation, and bracing panels, which brace a house against lateral loads, were first used in high-wind and earthquake areas and there they have been most widely implemented. Both are now required by model building codes across the country, but an inspector should also bone up on local building codes regarding these devices, as local codes may be more stringent.

ANCHOR BOLTS are installed in the forms before the wet concrete is poured in modern foundations. The threaded portions of the bolts protrude above the

---

GIVING PADS ROOM TO MOVE

PADS SHOULD BE CONSIDERED PART OF the foundation, not the basement floor. Consequently, a pad must be sized for the cumulative loads it will bear. It's common to see 6-in.- or 8-in.-thick pads with a lot of steel, whereas floors are typically 4 in. thick, reinforced with steel wire mesh rather than rebar. To prevent the greater loads on a pad from punching it through the concrete floor, the pad should be poured with an expansion joint around it. Note cracks around pads: Water could enter through them or the pad could continue to sink, creating structural issues.

Left: a rusty, ineffective and outdated mudsill anchor bolt. *Right*: a new bolt with a steel, square-plate washer that has been epoxied into the concrete below.

WALL SHEATHING AND SUBFLOORING

SHEATHING AND SUBFLOORING ARE NOT framing per se, but they stiffen framing members and help distribute loads. So inspectors should note water damage and deterioration to wall sheathing and subflooring. On older houses, 1-in.-thick boards were frequently used as both sheathing and subflooring, though plywood and OSB were widely used by the mid-twentieth century. Of the three materials, exterior-grade plywood is the most resistant to water damage but only up to a point. Water stains and rot are frequently found in the subflooring beneath kitchen and bathroom fixtures, where waste pipes have leaked or toilet wax rings have failed. The same is true of wall sheathing, particularly where it is less than 8 in. above grade. If plywood or OSB panels are starting to delaminate, they must be replaced.

top of the foundation walls and the predrilled mudsills are put in place and bolted to them. Anchor bolts can also be used to retrofit existing foundations, by drilling through the mudsills into the concrete, blowing clean the holes and inserting bolts. Retrofit bolts are secured mechanically by expanding the wedges of an expansion bolt (wedge anchor) or by gluing the bolt by filling the hole with epoxy cement. Epoxy-secured bolts are considered much stronger than expansion type as they do not come loose over time.

Whatever the type of anchor bolt or hold-down used, its nut must be tightened all the way down.

NOTE: If the concrete is of poor quality or the foundation is brick, it may not be possible to use anchor bolts; in which case, the foundation may need to be replaced.

The modern standard is for bolting at least every 6 ft., with bolts placed within the last 12 in. of each mudsill. In Seismic Zones 3 and 4 special 3/16-in.-thick plate washers measuring 2 in. by 2 in. are now required. Houses greater than one story or on hillsides may require more bolts. Many older houses have fewer bolts than would be recommended by modern standards. Note any bolts, nuts, or washer plates that are excessively corroded, as strong earthquake shocks could snap rusted bolts.

BRACING PANELS (also known as shear paneling) are required, according to code, on all exterior walls of a nonengineered or conventionally designed single-family home to brace walls against lateral loads caused by wind, earthquakes, and so on. Bracing may also be required on some interior walls.

Plywood bracing panels are typically used on the walls between the foundation and floor framing and around garage door openings. Code further specifies that the "braced wall panels be located near each end of a wall and at least 25 ft. on center. Designated wall bracing must also make up a certain percentage of overall wall length based on several factors including wind requirements, seismic category, and method used."

The panels should be nailed all the way around their perimeter and to intermediate members (studs and plates) behind them. It may be necessary to add blocks between the vertical studs to provide nailing surfaces for all edges of the plywood. Minimum nail spacing is usually 6 in.; engineers often recommend nailing every 3 in. or 4 in. for greater strength. Ventilation should be provided in each stud bay when shear paneling is added to the inside of exterior sub-area walls. Ventilation is usually provided by drilling 2-in.-dia. holes in the plywood at the top and bottom of each stud bay.

WHAT TO LOOK FOR

- Note the size and spacing of substructure framing.
- Are there wood scraps and debris under the house?
- Note holes and notches cut into joists. Are their size and location acceptable or do they exceed code limits? Do joists sag?
- If substructure framing includes engineered lumber, are I-joist flanges drilled or notched? Are web stiffeners installed between I-joist flanges?
- Inspect mudsills, floor joists, girders, wood posts, and pony-wall studs for signs of water damage or rot. Does any framing come in direct contact with dirt or damp concrete?
- Is the mudsill at least 8 in. above grade?
- Is rot present where girder ends rest on the foundation?
- Are there water stains or water-damaged sub-flooring beneath kitchen or bath drains?
- Are mudsills securely bolted to foundations? Were square plate washers used?
- If structural steel devices such as hold-downs are used, are all holes filled with bolts and do all bolt heads make contact with the device?
- Per local codes, is substructure framing adequately bolstered with bracing panels?
- Is any structural steel—whether joist hangers, anchor bolts, or washer plates—corroded?

Insect Infestation

If you see signs of an insect infestation, hire a pest-control professional to assess and suggest a remedy. Pesticides are often toxic, and anyone unfamiliar with insect habits may not destroy all their nesting sites or may apply pesticides inappropriately or unnecessarily. Moreover, local codes may require a professional.

Subterranean termites live in large underground nests. Their bodies are soft and they avoid exposure to air by constructing crawl tubes out of the wood they chew up. Subterranean termites are attracted to heat, so you'll often find them near furnaces and water heaters.

It's often difficult to tell whether an infestation is active. For example, if a subterranean termite infestation is inactive, a prophylactic treatment may suffice. But if the infestation is active, the remedy may require eliminating the conditions that led to the infestation (such as excessive moisture and earth–wood contact) and an aggressive chemical treatment. Treatment usually consists of applying a chemical barrier on the ground that repels the termites or a treated zone whose chemical doesn't repel them initially but later kills or severely disrupts them. More information can be found online, for example, at www.livingwithbugs.com.

TERMITES

Termites, the most famous of insect pests, include dry-wood, subterranean, and Formosan types. Because subterranean termites need access to moisture in the soil, they build distinctive dirt tubes up along the surface of foundations. When they eat into the wood, they usually proceed with the grain. Termites swarm in spring or fall. Discourage the return of subterranean termites by lowering soil levels around foundations, footings, and the like.

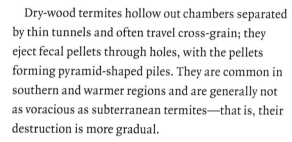

Dry-wood termites do not live in the ground and are often found inside walls or attics. Their existence can be detected by the presence of their frass (wood-colored droppings).

Small, very round holes like these are typically made by powder-post beetles, which are common in coastal areas. The holes are called "emergent holes" because they show where the beetles come from, not where they may be currently. These beetles favor hardwoods so they eat furniture, too.

Dry-wood termites hollow out chambers separated by thin tunnels and often travel cross-grain; they eject fecal pellets through holes, with the pellets forming pyramid-shaped piles. They are common in southern and warmer regions and are generally not as voracious as subterranean termites—that is, their destruction is more gradual.

Fumigation is effective for dry-wood termites, but it's ineffective for treating subterranean termites because their colonies are located in the ground and fumigation gas does not penetrate the soil.

Formosan termites, whose colonies may exceed 1 million individuals, are wreaking havoc along the Gulf Coast of the United States; they live in the ground or in buildings and build huge, hard nests.

CARPENTER ANTS

Carpenter ants are red or black, ¼ in. to ½ in. long. Sometimes confused with termites, these ants have narrow waists and, when winged, wings of different sizes. While they do tunnel in wet or rotting wood, they do not eat it as food and are therefore less destructive than termites. To locate their nests, look for borings rather like coarse sawdust. Professionals will often drill into nests and spray them with an insecticide safe enough for inside use; dusting with boric acid is another common treatment.

POWDER-POST BEETLES

Powder-post beetle holes look like tiny BB-gun holes; their borings resemble coarse flour. Because these insects favor the sapwood, evidence of borings may be only superficial until you prod with a pocketknife. Still, holes are not a sure sign of an active infestation. One approach is to remove the damaged wood, sweep up borings, paint the area, and monitor it for a year. If holes reappear, it's an active infestation: A professional will need to fumigate the wood or apply a pesticide.

WHAT TO LOOK FOR

- Pay close attention to wood in direct contact with the soil or where water collects, such as windowsills and doorsills, deck and porch framing, fence posts, and garage door frames.
- Note also wood in direct contact with concrete or masonry surfaces, including mudsills and the bottoms of stair stringers, and wood posts.
- Crawl spaces are especially prone to infestation because they are frequently moist, so inspect them carefully.

FUNGI AND WATER DAMAGE

FUNGUS CAN BE FOUND GROWING ON WOOD almost anywhere the wood is wet. It will not usually grow further after the source of water has been eliminated. Serious decay or fungus damage to structural members almost always requires their replacement. Minor damage can be treated locally.

Whether structural damage is caused by insects or rot fungi, excess water is usually at the heart of the problem. Before treating the specific agent causing the deterioration, reduce excess water by maintaining gutters, improving drainage, grading the soil away from the building, eliminating wood–soil contact, and improving ventilation.

The fungi that rot wood reproduce by airborne spores, so they're virtually everywhere. But they can't establish colonies on wood with a moisture content (MC) less than 28%; and they go dormant if the MC drops below 20% or the air temperature drops below 40°F. Household molds, also caused by fungi, thrive in a similar moisture and temperature range. So if moisture meter readings in the basement or crawl space are too high, reducing excess moisture may solve both wood rot and mold problems.

Fungus can be found growing almost anywhere that wood is wet. Usually, the fungus will not continue growing after the source of water has been eliminated.

- Note signs of infestations such as sandy, brown tubes (subterranean termites), small piles of tiny gray pellets beneath infested wood (dry-wood termites), shredded wood debris beneath nests (carpenter ants), and clusters of small round holes and light-colored powdery debris (powder-post beetles).
- Probe suspect wood to see how bad the infestation is. If you find signs of an infestation, have a pest-control professional do a report and make recommendations.

Finished Basements

Although finished basements are often covered with drywall and flooring, a careful inspector can still learn quite a bit about underlying conditions, especially moisture problems. If a finished basement is being billed as living space, the inspector should also get out the tape measure and see if that space conforms with local fire-safety codes—notably, if basement windows are large enough (and low enough) to allow occupants to exit quickly.

SIGNS OF SEEPAGE

The best place to look for signs of persistent moisture is along the base of walls. Look for discolored drywall and water-stained baseboards. Drywall stains may vary from brownish water marks to the familiar black speckles of mold. If the room is paneled, there may be a gray discoloration in the corners and along the base of panels. If the basement is furnished, try to get access behind sofas or bookcases placed against walls, for by blocking air circulation, large objects can trap moisture and promote mold. Use your nose, too, to detect musty smells.

Walk around the basement and note places where the flooring flexes excessively or seems spongy. If there is wood flooring or carpeting, it's likely that a subfloor of 2×4s and plywood was laid over the original concrete floor. If there is seepage or another unresolved moisture issue still lurking, the wood subflooring can rot. If there are resilient tile floors, they may be installed directly over the concrete slab,

Chances are, a sofa stood against this damp wall for a long time, blocking air flow that might have dried it. The moldy drywall should be replaced and the moisture source located and corrected.

Carpeting over old concrete floors often conceals moisture-related damage. Newly installed carpet is a red flag for inspectors, so get permission to pull up a corner and look underneath.

in which case you may be able to see efflorescence between tile joints.

If the floor is covered with carpet, a particularly bad choice for damp basements, ask if you can pull up a corner or a section along an exterior wall. If the area is persistently damp, you'll probably find sodden underlayment pads, rusted tackless carpet strips, and mold on the underside of the carpet. It should be removed.

BASEMENT EGRESS WINDOWS

To enable occupants to exit quickly in case of a fire, building codes require a method of escape—egress—for sleeping rooms on every level of the house, including the basement. Because egress windows must also be large enough to allow a fully equipped firefighter to enter, codes specify the size of the egress—typically, at least 20 in. wide and at least 24 in. tall, with a combined net-clear opening of 5.7 sq. ft.

To make it possible to climb out of an egress window, codes generally specify a maximum sill height of 44 in. above the floor, although a 32-in. sill height seems more reasonable if there are kids or elders present. (Check your local codes; some require two egress points for basement in-law units.) Installing an egress window in a concrete foundation wall is a job for a pro and may require the installation of an egress well.

Window wells are important outside basement bedrooms. They need to be large enough to provide a means of escape in a fire; the well height is typically limited to 44 in.

WHAT TO LOOK FOR

- Does the finished basement smell moldy? Is there a dehumidifier?
- Scrutinize the bottoms of walls for stained or moldy drywall, discolored baseboards, or wood paneling.
- If possible, pull large furnishings away from walls and look for mold behind them.
- Do any floor sections feel spongy or have excessive give as you step on them?
- Do basement windows meet minimal egress requirements?

CHAPTER 6

ELECTRICAL SYSTEMS

ELECTRICITY IS NOTHING TO FEAR, but it must be respected. If you are a homeowner new to home wiring or someone inspecting a house for the first time, hire a trained inspector or a licensed electrician to inspect the interior components of service panels and subpanels.

There is much that a nonprofessional can learn from a *hands-off look* at incoming service cables, the condition of unopened panels, and electrical wiring runs that are visible in attics or basements. Moreover, by using a noncontact voltage tester and a plug-in circuit tester, an amateur can safely determine if house receptacles are correctly wired.

But untrained individuals should not touch electrical panels or the cables feeding them and *never* remove the cover of a service panel or subpanel or go snooping inside. Even with the main fuse or main breaker turned off, there are cables inside a panel that will still be hot (energized) and that could deliver a fatal shock.

When inspecting components of an electrical system, observe this caution: *Before removing outlet covers or switch plates, or working on any electrical device, turn off the power at the service panel—and then test with a voltage tester to make sure the power really is off.*

Safely Inspecting Electrical Systems

Understanding electricity is the first step to safely inspecting electrical systems. The second is using a voltage tester to detect the presence of electrical current and avoid shocks.

You can wear street clothes for most of an inspection. But when inspecting electrical systems it's wise to wear safety glasses and insulating gloves. Trained inspectors examining potentially energized electrical panels should read "Personal Protection Equipment" on p. 123, which contains National Electrical Code® (NEC) recommendations that protect a person from arc flash and shock hazards.

UNDERSTANDING ELECTRICITY

Electricity (flowing electrons called current) moves through a wire, like water in a pipe. The flow of water is measured in gallons per minute; the flow of electrons is measured in amperes or amps. Water pressure is measured in pounds per square inch, and the force behind the electrons in a wire is measured in volts.

The larger the pipe, the more water that can flow through it; likewise, larger wires allow a greater flow of electricity. A small-diameter pipe will limit the flow of water, compared to a larger pipe; similarly, wiring that is too small will resist the flow of current. If that resistance (measured in ohms) is too great, the wires will overheat and may cause a fire.

Think of alternating current (AC) electrical systems as a loop that runs from a generation point (or power

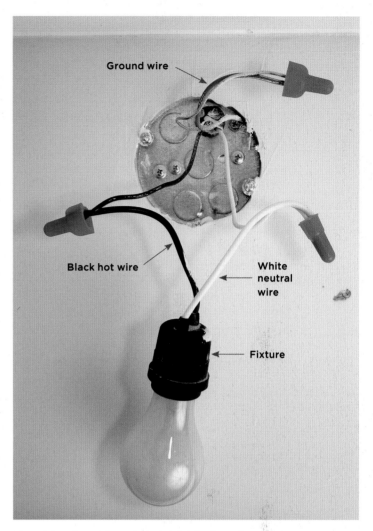

Electricity always flows in a circuit. The hot wire carries the current from the power source to the fixture, and the neutral wire returns it to the power source.

READ UP

THE SAFETY ALERTS AND PRACTICES explained in this chapter will go far to protect you, but the best protection is knowledge. We strongly recommend that readers also visit the OSHA/NIOSH website on electrical safety: www.cdc.gov/niosh/docs/2009-113.

BASIC ELECTRICAL INSPECTION TOOLS

INSPECTOR BRIAN COGLEY (p. 3) **CAN** complete the electrical part of an inspection with a circuit analyzer and this handful of tools. In his own words, here is how he uses them.

"I use the **small screw gun** mostly to remove mechanical screws when I am inspecting a multiunit residence and I have a lot of panels to look at. I probably save myself a half hour of time it would take me to turn all those panel screws by hand. Otherwise, my **multibit screwdriver** can do the job, with a little help from an **offset screwdriver** in tight spots.

"My primary use for a **utility knife** is to score around the edges of electrical subpanels that have been painted over. With a nice sharp razor you can score the paint around the edges and get the panel cover off cleanly.

"I like having **extra panel screws** on hand because now and again you drop one and there may be bushes below you or a storage room full of junk below. The main thing is to put back what was there—to replace whatever it was that you might have lost. Besides, you wouldn't want to leave a panel loose, for liability reasons.

"**Extra fuses.** Sometimes, for reasons beyond your control, a fuse will blow while you're there inspecting. You can't just say, 'Oh, well,' when the lights go out. So I like to carry several different size screw-in fuses . . . just in case.

"I don't use a **multimeter** very much for inspections, but it can be useful to figure out voltage drop when a large appliance is turned on or, say, what's going on with a 240-volt breaker for a dryer or a range. I don't have to solve the problem, but if I can ascertain that something is definitely amiss, then I can refer it to a licensed electrician."

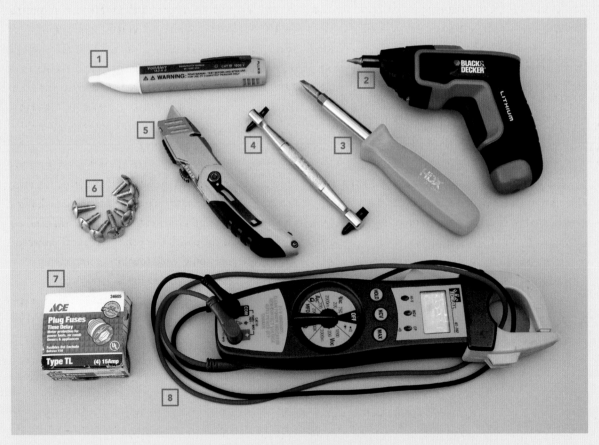

Electrical inspection tools: 1, noncontact voltage tester; 2, small screw gun; 3, multibit screwdriver; 4, offset screwdriver; 5, utility knife; 6, panel screws; 7, fuses; 8, multimeter.

source) through a load (something that uses electrical power, such as a light bulb) and back to the generation point. In a home, the electrical current from a power company is split into smaller loops called circuits. In typical circuit wiring, a hot wire (usually black or red) carries current from the service panel to one of the various loads, and a neutral wire (typically white or light gray) carries current back to the service panel.

USING A NONCONTACT VOLTAGE TESTER

A noncontact voltage tester is a popular battery-operated voltage tester that is reliable, inexpensive, and small enough to fit in a shirt pocket. Its tip glows (and it may beep, depending on the model) when the plastic tip is brought close to or touched to a hot (energized) screw terminal, receptacle slot, wire, or other conductor.

Each time you use a noncontact tester—or any voltage tester—test that it's functioning properly first on a receptacle that you know is hot.

A noncontact voltage tester will usually glow when its tip is merely near an energized conductor—that is, it can "read" current through a wire's insulation or through a cover plate. Thus you can often detect electrical current at a switch, fixture, or service panel without removing the outlet or panel cover.

TESTING A RECEPTACLE/OUTLET. After shutting off power at the panel, insert the tester tip into the narrow (hot) slot of a receptacle. If the tester tip does not glow, there is probably no voltage present. To be sure, insert the tester tip into the receptacle's wide (neutral) slot and into the grounding slot. This should protect you in case the receptacle was incorrectly wired.

TESTING TO SEE IF A PANEL OR SUBPANEL IS ENERGIZED. Cut power inside a service panel by switching off the main breaker or by removing the main fuse in a fuse box. This deenergizes the panel's hot buses. To cut power to a subpanel, flip off the subpanel breaker in the service panel and lock the service panel so no one can turn the subpanel breaker back on.

Always test before touching electrical components that may be hot (energized). Here, the glowing tip of a noncontact voltage tester (sometimes called an inductance tester) indicates that a wall receptacle is hot.

NOTE: Only a trained professional should remove the cover of an electrical panel. Modern service panels rated for exterior use have a hinged, weatherproof door and an inside cover. Opening the panel door to flip a breaker on or off is an everyday event, but removing the inside cover of a panel can have serious consequences because it exposes energized elements inside the panel. Thus, only a trained professional should remove a panel cover.

Before removing a subpanel cover, touch the tester to several breakers in the on position. If the tester tip doesn't glow, the panel is probably deenergized. But keep testing to be sure: Remove the cover and test again inside the panel. Once the cover is off, however, an inspector should avoid touching components inside the panel: His or her job is observing.

IMPORTANT: The only way to be 100% safe is to *disconnect* power to a panel and test to be sure the power is off. However, home inspectors rarely disconnect power to panels unless the house is vacant and clear of furniture. Homeowners often have computers, timers, security systems, and other devices that require power full-time; so shutting them all down during an inspection is not practical.

Trained professionals can inspect a subpanel safely if they first turn off the subpanel disconnect in the service panel, and then use a voltage tester to verify that the power is off.

Here, a noncontact voltage tester indicates that subpanel breakers are energized. As its name suggests, a noncontact tester often does not need to be in direct contact with an energized conductor to detect current nearby.

After shutting off the subpanel disconnect in the service panel—and locking it to keep others out of the panel—an inspector tests the subpanel again. This time, the tester indicates that there is no power present.

WHEN THE PROS SAY NO

Professional home inspectors like a challenge. But every now and then they come on conditions so risky that the only wise course is to say no. If you encounter any of the following conditions, request that they be fixed before resuming the electrical part of your inspection.

POTENTIAL SHOCK HAZARDS. If you see standing water or wet soil *and* improper wiring, don't enter the basement or crawl space. Water or dampness alone is no reason to stay out, but exposed wire splices (not inside a covered box), improperly supported wire runs, or other evidence of substandard practices is a sign that there may be shock hazards as well. Most licensed electricians won't enter such spaces either.

Always test to be sure. If you do inspect under the house, it's a wise precaution to touch a noncontact voltage tester to metal water supply pipes, metal ducts, the water heater housing, and any other metal surfaces that could become energized by a ground fault.

Be very suspicious of loose wire ends. A licensed electrician should remove all old, apparently unused wiring. Wires that look dead can become energized by connections made at other locations. Use a tester, if available, to check any old exposed wiring.

FOUR REASONS TO STAY OUT OF PANELS!

TRAINED PROFESSIONALS ROUTINELY remove panel covers so they can inspect the electrical components inside service panels and subpanels. Untrained amateurs, however, should stay out. Here are four reasons for this caution:

- Just removing or replacing a panel cover can be risky. Some older panels have no protective covering over the energized bars that supply power to the main panel. Inspectors need to be very careful when replacing the inside cover in such panels to avoid a minor explosion or electrocution should the cover touch these bars by mistake.

- There is no easy way for a nonprofessional to be certain that an electrical panel is correctly grounded, and thus a great shock risk exists.

- In most service panels, there is a small area near the main breaker that stays energized even after that breaker is set to an off position. Accidentally touching that area could shock and possibly kill you.

- Local building codes may specify that any panel work be done by a licensed electrician. Work not done by a licensed electrician may nullify appliance or equipment warranties or even void a homeowner's insurance should a mishap occur.

The inside cover of this panel has been removed by the inspector to examine the wiring inside. Some outdated panels have no protection on the energized (hot) vertical bars exposed inside the panels near the top (upper arrows). Inspectors and electricians need to be very careful when replacing the inside cover in such panels to avoid a minor explosion or electrocution should the cover come in contact with these exposed bars by mistake. (The supply cables of a panel usually enter at the top of a panel; here they enter from the bottom. Inspectors see many strange things.)
Note: The bare wire ends terminating to lugs in the main disconnect (lower arrows) are *always* hot, even when the disconnect is turned off.

A correctly grounded electrical system (see p. 137) should protect you against ground faults, but again, you should not assume that a system is correctly wired. (That's one of the things you will learn in the course of your inspection.) If your voltage tester indicates electrical current in things that shouldn't be energized, leave the space.

STAY OUT OF THE RAIN. If it's rainy or misty outside, it's often wise to reschedule an inspection. Roof surfaces become slick, and electricity's behav-ior can become unpredictable. In such conditions, especially stay away from high-voltage conductors such as the cables in an overhead service entrance (see p. 124). Electricity can arc (jump) to nearby objects, such as a person on a metal ladder, with fatal consequences.

LIMITED ACCESS. Trained inspectors often inspect panels that are inconveniently located (such as in closets), but an inspector should not tolerate a location that is so inaccessible or tight that it would

Electrical panels should never be installed where access is limited and especially not inside clothes closets where a fire could easily start if an electrical short occurred.

be unsafe. "Unsafe" is a judgment call, obviously. The NEC requires that a panel location have minimum clearances of 78 in. of headroom, 36 in. of free space in front of the panel, and 30 in. across the face of the panel. The panel should be installed at a comfortable height, meaning that no breaker handle should be higher than 72 in. These clearances ensure enough room to work comfortably on a panel or, as important, enough room to get away from the panel immediately if there is a mishap.

WHEN A PANEL IS PAINTED OVER

REMOVING PANEL COVERS THAT HAVE BEEN painted over may damage the finish surface and rip the drywall surfaces. To avoid such damage, inspectors should use a utility knife to score around the perimeter of the panel. That will break the paint seal.

OUTDATED BRANDS OF PANELS. If it's obvious that a panel is outdated and should be replaced, some inspectors won't even bother to open it. Federal Pacific and Zinsco panels, for example, are two older brands that have a host of well-documented failures. Here the issue is more about time than inspector safety per se.

WHAT TO LOOK FOR

- If it is rainy or misty outside, defer inspecting exterior service panels and stay away from high-voltage service cables.
- Where is the service panel (entrance panel) located? Where are subpanels (if any) located?
- Are all electrical panels in dry, accessible locations? Is dampness present or are there water stains on the walls or the floor near the panels? Is there rust on the panel(s)?
- Is there enough clearance to quickly get away from the panel should a mishap occur?
- What is the general level of workmanship? Does it look professionally done or makeshift?
- What is the condition of wiring around the panel(s)? Are electrical connections in covered boxes or are they exposed? Are cables adequately supported or do they sag?

Electrical Service

Power from the utility service is commonly delivered through three large wires, or conductors, which may enter the house overhead or underground. Overhead service wires are called a service drop. The drop runs to a weatherhead atop a length of rigid conduit. When fed underground, service conductors are installed in buried conduit or run as underground service-entrance (USE) cable.

Whether it arrives overhead or underground, three-wire service delivers 120 volts to ground and 240 volts between the hot (energized) conductors. Three-wire service consists of two insulated hot conductors wrapped around a stranded bare aluminum wire with an internal steel messenger cable—the bare aluminum wire also serves as a neutral. Two-wire service, which is still found on some older homes, is

PERSONAL PROTECTION EQUIPMENT

A QUALIFIED PERSON TESTING OR WORKING in a potentially energized electrical panel must wear personal protection equipment (PPE) as specified in NFPA 70E® PPE Hazard Level 1, Table 130.7 (C) (16). "The PPE requirements of 130.7 are intended to protect a person from arc flash and shock hazards." This protective equipment includes the following:

- Hard hat
- Arc-rated long-sleeve shirt and pants or arc-rated coverall
- Arc-rated face shield or arc flash suit hood
- Safety glasses or safety goggles
- Hearing protection (ear canal inserts)
- Heavy-duty leather gloves over rubber insulating gloves
- Leather work shoes

Reproduced with permission from NFPA70E-2012, *Electrical Safety in the Workplace*, Copyright © 2011, National Fire Protection Association. This reprinted material is not the complete and official position of the NFPA on the referenced subject, which is represented only by the standard in its entirety.

Personal protection equipment is required when working in a potentially energized electrical panel, per the National Fire Protection Association (NFPA).

inadequate for modern needs because it delivers only 120 volts.

Service conductors are attached to a meter base and then to the service panel. Straddling the two sets of terminals on its base, the meter measures the wattage of electricity as it is consumed. The service panel also routes power to various circuits throughout the house.

The utility company will attach the service drop and install the meter. The homeowner is responsible for everything beyond that, including the meter base and breaker panel, which a licensed electrician should install.

SAFE ENTRANCES

TREE TRUNKS AND BRANCHES can damage electrical cable, so they should never come in contact. In time, branches can fray cables' insulative sheathing, exposing bare wire. As the wiring between power poles and building is typically the responsibility of the local utility, it should trim trees away from wires. Before anyone works near such wires, they should first call the power company to disconnect the power. The power company should also be contacted to repair damaged or frayed wires.

OVERHEAD SERVICE WIRES must also be high enough to prevent contact: a minimum 12 ft. above a

SERVICE ENTRANCES

Aerial Service Entrance

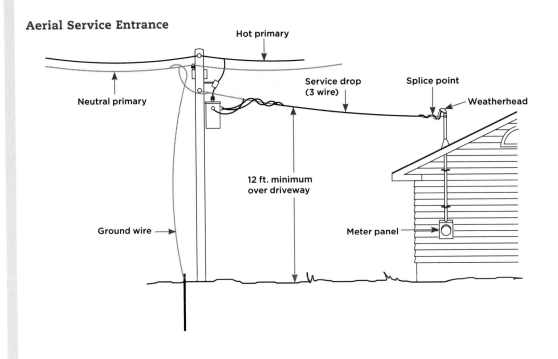

Hot primary

Neutral primary

Service drop
(3 wire)

Splice point

Weatherhead

12 ft. minimum
over driveway

Ground wire

Meter panel

Buried Service Entrance

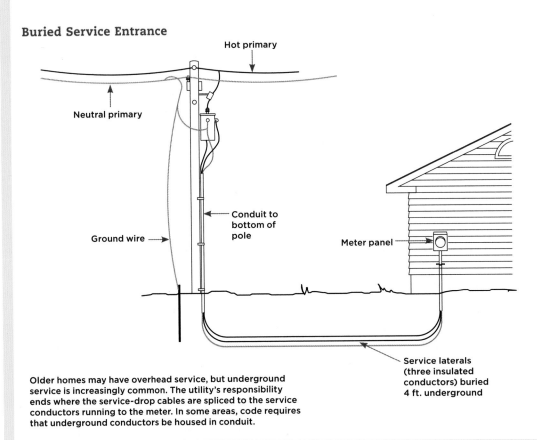

Hot primary

Neutral primary

Conduit to
bottom of
pole

Ground wire

Meter panel

Service laterals
(three insulated
conductors) buried
4 ft. underground

Older homes may have overhead service, but underground service is increasingly common. The utility's responsibility ends where the service-drop cables are spliced to the service conductors running to the meter. In some areas, code requires that underground conductors be housed in conduit.

SERVICE ENTRANCE TO THE EAVES SIDE

When the service drop extends over eaves, the service riser or conduit runs up through the eaves. The roof jack or metal flashing at this connection is usually caulked or sealed.

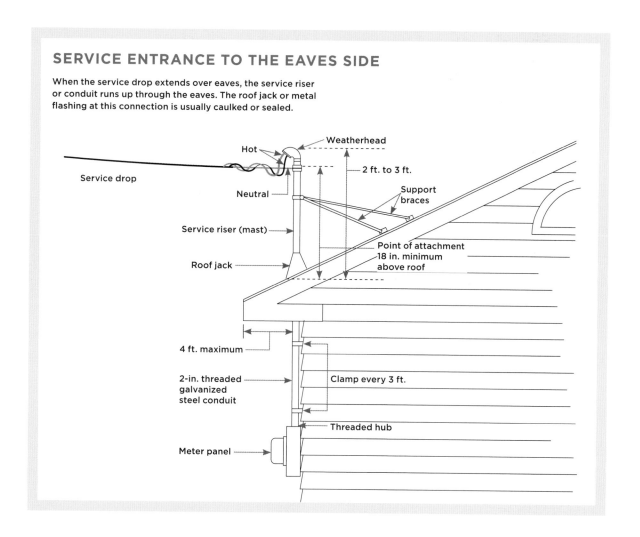

Weatherhead

Hot

Service drop

Neutral

2 ft. to 3 ft.

Support braces

Service riser (mast)

Point of attachment 18 in. minimum above roof

Roof jack

4 ft. maximum

2-in. threaded galvanized steel conduit

Clamp every 3 ft.

Threaded hub

Meter panel

Overhead electrical service wires should not be in contact with trees or other vegetation as branches can rub on wires and damage the insulation. In a storm, falling branches could damage wires and/or cause power outages.

driveway, at least 10 ft. above a pedestrian walkway, and 18 ft. above a street or swimming pool. Overhead service wires should be no closer than 3 ft. from the side or bottom of an operable window. Wires passing over a low-slope roof (less than 4-in-12) should clear the roof by 8 ft.; for slopes greater than that, a 3-ft. clearance will suffice. When the service drop approaches over roof eaves, the minimum clearances shown in "Service Entrances" on the facing page should be maintained. There are some exceptions to these rules; the utility provider typically has jurisdiction in such matters.

UNDERGROUND SERVICE CONDUCTORS are becoming more popular because street power poles are unsightly and buried electrical cables are somewhat safer than energized wires running overhead.

Underground services are becoming more popular as the power poles are being removed. This conduit has punched through the bottom of the panel, perhaps because of building settlement or seasonal soil movement upward. This installation should be reviewed by the utility provider and a qualified electrician, and repaired as needed.

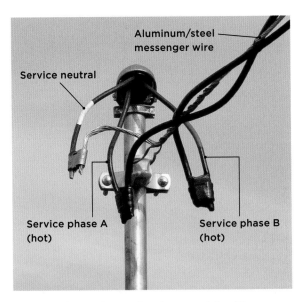

A typical three-wire service drop consists of two insulated hot conductors wrapped around a stranded bare aluminum wire with an internal steel messenger cable—the bare wire also serves as a neutral.

Nonetheless, homeowners or contractors should call 811 before digging near buried service cables. Local utility companies will be notified about your intent to dig and in a few days will send a locator to mark the approximate location of your underground lines, pipes, and cables, so you'll know what's below and be able to dig safely. Underground service conductors may also be susceptible to house settling, as shown in the left photo above.

SOLID ATTACHMENTS

The connection between the utility company's wires and the wires at the weatherhead should be insulated and secure. The conductors entering the weatherhead should be in separate holes of an insulating bushing, and should be arranged with a drip loop so water does not run into the service mast. Cable sheathing should be intact. Have an electrician examine any worn or damaged wires near the weatherhead for repair or replacement; the service drop is the responsibility of the utility company.

The service mast (service riser), which is the homeowner's responsibility, should be supported by braces as needed to offset the weight and tension of the incoming service wires. Service masts should be vertical; note leaning masts on your inspection report. In many cases, the braces of leaning masts have been bolted to roof sheathing only; ideally, bracing bolts should anchor to framing beneath sheathing. Bent service masts are usually too small in diameter, too tall, or insufficiently braced; a licensed electrician should assess their condition and repair or replace them.

On older houses, you may also see service entrance cables attach to porcelain insulators screwed to siding, eaves, or trim. If the insulator screws into framing behind the trim, the attachment may be secure. Where a porcelain insulator is screwed only to trim, over time the weight of incoming cables can pull the trim away from the building. This is hazardous.

ELECTRIC METERS

Electric meters (and certain covers on a service panel) are sealed by the utility company to prevent tampering. A broken or missing seal on the meter or on other panel components may indicate an attempt to bypass the meter or a past alteration of the service without notifying the utility provider. The utility company should be contacted to reseal the meter.

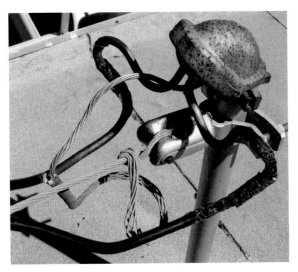

This is a potentially very hazardous condition. The tape used to wrap connections has worn, exposing energized wires inside. A homeowner removing roof debris or a roofer could inadvertently touch these connections and be electrocuted. Connections need to be rewrapped or replaced with more weather-resistant connectors. Also, note that the service neutral (stranded bare cable) has rubbed through the insulation of a hot conductor, creating a short.

The porcelain insulator for an outdated 60-amp service drop has pulled free from the building. Chances are, the insulator was screwed only to trim and over time the weight of service cables pulled the insulator out, straining connections and creating a hazard.

A length of rigid conduit typically protects service conductors as they enter the meter base. Examine the fitting where the conduit enters the base to ensure that it is watertight; write up cracked or missing rubber seals or a meter base that is not securely attached.

WHAT TO LOOK FOR

- Is there three-wire service running to the house—two insulated hot conductors wrapped around a stranded bare aluminum/steel wire? Or is there outdated two-wire service?

- Do trees make contact with overhead service conductors? The utility company should be contacted to cut back trees and repair or replace any damaged wires.

- Do overhead service wires maintain the minimum clearances spelled out in the text and shown in the illustrations on pp. 124–125?

- Are service conductors and their sheathing intact or are any wires worn or damaged?

- Do service conductors enter the weatherhead through separate holes of an insulating bushing? Is there a drip loop?

- Is the service mast upright or leaning?

- Is the meter sealed? Is conduit fitting to the meter base watertight?

Service Panels and Subpanels

At the main panel, the two hot cables from the meter base attach to lugs or terminals on the main breaker. The incoming neutral cable attaches to the main lug of the neutral/ground bus. In the main panel, neutral/ground buses must be connected together, usually by a wire or metal bar called the main bonding jumper.

NOTE: In subpanels and all other locations downstream from the main service panel, ground and neutral components must be electrically isolated from each other. (*Downstream* = away from the power source.)

CIRCUIT PROTECTION

Each fuse or breaker is rated at a specific number of amps (15-amp and 20-amp breakers or fuses take care of most household circuits). All current produces

INSIDE A SERVICE PANEL

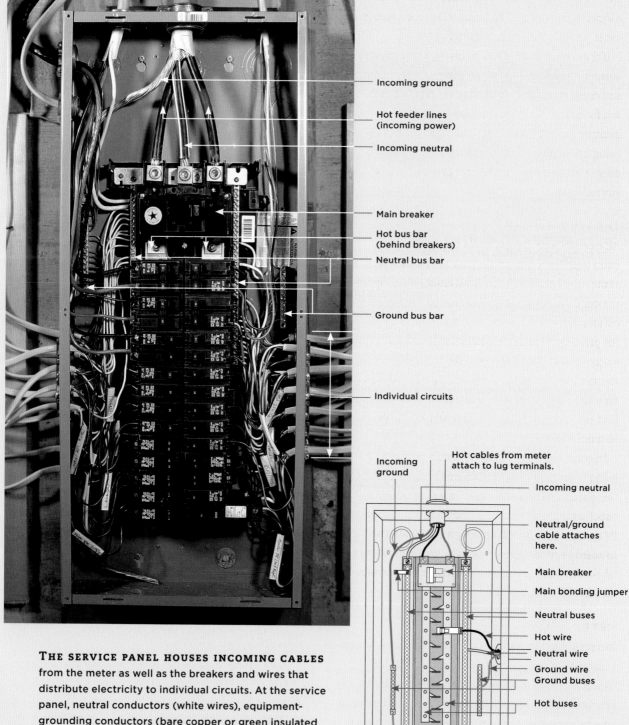

Incoming ground

Hot feeder lines
(incoming power)

Incoming neutral

Main breaker

Hot bus bar
(behind breakers)

Neutral bus bar

Ground bus bar

Individual circuits

Incoming
ground

Hot cables from meter
attach to lug terminals.

Incoming neutral

Neutral/ground
cable attaches
here.

Main breaker

Main bonding jumper

Neutral buses

Hot wire

Neutral wire

Ground wire
Ground buses

Hot buses

Grounding electrode
conductor

Knockouts for circuit
cables on all sides of
panel box

THE SERVICE PANEL HOUSES INCOMING CABLES
from the meter as well as the breakers and wires that
distribute electricity to individual circuits. At the service
panel, neutral conductors (white wires), equipment-
grounding conductors (bare copper or green insulated
wires), the meter service panel, and the grounding
electrode system (grounding rods) must be bonded
together.

some heat, and as current increases, the heat generated increases. When a circuit becomes overloaded or a short circuit occurs, the breaker trips or a fuse strip melts, thereby cutting voltage to the hot wire.

If there were no breakers or fuses, and if too much current continued to flow, the wires would overheat and could start a fire. Amperage ratings of breakers and fuses are matched to the size (cross-sectional area, measured as gauge) of the circuit wires. Overfusing—using a fuse rated higher than the wire it protects—is dangerous because circuit wires could overheat and start a fire.

THE MAIN BREAKER

All electricity entering a house goes through the main breaker or breakers, which are usually located at the top of a main panel. In an emergency, flipping the main breakers (main disconnects) to off will turn off all power to the house. The main breakers are also the primary overcurrent protection for the electrical system and are rated accordingly. (The rating is stamped on the breaker handles.) If the main breaker for a 200-amp panel senses current that exceeds its load rating, the breaker will automatically trip and shut off all power.

In some regions, photovoltaic solar systems are being installed on homes. Where these systems exist, the main breaker will not always de-energize the panel, as the solar system is another source of power. PV systems vary greatly in design and should be handled by trained professionals. Required warning labels should be present to alert those at the panel location of the secondary power supply.

METER/MAINS

Increasingly common are meter/mains, which house a meter base and a main breaker in a single box. Meter/mains allow a homeowner to put the main breaker outside the house, where it can be accessed in an emergency—if firefighters need to cut the power to the house before they go inside, for example. When meter/mains are used, electricians often locate a panel with the branch circuit breakers (called a sub-panel) in the garage or another centralized location inside that is easy to access, such as a laundry room.

FUSE BOXES

Many older homes still have fuse boxes. Fuses are the earliest overcurrent protection devices, and they come as either Edison-type (screw-in) fuses or cartridge (slide-in) fuses. Edison-style fuses are more common. They have little windows that let you see a filament. When the circuit has been overloaded and the fuse is blown, the filament will be separated.

A fuse with a blackened (from heat) interior could mean a short circuit—a potentially dangerous situation that a licensed electrician should repair. The less common cartridge fuses are used to control 240-volt circuits and are usually part of the main disconnect switch, or serve heavy-duty circuits for an electric range or a clothes dryer.

In a main fuse box, the hot conductors from the meter attach to the main power lugs, and the neutral cable to the main neutral lug. Whether the panel has breakers or fuses, metal buses run from the main breaker/main fuse. Running down the middle of the panel, buses distribute power to the various branch circuits either through fuses or through breakers. The neutral/ground buses are long aluminum bars containing many terminal screws, to which ground and neutral wires are attached.

WHAT TO LOOK FOR

- Is there a fuse box or breaker panel? Is there also a subpanel?
- Where are panels located? Are they easily accessed? Panels in clothes closets or storage areas that contain flammable materials are typically code violations.
- Is there a main breaker outside the house that can be accessed in an emergency?
- What is the capacity of the main disconnect breakers or fuses in the main panel? (The amperage capacity will be stamped on the panel's main breakers or fuses.)

This undersize 30-amp main switch and fuses are the service panel for a whole house. Moreover, this lever main panel does not have a dead-front cover to protect users from shocks—energized connections can easily be touched. The panel should be replaced at once.

Inspecting Fuse Boxes or Breaker Panels

By inspecting the condition of an unopened panel and the wiring that's visible in the basement or attic, nonprofessionals can get a good overview of the electrical system's condition. If the system seems unsafe or inadequate, a licensed electrician should open and inspect the panel.

NOTE: Only a trained professional should remove the cover of an electrical panel.

ASSESSING PANEL CAPACITY

You can assess the capacity of service panels and subpanels without removing panel covers. Look for the following issues.

INADEQUATE CAPACITY. In older houses it is not uncommon to find a 30-amp or 60-amp service. A 30-amp main capacity is inadequate and should be upgraded; 60-amp services are marginally OK as long as there are no electric heaters, air-conditioners, or electric ranges. Since 1960, the minimum capacity for a new detached dwelling is 100 amps. Modern single-family residences typically have an electrical capacity of 125 amps; larger new houses may have capacities of 200 amps or more.

PROVIDING 120 VOLTS ONLY. Older two-wire service, which provides only 120-volt service (see p. 122), was once common. But 120-volt service is not adequate for many modern appliances. Even if the house wiring has not been altered since original construction, the service should be upgraded.

BREAKER PANEL FULL. If there is no room to add circuit breakers, have an electrician do load analysis of the panel and recommend an upgrade.

LIGHTS DIM. Lights dimming when a refrigerator or other large appliance's motor kicks in—or when several appliances are running at the same time—is common in older homes when lights and appliances are on the same circuit. Big energy users should be on dedicated circuits. Have an electrician add circuits or upgrade the service panel.

FREQUENTLY BLOWN FUSES usually indicate that circuits are loaded beyond capacity or that there is a persistent short circuit. If a properly rated fuse blows when an appliance starts, the startup load of the appliance may be too great for the type of fuse; try replacing it with a time-delay fuse of the same rating. If a time-delay fuse doesn't solve the problem, call an electrician.

OVERFUSING, or using a fuse (or breaker) rated higher than the wire it protects, is dangerous because the wire could overheat and catch fire. If you see only 30-amp fuses installed in a panel—with no 15-amp or 20-amp fuses protecting general household and lighting circuits—chances are that the panel is overfused. (There's more about overfusing on p. 134.)

WHAT TO LOOK FOR

- Is the service entrance two- or three-wire? What's the capacity of the main breakers or fuses?

- Is there room in the entrance panel to add circuits?

- Do lights dim or fuses blow when large appliance motors start up? Do fuses blow often?

- Does the panel seem to be overfused?

INSPECTING PANEL CONDITION— COVER ON

You can get a good sense of an electrical panel's condition without removing panel covers. The following are some conditions to look for.

LOOSE WIRING NEAR PANEL. Wires entering panels and boxes should be secured to adjacent framing within 12 in. of the panel or fuse box. Loose wiring and other substandard practices suggest an electrical system that has been modified by a non-professional. Because there may be more defects in concealed areas, the system should be inspected by a licensed electrician.

RUST AND CORROSION on the outside of a service box or on the armored cable or conduit feeding it can indicate corroded connections inside. Such connections can lead to arcing and house fires, so have a licensed electrician replace the fuse box or panel. Likewise, if you see scorch marks on breakers or a panel—or near a receptacle cover—have a pro examine it.

MULTIPLE WIRES ATTACHED TO PANEL LUGS. A single wire should terminate at each panel lug. Terminating additional wires beneath one lug can cause loose connections and arcing, which could be a fire hazard. Lacking circuit-breaker overload protection, additional wires could melt (instead of causing a breaker to trip) if there were shorts or overloading.

OPENING(S) IN A PANEL FACE. The inner covers of circuit breaker panels have twist-out tabs that can be removed for each breaker location. Unused openings can allow contact with the live

Here, main panel lugs secure multiple wires; each lug should secure only one. Adding wires can cause loose connections and arcing and create a fire. Also, the wires added to the main panel lugs do not appear to have any circuit breaker overload protection, so wires could melt.

This panel cover has a missing twist-out where a breaker was removed and not replaced. Such openings are potential shock hazards and should be filled with special cover plates. In addition, the panel is an outdated Federal Pacific brand, widely regarded as unsafe.

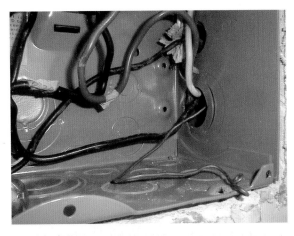

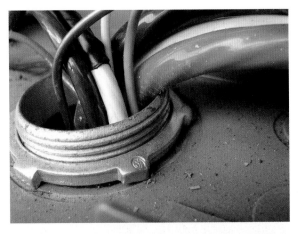

At right, circuit wires enter through a knock-out hole missing a cable clamp. Such wires could get yanked, endangering electrical connections, or they could have their insulation sliced by sharp box edges. Holes in boxes also provide access to rodents attracted to the panel's warmth.

The ends of metal conduit are often sharp, so bushings are often used inside conduit ends to protect the relatively thin insulative sheathing of electrical cables as they enter a panel.

(energized) electrical components behind the panel cover. Clips can be purchased to fill such openings. A similar danger exists in fuse panels with empty fuse sockets. Empty sockets should be filled with fuses even though not in use.

PANEL COVERS WITH MISSING PARTS, gaps, or that fit poorly are unsafe. So if you see covers that have been cut to fit a breaker, housing knockouts that are missing, bus bars that are visible when the panel cover is on, or mismatched components, hire a licensed electrician to assess and correct those problems.

OPEN KNOCK-OUT HOLE(S). Panel boxes have knockouts in the sides, bottom, and top that can be removed to provide holes for the wires to enter. Typically, cable connectors (clamps) are inserted into knock-out holes. Unused holes can be filled with special covers to maintain the fire integrity of the panel and to prevent entry of insulation, vermin, or insects.

CABLES UNPROTECTED AT HOLE(S). Cable wires should be protected with bushings and/or strain relief clamps where they enter panel box holes or openings. A missing cable connector (clamp) may also allow the sharp edge of the panel to slice

through thermoplastic cable sheathing, which could energize the panel (if the grounding of the system is not correct) and electrocute anyone who touches.

NO INSIDE COVER. The energized wiring and terminals inside modern panels should not be accessible when the panel cover is open. The "dead front" is an inside cover designed to protect panel users from electrical shock when operating a breaker or replacing a fuse. Missing covers should be replaced. Older fuse panels that do not have dead-front covers, such as the lever main panel shown in the photo on p. 130, are unsafe and should be replaced.

OLDER, OUTDATED PANEL AND BREAKERS, such as Federal Pacific and Zinsco, have a host of well-documented failures and so should be carefully checked and, where necessary, replaced.

WRONG BRAND OR TYPE OF BREAKER. Panels with several brands of breakers should raise a red flag. Many brands of circuit breakers can be made to fit other brands of panels, but only the types for which the panel has been tested and approved should be used. Modern panels often have a rating sheet inside the panel listing the types and brands that are acceptable. Using other breakers increases the likelihood of arcing and other hazards.

This panel has at least two strikes against it. Because an incoming conduit leaked water, many of the panel's breaker terminals are corroded or rusted. When you see several different breaker brands, be suspicious. Some of the breakers may not be approved for use in the panel.

MISSING HANDLE TIES. When two breakers are paired to protect a single 240-volt circuit, the breaker switch handles should be mechanically connected to operate in unison. A simple connector can be installed by an electrician to ensure that both breakers trip at the same time. Handle ties are also required when two breakers protect multiwire branch circuits, such as for a combination dishwasher and garbage disposer receptacle.

AN OVERSIZE FUSE OR BREAKER may not melt wires where you can see them, but there may be damaged wire insulation in places not readily visible. Anytime the inspector finds a fuse or breaker that's too big for the circuit, an electrician should inspect the system. Installing Type S fuse socket inserts in older panels can allow the installation of modern porcelain fuses. In general, however, it is best to replace all old fuse panels with modern circuit breaker panels to provide a safer system.

"PENNYING" A FUSE is another unsafe way to deal with an overloaded circuit that keeps blowing fuses. In this case, someone unscrews a fuse, inserts a penny or a blank metal slug into the bottom of the

socket—a dangerous act in itself—and then re-installs the fuse. The penny allows current to bypass the fuse and the protection it offers. Here, again, have an electrician examine the circuits for damage to the wire insulation.

A PROPERLY GROUNDED PANEL will have a large grounding wire running from the panel to a grounding electrode (which could be a metal underground water pipe, a ground rod driven into the earth, or an Ufer electrode). For the entire electrical system to be grounded, there must be a continuous ground wire or other effective grounding path running from each device or fixture to the service panel and, by extension, to the grounding electrode. Cold-water and gas pipes must also be connected (bonded) to the grounding bus in the panel.

See "Grounding Basics" on p. 137 for more information about this vitally important topic.

WHAT TO LOOK FOR

- Is wiring near the panel(s) installed in a neat, workmanlike manner?
- Are panels rusted, corroded, scorched, or otherwise damaged?
- Are there unused openings in the panel face or open knockouts around the sides, top, and bottom of the panel box? Are energized wires or terminals visible through such openings?
- Are cable wires protected with bushings and/or strain relief clamps where they enter panel box holes or openings?
- Do older fuse panels lack inside covers?
- Are breaker panels or equipment outdated or discontinued brands? Does the panel contain different brands of breakers and, if so, are they approved for that panel?
- Does the panel wiring have adequate overload protection?
- Is there any evidence that someone has tried to penny a fuse?
- Is the panel properly grounded? (See p. 137 for more information.)

Screws that come with new panels have blunt ends designed to avoid damaging wires. When such screws get lost, remuddlers sometimes use drywall or wood screws to secure covers. Very dangerous! The screws' sharp points can puncture the insulation of energized wires.

White wires inside an electrical panel are the ones most likely to show signs of overheating. Power enters the system through black (hot) wires and, after being partially used, it returns along the white (neutral) wires. Some wiring configurations will allow one neutral wire to carry the return load from two hot wires. If not wired correctly, these configurations can overload the neutral wire and cause it to melt.

INSPECTING PANEL CONDITION—COVER REMOVED

Inspecting some conditions requires removing panel covers and having a look inside.

NOTE: Only a trained professional should remove the inside cover of an electrical panel. Look for the following conditions inside a panel.

SCORCHING/MELTING. Discolored breakers or melted wire insulation indicates excessive heat caused by wiring or component failures. Melted wire insulation is often caused by overfusing (discussed next) or by loose connections in which electricity arcs (jumps) between conductors. Because electrical arcs are usually hot enough to melt metal, arcing is a serious fire hazard.

OVERSIZE BREAKERS/BUSES (aka overfusing). Fuses and circuit breakers are rated to allow a specific amount of current in the circuit before tripping or burning out. When the wrong size breaker or fuse is used, there is a potential for the wiring to overheat, creating a fire hazard. For example, a 14-gauge wire is rated to safely draw 15 amps before the wiring overheats and a 15-amp fuse or circuit breaker on this circuit will blow when overloaded. Using a larger

Overfusing and double-wiring are common in older fuse panels. The green and yellow fuses shown are 30-amp, the red fuse is 20-amp. The red 20-amp fuse (lower left) is too large for the 14-gauge wire attached to it, which should be protected by a 15-amp fuse. Oversize fuses can overload wires, causing them to melt or start a fire.

Too many wires in an electrical panel may cause the panel cover to pinch wire insulation, creating a potential short or shock hazard. Any service panel this full should be replaced with a larger panel or supplemented by a subpanel installed nearby.

ALUMINUM CIRCUIT WIRING

THE SERVICE ENTRANCE WIRES THAT FEED A service panel are typically three large aluminum or copper conductors that terminate in proper-rated lugs.

Aluminum circuit wiring, however, can be a fire hazard unless it is correctly terminated with a proper connector such as a COPALUM connector or CO/ALR-rated outlets and switches. If it is incorrectly terminated in a copper device, the two metals can corrode and expand and contract at different rates each time the circuit is under load. This can lead to loose connections, arcing, overheating, and house fires.

While not a code requirement, it's best to apply antioxidant paste to all large aluminum wiring terminations to prevent corrosion in the wiring. Corrosion can cause poor connections and overheating. In some cases, the antioxidant coating may be present but not readily visible.

breaker or fuse, such as one rated at 20 amps or 30 amps, will not provide adequate protection. (Twelve-gauge wire takes a 20-amp fuse.) In fact, it is a dangerous condition and a serious code violation.

IMPROPER WIRE COLOR CODING. The insulation on individual wires is color coded to indicate its proper use: red or black for hot wires, white wires for neutrals, green or bare copper for grounds. Improper color coding may indicate modifications by a nonprofessional; a licensed electrician should inspect the system.

EXCESS WIRE IN PANEL. An excessive amount of wiring in a panel can cause overheating and wire damage, creating a potentially hazardous condition. In some overcrowded panels it is difficult to replace a panel cover without damaging wire insulation, creating a shock hazard.

DAMAGED WIRE INSULATION. Wire insulation that is damaged is potentially hazardous. It should be repaired or replaced by a qualified electrician.

EXCESS CABLE SHEATHING or wrapping on electrical cables is substandard practice and may indicate work by a nonelectrician. While not a code requirement, professional electricians will typically leave only ½ in. of sheathing at each cable clamp inside a panel box.

LOOSE END WIRE(S) can come in contact with energized components, creating a shock or fire hazard. Just because a loose end wire does not test energized, doesn't mean it is safe.

DOUBLE WIRING (aka double tugging). Attaching more than one wire to a single breaker, fuse, or bus bar terminal can cause loose connections, arcing, and overheating. Most terminals are designed to hold only one wire, and attaching more than one may be hazardous. Double wiring is usually done because a panel is full; upgrading equipment is a far safer solution.

SAME POLE MULTIWIRE CIRCUIT(S) are pairs of 120-volt circuits that share a common neutral wire. To prevent overloading the neutral, the pairs of hot wires must originate from different poles in the panel (so there is 240-volt potential between them). Same

The three single-pole breakers at left all have two wires attached to them, which is unsafe. A single wire should attach to each breaker terminal. Multiple wires attached to the same terminal can become loose, arc, and create a fire hazard. Chances are the panel is full and should be replaced by a panel with larger capacity.

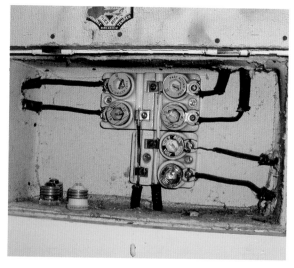

This panel has "fused neutrals," in which both the hot and neutral wires are fused. This arrangement is outmoded and unsafe because a loose or missing neutral fuse could make an energized circuit appear dead, thus creating a shock hazard. Also, many old wood-framed panels such as this one were wrapped in asbestos, an environmentally hazardous material.

pole multiwire circuits can typically be corrected by relocating the wires to different breakers or fuses within the panel.

SERVICE PANEL NOT BONDED. The service panel housing (box), neutral wires, and grounding wires should be bonded together (securely connected) inside the main service panel. Correct bonding is shown in the photo on p. 128. However, *in subpanels*, neutral wires must be isolated from the panel housing and grounding wires.

IMPROPER GROUND NEUTRAL. Subpanel neutral wires must be isolated from the panel housing (box) and grounding wires to prevent current from being carried on the grounding wires and components. In subpanels, grounding wires should not connect to the neutral wires and should have their own bus or terminal attached to the panel. Older subpanels installed before the use of three-hole outlets may need new feed wires to provide separate paths for the neutral and grounding wires.

FUSED NEUTRALS. Fuses are installed on both hot and neutral wires in some older fuse panels. While this might seem to provide added safety, the

opposite is true. If the neutral fuse blows, the circuit would be hot but would appear dead, creating a hazardous condition. This condition indicates an outdated and potentially hazardous system. Fused neutral panels often also have exposed electrical connections, creating an additional safety hazard. All old, outdated, or unsafe panels should be replaced.

WHAT TO LOOK FOR

- Are any panel breakers or wires scorched or melted?
- Are breakers or fuses correctly matched to the circuit wires they protect? Or are breakers or fuses oversize for the wires they should protect?
- Does the panel contain improper wire color coding?
- Does the panel contain excess wires? Could wire insulation be pinched or damaged when the inside panel cover is replaced?
- Does the panel contain loose-end wires?
- Are any circuits wired with 14-gauge or 12-gauge aluminum wiring?

- Do you see more than one wire attached to any single breaker, fuse, or bus bar terminal?
- Where multiwire branch circuits share a common neutral wire, do pairs of hot wires originate from opposite poles (phase A and phase B) in the panel?
- Are the main service panel housing (box), neutral wires, and grounding wires securely bonded (connected together) in the main service panel?
- Are subpanel neutral wires isolated from the panel housing (box) and grounding wires?
- If there is an older fuse panel, are fuses installed on both neutral and hot wires? Panels with fused neutrals are hazardous and should be replaced immediately.
- Is the panel properly grounded? (See the next section for more information.)

Grounding Basics

Because electricity moves in a circuit, it will return to its source unless the path is interrupted. The return path is through the white neutral wires that bring current back to the main panel. Ground wires provide the current with an alternative low-resistance path for fault currents—abnormal electrical flows such as short circuits.

WHY GROUNDING MATTERS

Why is having a grounding path important? Before equipment-grounding conductors (commonly called ground wires) were widespread, people could be electrocuted when they came in contact with voltage that, due to a fault like a loose wire, unintentionally energized the metal casing of a tool or an electrical appliance. Ground wires bond all electrical devices and potentially current-carrying metal surfaces.

This bonding creates a path with such low impedance (resistance) that fault currents flow along it, quickly tripping breakers or fuses and interrupting power. Contrary to popular misconceptions, the human body usually has a relatively high impedance (compared with copper wire); if electricity is offered a path with very low resistance—the equipment grounding conductor—it will take the low-resistance

AVOIDING ELECTRICAL SHOCKS

GROUND FAULTS CAN KILL! CURRENT flowing unintentionally to ground ("earth") is called a ground fault. The ground wire in an electrical system is intended to be a low-impedance path to ground, to safely carry the current of a ground fault until a circuit breaker trips. You, however, can also be a path to ground should you come in contact with an energized conductor. In this case, you would become part of the circuit, with current flowing through you. **So be careful:** Only a little current flowing through your heart can kill you. When inspecting electrical systems, *always test first* to be sure that potential conductors are not energized.

STAY OUT OF THIS LOOP!

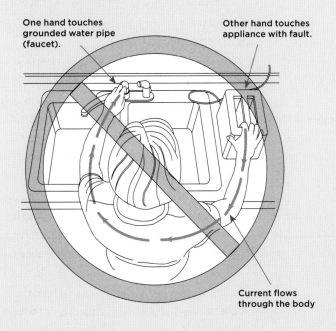

One hand touches grounded water pipe (faucet).

Other hand touches appliance with fault.

Current flows through the body

path back to the panel, trip the breaker, and cut off the power.

Effective bonding of all metal components is created by ground wires (equipment grounding conductors) that connect to every part of the electrical system that could become energized—metal boxes, receptacles, switches, fixtures—and, through three-pronged plugs, the metallic covers and frames of tools and appliances.

Grounding conductors, usually bare copper or green insulated wire, create an effective path back to the main service panel in case a metal component becomes improperly energized. Bonding allows fault current to trip the breaker and disconnect the power to the circuit.

THE NEUTRAL/GROUND BUS

In the main service panel, the ground wires attach to a neutral/ground bus bar, which is bonded to the metal panel housing via a main bonding jumper. If there's a ground fault in the house, the main bonding jumper ensures the current can be safely directed to the ground, away from the house and the people inside. It is probably the single most important connection in the entire electrical system.

Also attached to the neutral/ground bus in the service panel is a large, usually bare, copper ground wire—the grounding electrode conductor (GEC)—which exits the service panel and clamps to a grounding electrode, usually either a ground rod driven into the earth, or an Ufer grounding electrode, a 20-ft. length of steel rebar or heavy copper wire in the footing of the foundation.

GROUNDING TO WATER PIPES. In many older houses, electrical services were grounded only to metal water pipes. When metal water piping functions as the ground, and any sections of metal piping have been replaced with plastic pipe, the grounding system should be upgraded with a driven rod. The gas piping and other metallic interior piping should also be bonded to the grounding system.

To ensure that the grounding is continuous along metal water piping, bonding jumpers must be used at the water heater, at gas meters, and at any point where nonconductive materials could interrupt electrical flow. When a dielectric union (see p. 155) is installed to prevent corrosion between, say, copper and galvanized steel pipes, continuity should be restored by a bonding jumper wire that jumps around the interruption. Though the jumper may reduce the

GROUNDING REQUIREMENTS

In a service panel, ground and neutral wires attach to a neutral/ground bus, which is bonded to the panel box. (In subpanels, ground and neutral wires and buses are electrically isolated from each other.)

A large copper ground wire bonded to the service panel is clamped to a grounding electrode (rod).

The main water pipe (and metal gas piping) must also be bonded to the grounding system, so that ground faults can be safely discharged should pipes become energized.

MAJOR GROUNDING ELEMENTS

The equipment-grounding system acts as an expressway for stray current. By bonding together conductors or potential conductors, the system provides a low-impedance path for fault currents. In a ground fault, the abnormally high amperage (current flow) that results trips a breaker or blows a fuse, disconnecting power to the circuit.

The NEC requires the interior metal water piping and interior metal gas piping be bonded so that if it becomes energized, the breaker will trip and cut power. An underground metal water pipe may be used as one of the grounding electrodes, and a grounding electrode run from the pipe to the panel within 5 ft. of where the pipe enters the building. Proper grounding and bonding reduces the chance that the grounding path will be interrupted if part of the piping is replaced with plastic. The primary grounding in new construction is typically a Ufer (steel rebar in the concrete footing) or a grounding rod driven into the soil at the building exterior.

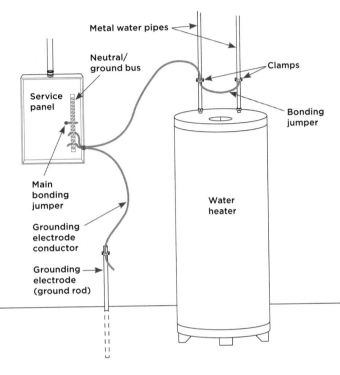

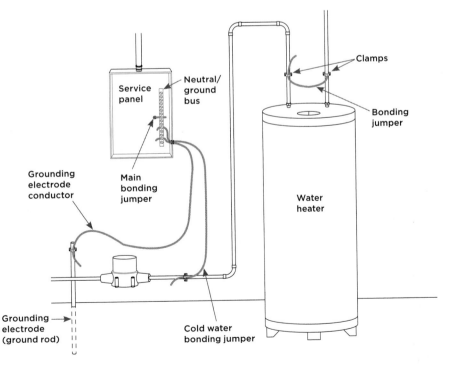

Failed ground! The dielectric union between galvanized steel water piping and copper piping is designed to keep the copper from corroding the steel piping. However, the plastic separator inside the union also interrupts the flow of electricity needed for a continuous grounding system. One fix is adding a second ground wire and clamp to the steel piping; another is installing a separate driven ground rod system.

This loose (and undersize) ground wire is a trip hazard, which could also damage the ground. Properly installed ground wires between the main panel and the grounding rod must be mechanically protected by being secured to the siding and/or running through conduit.

ability of the dielectric union to prevent corrosion, electrical safety is a greater priority.

PROTECTING THE GROUND WIRE. The GEC that runs between the service panel and a ground rod or pipe should be protected against mechanical damage. The ground wire must be securely clamped to the rod or pipe to ensure good electrical conduction. The ground wire can be installed in conduit or can be secured to the building surface to reduce the possibility of damage. When a metal conduit is used to protect the ground wire, the conduit itself must also be bonded to the grounding rod.

PREVENTING TRIP HAZARDS. Ground rods should be fully driven into the earth. If the rod has been cut or not fully driven, it will not be as effective as it should be. It is possible to correct inadequate grounding by adding a second grounding rod. Also, the rod should be located away from walkways or other areas where someone could trip over it. Ideally, a rod should be driven into the bottom of a 1-ft.-deep hole that is then covered with gravel.

THE GROUNDING ROD. The grounding electrode system (GES)—commonly called ground rods—connects to the building's equipment grounding system at the service panel. As such, the GES's primary function is to provide a low impedance path to ground (earth), so that in the event of a fault in the system, the fault current will pass through that low impedance path rather than through, say, someone using an electrical appliance inside the house.

SIZING. The National Electrical Code requires grounding electrode conductor size to be based on the sizes and types of conductors in the service. Typically, residential GECs are size 6 American wire gauge (6 AWG) copper. Ground rods are typically $\frac{1}{2}$-in. or $\frac{5}{8}$-in. copper-clad steel rods at least 8 ft. long. The Ufer or concrete-encased electrode is the preferred grounding electrode and must be used if present in new construction.

WHAT TO LOOK FOR

- Are the main service panel housing (box), neutral wires, and grounding wires securely bonded (connected together) in the main service panel? A main bonding jumper (p. 138) should bond the neutral/ground bus to the service panel housing.

- Do all ground and neutral wires in the main service panel attach securely to a neutral/ground bus? Are all bus lugs (screws) tight? Are there any signs of corrosion, scorch marks, or melted wire insulation where wires attach to lugs?

- Is there a large (usually bare) copper ground wire (the GEC) attached to a neutral/ground bus in the service panel?

- After it exits the service panel, does the GEC attach to a driven ground rod or to an Ufer grounding electrode in the footing of the foundation?

- If the house is older, does the GEC from the service panel attach only to metal water pipes? If so, is the metal piping continuous or is it interrupted by sections of plastic pipe or other nonconductive materials?

- Are dielectric unions used to prevent corrosion between galvanized steel and copper water piping? Because the plastic separator inside these unions will interrupt the flow of electricity, a bonding jumper must be installed to bypass the union and be securely clamped to the piping on both sides.

- Are gas pipes and other metallic interior piping bonded to the grounding system?

- Does the bonding system include bonding jumpers to create a continuous bond at water heaters?

- Is the GEC protected from mechanical damage where it runs between the service panel and a ground rod or metal water pipe? If the GEC is protected by metal conduit, is the conduit itself bonded to the ground rod?

- Is the ground rod driven fully into the earth? Is the ground rod a trip hazard?

Assessing Circuit Wiring

Circuit wiring may be visible as it nears electrical panels and as it runs through attics and basements. Although home inspectors do not typically remove the covers of junction boxes, doing so will allow you to examine the condition of wires and wire splices

inside—without touching them. You could turn off power to receptacles to examine the condition of circuit wiring. But most inspectors simply use a circuit analyzer (see p. 146) to determine if outlets are correctly wired.

Deteriorated sheathing is a potential shock hazard, so note brittle fiber insulation and bare wire but avoid touching it. If cable sheathing has been chewed on by mice, rats, or squirrels, it should be replaced.

SECURING CABLE

NM cable (cable protected by nonmetallic sheathing) must be stapled within 8 in. of single-gang boxes that don't have cable clamps, and within 12 in. of other boxes, and supported by stapling or another method at least every $4\frac{1}{2}$ ft. (54 in). A cable running through a drilled hole in the framing is considered supported. Sagging wire is potentially hazardous because it can

As a general rule, Romex (nonmetallic) cable should be secured to framing within 12 in. of outlet or junction boxes. Wiring as loose and amateurish as that shown here is a red flag that there are likely other wiring mistakes lurking, some possibly hazardous, that a qualified electrician should investigate.

Wire splices must take place in a covered box (unlike here), and Romex cable must be secured to framing within 12 in. of a junction box.

Electrical conductors entering a metal box must be secured by cable connectors (clamps), which are missing here. Clamps prevent connections from being pulled apart and protect wire insulation from being sliced by sharp box edges. Last, clamps should tighten down on cable sheathing, not individual wires.

become strained, stressing the electrical connections. Likewise, all junction boxes should be securely mounted.

Electrical cables that run through holes drilled in studs or joists must be at least 1¼ in. from the face of framing members to avoid being punctured by nails or screws when finish surfaces are installed. Cables closer than 1¼ in. should be protected by metal nail plates.

All NM cable entering metal boxes must be gripped by cable clamps. Single-gang plastic boxes do not require the strain relief of cable clamps, but double-gang (and larger) plastic boxes have integral plastic tension clamps that provide some strain relief on cable.

ALUMINUM CIRCUIT WIRING

Small-gauge aluminum circuit wiring (10 gauge or 12 gauge) can be a fire hazard unless it is correctly spliced to a copper wire with a COPALUM® connector, or terminated to CO/ALR-rated outlets and switches. If it is incorrectly terminated in a copper-rated-only device, the two metals will expand and contract at different rates each time the circuit is under load. This can lead to loose connections, arcing, over-heating, and house fires. Aluminum-to-aluminum splices require special splicing techniques, either

COPALUM connectors or another listed and approved method.

WIRE SPLICES

Wire splices (whether copper to copper, copper to aluminum, or aluminum to aluminum) must be housed within a covered junction box or outlet box. Wires that are spliced outside a box or inside an un-covered box can be a fire hazard because of the dangers of arcing. Loose connections not contained in a covered box can easily ignite combustibles nearby because arcs approach 2000°F.

CABLE CLAMPS

Every wiring system, whether nonmetallic (Romex), metal clad, or armor clad, has clamps (connectors) specific to that system. Clamps solidly secure cables to boxes to protect connections inside the box, so wire splices or connections to devices cannot get yanked apart or compromised. Cable clamps in metal boxes also keep wires from being nicked by burrs created when metal box knockouts are removed.

KNOB-AND-TUBE WIRING

Knob-and-tube wiring, although outdated, is usually safe unless individual wire insulation is deteriorated, splices are incorrectly made, the wiring is overloaded, or buried in thermal insulation. Typically, splices that were part of the original installation will not be in a junction box but must be wrapped with electrical (friction) tape and supported by porcelain knobs on both sides of each splice. Nonoriginal splices must be housed in covered boxes. Have knob-and-tube wiring assessed or modified by an electrician familiar with it; it's quirky stuff. The NEC does not allow knob-and-tube wiring to be buried in insulation but several states now allow buried knob-and-tube wiring to encourage adding insulation for energy conservation. They typically require that the wiring be examined by an electrician before it is covered.

Knob-and-tube wiring lacks an equipment ground (a separate grounding wire), so it offers no protection should a faulty appliance get plugged into a receptacle. On the other hand, a knob-and-tube system is run completely on insulators, which is a plus. The conductors of knob-and-tube wiring were copper, coated with a thin layer of tin (to protect the copper from sulfur in the rubber wire insulation). Uninformed inspectors often mistake the tinned copper wire for aluminum wire.

EXTENSION OR ZIP-CORD WIRING? NEVER!
Extension cords, lamp cord wiring (zip cord), and other temporary wiring should not be used for permanent installations. Such wiring should be replaced by a qualified electrician.

WHAT TO LOOK FOR

- Are wiring runs neat and workmanlike or do loose wires sag from joists?
- If electrical cable runs through joists or studs, is it at least 1¼ in. back from the edges of framing members? If cables are closer than 1¼ in., are metal nail protection plates used?
- Do all electrical wire splices take place in covered junction or outlet boxes? Write up any splices outside boxes, boxes with no covers, or boxes with missing (unfilled) knockouts.
- Do any circuit wires entering metal outlet or junction boxes lack protective connectors?

Knob-and-tube is an outdated wiring method where porcelain knobs secure the wire and keep it from overheating wood at framing holes. The splices shown here are not to code and not safe. Any changes in wiring types—such as splicing Romex cable to knob-and-tube—must occur in a box and are subject to other code specifics.

- Is there any apparently nonfunctional old wiring? It should be removed so that it is not mistakenly spliced to newer (energized) wiring or energized by an old switch or panel.
- Does the house contain old knob-and-tube wiring? Is its insulation in good condition? Has the knob-and-tube wiring been spliced to new wiring types? Are such splices contained in covered boxes?
- In attics and other locations where old fiber-sheathed wiring is visible, is wire insulation brittle or cracked?
- If you see extension cords or lamp cord used as permanent wiring, write it up!

Indoor Outlets

An outlet is a location where electricity is used, such as a duplex receptacle, a light, a fan, or a kitchen appliance.

GENERAL-USE CIRCUIT REQUIREMENTS

General-use circuits are intended primarily for lighting, but small loads that are connected via a cord and plug, such as televisions, fans, and vacuums, are allowed—as long as the power they draw doesn't exceed the capacity of the circuit.

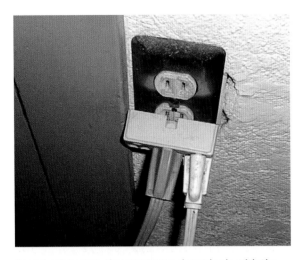

Scorched receptacles warrant a closer look, with the power turned off. Scorching may be caused by loose connections (arcing), overfusing (p. 133), overloaded circuits, or in some older houses, overheated aluminum circuit wiring. The extension plug suggests overloading. An electrician should identify the cause and survey the house for similar symptoms.

LIGHTING AND SMALL LOADS. Though 14-AWG wire is sufficient for lighting, electricians often run 12-AWG wire on general-use circuits to accommodate future uses. Lighting loads are calculated at 3 watts per square foot, or roughly one 15-amp circuit for every 500 sq. ft. of floor space. When laying out lighting circuits, an electrician should not put all the lights on a floor on one circuit. Otherwise, should a breaker trip, the entire floor would be without lights.

RECEPTACLES. There must be a receptacle within 6 ft. of each doorway and located at least every 12 ft. along each wall. (This is also stated as, "No space on a wall should be more than 6 ft. from a receptacle.") Any wall at least 2 ft. wide must have a receptacle; and a receptacle is required in hallway walls 10 ft. or longer. In new construction, any foyer of more than 60 sq. ft. must have a receptacle on any wall 3 ft. or longer.

OUTLETS. The NEC does not specify a maximum number of lighting or receptacle outlets on a residential lighting or appliance circuit, though local jurisdictions may. Figure roughly 9 outlets per 15-amp circuit and 10 outlets per 20-amp circuit.

LIGHT SWITCHES. In new construction there must be at least one wall switch that controls lighting in each habitable room, in the garage (if wired for electricity), and in storage areas (including attics and basements). Near each exterior door with grade-level access, there must be a switch controlling an outside light. Three-way switches are required at each end of a corridor and at the top and bottom of stairs with six steps or more. When possible, switches should be near lights they control. It should be noted that a light switch may control a receptacle (considered "lighting") in habitable rooms, except in kitchens and bathrooms.

GFCI PROTECTION. The NEC requires GFCI protection for all bathroom receptacles, all receptacles serving kitchen counters, all outdoor receptacles, receptacles in unfinished portions of basements, garage receptacles, and receptacles near pools and hot tubs. (Check the most recent NEC for a complete listing.)

AFCI PROTECTION. Arc fault circuit interrupters (AFCIs) are relatively new safety devices designed to detect electrical arcs from cracked, broken, or damaged electrical insulation and to shut off power to the circuit before the arcing leads to a fire. They are required in new construction for 15-amp and 20-amp branch circuits having outlets in dwelling family rooms, dining rooms, living rooms, parlors, libraries, dens, bedrooms, sunrooms, recreation rooms, closets, hallways, or similar rooms or areas. An outlet can be a lighting outlet or another point on the circuit where electrical equipment is supplied with current. Hard-wired smoke alarms are outlets and require AFCI protection. It has been found that some older knob-and-tube wiring may cause these new breakers to trip, and it may be necessary to replace such wiring for the new AFCIs to function properly. New electrical codes now require AFCIs in accessible kitchen and bathroom circuits.

NEW CONSTRUCTION REQUIREMENTS ROOM BY ROOM

Kitchen and bath appliances are heavy power users, so their circuits must be sized accordingly.

BATHROOM CIRCUITS. Bathroom receptacles must be supplied by one or more 20-amp circuits. The NEC allows a 20-amp circuit to supply the receptacles of more than one bathroom or to supply the receptacles, lights, and fans (excluding heating fans) in one bathroom. Receptacles in bathrooms must be GFCI protected, either by a GFCI receptacle or a GFCI breaker. If a bathroom does not have a window at least 3 sq. ft., half of which is operable, a mechanical exhaust fan must be provided.

SMALL-APPLIANCE CIRCUITS. There must be at least two 20-amp small-appliance circuits in the kitchen serving the kitchen countertops. No point along a kitchen countertop should be more than 2 ft. from an outlet—in other words, space countertop receptacles at least every 4 ft. Every counter at least 12 in. wide must have a receptacle.

KITCHEN LIGHTING. Adequate lighting is particularly important in kitchens so people can work safely and efficiently. Kitchen lighting should be a good balance of general and task lighting. Many jurisdictions have energy-efficiency requirements for lighting in kitchens, but assessing lighting-code requirements is not typically part of a home inspection.

BATHROOM LIGHTING. It is important to illuminate the face evenly in mirrors. Common practice is to place good-quality light sources either above the vanity mirror or on either side of it. Many jurisdictions also have energy-efficiency requirements for lighting in bathrooms, including the use of high-efficacy lighting and vacancy sensors. Here again, lighting code compliance is not part of a home inspection.

MISCELLANEOUS LIGHTING. Bare incandescent light bulbs should not be used as closet light fixtures because they get hot and could ignite clothing and other combustibles. Fluorescent lights are a better choice, as they are cooler and require less clearance from storage areas. Old-style light fixtures in which bulbs hang from a single lamp cord are hazardous because hot wires can become frayed, creating a shock hazard. Homemade zip-wire or extension cords should not be used to power perma-

This light fixture is missing the porcelain ring that protects bulb changers from touching the threaded metal fixture base. This fixture should be removed and replaced with a florescent fixture whose cool bulbs are more appropriate for use in a clothes closet.

nent ceiling light fixtures. (The latest electrical codes now refer to all light fixtures as "luminaires")

DEDICATED CIRCUITS. All critical-use and fixed (stationary) appliances should and in most cases must have their own dedicated (separate) circuits. These fixed appliances include the water pump, freezer, refrigerator, oven, cooktop, microwave, furnace and/or whole-house air-conditioning unit, window air conditioners, and water heater. Laundry room receptacles must be on a dedicated circuit; so must an electric clothes dryer.

MISWIRED MISCELLANY

Home inspectors come across certain wiring mistakes again and again. Fortunately, most are easy to detect and repair.

THREE-PRONG ADAPTERS IN TWO-HOLE OUTLETS. Three-prong adaptor plugs installed in a two-hole outlet may not provide an effective ground connection. To be sure safe grounding is present, the outlet should be rewired with a three-wire cable that includes a ground wire; or the two-hole outlet can be replaced with a GFCI receptacle.

UNGROUNDED THREE-HOLE OUTLET, aka an open ground, is common in older buildings and typi-

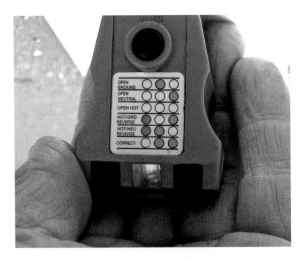

Circuit analyzers, sold in most hardware stores, can check the wiring of all receptacles. "Open ground" means that the third hole of the receptacle is not connected, a common problem when an original two-hole outlet has been replaced with a three-hole type.

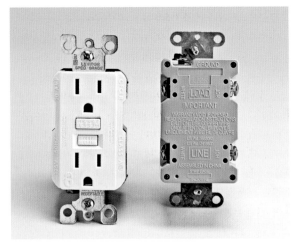

GFCI receptacles have two sets of terminals, marked "line" and "load." Cable attached to line terminals protects the receptacle location; cable attached to load terminals provides current to and GFCI protection for outlets downstream (away from the power source).

cally occurs when two-hole receptacles are replaced with three-hole types without adding a grounding wire. Code requires that an ungrounded three-hole outlet be labeled as such. Ideally, the outlet should be rewired with a three-wire cable that includes a ground wire or the two-hole outlet can be replaced with a GFCI receptacle. A circuit analyzer will identify open grounds.

REVERSE POLARITY. Receptacles, plugs, and fixtures are polarized so they can fit together only one way. A receptacle's brass screw terminal connects to hot wires and, internally, to the hot (narrow) prong of a polarized plug. The receptacle's silver screw terminal connects to neutral wires and, internally, to the neutral (wide) prong of a polarized plug. Finally, the green ground screw connects to the ground wire and the grounding prong of the plug. Reverse polarity is a defect where the hot and neutral wires to an outlet are reversed. This potential safety hazard is usually easily corrected. A circuit analyzer will identify reverse polarity.

LINE-LOAD REVERSAL. GFCI receptacles have two sets of terminals, marked "line" and "load." Cable attached to the load terminals provides current to and GFCI protection for outlets downstream (away

Standard wall-mount receptacles should not be installed in floors or in other horizontal surfaces; this outlet should be replaced with a special receptacle in a proper floor-mounted box.

from the power source). If the line and load connections are reversed (a common defect), the GFCI test button will operate properly and downstream outlets may be protected but the GFCI outlet itself will be not protected. To see if the GFCI receptacle is correctly wired, insert a circuit analyzer into the device and press the test button. If the button pops out yet there is still power at the receptacle, the most likely cause is line-load reversal.

IMPROPER FLOOR RECEPTACLES. Standard wall-mount receptacles are not designed to support weight, so any installed in floors should be replaced with special receptacles in floor-mounted boxes.

MISSING, DAMAGED, OR LOOSE COVER PLATES. All switches and outlets should have intact cover plates to protect wiring connections in outlet boxes. Wall and ceiling light fixtures should also have bases or canopies that protect wiring connections. Any cover plates that are cracked, melted, or damaged should be replaced.

WHAT TO LOOK FOR

- Are receptacles spaced at least every 12 ft. along walls? Does every wall at least 2 ft. wide have a receptacle? Do hallway walls at least 10 ft. long have a receptacle?
- Does each habitable room have at least one wall switch that controls lighting? Do the garage and storage areas have a light switch?
- Does a switch control each outside light near an exterior door with grade-level access? Are there three-way switches at each end of a corridor and at the top and bottom of stairs with six steps or more?
- Do all bathroom receptacles, kitchen-counter receptacles, outdoor receptacles, receptacles in unfinished portions of basements, and garage receptacles have GFCI protection?
- Is there GFCI protection for receptacles near pools and hot tubs?
- In homes built within the last decade, do all branch circuits in bedrooms and living spaces have AFCI protection?
- Are bathroom circuits supplied by 20-amp circuits?
- Are there at least two 20-amp circuits serving kitchen countertops? Is there a countertop receptacle at least every 4 ft.? Does every counter at least 12 in. wide have a receptacle?
- Are critical-use and fixed appliances on dedicated circuits?
- Are extension cords used as permanent circuits? Are octopus plugs or three-plug adaptors used to increase the number of appliances plugged into two-hole receptacles?

ELECTRIC HEATER SAFETY

ELECTRIC WALL AND BASEBOARD HEATERS should not be covered by draperies, furnishings, or other items. Proper clearances vary by make and model. Consult the owner's manual for clearance requirements. Care should be taken to prevent electrical cords from falling into the heaters. In modern construction, electrical outlets are not allowed directly above a baseboard heater. Electric wall or baseboard heaters may have hot surfaces, and barriers may be needed to prevent small children from contacting them.

- Does a circuit analyzer indicate open grounds or reversed polarity at any outlets?
- Are all GFCI receptacles correctly wired or do some show line-load reversal? (Best to have a licensed electrician check and repair all if your random inspection finds miswiring.)
- Are standard wall-mount receptacles installed in floors?
- Are cover plates on switches or outlets missing or damaged?

Outdoor and Garage Outlets

Moisture is the biggest concern for electrical outlets located outdoors or in locations subject to dampness or open to the weather. Wiring, boxes, outlets, switches, and light fixtures that are exposed to weather must be rated for such locations to prevent water entry, hazards, or damage. Using NM (Romex) cable outside, for example, is a code violation.

In addition, the NEC requires GFCI protection for all outdoor receptacles, receptacles in unfinished portions of basements, garage receptacles, and receptacles near pools and hot tubs. (For a more complete listing, see the most recent edition of the National Electrical Code.)

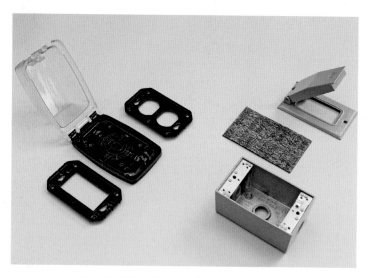

Raintight (weatherproof) covers include a weatherproof-in-use receptacle cover with adapter plates (left) and a weatherproof box with a gasketed cover (right).

Exterior wall-mounted light fixtures are often not properly caulked to the wall behind, which may allow rain to enter the electrical box or soak wall framing. Sealing this gap with a high-quality caulk will prevent moisture entry at this location.

Inspectors should also note the following issues.

OUTDOOR COVERS. Receptacles in damp or wet locations must be listed as weather-resistant types. Electrical outlets in damp locations such as protected (roofed) porches are required to have a gasketed weatherproof cover. Receptacles in wet locations require in-use covers.

CAULKING TO SIDING. Outlet boxes must be rated for exterior use and should be well caulked with siliconized caulk to prevent water from entering wiring-access holes behind outlet boxes. As is true with any outlet, exterior boxes should be solidly attached.

GARAGE RECEPTACLES. Standard three-hole receptacles may not be durable enough to withstand the repeated plugging and unplugging of heavy appliance plugs; heavy-duty nylon receptacles with reinforced yokes will last longer in garages and workshops. Because fuel and solvent fumes tend to collect near garage floors, where an electrical spark could start a fire, garage receptacles should be at least 18 in. above garage floors—though this is not code required.

OUTDOOR LIGHTING. Low-voltage walk and trail lights will decrease the chance of falling. Motion-actuated security lights should be at least 10 ft. high, to prevent an intruder's unscrewing a bulb.

WHAT TO LOOK FOR

- Are outdoor or garage outlets GFCI protected—by GFCI receptacles at the point of use or by GFCI breakers that protect a whole circuit? (By the way, GFCI breakers are less prone to nuisance tripping by high ambient moisture, as some GFCI receptacles are.)

- Are all wiring, boxes, outlets, switches, and light fixtures used outside exterior rated? Write up any interior components (such as Romex) used outside.

- Are receptacles used in damp or wet locations protected by outdoor covers?

- Are outlet, switch, and light fixture boxes caulked to prevent water entry behind them?

- Are garage receptacles at least 18 in. above the garage floor?

- Are there walk or trail lights?

- Are security light bulbs low enough to be unscrewed by an intruder?

CHAPTER 7

PLUMBING

A PLUMBING SYSTEM IS A LOOP OF SORTS, created by supply (or delivery) pipes that carry potable water to the house and its fixtures, and by DWV pipes, which carry waste water, effluvia, and sewer gases away from the fixtures—sinks, toilets, bidets, lavatories, washing machines, and so on.

These two systems within a system are quite different from each other. DWV pipes are larger and must slope so waste can fall freely (by gravity) and sewage gases can rise and exit through vents. By contrast, smaller water supply pipes deliver water under pressure, so there's no need to slope them.

Over the years, rust accumulates inside steel piping and eventually affects water flow. House water pressure may be good, but the low volume of water in constricted pipes will cause flow to drop significantly, sometimes to a trickle, when several fixtures are used at the same time.

Water Supply Piping

Water supply systems have many parts, but conceptually they're simple. After a brief overview of supply system elements, we'll get into the nitty-gritty of inspecting it all.

SUPPLY PIPE OVERVIEW

The pipe that delivers water to a house (from a city water main or an individual well) is called the house service main, or just house main. In cold regions, the house main runs below the frost line and enters the building through its foundation. Typically, a 1-in. house main is controlled by a main shutoff valve after it enters a building; municipal hookups may enter a water meter first.

On the other side of the shutoff valve, the house main continues as the main cold water supply, commonly ¾ in. in diameter. At some point, the main supply pipe enters a tee fitting, where it splits. One leg continues on as a cold water trunk line and the other feeds into the water heater, where it emerges as the hot water trunk line. From the ¾-in. hot and cold trunks run various ½-in. branch lines that serve fixture groups. Finally, individual risers (supply

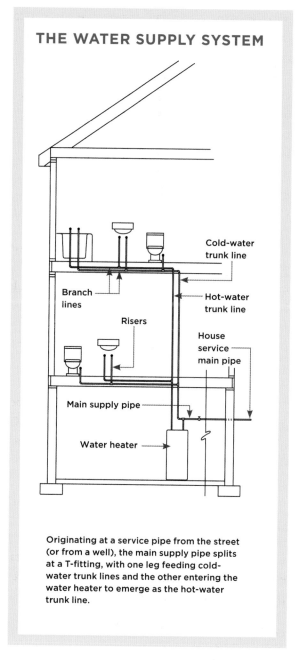

THE WATER SUPPLY SYSTEM

Originating at a service pipe from the street (or from a well), the main supply pipe splits at a T-fitting, with one leg feeding cold-water trunk lines and the other entering the water heater to emerge as the hot-water trunk line.

tubes) run from branch lines to fixtures. Risers are ⅜ in. dia. or ½ in. dia. and connect to fixtures with threaded fittings. By decreasing in diameter as they get farther from the trunk lines, supply pipes help maintain constant water pressure.

NOTE: Because many fixtures supply hot and cold water, hot water and cold water pipes usually run parallel throughout the house. But they should be kept at least 6 in. apart so they don't transfer heat (or cold) to each other; insulating hot water pipes will conserve heat too.

PIPE TYPES. Before the 1950s, supply pipes were usually galvanized steel, joined by threaded fittings, but steel pipes corrode and corrosion constricts flow. (Threaded brass was used less often because it was more expensive.) Consequently, rigid copper piping, which corrodes more slowly, soon replaced galvanized steel. Joined by sweat fitting (soldering), copper was also easier to install and has been the dominant supply piping since the 1950s.

In the 1970s and 1980s, several types of rigid plastic pipes were introduced for indoor water supply, with mixed success. PB (polybutylene) piping was plagued by deterioration and leaks and so was discontinued, PVC is allowed as drainpipe but not as supply, and chlorinated polyvinyl chloride (CVPC) supply pipe is accepted by some building codes and spurned by others. (One suspects a bit of acronym fatigue.)

These days, it looks like King Copper will finally be dethroned by flexible cross-linked polyethylene (PEX) piping. In contrast to the trunk-and-branch distribution common to rigid piping, PEX tubing systems feature a ¾-in. main water line that feeds into a manifold, out of which small supply lines run directly to fixtures. Because it doesn't rely on large pipes to distribute water, PEX delivers hot water quickly to fixtures, saving water and energy. And as copper gets ever more expensive, PEX looks better and better. We talk more about PEX on p. 156.

MORE ABOUT WATER MAINS AND METERS

Most homes get water from a utility company, so here's what inspectors typically encounter. Utility water mains run from the street to the property line for each house, where a curb valve (shutoff valve) controls the supply to the house. If a resident doesn't pay the water bill, the utility shuts the curb valve. The supply pipe that runs from the curb valve to the house—the house service main—is the homeowner's responsibility.

The main water shutoff valve should be in an accessible location so residents can find and shut it off if there is a serious water leak. Single-lever ball valves are much easier to operate than this old twist type, so it would be advisable to replace it.

Water meter locations vary. Some are located in the unpaved area next to the front sidewalk (near the curb valve), whereas others are located in a side yard near where the service pipe enters the house. Most often, however, water meters are located inside the house where the house main emerges, near a foundation wall. (That length of piping is sometimes called the inlet.) Meters measure total consumption, so they are located before the water main branches to become cold and hot water trunk lines.

There should also be a main shutoff valve inside or outside of the house, which enables the resident to shut off water to the whole house should there be a serious leak or the water supply system needs to be worked on.

INSPECTION POINTS

The inspector needs to determine the location, size, composition, and condition of the observable service piping. There may be other devices present, such as pressure regulators or antisyphon valves, which we'll discuss in the next section.

MAIN WATER SHUTOFF VALVES should be accessible so that the water can be turned off quickly in an emergency, and of course, they should be in good working order. In reality, home inspectors must frequently hunt to find inlet pipes or shutoff valves, and when they do, the valves are frequently so encrusted with paint that they can't be turned. Scraping the paint off valve spindles usually frees them but replacing an old valve with a single-lever ball valve is money well spent because the valve opens (and shuts) with a quarter turn.

HOUSE MAINS should be at least ¾ in. inner diameter (I.D.), with 1 in. I.D. desirable. If you use calipers to measure the outside of a 1-in.-I.D. pipe (measure the pipe, not a fitting), you should get a 1¼-in. outer diameter (O.D.) reading. Houses with main pipes less than ¾ in. I.D. will experience reduced flow when several fixtures are used at the same time.

THE TYPE OF PIPE may be difficult to determine if the house main is buried or encrusted with paint. Scrape off a bit of paint to expose the bare pipe,

though take care not to nick it. The house main will most likely be galvanized iron or brass (a magnet can distinguish between the two), copper, or in older homes, lead. Some utilities install plastic piping, which is easily distinguishable from metal pipe once a small area of paint is removed. (Look also where plastic service pipe emerges from the soil, it is usually not painted there.)

PIPE CONDITION is most often revealed by corrosion or leaking at pipe fittings and valves, though badly deteriorated supply pipes may also show pinhole leaks along their lengths. If supply pipes are galvanized steel (50+ years old), it's more or less a given that they should be replaced, especially if rust is widespread and water flow is poor. If supply systems contain both galvanized ~~steel and~~ copper, corrosion will be accelerated even if dielectric unions have been installed where steel pipes meet copper. Dilute copper in the water system will accelerate galvanic action (corrosion) inside the steel pipes and hasten their end.

WHAT TO LOOK FOR

- Is house water supplied by a utility company or a private well? If a private well, a qualified well specialist should check the well equipment and flow rate at the time of purchase. Water quality should also be checked annually by the local health department. Residents can also take a sample and send it to a laboratory for testing.

- If a utility supplies the water, locate the water meter and check for leakage or corrosion.

- Locate the house main and measure its outer diameter. Is the pipe's inner diameter at least ¾ in.? What is the pipe made of?

- If the house main is lead, write it up; it should be replaced. Lead is a known health hazard.

- Locate the main shutoff valve for the house. Is it accessible? Does its handle turn freely so that water can be shut off quickly in an emergency? If the pipe is encrusted with paint and hard to turn, note that on your report.

LEAD SERVICE PIPES

LEAD SERVICE PIPE IS EASILY RECOGNIZABLE because it is soft. When scraped with a metal edge, the exposed pipe surface will be silver gray. Lead pipe joints also have distinctive shapes, as they balloon (bulge) gently. Typically there will be a bulge joint where the lead pipe emerges near the foundation, or where the pipe joins a water meter.

Water-supply systems with lead inlet pipes should be tested by the local health authority; such tests are typically free or low cost. Lead is a neurotoxin, so although lead water pipes may leech minuscule amounts into the water supply, over time the cumulative health effects of drinking lead-tainted water could be serious. So homeowners should have the water analyzed and the lead service pipe should be replaced. Because service pipes are typically the homeowners' responsibility, they often assume replacement costs.

To determine house water pressure, screw a pressure gauge onto an outside faucet and turn the faucet on. Water pressure typically ranges from 40 psi to 80 psi, so this reading is on the high end of normal.

Water pressure regulators are designed to lower excessive pressures that can damage attached fixtures and appliances. Regulators are common where the neighborhood water pressure is over 80 psi.

WATER PRESSURE AND FLOW

While surveying the exterior of the house, check the water pressure by screwing a water pressure gauge onto an outside faucet, then turn the faucet on.

Pressures between 40 psi and 80 psi are in the normal range. Low pressure may be a result of the building's location in relation to the utility's reservoir or because the utility service pipe is constricted. The local utility company can usually be contacted to determine what pressure is provided to a particular street and address.

If the water pressure exceeds 80 psi, a water pressure regulator should be installed to lower the excess pressure, which can damage pipe fittings, valves, fixtures, and appliances. The regulator has an adjustment screw to raise or lower the water pressure. Regulators should be on the house side of the main shutoff valve. Modern regulators should have a sand screen to prevent the regulator from becoming clogged. Such screens require routine cleaning to prevent a reduction in available water flow.

LOW FLOW. Water pressure and water flow are not the same thing. If water pressure is low, the flow will be low, but it is possible to have normal pressure and low flow, usually because of mineral buildup or corrosion inside supply pipes. The mineral content of the water may be a factor in how quickly deposits form inside supply pipes, but more often the key indicator is the pipe material itself.

As was noted earlier, galvanized steel supply piping was widely installed till the 1950s, which, at this writing, was 60 years or 70 years ago. In the best of conditions, that would be the outer limits of galvanized pipe life, so if there is galvanized pipe anywhere in the supply system, it is almost certainly the cause of low flow.

To test water flow, test cold water faucets and hot water faucets separately. Open at least two cold water faucets and flush a toilet at the same time. If piping is constricted, flow from the faucets should decrease dramatically. Make a note if it does. Do the same by opening several hot water faucets and running a hot shower. If hot water flow is dramatically less, the problem may be exacerbated by mineral deposits in the water heater. The effective life of a water heater is 10 years to 15 years in the best of conditions.

To recap, even a small section of constricted pipe can affect the flow to a number of fixtures, so survey as much of the water supply piping as you can, noting not only the type of pipe and its diameter but its condition as well. In addition to corroded galvanized steel piping, kinked copper tubing or too-tight bends can also reduce water flow.

WHAT TO LOOK FOR

- What is the water pressure? If it is between 40 psi and 80 psi, it is within normal range.
- If the pressure is excessive, is there a water pressure regulator on the house side of the main shutoff valve? The regulator could be faulty.
- Is water flow adequate when several faucets are open? Test both cold water and hot water.
- Scan water supply piping for outdated galvanized steel piping, kinked copper tubing, or bends that are tight enough to constrict and reduce water flow.

SURVEYING SUPPLY PIPE

Now that you have determined the water pressure, tested water flow, and identified possible constrictions, survey supply piping throughout the house. Of course, many supply pipes will be hidden in the walls, but by inspecting them where they are visible, you'll get a good sense of what's there, how carefully it was installed, and how much longer it will be serviceable.

This dielectric union has a plastic washer inside to prevent direct contact between the copper and galvanized steel piping. Nonetheless, over time, dilute copper in the water will corrode the steel piping. The only long-term solution is replacing the steep piping.

Crawl spaces, unfinished basements, and attics are good places to inspect supply pipes, as is the top of the water heater, where pipes attach. Cabinets under sinks and lavatories frequently house supply risers and shutoff valves. In older homes, there is frequently an access panel on the back side of a tub's water wall (where pipes are grouped). Access panels are usually small (2 ft. sq.) and frequently tucked into a closet or a hallway; panels are usually held in place by a screw in each corner. Once the panel is removed you can see the head of the tub, an overflow-and-drain assembly, and supply risers that go up to a shower diverter valve.

LOOK FOR SUPPORT. Regardless of the pipe material, supply pipes must be adequately supported. Inadequately supported pipe puts stress on joints and fittings. Horizontal runs of copper supply pipe should be supported at least every 6 ft., but if pipes run perpendicular to joists, plumbers usually secure the pipe every second or third joist. Horizontal runs of CPVC supply pipe should be supported every 3 ft. PEX tubing should be supported every 32 in. on horizontal runs. In most cases, however, eyeballing pipe is sufficient: If pipe runs sag or you can sway pipes by touching them, they need more support.

ONE APPROACH TO IMPROVING FLOW

TO REPAIR MAJOR FLOW RESTRICTION, IT may be necessary to replace all galvanized piping. But homeowners may want to try replacing *some* of the pipes first. It may be sufficient to replace exposed horizontal hot water piping before going to the extra expense of opening up interior walls to replace the vertical piping within them. It may also be cost-effective to install new piping whenever old piping is exposed, such as when new shower walls are installed.

PIPE REPAIRS generally don't last, so leaking or otherwise defective pipes or fittings should be replaced. Occasionally, one sees plastic pipe cement slathered onto a pipe or rubberized patches held on with, say, ring clamps but chances are the pipe still leaks. To get a sense of how long the condition has persisted, look for water damage nearby.

GALVANIZED STEEL PIPE has been discussed at length, so suffice it to say that it's probably time to replace it—all of it. Galvanized pipes tend to fail (rust out or corrode) at fittings first. When galvanized steel is joined to copper pipe, a dielectric union should be used to join the dissimilar metals. But again, dielectric unions just slow the *rate* of corrosion; dilute copper in the water will continue the electrolysis inside the galvanized pipe. When corrosion is far advanced, galvanized steel piping may also rust and split along its lengths.

NOTE: When water pipes are bonded (see p. 138), a copper jumper wire should be clamped to pipe on both sides of the dielectric union to ensure a continuous electrical ground.

COPPER PIPE is very durable, with copper water supply systems expected to last 100 years as long as the water chemistry is favorable. In fact, about the only thing that shortens copper's life is very hard (acidic) water, which can pit the inside of copper pipe and in time produce pinhole leaks. If you observe pinhole leaks and excessive blue-green deposits at fittings, the water should be analyzed. As with most rigid piping, if failure occurs, it is most common at fittings. On occasion, an inspector will observe leaky copper joints with excessive solder—the mark of an inexpert plumber. One or two passes should draw the solder into the joint and create a tight seal; too much solder actually creates a weaker joint. Inspectors in cold regions should scrutinize copper pipes for splits or fractures, especially if a house has been uninhabited and unheated for a while as freezing water can split pipes.

POLYBUTYLENE is a gray plastic water supply pipe widely installed in the United States from 1978 to 1995. Unfortunately, the piping and its fittings

WATER SOFTENERS

THE FUNCTIONALITY OF WATER SOFTENERS or water treatment systems is not typically included in a home inspection. If hard water is common to the area or you see conditions, such as degraded copper supply pipes, that suggest hard-water problems, have the water quality tested to determine if treatment is advisable.

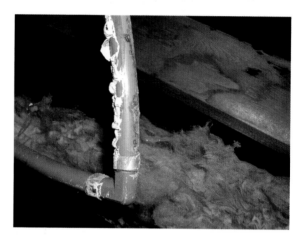

Polybutylene (PB) water supply piping is no longer used because chemicals in water supplies (such as chlorine) cause the piping to deteriorate. Leaking is usually apparent around fittings first. PB piping should be replaced.

deteriorated due to adverse reactions with oxidants in the water supply, such as chorine. The damage took time to become manifest because the deterioration began inside the piping, but eventually the PB became brittle, split, and leaked. If your inspection finds PB piping, prospective buyers should be warned that it will probably need to be replaced. The period for filing PB-related claims has passed.

CPVC SUPPLY PIPE. Most plumbing codes allow CPVC for hot and cold water lines, but check with local authorities to be sure. CPVC is a good choice for hard-water areas, because, unlike copper, CPVC won't be corroded by chemicals in the water.

PEX flexible plastic tubing is becoming more popular because it is easier to install than rigid copper. Shutoff valves are clustered at an accessible manifold installed in a laundry or bathroom wall compartment, rather than in hard-to-access locations beneath individual fixtures.

NOTE: CPVC is a different material from PVC, which is widely used as drain and waste pipe; PVC may not be used as supply pipe, however, because it releases carcinogens.

PEX is a flexible tubing system that's been used in Europe for radiant heating and household plumbing since the 1960s. It wasn't widely used in potable-water systems in North America until the late 1990s. But within 5 years it had captured 7% of the market, even though it was unfamiliar to most plumbers and cost roughly the same as copper. Every year PEX gains a larger share of residential installations, and it is now approved by all major plumbing codes, though not by all states. As PEX tubing, tools, and techniques become more widespread, more and more weekend plumbers will be installing it. And as global prices for copper continue to soar, PEX will become ever more popular.

PEX tubing runs to fixtures from hot and cold water manifolds with multiple takeoffs. Most of the fitting is simple, consisting of crimping steel or copper rings onto tubing ends. Because most leaks occur at joints, fewer fittings also mean fewer leaks.

During your inspection scrutinize the crimped fittings that join tubing to manifold nipples and adaptors to fixtures.

Two things inspectors should note: First, PEX can break down when exposed to direct sunlight (within 30 days to 90 days), so it must be installed and covered quickly. Manifold assemblies are typically located in basement rooms with a door, to minimize exposure to sunlight. Second, although PEX can withstand high water temperatures, it will melt when exposed to open flame. It must not be directly connected to gas- or oil-fired water heaters and must be kept away from flue pipes, recessed lights, and other sources of excessive heat.

WHAT TO LOOK FOR

- Are supply pipes adequately supported?
- Are hot and cold water supply pipes at least 6 in. apart?
- Write up any leaks, corroded pipes, or temporary patches you find. Pipe joints and fittings usually leak first.
- Are supply pipes all the same material or has the supply system been pieced together out of different materials?
- If the supply system contains galvanized steel pipe and copper, do the different pipes connect directly or are dielectric unions used? Are connections corroded? Does a copper jumper wire clamp to both sides of any union to ensure a continuous ground?
- If copper supply pipe shows excessive blue-green deposits around fittings and pinhole leaks elsewhere, hard (acidic) water is probably the cause. Water should be tested.
- If there is rigid plastic supply pipe present, is it a code-approved plastic?
- If PEX piping is used, is it protected from sunlight and UV degradation?
- In cold regions, supply pipes in unheated areas such as crawl spaces and garages may split and leak if water is left in them. Do you see signs of previous leaks or water damage?

Backflow prevention devices are often required when there is a potential hazard for a cross-connection, in which contaminated water could be drawn into the water supply. These devices need periodic maintenance, including removing any trapped debris.

OUTDOOR FAUCETS AND PIPING

Inspectors don't usually spend much time on outdoor supply piping, but faucets and sprinkler systems deserve some time because either can be damaged by freezing temperatures or allow cross-contamination (mixing of potable and contaminated water) if incorrectly detailed.

FREEZE-RESISTANT OUTDOOR FAUCETS

(hose bibs) won't freeze if a resident forgets to drain outdoor water lines before temperatures drop below freezing. Typically, such faucets have a stem that extends into a heated area of the house. The stem slopes downward toward the heated area so it naturally drains, and on the bottom of the stem is a valve that shuts off water flow. Devices vary, but most also have an antisyphon device that screws to the faucet spout. The antisyphon device prevents water from being drawn back into the faucet and freezing, but it also serves the important function of preventing contaminated water from being drawn back through the garden hose, should a drop in water pressure cause a reversal of water flow. Point being, even if the house is in a temperate region, outdoor faucets should at least have an antisyphon device.

UNDERGROUND LAWN SPRINKLER SYSTEMS

should also have antisyphon devices (vacuum breakers) on every water supply line. Because spray heads on sprinkler systems routinely sit at or slightly under ground level, they are frequently immersed in dirty water, which could get fouled by fertilizer or other contaminants. Should a drop in house water pressure reverse the water flow in supply lines, contaminated water could be sucked into supply pipes that contain house drinking water. Vacuum breakers on sprinkler systems must be at least 6 in. above the highest sprinkler head on the system. For convenience, vacuum breakers are usually located next to the house, along a foundation wall.

Inspectors should also survey sprinkler systems for leaks, broken heads, and PVC plastic supply pipe exposed above ground. Sunlight's UV rays degrade PVC plastic, so sprinkler system piping made of PVC should be kept painted or placed entirely underground.

WHAT TO LOOK FOR

- Do outdoor faucets in cold regions have freeze-resistant faucets?

- Do outdoor faucets (in all regions) have antisyphon devices to prevent cross-contamination of the house water supply?

- Does the lawn sprinkler system have an antisyphon device (vacuum breaker) at least 6 in. above the highest sprinkler head on the system?

- Scrutinize lawn sprinkler systems for broken pop-up heads, leaks, and exposed PVC piping.

Water Supply at Fixtures

A home inspector should operate every plumbing fixture because there is a lot of information to be gotten there. The following sections offer a stripped-down list of conditions to look for; for more information about bathroom and kitchen fixtures, see Chapter 12.

WATER FLOW

Turning on hot and cold water at individual fixtures will help you fine-tune your survey of where the supply system is constricted. You may find, for example, that though trunk lines have been upgraded, the risers to individual fixtures were not replaced. Inadequate flow and rust stains on fixture surfaces usually indicate galvanized piping that needs to be replaced. If the water supply comes from a private well, you may find that the flow pulses. If so, the system's pressure tank may be waterlogged (see p. 175).

FIXTURE AND TAP CONDITION

Note fixtures that are stained, chipped, or cracked and taps that are hard to operate or missing parts. Standing water at the base of a faucet handle usually indicates a worn washer; itself an easy repair, but if it has been leaking for a long time, there may be water damage in the cabinet under the lavatory or sink.

STAINS AND DEPOSITS

Blue-green deposits in tubs, lavatories, or the toilet tank or bowl are probably caused by hard (acidic) water dissolving the insides of copper pipes. In time this condition will damage the supply system, so residents should have the water analyzed and, as needed, install an acid-neutralizing filter or water softener on the house main. White deposits on kitchen and bath faucets suggest hard water reacting to metal in the faucets.

DANGER: STEAM ALERT!

IF YOU EVER OBSERVE STEAM—NOT WATER— coming from a faucet or showerhead, leave the faucet open, leave the house *immediately*, and call a plumber from a phone outside the house. Quite likely, the water heater's TPR valve has failed and the unit may be about to explode. This is an extremely dangerous situation.

IS THERE AN AIR GAP?

There should be an air gap between the top of the sink, lavatory, or tub and the opening of the fixture spout. Otherwise, when the fixture is full, the spout would be underwater and back-syphoning could occur. That is, the waste water in the sink or tub could flow back into the water supply system. This is another example of cross-contamination.

WATER HAMMERING

If you turn faucets off suddenly, you may hear a metallic banging or knocking noise, called water hammering. Because water cannot be compressed, when a faucet is suddenly closed, moving water slams against the pipe, which may then hit wood framing. In a well-plumbed house, fixture supply pipes will terminate in air chambers or antiknock coils that cushion the oncoming water. Air hammering is annoying, but is not considered serious. Remedying it, however, can be costly because it means opening the walls, altering pipes, and patching walls.

HOT WATER CONCERNS

At each fixture with a hot water supply, allow the water to run till hot water issues from the tap. If the water from the spigot takes a long time to get hot, supply pipes may be running through an unheated area; insulating the pipes will reduce heat loss. If there is a popping sound when hot water runs, that noise may be caused by pipe support straps that are too tight: as the pipes expand from the heated water, they may snag and then suddenly release.

EXCESSIVELY HOT WATER

Hot water supply that is too hot (or not hot enough) can usually be corrected by adjusting the thermostat on the water heater. Typically, water heaters are set at 120°F. If turning up the thermostat doesn't produce hot enough water, or enough hot water, the unit's anode rod(s) may need replacing, a relatively inexpensive fix.

It is common to find leaky under-sink supply valves and angle stops. This valve and possibly the attached piping need to be replaced; a short threaded brass pipe would be a better wall connection.

ANGLE STOPS

Every fixture supply riser should have an angle stop (shutoff valve). Angle stops are helpful if one needs to repair or renovate a fixture. Because angle stops are not used much they tend to seize up, so many inspectors don't try to see if they work.

WHISTLING TOILETS

If you hear a whistling sound as a toilet refills, the fill valve should be adjusted. Ditto, if water continues to run after the tank is full.

MEANWHILE, UNDER THE SINK

While you're inspecting fixture water supply pipes, have a look at their drains, too. If you see drips, pots to catch drips, makeshift repairs, or nonstandard drain assemblies, you should probe the area for water damage (see also p. 172).

WHAT TO LOOK FOR

- If some fixtures have lower flow than others, note them on your report and try to explain why. If there's a private well, pulsating flow may indicate a waterlogged pressure tank.
- Note stained, chipped, or cracked fixtures and faucets that are hard to turn or missing parts.

- Is there standing water at the base of faucet handles after operating them? Any signs of water damage in cabinets below?
- Is there an air gap between the top of every fixture and the opening of its spout?
- Do supply pipes hammer when you close faucets suddenly?
- Does it take a long time for hot water to reach some faucets? Are hot water pipes insulated?
- How hot does the water get at each faucet?
- Is there an angle stop for each supply riser?
- Do toilets whistle while they work? Does water continue to run after the tank has filled?

Water Heaters

In most homes, a tank-type water heater produces hot water for bathing, laundry, and other household uses; though tankless water heaters are becoming more common. We should note from the onset that water heated to 120°F is adequate for most tasks. Setting a water heater thermostat higher, say, to 140°F, risks scalding users, wastes energy, and shortens the life of the unit. (Dishwashers have integral heating elements that boost water temperatures *inside the unit* for more effective cleaning.)

HOW LONG WILL IT LAST?

How long a water heater will last depends on several factors, including its type—electric, gas, or oil—how long it has been in service, how high it has been set, how well it has been maintained, and what the water conditions are.

LONGEVITY BY TYPE. On average, electric water heaters last longer (10 years to 15 years) because their heating elements are immersed in the water being heated, whereas oil- and gas-fired units apply flame to the bottom of a tank and thus heat the water inside by conduction. Open flame is hard on metal because it expands each time it is heated and contracts each time it cools. So oil- and gas-fired units often get only 8 years to 10 years before they start leaking. The actual lifespan depends much more on the amount of use and maintenance effectiveness than on a particular unit's age in years.

HOW OLD IS IT? Once you know how long the unit should last, find out when it was installed. A stamped metal data plate atop the water heater typically contains the capacity of the unit, a serial number, and a date of manufacture. The date of manufacture is not always obvious: It may be stated clearly or may be part of a serial number (0499, for example, may indicate that it was made in April 1999). A plumbing parts supplier may be able to explain the code or you can contact the manufacturer directly. The actual date of installation is trickier because the unit may have sat in a distributor's warehouse for a year or two. Ask the homeowner for installation records. Installing a water heater usually requires a permit, so the local building department may also have a record, if a permit was pulled.

WHAT'S THE THERMOSTAT SETTING? As we noted, running a water heater at higher temperatures can shorten its life. So read the thermostat setting. If it's 140°F or above (!), it may have been compromised. Granted, its current setting may not have been what it was set at for most of its operating life, but a higher setting suggests either that the unit has been cooked or that its setting has been boosted recently because it is not delivering hot enough water.

WATER CONDITIONS. Hard (acidic) water tends to shorten the life of water heaters. Typically, water heaters contain anode rods that react with minerals in the water, so that corrosion accretes to (builds up on) the rods rather than to the tank lining. If a middle-aged water heater is not recovering fast enough or generating enough hot water, replacing the anode rod(s) usually does the trick.

SEDIMENT BUILDUP. In time, mineral deposits and sediment will build up in the bottom of a tank. In gas- and oil-fired units, solid matter in the bottom of the tank acts as an insulator between the open flame and the water, which wastes energy because the water takes longer to heat. This sediment accumulation can also lead to premature leakage and failure as it causes the base of the tank to overheat. When an older water heater fires up, an inspector will sometimes hear the tank rumbling. It's nothing to fear but is a definite

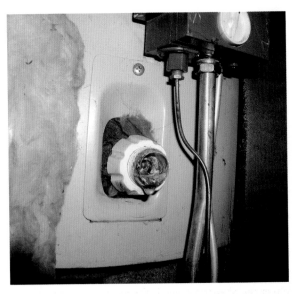

Storage-type water heaters usually have a drain valve that should be opened periodically to remove deposits that collect in the bottom of the tank. Deposits can cause overheating above the flame and shorten the useful life of the water heater.

sign that there's a lot of sediment in the bottom of the tank.

Draining the tank periodically reduces sediment, but eventually deposits harden. Ideally, water heaters should be drained annually. Owners should attach a garden house to the valve near the bottom of the tank, turn off the water supply, and then open the valve until the water runs clear.

It is not unusual to find a sheet metal pan beneath the water heater to collect any leakage from the tank or the TPR valves. Such pans should have drain piping that leads to an approved drainage location. It is a good idea to install a moisture sensing alarm in the pan or on the floor near the water heater to notify occupants of any water leakage or TPR discharge.

WHAT TO LOOK FOR

- What type of water heater is it? What is the Btu capacity of the unit? How many gallons?
- Find out when the unit was installed, either from homeowner records or code permit or by adding a year or two to the manufacture data on the data plate.

- What is the thermostat setting?
- What are the prevailing water conditions in the area?
- You may want to drain a bit of water from the tank: Is it clear or turbid? Does the tank rumble when the burner kicks on? Draining water can cause the valve to drip afterward. It's a good idea to carry a few small threaded caps for use if a valve leaks after use.

TPR VALVE

All water heaters must have a TPR valve to protect residents from a tank that could explode. If the thermostat fails and the energy source stays on, the water temperature and pressure will continue to rise. When the pressure exceeds the capacity of the tank, around 300 psi, the tank bursts and the superheated water flashes to steam with explosive force. The steam expands to over 1,600 times the volume of the liquid water and turns the water heater into an unguided missile. Exploding heaters have been known to reach heights of 500 ft. and lift houses off their foundations.

SENSOR PROBE. Each TPR valve has a sensor probe that should extend into the top 6 in. of water in the tank. In other words, the threaded body of the valve must screw directly into the tank. A TPR valve should *not* be mounted above the tank (as shown in the right photo below) or installed in either the hot water outlet pipe or the cold water inlet pipe. Even if the valve is in good working order, it cannot offer full protection from an incorrect location because the probe cannot sense the hottest water in the tank.

DISCHARGE PIPE. To avoid scalding someone standing near the tank should a TPR valve open, a discharge pipe attached to the valve should terminate not more than 6 in. above the floor. The discharge pipe must be *rigid* piping with the same diameter (at least ¾ in.) as the valve. (A smaller pipe may not allow pressure to discharge quickly enough.) There should be a pan or bucket beneath the opening of the pipe so that the resident can see the discharged water. When a TPR valve discharges, it indicates a condition (such as excess pressure or too high temperatures) that needs to be checked. If discharge water empties down a drain or a utility sink, the resident won't know about the potential problem and could be burned by a high-pressure steam discharge.

All water heaters must have a TPR valve. The valve's sensor probe must extend into the top 6 in. of water in the tank, where the water is hottest.

The TPR valve at the left has a temperature probe below that should extend into the top of the water heater tank. Mounting the valve well above the tank as it is here will cause it to malfunction and not release under excessively hot water conditions.

SUPPLEMENTAL EXPANSION TANKS

THE PROBLEM OF A TPR VALVE LEAKING because of relatively minor fluctuations in water heater tank pressure can be solved by adding a water expansion tank. Required for new installations in some areas, expansion tanks are designed to absorb the increased volume of water created by thermal expansion; such tanks also help maintain a balanced pressure throughout the water supply system. They prevent plumbing system and/or water heater damage and unnecessary TPR valve discharge.

TPR discharge piping should be at least ¾ in. in diameter. Outdated copper tubing such as this should be replaced.

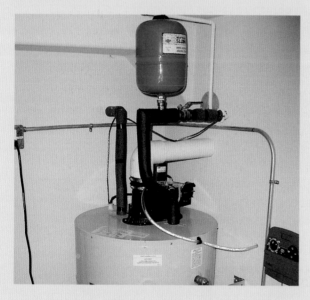

This modern high-efficiency water heater uses a power vent to exhaust fumes through the PVC plastic flue pipe.

DISCHARGE DOWN! The TPR valve opening and its discharge pipe must slope downward. A valve installed pointing up could fill with standing water, causing it to malfunction. If the water heater experienced excessively high pressure or temperature, it could explode.

LEAKY TPR VALVE. Another benefit of having a pan or bucket under the discharge valve is observing valve leakage. In general, leaking TPR valves may be

defective and should be replaced. But leaks may also result from minor spikes in tank pressure as when barometric pressures are low. In time, minor leaks can allow debris in the water to keep the valve from closing fully. The experts offer conflicting advice: Some favor opening the valve periodically to flush out debris and others advise replacing any valve that leaks for whatever reason.

ANOTHER CHOICE. The Watts® 210 valve, an alternative to the standard TPR valve, is common in areas where there is no convenient downslope drain location, needed with TPR valves. The Watts 210 valve has a temperature probe at the water heater and a water discharge at the building exterior, typically near a hose faucet. Check local codes to be sure Watts valves are compliant.

WHAT TO LOOK FOR

- Is the TPR valve's sensor probe immersed in the top 6 in. of the tank? If the valve is incorrectly installed, the water heater is not protected.
- Does the TPR valve have discharge piping? Does the discharge valve piping terminate within 6 in. of the floor?
- Is there a pan or bucket under the discharge valve so that leaks or discharged water will be visible to the resident?

- Does the discharge piping slope downward so there can be no standing water in the pipe or the valve?
- Is the TPR valve leaking? (Look for water in the discharge-pipe container or touch a finger to the bottom of the pipe to see if there's water.)

FLUE PIPES AND VENTING

Oil- and gas-fired water heaters need flue pipes to vent combustion gases safely out of the house; electric heaters do not need flue pipes. To see if an oil- or gas-fired water heater is operating correctly and flue pipes are venting properly, open a hot-water faucet and let the water run till the burner ignites. If the water heater's burner does not ignite within 5 minutes or 6 minutes, something's wrong. Shut the faucet and have a qualified plumber inspect the unit.

FLUE PIPES MUST BE INTACT and single-wall-type pipe connections securely joined with screws. Split or separated pipe sections can allow exhaust gases to escape. Exhaust gases typically contain several toxic gases including carbon monoxide, which is odorless and extremely poisonous. If a flue pipe terminates in a masonry chimney, there should be no gaps where exhaust gases could leak. If you see dark water stains or creosote-like stains on the outside of the flue pipe, the chimney may need a chimney cap (see p. 210) to keep rain from running down the inside of the chimney.

FLUE PIPING SHOULD SLOPE UPWARD so that heated uncombusted gases can rise naturally and exit. Piping should be supported every 4 ft. and maintain a minimum ¼ in. per 1 ft. upward slope. Because combustion gases also contain water vapor, water could condense and rust out pipe sections that sag or don't slope up. The slope must be continuous, that is.

NOTE: Some newer, high-efficiency water heaters use fans to exhaust fumes through PVC plastic flue pipe; these powered vent pipes may not need to slope up. Check the manufacturer's installation specifics.

METAL FLUE PIPE GETS HOT so maintain safe distances from combustible materials. If single-wall metal flue piping is used, there should be a minimum 6 in. between the flue pipe and wood framing. Ideally, the flue should be upgraded to double-wall, Type B flue piping. Where a metal flue pipe exits an exterior wall, it should do so with a double-wall, insulated wall-adaptor (aka thimble). On your inspection report, note any scorched wood near any flue pipe(s).

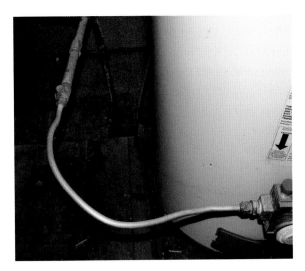

Small-diameter aluminum tubing is not suitable for water heater gas supplies; it should be replaced with ¾-in. flexible gas connector. For more information about gas piping, see Chapter 8.

IS THE CHIMNEY CLEAR?

THOUGH IT'S NOT A ROUTINE INSPECTION task, an inspector may want to remove the vent thimble, where the vent pipe inserts into a masonry chimney. (Turn the water heater off first.) Use a flashlight and mirror to check the chimney interior. All manner of debris can accumulate in the bottom of a chimney—from soot to nests—and that debris can block a chimney, hamper draft, and possibly force carbon monoxide into living areas. The National Fire Protection Association suggests annual chimney and flue inspections—or whenever a fuel-burning appliance is vented into a chimney. The Chimney Safety Institute of America (www.csia.org) offers a state-by-state listing of chimney services with certified staff.

When a new water heater is installed the old flue draft diverter should be removed. Here a double diverter has caused the spillage of superheated flue gases. The (melted) black foam insulation on the cold water heater supply is not necessary and should be removed.

Rusting at the base of this water heater indicates poor venting of flue gases. This water heater is near the end of its useful life and should be replaced.

CHECK THE DRAFT. After the burner fires for a few minutes, hold your hand 4 in. to 6 in. away from the draft diverter. If there is a decent draft, you won't feel much: perhaps a flow of air toward the diverter, but not hot air. If, however, you feel hot exhaust on your hand, the flue may be blocked or there may be negative pressure in the house, also known as backdrafting, in which exhaust gases are pulled back into living spaces.

In older houses, the most common cause of backdrafting is a water heater that is housed in a laundry room with an exhaust fan and/or a clothes dryer. The draft of the fans creates a negative pressure (a partial vacuum) in the room, which sucks exhaust air back down the flue. If this condition has existed for a while, you may see rust stains on water heater pipes near the diverter. One possible fix is moving the water heater to a separate room.

Backdrafting may also be a cause of a water heater's rusted-out bottom, as shown in the right photo above. Water vapor not being vented is collecting near the water heater and being drawn into the burner area.

SCORCH MARKS on the bottom of a gas-fired water heater are an example of flame rollout, in which flames flare outside the burner area. The most common cause of rollout is a missing access cover, although a specialist should check the adjustment of the pilot light and check to be sure the unit has adequate fresh air for robust combustion. Note any combustibles stored near an oil- or gas-fired water heater; they should be moved well away from the area.

WHAT TO LOOK FOR

- Run hot water till the water heater burner kicks in. If it doesn't ignite within 5 minutes or 6 minutes, shut off the unit and have a plumber check it.

- Is the water heater flue pipe intact along its length? Is it free from rust, splits, and separations? Are sections screwed together?

- If the flue pipe terminates in a masonry chimney, does the pipe fit tightly to the chimney thimble or are there gaps? Are there dark water stains, rust, or creosote leakage on the flue pipe? Gently pull the pipe from the chimney thimble and examine the chimney for signs of blockage.

- Does the flue pipe slope upward? Is it supported at least every 4 ft.?
- Is the metal flue pipe single wall or, preferably, Type B double wall? Is there at least 6 in. between single-walled metal flue pipe and combustible surfaces such as wall or floor framing? If double-wall flue pipe, is there at least 1-in. clearance?
- If the flue pipe vents directly through an exterior wall, does it do so through a proper wall adaptor? Is any of the framing near the flue pipe or wall adaptor scorched?
- Is there a draft diverter atop an oil- or gas-fired water heater?
- After running the unit's burner for a few minutes, do exhaust gases vent properly? Or are there fuel fumes, a weak draft, or other signs of possible backdrafting?
- Does the water heater share a room with a clothes dryer or other vented appliances?
- Are there rust marks or scorch marks near the bottom of the water heater?
- Are combustibles stored near an oil- or gas-fired water heater? They should be moved.
- Insulating blankets should be removed from water heaters. They trap moisture and may interfere with flue drafting.
- If the water heater is in a seismic region, is it strapped to framing?

WATER HEATER SUPPLY PIPE ISSUES

Here are a few supply pipe–related issues you may encounter when inspecting a water heater.

REVERSED WATER LINES. Openings in the top of most water heaters have cold or hot stamped next to respective openings for cold water inlet pipes and hot water outlet pipes. It's all pretty straightforward, but inattentive plumbers frequently reverse the lines. Attaching supply pipes correctly matters because inside the water heater are dip tubes of different lengths. The cold water dip tube empties near the bottom of the tank, so that as the water is heated it rises in the tank, to exit through a shorter dip tube near the top of the tank.

Reverse the supply pipes and cold water will enter the top of the tank, mix with somewhat heated water,

REMOVE INSULATING BLANKETS

INSULATING BLANKETS, VERY POPULAR during periodic energy crises, are now prohibited by many water heater manufacturers because they can retain moisture and cause rust. Covering the top of a water heater was never a wise idea because it obstructs the flow of air into the draft diverter and blocks proper venting of flue gases. All such blankets should be removed and the water heater checked for excessive rust and proper venting.

Insulating blankets should be removed and the unit checked for rust.

and exit (incorrectly) through a dip tube at the bottom of the tank. So when a resident opens a hot water faucet, the water that flows out isn't very hot. In response, the resident increases the heater thermostat setting, which wastes yet more fuel and shortens the life of the water heater.

It's pretty easy to detect reversed water pipes at the water heater by touching the hot water supply pipe. It won't be very hot. (Touch both outlet and inlet pipe

PIPE INSULATION on hot water pipes will keep heat from dissipating, especially if they pass through unheated areas or feed distant fixtures. Thus hot water will get there quicker. Pipe insulation will melt if too close to flue pipes or the diverter, so install pipe insulation a safe distance above, and away from, such hot venting elements.

WHAT TO LOOK FOR

- Are faucet water temperatures considerably lower than the thermostat setting on the water heater? Check the hot and cold openings atop the unit: Perhaps inlet and outlet pipes have been reversed.

- Inlet and outlet pipes that attach to the water heater should be flexible piping, not rigid.

- If water from an electric heater isn't very hot, check the breaker that controls the unit first, then the high-limit switch near the water heater. Then suspect a failed heating element or a temperature sensor.

- If hot water smells like rotten eggs, bacteria have reacted with the anode rod. The rod should be replaced and the water heater flushed with bactericide.

- Are hot water pipes insulated? Is any of the foam insulation above the water heater melted?

TANKLESS WATER HEATERS

Tankless water heaters, also known as on-demand, instant, or flash water heaters, don't have storage tanks for heated water. When someone opens a hot-water faucet and water begins to flow through a tankless heater, a flow sensor ignites the unit's burner and a heat exchanger honeycombed with coiled water pipes heats up almost instantaneously. When the faucet or shower valve shuts off and the water stops flowing, the sensor shuts off the burner.

Tankless water heaters are generally more complicated and more expensive to install than a traditional tank heater but, on the whole, less expensive to operate because there's no energy wasted keeping a tankful of water hot round the clock. In other words, tankless water heaters consume energy only when

fittings for comparison.) To be more exacting, compare the thermostat setting to the temperature of hot water coming from a nearby faucet. Especially if the water heater is new, you've discovered the problem.

RIGID INLET AND OUTLET PIPES are a code violation in some regions. Flex water piping will resist breaking in the event of an earthquake. By the way, leaky fittings atop a water heater are not unusual and can be a serious problem. A plumber should tighten or replace the fittings, and the resident should monitor the fittings periodically

WATER NOT HOT: ELECTRIC UNIT. First make sure the water heater breaker has not tripped, check for reversed supply lines, then have a plumber assess the heating elements and temperature sensor to see if either has failed. Frequently the cause is a power failure or a high-limit switch near the water heater that has tripped.

HOT WATER THAT SMELLS LIKE ROTTEN EGGS is usually caused by bacteria in the water reacting with an anode rod in the water heater. This condition is more likely to happen in a home with a private well, but it has become less common. The tank should be flushed with a bactericide such as bleach, drained thoroughly, refilled, and retested. The anode rod should be replaced.

Tankless water heaters consume energy only when hot water is needed—that is, when a hot-water faucet or shower valve is opened. Gas-fired units must be located where a vent can be run to the outside.

hot water is needed. About the size of a suitcase, tankless units are a great favorite when space is tight, too. They are typically wall mounted.

Their other great draw is that properly sized tankless units never run out of hot water. (Endless hot water is not free, of course.) As a rule of thumb, a tankless unit with 140,000-Btu input will suffice for a one-bath home with one or two users; a 190,000-Btu input should do for a two-bath home with two to four people.

Because tankless heaters are technologically complicated yet compact, there's not a lot to inspect. In fact, a plumber trained in tankless technology should inspect the unit periodically. If the unit is gas fired, it must be located where a vent can be run to the outside. Depending on the type, tankless water heaters may have separate intake and exhaust pipes, whereas others will have a single concentric direct-vent pipe—a pipe within a pipe—to supply fresh air and exhaust combustion gas. The pipe will have an optimal pitch to carry off combustion condensation, which the manufacturer will specify. If hard-water conditions exist, the unit should be flushed regularly to prevent mineral buildup on the heat exchanger.

WHAT TO LOOK FOR

- What's the Btu rating of the tankless water heater?
- If the unit is gas fired, is it located so it can vent easily to the outside?
- Does the tankless water heater have separate intake and outtake pipes or a single concentric direct-vent pipe? If the latter, does the pipe slope meet manufacturer recommendations?
- If the house has hard water, is the unit regularly flushed to prevent mineral buildup?

DWV pipes

The DWV system carries wastes and sewage gases away from the house. Every fixture has a drain trap designed to remain filled with water after the fixture empties. This residual water keeps sewage gases from rising into living spaces. (Toilets have integral traps.) As trap arms leave individual fixtures, they empty into branch drains or directly into a soil stack, which, at its base, turns and becomes the main drain. The main drain then discharges into a city sewer main or a septic tank.

Drainpipes also may be differentiated according to the wastes they carry: soil pipes and soil stacks carry fecal matter and urine, whereas waste pipes carry waste water but not soil. Stacks are generally vertical pipes, although they may jog slightly to avoid obstacles.

VENTING SPECIFICS

Venting is the V in DWV. Without venting, wastes would either not fall at all or, in falling, would suck the water out of fixture traps, allowing sewage gases to enter living spaces. Vents admit an amount of air equal to that displaced by the falling water. Thus every fixture must be vented. In most cases, the trap arm exits into a tee fitting whose bottom leg is a branch drain and whose upper leg is a branch vent.

THE DRAIN, WASTE, AND VENT SYSTEM

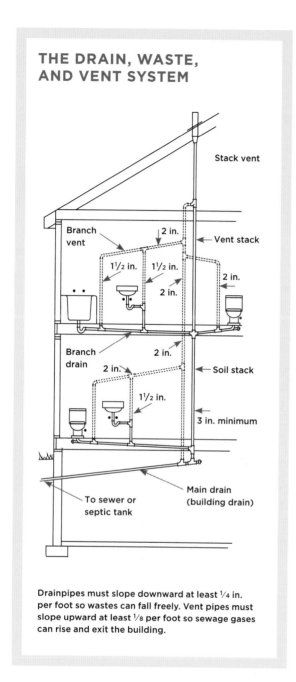

Drainpipes must slope downward at least 1/4 in. per foot so wastes can fall freely. Vent pipes must slope upward at least 1/8 per foot so sewage gases can rise and exit the building.

A DRAIN TRAP

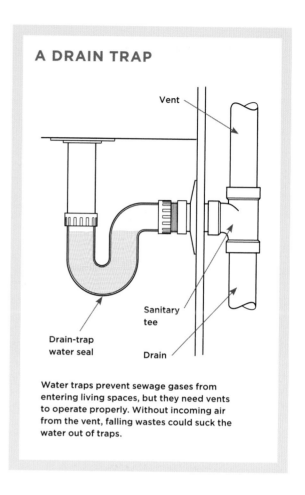

Water traps prevent sewage gases from entering living spaces, but they need vents to operate properly. Without incoming air from the vent, falling wastes could suck the water out of traps.

from entering the house, vents must terminate at least 3 ft. above an operable window or a minimum of 10 ft. horizontal distance from an operable window at the same level.

As you inspect the exterior of a house, scan the roof for plumbing vent stacks. If you don't see at least one, either the stack(s) terminates in the attic—a code violation—or the DWV system is not properly vented.

DRAINPIPES

DWV pipes may be of any number of materials. An older house may have drain and vent pipes with sections of cast iron, galvanized steel, copper, or plastic. DWV pipes installed these days are mostly plastic: white PVC or black acrylonitrile butadiene styrene (ABS). No-hub couplings (also known as hubless connectors) are the fitting most often used to join different DWV pipes; their inner neoprene sleeves

Branch vents continue upward, often joining other fixture vents, until they join a vent stack, which exits through the roof.

Because vents must admit enough air to offset that displaced by falling water, vents are approximately the same size as their companion drains. Branch vents and drains are usually 1½-in. or 2-in. pipes, and main stacks and drains are 3-in. pipes. To keep septic gases

VENT TERMINATION

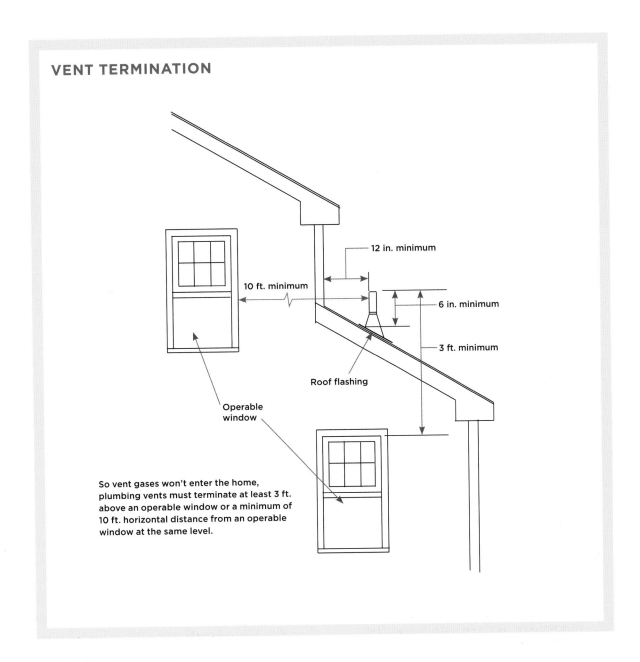

12 in. minimum

10 ft. minimum

6 in. minimum

3 ft. minimum

Roof flashing

Operable window

So vent gases won't enter the home, plumbing vents must terminate at least 3 ft. above an operable window or a minimum of 10 ft. horizontal distance from an operable window at the same level.

seal junctions tightly when their outer band clamps are snugged down.

Drainpipes must slope downward (fall) at least 1/4 in. per foot so that waste will be carried out; whereas vent pipes typically slope upward a minimum of 1/8 in. per foot. All pipes need to be properly supported. The general rule is that plastic DWV pipe must be supported every 4 ft., cast iron every 5 ft. and at least within 18 in. of each hub, threaded steel-cast iron every 12 ft., and copper piping 1 1/2 in. or larger at 10-ft.

intervals. Note any missing or broken pipe supports in your inspection report as well as pipe sections that lack adequate downward slope. When metal strapping is used to support plastic piping, the piping should be insulated from the strapping to protect it from abrasion and damage.

If at any point you see larger-diameter drainpipes emptying into smaller ones, write it up. The smaller pipe sections need to be replaced to avoid blockage in the lines.

Small pinhole leaks are common in older cast-iron waste piping. Piping such as this should be checked periodically and replaced if leaks are found.

All piping needs to be properly supported. ABS plastic needs support every 4 ft., cast iron every 5 ft. and at least within 18 in. of each hub, threaded steel-cast piping systems every 12 ft., and copper piping 1½ in. or larger in diameter should be supported at 10-ft. intervals. This pipe is sagging because it is inadequately supported.

OLD SEWER PIPING

CLAY TILE PIPING WAS USED IN MANY OLDER waste systems between the building and main sewer. These pipes, called sewer laterals, are buried in the ground and not accessible to inspection. Clay pipes are easily damaged and can be blocked by tree roots, or may crack from soil movement, causing sewage to back up into house fixtures. Older cast-iron or steel waste piping is susceptible to rusting and may also need replacement. If possible, determine if there is any history of clogged drains or waste system repairs. Older sewer laterals should eventually be replaced. Prospective home buyers should have sewer laterals examined for defects by a qualified plumber using special video equipment designed for this purpose.

INSPECTING DWV PIPES

Large drains can usually be inspected in crawl spaces or unfinished basements. Obviously, in houses with finished basements or houses built on slabs there won't be much to see; so your DWV inspection will be confined to attics (if any) and cabinets under sinks and lavatories.

FILL, FLUSH, DRAIN, REPEAT. Inspecting DWV pipes is pretty straightforward. Run the water in a sink, lavatory, or tub and see if it drains quickly and completely. For sinks and lavatories, look at traps and drainpipes in the cabinet underneath for wetness or leaking. In addition to looking, listen, and smell. A draining fixture should not cause gurgling in an adjacent fixture, nor should flushing or draining one fixture suck the water out of another fixture's trap. Both symptoms are signs of clogged, undersize, or missing vents. Waste and drainage systems should be airtight, so have a plumber investigate persistent sewage smells.

DWV PIPE CONDITION. DWV pipes should be airtight and free of gaps, cracks, and leaks. Fittings tend to be the most vulnerable points along any system, so inspect them carefully for cracks, leaks, or smells. Surface rust is acceptable on cast-iron pipe, but pinholes and leaking or corroded fixtures are not; they should be replaced.

Rigid plastic DWV pipe is durable if it is correctly installed and supported. The most common causes of plastic pipe leaks are insufficiently cemented fittings, followed by cracks due to inadequate supports. However, defective ABS rigid plastic pipe installed as DWV lines from 1984 to 1990 resulted in a major class-action settlement. Defective ABS pipe tended to crack around its circumference, especially near

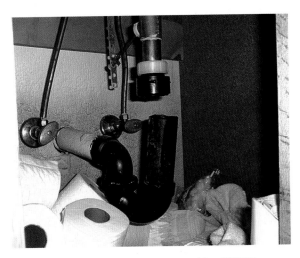

Defective ABS rigid plastic pipe used for DWV lines was subject to a major class action settlement in the 1980s. As is shown here, ABS pipes were breaking near the joints, causing leaks and damage. The cause was identified as a production issue; settlement money for these defects is no longer available.

joints. The cause of the failure was a production issue (poor quality); settlement money for damages is no longer available.

NOTE: PVC and ABS piping must be cemented with the adhesive specified for each pipe type. In other words, one may not use PVC cement to join ABS pipes. If you see black ABS fittings slathered with whitish PVC cement, scrutinize it for leaks and write it up.

DWV PIPE REPAIRS. To ensure that DWV systems are airtight, damaged pipes cannot be repaired, only replaced. If you see repair materials clamped, glued, or puttied into fittings or along pipe lengths, they should be replaced as soon as possible to avoid leaks.

WATER STAINS, WETNESS, OR ROT BELOW. Water-stained or wet subflooring and framing below fixtures should be inspected to see if there is active leaking or sewage odors. Damaged materials should be replaced, especially below tubs or toilets, so that these weighty fixtures are adequately supported. When inspecting toilets, try to gently rock the toilet base to see if it is well supported; there should be no movement.

WHEN A HOUSE IS DOWNHILL FROM A municipal sewer main, or a basement toilet is below the main house drain, it's sometimes necessary to pump wastes *up* to the main sewer drain. Pumping wastes uphill requires a sewage ejection system with a tank, pump, air vent, and various controls or valves. Because the tank is typically installed below the basement floor, all an inspector can see is a gasketed tank cover with discharge and vent pipes rising out of it. There should be no leaks or smell around the unit.

The sewage ejector discharge piping that runs uphill should not connect to upper-level waste piping horizontally but should be located above it, so the waste water flows down into the piping system by gravity in order to prevent any pressurization of the waste piping by the ejector pump. Ejector pump systems are reliable, so an inspector is usually most concerned with how noisy the system is because that may be a big concern to a house buyer. So flush a toilet or two till the sewage ejector pump starts.

When the main sewer piping system runs above a house, it's sometimes necessary to use a sewage ejector with a tank, pump, and air vent to properly drain lower level bathroom fixtures. The discharge piping should terminate above the main waste piping and then flow downward to prevent any pressurization of the waste piping system. When buying or inspecting a home, always run enough water into the tank to cause the pump to operate.

Repairs such as these are only temporary; defective sections and fittings need to be replaced.

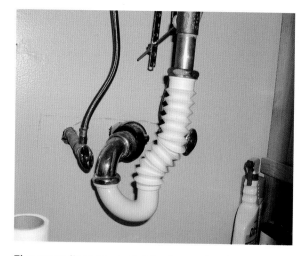

Flex waste lines are available at many hardware stores but do not comply with most modern plumbing codes, which specify that only smooth wall piping is suitable in a drain line.

INSPECTING FIXTURE TRAPS

A trap is a U-shaped drain section required on all plumbing fixtures except toilets. The trap holds water to block sewer gas, which otherwise could flow up from the main sewer piping into the building. Sewer gas (methane) may have an odor or it may be odorless; it can be explosive. If a trap is not properly installed, the water can be siphoned out and sewer gas may enter living spaces. The horizontal pipe or arm should flow downward at a gentle slope (¼ in. per foot) to the vertical drain–vent connection.

Look for the following fixture trap and drain conditions during your inspection.

A BUCKET UNDER A SINK TRAP. A leak that no one bothered to fix. Most likely, trap fittings need to be tightened or washers replaced. Check the sink drain stems, too. If you see wrench marks on fittings, this is a long-term problem.

TWO SINKS, TWO TRAPS. Two adjacent sinks should empty into only one trap. This is a common problem beneath kitchen sinks with two basins; having two traps means that both will function poorly when they drain. Only a single U-shaped trap is permitted below bath and kitchen sinks.

FLEX WASTE LINES are available in many hardware stores but they do not meet most plumbing codes, which specify that only smooth piping is suitable in a drain line. While technically incorrect, they are cheaper and easier to install and usual function well, till they clog.

HIGH WASTE-OUTFLOW PIPE. Waste-outflow pipes must be lower than the flood level of the attached trap. The outflow shown in the top left photo on the facing page is problematic because it is higher than the garbage disposal trap. This configuration would cause waste water to stand inside the disposer and perhaps spray upward into the kitchen sink. Adding a disposer to an older kitchen sink with a high waste outflow often causes this problem. The only sure fix is opening the wall and installing a new, lower sanitary tee or removing the disposer entirely.

SEWER ODOR AT CLOTHES WASHER DRAIN OVERFLOW. The plumber may have forgotten to install a trap. Clothes washer drains (stand pipes) should be located so the trap is between 6 in. and 18 in. above the floor, and the vertical pipe 18 in. to 42 in. above the trap. The piping itself should be larger in diameter than the washer drain; newer clothes washers need a 2-in. drain. If an older clothes washer drain overflows, the drain is probably undersize or clogged.

The upper right (horizontal) drainpipe needs to be lower than the flood level in the attached trap. This configuration will allow waste water to stand inside the disposer and perhaps cause drain water to spray upward into the kitchen sink.

This modern air-admittance valve acts as a vent, allowing air to flow into the waste piping system. Such valves are useful in attics, in subfloor areas, and below island-cabinet sinks.

This is a classic S-trap, which has no vent to prevent siphoning waste water out of the trap. Thus sewage gases could rise into living spaces.

PUTTIED TRAP OR DRAIN JOINTS. Using putty to repair leaks is not approved and will leak soon. It's better to remove all pipe sections and install proper washers and fittings or even new piping.

AIR-ADMITTANCE VALVES ARE OK. Modern air-admittance valves are a mechanical way to vent inaccessible drains, which most codes now allow. Air-admittance valves are particularly useful in subfloor areas, below island-cabinet sinks, and in attics where vent piping does not need to penetrate the roofing system.

WHAT TO LOOK FOR

- When inspecting the house exterior, scan the roof for vent stacks. Do they terminate at least 3 ft. above operable windows?

- What are drainpipes made of? What is their general condition? Look for pinholes, cracks, and leaks, especially where pipes join fittings.

- Does every fixture (except toilets) have a drain trap?

- Run water in fixtures and note any whose traps or drains leak. Does it look like the leak has existed for a while? Look for water stains or damage in cabinets under sinks and lavatories.

- Do all drainpipes slope downward at least ¼ in. per foot? Are pipes adequately supported or do some sections sag?

- Note wherever you see larger-diameter drainpipes emptying into smaller ones.

- Note pipe repairs; faulty fittings or pipe sections must be replaced.

- Note flexible waste lines used instead of traps; they should be replaced.

- Is there a sewage smell where a clothes-washer drain feeds into a laundry standpipe?

Private Wells and Septic Systems

Private (on-site) wells and septic systems need a bit of land, so they are usually located in rural or suburban areas.

PRIVATE WELLS

Private wells (also called freshwater or groundwater wells) serve different needs. In rural areas they primarily provide drinking water and/or irrigation for crops. In suburban locales private wells typically supply water for lawns and gardens, as a backup during droughts. The first, best advice to give anyone interested in buying a property with a private well is to get the water tested. Water quality matters even when wells are used to water lawns; for example, children often play or drink from lawn sprinklers. Wells that provide drinking water or other critical uses should also be checked to see how deep they are and what the flow rate is in dry weather.

Both shallow wells (less than 25 ft. below the surface) and deep wells (more than 25 ft.) can become contaminated and either will be expensive to replace because that means drilling a new well. Moreover, if the contaminants are chemical pollutants in the aquifer (subterranean rock layers where groundwater collects), there's not a lot that can be done short term.

Public-health and water-quality authorities in the area should have reports of regional water pollution, including maps of affected areas. A Google™ search of Internet articles may yield more recent information on the problem though, of course, the science behind that plethora of materials will vary considerably. "Consider the source," as the saying goes.

A home inspector should ask homeowners for water-testing reports. Beyond that, you can't tell a lot from a glass of tap water. It may taste OK, be clear and odorless, and still be polluted. (Many pollutants are odorless and colorless, especially when diluted in a vast aquifer.) On the other hand, if the water stinks, is turbid (cloudy), or tastes bad, note that in your inspection report. Shallow wells are more prone to show such conditions, especially in wet months when the ground around a shallow well becomes sodden;

This well appears relatively new. It is fairly common to have the starter and motor completely exposed, at least in areas where snow isn't going to interfere. As long as the motor and other enclosures are NEMA 3 and the wiring is suitable for wet locations, it isn't a problem.

then rotted leaves and, say, drowned earthworms can lend a distinctive tang to potable water. Shallow-well conditions may clear up on their own or may need inexpensive intervention such as flushing the cistern, but in any event, the homeowner should have the water tested.

Three basic pump types service private wells: jet, piston, and submersible. Any of these can be used in shallow or deep wells. In practice, jet or piston pumps are usually situated atop shallow wells, and submersibles immersed in deep wells.

JET PUMPS are centrifugal pumps that feature an impeller wheel that increases the pressure and velocity of water being drawn from the well. As the pump motor turns the impeller, it sucks up water from the well and creates pressure in the water supply pipes. A shallow-well jet pump typically has only one pipe running into the well. (Deep-well jet pumps have two pipes.) Jet pumps atop a shallow-well platform need to be encased in an insulated housing to protect them from freezing in the Frost Belt. Otherwise, water will freeze inside the pump and split it, requiring replacement.

PISTON PUMPS are no longer installed and are increasingly difficult to get parts for. That said, they are pretty reliable. Piston pumps have been likened to motorized hand pumps because both feature a two-stroke piston that sucks up water on one stroke and discharges it on the next. If the pump casing leaks or its pulley systems are rickety, the pump may need to be replaced before too long. Piston pumps should also be protected by an insulated housing in cold regions.

SUBMERSIBLE PUMPS are designed to be immersed, so both their electric motor and centrifugal pump operate under water. A single pipe runs from the pump to an above-ground storage tank, typically placed in an insulated well house or in the basement of a house. Submersible pumps are powerful, efficient, reliable, and because they operate in a well, quiet. Their downside is that if the pump or its motor fail, the whole apparatus—wire, water piping, and pump unit—must be pulled out of the well and brought up to the surface. Lightning strikes can knock out submersible pump motors, so an electrician should install a lightning arrestor to protect the power feed to the motor.

PRESSURE TANKS are storage tanks located in a well house or a basement that act as reservoirs so that pumps don't have to cycle (start and stop) so often. (Short-cycling shortens the life of pumps.) Because water can't be compressed, pressure tanks contain air bladders, typically a rubberized or plastic lining, that can expand and contract as water pressure varies.

It works like this: when someone opens a tap and water is withdrawn from the tank, the bladder expands till, at some point, the pressure inside the tank decreases sufficiently to start the pump again. Water enters the tank, the bladder constricts, and the pump stops running when a preset pressure is reached.

The pressure tank has a pressure gauge, a pressure switch, and an automatic pressure relief valve to prevent excessive pressure buildup in the tank. As noted, the pressure varies as water is withdrawn or pumped into the tank: 30 psi to 50 psi is a normal pressure range. The pressure tank and its devices should be checked periodically by a pump service company to be sure they're working.

Because a submersible pump is located deep in a well, an inspector can't hear the pump running. So as a resident or a helper opens several faucets, the inspector should stand by the pressure tank noting the pressure gauge to make sure that it starts when the gauge needle drops to the lower pressure limit and stops when the needle reaches the upper limit. At the same time, the inspector will be able to hear the pressure switch clicking on and off. There's typically a 20-psi difference between upper and lower limits—that is, the start and stop readings.

If the pressure switch clicks on and off too often, the tank air bladder may be waterlogged. In other words, the tank is full of water, so that even small water withdrawals at a faucet will start the pump. The bladder should be replaced, which is not an expensive repair. If the pump switch does not start at the lower limit or stop at the upper limit, the gauge may be malfunctioning and should be replaced. And, of course, if the gauge indicates excess pressure in the tank (anything above 60 psi), a pump service company should assess the system.

Note pressure tanks that are rusting or leaking; leaking tanks may need to be replaced if they cannot hold requisite pressures. Last, if the pressure tank is in an outside well house, it should be insulated and heated as necessary to prevent damage to the tank in regions with freezing temperatures.

SEPTIC SYSTEMS

Septic systems typically consist of a watertight septic tank (holding tank) that house sewage empties into and an array of perforated piping called a leaching field that disperses effluents (waste liquids) into the ground. Septic tanks are often cast concrete but may be fiberglass or steel. Wastes from the house main drain flow along downward-sloping pipes to the inlet pipe of the septic tank; there, bacteria break down wastes so that sludge settles to the bottom and effluents rise to the top and exit through an outlet pipe connected to the leaching field.

Leaching fields are complex and may need to be engineered. Leaching field design must consider the size of the household, the volume of wastes, the size of the septic tank, the size and slope of the site, soil composition, groundwater levels, and more. A soils engineer does a series of perc tests to determine the site's percolation rate: the rate at which effluents are absorbed by the soil. Because groundwater levels vary from year to year, sizing a leaching field is a somewhat inexact, if essential, science.

With good design and a modest amount of maintenance, septic systems should be trouble free for years. When systems do fail, it's usually because too much water has been flushed through the tank or an exceptional amount of groundwater has saturated the soil. (Rain runoff from roof, gutters, and downspouts should not be discharged into a septic system but rather through a separate storm drain system.) When a septic system is flooded, waste solids flow out into the leaching field, rather than settling to the bottom of the septic tank. The results range from a patch of exceptionally lush grass over the leaching field to stinky, boggy ground under foot. If you encounter such conditions during your inspection, ask the homeowner where the septic tank and leaching field are located.

On average, a septic tank should be inspected every 3 years to 5 years and pumped out periodically to remove sludge buildup. If the tank isn't pumped out and the sludge level gets too high, there will be no room for additional sewage to separate. In effect, raw sewage will flow across the top of the septic tank and into the leaching field, where waste solids may eventually fill the gravel beds and the perforated pipes. That's a big problem, requiring a new leaching field, which could have easily been avoided.

WHAT TO LOOK FOR

- Does the homeowner have records of annual water-quality tests? When was the last time well water was tested for contamination?
- Is water from the tap clear or cloudy? Does it smell?
- If there is an above-ground pump, is it leaking? If the region gets freezing temperatures, is the pump located in a basement or in an insulated outbuilding?
- Does the well water pressure tank have a pressure relief valve? Is the tank leaking?
- Run the water and watch the pressure tank gauge. Do readings stay within a 30-psi to 50-psi range? Does the pressure switch operate normally or does it click on and off too often?
- When was the septic tank last emptied?
- Ask the homeowner where the septic tank and leaching field are located.
- Do you observe especially lush vegetation, boggy ground, or sewage smells around the septic tank or leaching field?

CHAPTER 8

HEATING *and* COOLING SYSTEMS

TO VETERAN HOME INSPECTORS, today's high-efficiency heating and cooling systems must look like a whole new world. Where once an inspector could remove a few sheet-metal screws to look inside a furnace, today the health of a heating system is more likely to be revealed by a set of digital readouts. Increasingly, a general home inspection will be followed by a heating, ventilation, and air-conditioning (HVAC) inspection performed by a specialist.

WHEN TO CALL IN AN HVAC SPECIALIST

GIVEN THE COMPLEXITY OF MODERN HEATING and cooling systems and the high cost of replacing them, there are times when a home inspector should call in an HVAC specialist to service and/or repair a system or to provide a more detailed assessment of its condition.

The key triggers for calling an HVAC specialist are visual clues that the system has not been serviced recently, such as dirty filters or blower compartments, signs of flue-gas leakage at the inducer motor, flue-vent leakage or spillage, and water or condensate leakage inside or near a high-efficiency condensing furnace. These symptoms can appear in a unit of any age: Homeowners with newer systems often do not have them serviced adequately.

A good heating contractor will put a tag on the furnace that includes the most recent service date. No service tag is an immediate tip-off. Most contractors recommend annual servicing, but once every two years is adequate if owners change filters as needed. Furnaces with air-conditioning systems in hot summer areas may need annual servicing. A number of potential defects can be discovered only during a detailed servicing, such as a cracked heat exchanger or a badly balanced distribution of heat or cooling throughout the house.

This cleanable fabric air filter hasn't been cleaned in a long time, which is no small matter. Clogged filters waste energy and can shorten furnace life. Units that haven't been maintained or serviced in a long time should be inspected by an HVAC contractor.

Inspecting modern furnaces has become a complex business. After carefully removing the furnace cover, look for rust or corrosion, flue spillage, and signs of maintenance or neglect. Photograph the unit so you can scrutinize it further when writing your report.

Overview: Central Heating Systems

Home heating can be divided into two broad categories: room heaters and central heating systems. Fireplaces, woodstoves, portable space heaters, floor heaters, and wall furnaces are examples of room heaters because they provide direct heat only to the rooms in which they are installed. In a central heating system, on the other hand, hot water, steam, or warm air are generated in one location and then distributed throughout the house. Though we will look at room heaters later on, most of this chapter is about central heating, especially forced-air systems.

FIVE COMMON COMPONENTS

Most central heating systems have these five components: (1) **thermostats** and other controls; (2) **burners** that get heat from natural or liquefied petroleum (LP) gas, fuel oil, or electricity; and (3) **heat exchangers** that transfer heat from the firebox to circulating air or water. If the heat exchanger transfers heat to water, it's a boiler; if it transfers heat to air, it's a furnace. If a blower fan moves the heated air, it's a forced-air heating system; if there is no fan, it's a gravity system. The same is true of boilers, which produce

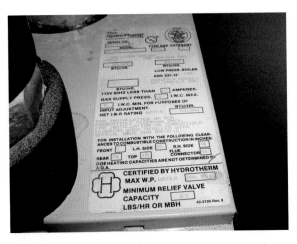

Furnace and boiler nameplates contain a wealth of information, including model numbers, fuel type, input and output Btu/hour, pressure limits, electrical specs, clearance requirements, and relief-valve capacity. With this information, you can probably find an operation manual online.

hot water or steam. Gravity hot water systems rely on convection to move the water, forced–hot water (hydronic) systems use circulating pumps, and steam moves under its own pressure. The other two components are (4) **pipes or ducts** to distribute the heated water, steam, or air to rooms throughout the house and (5) **outlets** in the form of either radiators or registers to deliver the heated water or air to a room; they can be adjusted to some degree.

FURNACE ACCESS AND CLEARANCES

If a furnace (or boiler) is enclosed in a compartment, the door to that compartment must be large enough to remove the appliance without having to remove any other permanent construction. (A door 2 ft. wide is typical.) There must be a working space at least 30 in. deep across the service end of the furnace.

Check the nameplate (see photo above) on the housing for minimum clearances around the furnace; alternatively, you can do an Internet search for the furnace model number to see if a PDF of the furnace's installation manual is available. Often, at least 1 in. of clearance at the sides and back will be required to provide adequate ventilation, though many high-efficiency units allow even less.

MOUNTING AND ENCLOSING EQUIPMENT

Heating and cooling appliances should be securely mounted and able to sustain both vertical and horizontal loads. Furnaces or furnace housing that shakes or rattles when the burner fires up or the blower fan starts may not be adequately fastened.

Exposed fly wheels, fans, pulleys, belts, and moving machinery should have a proper metal enclosure to protect people or pets from being injured.

The furnace housing should be intact. Examine it for damage or rust if the furnace is sitting on a basement floor or located in a damp subfloor area with earlier signs of standing water.

Gas-fired appliances (that are not direct vent design) must not be installed in bedrooms, bathrooms, or storage closets. Adequate fresh air intake is necessary for optimal combustion.

GARAGE FURNACE REQUIREMENTS

Furnaces may be safely located in a garage if they are protected from damage and isolated from combustibles such as fuel fumes or stored chemicals.

Appliances in garages that house vehicles must be protected from impact or elevated above the normal path of vehicles.

Heating equipment that generates a spark, flame, or glow must have its ignition source at least 18 in. above the floor level of a garage. (Fuel fumes and other combustibles, being heavier than air, tend to collect near the floor.)

If a heating appliance is enclosed in a separate sealed compartment within a garage, the appliance may be installed at floor level if the compartment has exterior access and combustion air is drawn from the outside rather than from the garage.

ATTIC FURNACE REQUIREMENTS

Attic furnaces need full access and a sturdy work platform so they can be easily serviced. Furnaces located in an attic require a minimum access opening of 22 in. by 30 in., or the dimensions of the appliance, whichever is larger. They should be no farther than 20 ft. from the access opening.

A solid floor at least 24 in. wide must run from the access opening to the furnace; in front of the furnace, the platform should be 30 in. deep, unless the furnace is closer to or at the attic access opening. The attic should have sufficient lighting and electrical outlets for furnace operation and maintenance. A light switch by the access opening is convenient.

THERMOSTATS AND MASTER SHUTOFFS

A thermostat is a temperature-sensitive switch that automatically keeps house temperatures within a preset range. When the air near the thermostat cools, the switch's contacts close to complete a circuit and turn on (send power to) a furnace or boiler. When the house heats up, the thermostat shuts off the heat. To maintain an even house temperature and avoid excess cycling, it's important to locate a thermostat on an interior wall away from drafts or hot sun. It's also important that homeowners clean thermostat contacts now and then because dust buildup will interfere with operation. When a thermostat cover looks fuzzy with dust, that's a good time to remove the cover, inspect the contacts, and blow dust off with compressed air.

To reduce fuel consumption, replace an older thermostat with an electronic clock-thermostat that can be set to reduce the heat at night and raise it in the morning. Such setbacks can save, on average, 10% to 15% of an energy bill. Thermostats have gotten very brainy, such as The Nest®, a smart thermostat with a wheel user interface, a Wi-Fi® connection, and several sensors, which learns a family's behaviors and fine-tunes settings accordingly. Some thermostats incorporate smoke alarms and carbon monoxide detectors, and most can be programmed distantly with a smartphone or tablet.

Every HVAC unit should also have a master shutoff switch ("disconnect") conveniently located so that power can be shut off quickly for maintenance. If the shut off is remote from the appliance, it must be clearly labeled as the furnace disconnect. Master shutoffs are also helpful when a unit is being repaired. By turning off the power, someone working

Heating outlets such as steam radiators or forced-air registers are often placed beneath windows so that rising heat can moderate cool air descending from window glass.

on, say, a blower fan, won't have it unexpectedly turn on in response to a thermostat signal.

OUTLETS

HVAC systems, including heating outlets, should be designed by a specialist. The size and number of outlets depends, in part, on house square footage, climate zone, furnace capacity, and how well the house is air sealed and insulated. As a rule of thumb, every room should have at least one heating outlet, with rooms larger than 150 sq. ft. having two or more.

Most jurisdictions require that all habitable rooms have heating capable of maintaining a minimum room temperature of 68°F at 3 ft. above the floor and 2 ft. from exterior walls. The installation of portable space heaters may not be used to achieve compliance.

Radiators or warm air registers are almost always located along exterior walls, beneath windows, so that cold air cannot intrude too far into living spaces without encountering the moderating influence of warmer air. In older forced-air heating systems, there will also be one or more return ducts (aka cold air returns), centrally located so that the air returning to the furnace ducting will not be all that cold.

BALANCING A CENTRAL HEATING SYSTEM

When it is installed, a central heating system should be balanced by an HVAC contractor so that heat is evenly distributed throughout the house. (All rooms may not have to be the same temperature, but rather a temperature appropriate to their use. For example, a workout room might be cooler.) Radiators or warm air registers near the boiler or furnace tend to be heat rich, whereas more distant outlets are heat starved.

To achieve a balance within a forced-air heating system, dampers inside ducting can be opened or closed; in hot water systems, throttling valves can be adjusted. Though a homeowner can make minor adjustments, the system should be rebalanced by a pro whenever a furnace or boiler is upgraded or rooms are added.

WHAT TO LOOK FOR

- What type of heating system does the house have? Is the heating adequate?
- How old is the heating system? A manufacturer's nameplate will usually include a model and serial number, which can be used to date the unit.
- Has the unit been regularly serviced? Look for a heating contractor's service tag.
- If the furnace is in a closed compartment, is it large enough to access or to remove the unit?
- If the furnace is in an attic, does it have solid flooring leading to and in front of it?
- Is there a master shutoff (disconnect) conveniently located, so that electricity to the furnace or boiler can be turned off quickly?
- Is the thermostat centrally located? Ideally, it should be on an interior wall, away from drafts and not placed too close to a heating register or radiator.
- Is there a programmable thermostat? Older thermostats may still work but may not be as efficient as newer electronic thermostats that can be programmed.
- If there are two or more thermostats, the house has zoned heating. Do all thermostats work?
- Are room heaters being used as well? What type?
- If the house has central heating, does each room contain at least a radiator or warm-air register along an exterior wall? Are return ducts centrally located?

Warm Air Heating Systems

Warm air systems have evolved over the years. Gravity-fed systems are the oldest, with large ducts that allowed heated air to rise on its own, without aid of a fan. Such furnaces typically had cast-iron heat exchangers, and their superheated flue gases typically exited up a masonry chimney. Before long, blower fans were added to speed the flow of heat to rooms, creating the first forced-air heating systems. But furnaces were still large and not very efficient.

As the cost of fuel rose, there was a push for greater efficiency. Mid-efficiency furnaces were the next development, in which blowers moved air more quickly across heat exchangers and extracted more heat from flue gases. The flue gas, now with less heat to rise out of the building, prompted the addition of another blower to induce draft in the flue.

The fourth type of warm air system, the high-efficiency, condensing furnace, has represented state-of-the-art technology for the last few decades, achieving up to 98% annual fuel utilization efficiency (AFUE). Condensing furnaces use a second heat exchanger to extract even more heat from flue gases. Flue gases that cool (about 100°F) don't rise very quickly, so condensing furnaces require a forced draft to exhaust combustion gases. (This is why they can be vented horizontally.) Condensing furnaces also provide a drain so condensate can exit the building—greatly reducing the likelihood that water vapor will rust out furnace parts.

NATURAL-GAS SAFETY

FUEL OIL, LP GAS, COAL, AND natural gas are among the most common fuel sources, but natural gas is by far the most commonly used fuel in modern furnaces in North America. Following are gas-related safety concerns that home inspectors frequently mention. Readers who want a more exhaustive treatment of gas-related safety issues should visit the website of the American Gas Association (www.aga.org). Last, local building departments have the final say for what's required in your area.

GAS PIPING

Approved gas piping includes rigid galvanized steel, rigid black steel, and CSST flexible gas tubing; some types of plastic piping are approved only for use outside and underground. Gas piping needs to be properly supported, typically every 6 ft. and at joints.

Unapproved piping includes cast iron, copper, brass, and aluminum, though some exceptions are made for copper and brass tubing for natural gas with low amounts of hydrogen sulfide.

GAS CONNECTORS

A gas connector is the flexible tubing that connects a gas-fueled appliance such as a furnace to rigid gas-supply piping. Modern connectors are typically corrugated and have a shiny gray plastic coating. Flexible stainless-steel or bright yellow connectors are also found on some new equipment.

UNAPPROVED CONNECTORS

Copper connectors may be subject to corrosion from sulfur compounds found in natural gas; corrosion flakes off the interior of the tubing and can clog pilot lights and other openings. Aluminum tubing connections, being soft, tend to leak. Corrugated brass connectors may corrode so should

not be used for exterior applications such as spa or pool heaters or on rooftop HVAC units; check local codes.

AUTOMATIC SHUTOFFS

Special valves triggered by vibration or uneven gas flow are now being required in seismic and hurricane risk areas. They will shut down the gas automatically. It's very important that the property residents know how to reset these devices after the triggering event, such as an earthquake, tornado, or hurricane.

WHAT TO LOOK FOR

- Gas meters, supply lines, and appliances must be protected from vehicle impact.
- A furnace located in a garage should be in an isolated compartment with its own source of fresh air or have its ignition source at least 18 in. above floor level.
- The only limitation on gas-piping unions is that they not be concealed.
- There must be an accessible drip leg before gas supply piping connects to an appliance if there is water vapor or sediment in the gas supply. (Check with utility company to ascertain.)
- Appliance connectors must be protected from damage; rigid piping, not a flexible connector, is required where a gas line passes through the furnace housing and house walls or floors.
- Gas piping cannot enter a building below grade (basement wall). If a gas line is otherwise passing through a concrete wall, it must be sleeved.
- A main valve is required ahead of the meter; the main meter valve must be accessible.
- A shutoff valve is required ahead of the gas connector to the appliance.

Gas meters, gas piping, and appliances need protection from impact whether located outside or in a garage. This concrete-filled bollard is designed to protect a meter and the gas piping from vehicle impact.

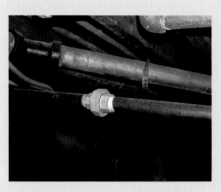

Gas pipe unions have two approved locations: next to an appliance or near the gas meter-to-house connection. Isolated unions such as this one might leak gas undetected.

Rigid gas supply piping should extend through the metal furnace walls. This flexible gas connector could be easily damaged by the sharp metal edges.

WARM AIR RISES, COOL AIR FALLS

Warm air rises, which is the basis of every convectional heating system from woodstoves to today's high-efficiency condensing furnaces. Heated in a furnace surrounded by sheet-metal housing, warm air is routed by supply ducts to rooms, where it enters via supply registers in floors, walls, or ceilings. Because warm air takes up more space and exerts more pressure, it displaces cool air in the room, which returns to the furnace to be reheated and recirculated.

Warm air systems work best if both the supply air and return air travel through ducts. In some older homes there are no return-air ducts—simply a plenum in a wall or a floor cavity—so cooler return air simply meanders downward from one floor to the next until it eventually reaches the furnace in the basement. Such outdated systems are inefficient and at times unsafe because the return air may contain combustion gases or draw dirt from the basement floor into the burner. Also, such undirected, cooler return air typically needs more fuel to reheat it.

Adding a blower fan to warm air systems to force air through the ducts was a great improvement because it delivered warmth more quickly to rooms, and because return air is always ducted in forced-air heating systems it requires less fuel to reheat and recirculate.

GRAVITY-FED SYSTEMS

Gravity-fed warm air systems, which lack blower fans, are outdated but you still see them in older houses. Gravity-fed systems typically feature large furnaces with several oversize ducts sticking out of the top of the housing, rather like octopus legs. The ducts are big to reduce air resistance. Lacking a fan to move the air, convection must do all the work of getting heat to the rooms. Rooms heat slowly, which is perhaps the main complaint of this system.

So many of these systems are still in use because they are quiet (no motors or rattling ducts) and need electricity only for thermostat and burner controls. (One suspects that they are also left in place because they are immense and would be hugely disruptive to remove.) Gravity-fed systems often lack air filters,

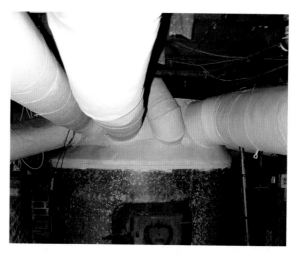

This old octopus-style, gravity-fed furnace is durable and quiet, but fuel inefficient. Moreover, its large ducts are wrapped in asbestos. Before long, it should be replaced with a new efficient furnace and new ducting.

because airflow is so sluggish that filters might stop it altogether. One can add a fan to a gravity-fed system but given the age and inefficiency of the burner, a homeowner is probably best advised to replace the system, including its ducts.

Speaking of which, the housing and ducts of an octopus furnace will probably be wrapped with asbestos. If it is in good repair and not fraying, it's probably safe. But homeowners should get a thorough hazmat assessment (see Chapter 14), including tests for airborne asbestos fibers at registers, especially if there are young children around.

FORCED-AIR ADVANTAGES

There are several reasons forced-air heating systems (including mid-efficiency and condensing furnaces) are the most commonly installed home heating setups.

Forced-air systems are clean, especially with gas-fired burners. If air filters are replaced regularly, registers are vacuumed from time to time, and ducting is sealed against leaks, the system's air quality will be good. Improved ventilation is an asset to house health.

In cold winter climates, integral humidifiers are packaged with many new forced-air systems; and humidifiers can usually be added to older systems.

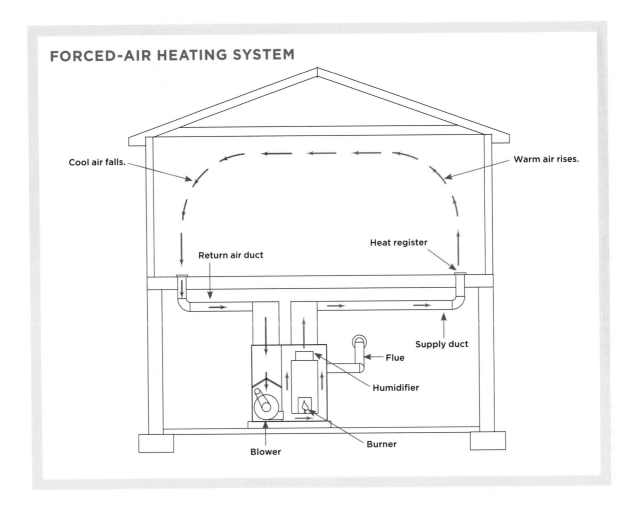

FORCED-AIR HEATING SYSTEM

Cool air falls.

Warm air rises.

Heat register

Return air duct

Supply duct

Flue

Humidifier

Burner

Blower

Central air-conditioning is an option. Because the system already has a blower fan and ducts to all the rooms, A/C can be easily added, though rooms with ceiling registers will deliver cooled air more efficiently. (Cool air falls.)

Forced-air furnaces are less expensive to install than hot water or steam boilers.

Homeowners can adjust individual duct dampers to increase or reduce heat to a room, though whole-house balancing should be done by an HVAC professional.

There are no pipes to freeze and burst during a power outage, and no leaks at radiators to damage flooring. So this system is especially well suited to the Snow Belt.

Forced-air heating systems

Forced-air heating (FAH) is also known as forced hot air, so you are likely to see either term used. FAH systems have become increasingly complex, but their essential elements are a furnace in which a burner heats a heat exchanger, vent flues that carry off exhaust gases, a blower fan to force the air through supply-air and return-air ducting to room registers that provide heat, and one or more furnace control switches.

INSPECTING A BURNER

In older furnaces (15 years or more), an inspector can look at the burner flame and the heat exchanger. Sometimes one must remove a screw or two to gain access, but it's easily done. Burners will vary according to the type of fuel and the age of the furnace,

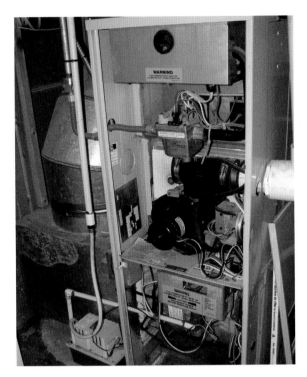

Modern Plus 92/95 condensing furnaces can extract up to 95% of the available heat; their exhaust gases are so cool that flues and vents are often PVC plastic. Because water vapor condenses in cool exhaust, the furnace must have special tubes or drains to carry the water to an approved exterior location. Though this furnace is relatively new, the bottom of its housing is rusting, perhaps because of leaky condensate pipe connections.

Heat exchanger cracks such as this one can leak carbon monoxide and other gases into living spaces. Fortunately, home CO alarms can alert occupants of excessive CO, prompting them to call a heating contractor.

but the basics will be the same. In newer systems, accessing the heat exchanger is more difficult and is typically done only by an HVAC specialist.

If the burner and heat exchanger can be accessed, the inspector should observe the flame. Does the flame lift off the burners? Is its color more yellow or blue? (Blue flames are hotter and indicate more complete combustion; yellow or orange flames indicate less complete combustion.) Is the flame lazy or erratic? (It should be steady.) Check for excessive flame roll-out at the heat exchanger opening when the burners ignite, which may be caused by improper burner or pilot adjustment or may indicate insufficient combustion air.

Observe the flame as the blower turns on. Look for flame deflection or movement, which may indicate a cracked heat exchanger, though some movement from blower vibration is normal. Look for soot, indicating incomplete combustion, both inside the furnace housing and at room registers. Fuel or exhaust smells in living spaces may be further indications of a cracked heat exchanger.

INSPECTING A HEAT EXCHANGER

The heat exchanger is the metal box that contains the burner flame and directs the flue gases to the vent pipe. The heat exchanger transmits heat from the flame inside the box to the air that moves over the metal box's outside surface. Each time the exchanger is heated its metal expands and then contracts, which eventually leads to metal fatigue and cracking. Poor air circulation due to dirty air filters or fan blades can also cause the exchanger to overheat and fail prematurely.

Some furnaces have several burner/exchanger covers that can be unscrewed for better access. An inspector should use a mirror and flashlight to examine the accessible portions of the heat exchanger before and after the furnace heats up. But be sure to close the blower compartment door before turning on the furnace.

Furnaces installed in the 1940s and 1950s often had heavy-gauge metal heat exchangers that were less

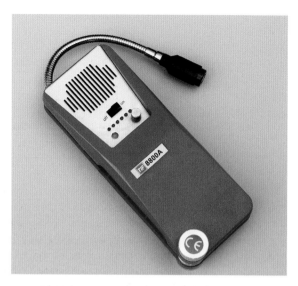

A combustible-gas leak detector can help locate heat exchanger cracks or flue-gas spillage or reassure homeowners that no leaks currently exist.

susceptible to cracking than furnaces made in the 1970s. In older furnaces the flame was also farther from the exchanger, making them less fuel-efficient but prolonging furnace life. Depending on the shape of the crack, a cracked heat exchanger could lead to excessive levels of carbon dioxide and carbon monoxide in the house, especially if the house construction is relatively airtight.

The danger of a cracked heat exchanger is often exaggerated. A crack in the heat exchanger does not necessarily mean that the furnace is unsafe to operate. However, existing damage will likely deteriorate till the unit becomes unsafe. For this reason, most heating contractors and utility companies recommend that furnaces with cracked heat exchangers be replaced.

If you suspect that there is a cracked heat exchanger, recommend a thorough examination by a heating contractor. Heat exchangers in some furnaces, especially horizontal models and modern high-efficiency types, can't be visually examined. Many HVAC contractors and home inspectors carry combustible gas detectors to assess small heat exchanger cracks. Residents should be advised to install CO alarms immediately outside of all bedrooms, especially if the furnace is old and worn.

Almost all furnaces that have been used regularly for over 20 years are highly inefficient; complete replacement with an energy-efficient system and new ducting should be considered. It's best to recommend that all older furnace's be serviced by a qualified heating contractor.

WHAT TO LOOK FOR

- Note the type of warm air system in the house. If you are not sure of the furnace's age, copy the manufacturer and model number from its nameplate and do an Internet search. (General condition is much more important than age in determining the furnace's potential lifespan.)
- Is there corrosion around the base of the furnace housing (look inside the housing as well)?
- If it's a gravity-fed system with large octopus ducts rising out of the top of the plenum, they are probably covered with asbestos. Is the asbestos intact or fraying? Have an expert in asbestos remediation inspect it to be sure it's safe to operate.
- Inspect the burner flame if possible. Does the flame lift off the burners? Is its color more blue than yellow?
- When the burners ignite, do flames roll out of the heat exchanger opening? Do scorch marks around the opening indicate an ongoing roll-out problem?
- When the furnace is running, check living spaces for exhaust or fuel smells.
- Use a mirror and flashlight to inspect visible parts of the heat exchanger.
- Can you see cracks or splits in the heat exchanger? Corrosion or rust?

FURNACE CONTROLS

In addition to the master shutoff switch discussed on p. 180, forced-air heating systems typically have three thermostatic (temperature-sensitive) switches as well: a main thermostat, a fan control (blower control), and a high-limit control (high-temperature limit control).

A MAIN THERMOSTAT communicates with the furnace burner. After the homeowner sets a temperature point for living spaces, thermostat sensors keep

This hydronic gauge shows temperature and pressure expressed in pounds per square inch. Before inspecting a furnace or boiler, familiarize yourself with normal operating ranges for that system.

house temperatures within a few degrees of the set point. To work correctly, the thermostat must be clean, level, and securely mounted. An inspector should note if the device is loose or damaged and then, after removing the cover, note if it is out of level or if its contact points are dusty. Excess dust can insulate thermostat contacts and block electrical current.

A FAN CONTROL usually has two settings at roughly 110°F and 125°F. The fan turns on when the temperature around the heat exchanger reaches the higher setting and off at the lower setting. If the temperatures are too close, the fan will blow cold air into the room. This is called short cycling. If the temperature difference is too great, heat will be wasted up the flue or vent and the delay may cause the heat exchanger to overheat.

If the furnace gets hot and several minutes pass before the blower turns on, this may indicate that the blower switch is defective. Tapping on the blower switch at the front of the furnace can sometimes cause it to turn on, but the switch should be replaced.

A HIGH-LIMIT CONTROL keeps the heat exchanger from overheating. When a preset temperature is reached, this control turns off the fuel to the burner. The factory setting on the high limit control should not be adjusted. If the fan control switch is defective and does not turn on, the high-limit switch should shut the burner down between 175°F and 200°F to prevent heat exchanger burnout or failure.

OTHER SWITCHES. Appliances with pilot light ignition systems should have a pilot safety control valve that automatically closes and shuts off the gas flow when the thermocouple at the pilot cools and ceases to generate the current necessary to keep the valve open. Fuel oil–fired systems use a bimetallic stack switch or more commonly a photoelectric cell to turn the fuel oil supply off if there is no ignition. Glow plugs or hot surface ignition systems are common in newer gas-fired systems. They are flameless and require a device to prove ignition before the gas valve will open.

WHAT TO LOOK FOR

- How old is the thermostat? Replacing old ones with new programmable models saves fuel.

- You may want to remove the thermostat cover. Is the unit securely mounted? Is it clogged with dust?

- If the gas burner shuts off before the blower comes on, the fan control may be defective.

- Does the older blower fan short cycle—that is, stop and start repeatedly within short time intervals? (Newer furnaces have inducer fans that turn on first and run continuously to vent exhausts, which is *not* a problem.)

CONDENSING FURNACES

To recap briefly: Conventional furnaces are roughly 60% to 65% fuel efficient, with most of the energy lost as superheated exhaust gases (450°F to 500°F) disappearing up a chimney. That waste was tolerable when fuel was cheap, but following the oil crises of the 1970s HVAC manufacturers got serious about producing a new generation of efficient furnaces.

Condensing furnaces extracted more heat from combustion gases with a more convoluted heat exchanger—in other words, increasing the exposure of the gas flame to the metal heat exchanger. Most condensing furnaces also have a second heat exchanger. Thus the temperatures of flue gases venting from high-efficiency furnaces range from 100°F to 110°F.

As noted earlier, prolonging the gas flame contact with heat exchangers increases drag and makes chimney drafts sluggish. This was solved by adding an induced draft blower to push flue gases out a sidewall or roof vent. Condensing or Plus 90 furnaces have exhaust gases that are so cool they are typically vented with PVC plastic or stainless-steel vent pipe, and conventional metal or masonry chimneys are no longer needed. PVC vent pipes can also be run almost horizontally, although a slight pitch is usually specified when the flue also provides drainage for condensation moisture.

Speaking of which, all combustion gases contain water vapor. And when flue gases are cooled down to, say, 110°F, water vapor condenses into water, which

Because every installation is not perfect, regular servicing is essential. This relatively new condensing furnace has leaking pipes that could cause substantial damage over time.

needs to be drained off by condensate pipes. Because this condensate contains chemicals from combustion, it is acidic, so it's important that it be directed away from furnace parts and the building itself.

Plus 90 furnace condensate piping should be at least ¾ in. in diameter and have a slope of ¼ in. per foot, discharging to an approved plumbing fixture or drain location. The left photo on p. 205 shows what happens when a condensate drain is allowed to drip onto siding, potentially a big problem and entirely unnecessary. Condensing furnace systems vary significantly, so review manufacturer's installation specs for each system.

COMBUSTION AIR

To safely operate furnaces and other heating appliances, there must be adequate separation between combustion and recirculating air. The opening to a return-air duct should be at least 10 ft. from the furnace firebox and draft diverter. The same distance should be maintained between a return-air duct and a water heater burner and its draft diverter (see the drawing on p. 190).

DESPITE THE SUPERIOR PERFORMANCE OF condensing furnaces, builders concerned about costs are still installing mid-efficiency furnaces (aka Plus 80s) because they satisfy minimum energy-efficiency standards. Plus 80s sometimes scrimp on details such as venting. In some models, condensate flows down the vent pipe and into the draft inducer or heat exchanger, causing corrosion and premature failure. It is not uncommon to find corrosion or deposits on or below the inducer motor inside the furnace.

This 85% efficient, draft-induced furnace is starting to rust because its design does not adequately drain the condensate that results from cooler flue-gas temperatures.

Furnaces in sealed closets or compartments should be provided with adequate combustion air from the building exterior. These closets, if located below attics or above crawl spaces, typically need air openings within the upper 12 in. and the lower 12 in. of the enclosure. Exterior air openings should be screened to prevent animal entry. Follow manufacturer specs when sizing pipe to bring in combustion air; 3-in. pipe is common for condensing furnaces.

Dust or dirt along the furnace compartment door edges may indicate a low-pressure area inside the furnace compartment and insufficient combustion air. Soot or signs of flame roll-out at the front of the burner compartment may indicate inadequate combustion air.

In larger rooms of ordinary tightness, the space itself can provide combustion air as long as there is at least 50 cu. ft. per 1,000 Btu. If bath fans, kitchen range hoods, clothes dryers, or fireplaces also draw that air, operating them at the same time may create negative pressure (see p. 215) in which combustion gases may be pulled back into living spaces (back-drafting). An HVAC contractor can use a digital combustion analyzer to check the condition.

BLOWER FANS

In forced-air systems, heated air is distributed by a blower fan mounted above, below, or beside the heat exchanger. In downdraft systems the blower is mounted over the heat exchanger. Counterflow or updraft systems have the blower mounted either below or beside the main furnace compartment.

Your HVAC inspection should include the blower fan compartment, which typically has an access door. If the furnace is older (10 years to 15 years), turn off the master shutoff switch before opening the access door so that the blower fan cannot start up and possibly injure you. Modern furnaces have an auto-disconnect switch that prevents blower operation when the door is open. (If a blower access door is loose or missing, write it up as a safety hazard: Flue gases could be drawn into the blower.)

After opening the access door, look for dust accumulation on the blower blades. Blades fuzzy with

MINIMUM DISTANCES TO AIR RETURN

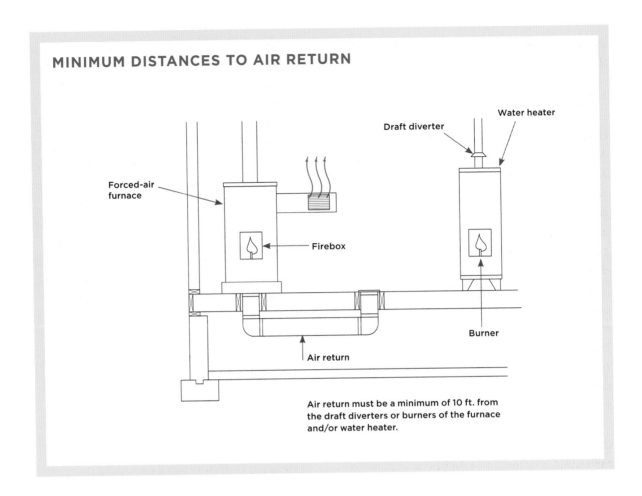

Air return must be a minimum of 10 ft. from the draft diverters or burners of the furnace and/or water heater.

Older forced-air heating systems rely on belt-driven blower fans; check their tension and wear. Fans with dusty blades don't move air efficiently, causing exchangers to overheat.

dust don't move air very well, which can significantly reduce furnace efficiency and overheat the heat exchanger. Older furnaces have squirrel-cage fans with blower motors that require regular lubrication and fan belts that need periodic adjustments. When you press gently on a properly adjusted belt, it should deflect between ½ in. and ¾ in. Check the fan belt for excessive wear, and the fan and motor for looseness, damage, and missing bolts. Modern furnaces have motor and blower assemblies that are self-lubricating and do not have belts.

Shut the blower access door, restore power, and turn on the heat. When the blower is running, listen for vibrations and squealing or banging sounds, which usually indicate worn bearings or a loose or damaged fan belt. While the blower is running, check each room to see if air is coming out of the registers. Inspectors cannot determine if the heat supply is adequate but they can state whether supply air is moving through the ducts and reaching the heat supply registers.

AIR FILTERS

Air filters should be checked monthly and changed or cleaned twice annually. Air filters remove dust from house air and prevent dust buildup on the blower blades, which can greatly reduce blower efficiency, decrease heat distribution, and lead to heat exchanger failure. Air filters are especially important in preventing dust accumulation on A/C evaporator coils. If a house is undergoing remodeling, filters should be checked periodically for extra dust.

ELECTROSTATIC FILTERS filter the finest particles and therefore need cleaning frequently. They should be washed in the shower or with a garden hose spraying in the opposite direction of the system air flow. Pleated disposable filters have a surface that is three times to four times larger and need replacing less often.

MEDIA TYPE FILTERS have large (3 in. to 4 in. thick) replaceable cartridges and require a special compartment. Considered to be the best solution for peo-

ple with allergies and chemical sensitivities, media filters are very efficient and require replacing much less often, perhaps once or twice a year, depending on interior air quality.

CHECK THE PLENUM. After removing the air filter, look into the plenum, typically a metal box where the air return ducting is attached, located above, below, or at the side of the furnace. Note the presence of dust, debris, asbestos (white or gray paper tape), and—if there is a light outside the plenum—air leaks. Some blower enclosures or plenums located at the bottom of the furnace have openings to the wood or concrete basement floor. These areas need to be covered and sealed to prevent moisture and dust from being drawn into the furnace air flow. There should be an airtight cover over the air filter slot if it is located in the return-air ducting.

WHAT TO LOOK FOR

- To prevent exhaust fumes from being sucked into ducting, air returns must be at least 10 ft. from burners and draft diverters of the furnace and water heater (if they share the space).

- If the furnace is in a sealed compartment, does it have a source of outside air? Soot or flame roll-out around the burner door may indicate insufficient combustion air.

- In airtight houses, negative pressurization can create backdrafting. Look for soot or warm, moist air near the underside of the furnace draft diverter.

- Does the blower fan have an access door? Write it up if it's missing.

- Are blower blades clean or clogged with dust? Dusty fan blades don't move air efficiently.

- If a fan belt runs between the fan and its motor, is it correctly adjusted?

- When the blower is running, do you hear squealing or banging sounds?

- What kind of air filter does the furnace have? Is it clean or clogged with dust?

- Remove the air filter and look inside the plenum. Are surfaces clean or filled with dust and debris? Can you see light where plenum seams have separated or where ducts join?

Large, replaceable media-type filters are considered more effective than the thin types and are preferred by many professionals.

SUPPLY AND RETURN-AIR DUCTING

In a forced-air system, supply ducting distributes heated (or cooled) air throughout the house. There are two primary configurations for supply ducting: an extended plenum system with a large rectangular duct that serves as a trunk line, with smaller branch ducts running to room outlets, and a radial distribution system in which each branch duct runs directly from the furnace. In either case, branch ducts may be rectangular or round and often have a damper to adjust airflow. As noted earlier, there will also be at least one centrally located return-air duct (cold air return) that circulates partially conditioned air back to the plenum to be reheated (or recooled).

CHECK FOR RUST. Furnace plenums and ducting should be at least 4 in. above the ground. Inspect ducting for its general condition, soil contact, holes or gaps, sagging or insufficient support, and asbestos insulation. If the furnace is installed in an area with flood lines (water stains or sediment residue), carefully check all sheet-metal components for signs of water stains or rust. Probe the bottom of a furnace plenum for damage if it is below an old subarea flood level.

DUCT SYSTEMS SHOULD BE AIRTIGHT, with joints sealed with metallic tape, mastic, gaskets, or other means. Fabric duct tape isn't durable; it becomes brittle and gets unstuck. Supply and air-return ducting and plenums in unheated areas should be insulated. Examine insulation for damage. Animals can pull insulation off pipes. If ducts are wrapped with fiberglass insulation, dark stains on the insulation indicate air leakage at ducting connections, which can significantly reduce heating system efficiency.

Furnace plenums and ducting should be at least 4 in. above the ground. Plenums that come in contact with the soil frequently rust out.

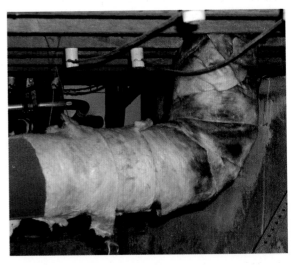

Old metal ducting in subfloor areas often rusts out in time. The black stains on the fiberglass insulation are caused by air leakage and indicate a significant waste of energy.

DUCTING MUST BE PROPERLY SUPPORTED.
Sheet-metal and rigid-fibrous ducting needs support every 6 ft. Soft ducting will sag at supports that are too far apart, cutting off the flow of air; it should have 1½-in.-wide galvanized strapping every 4 ft.

FREE AIRFLOW THROUGHOUT THE BUILDING is essential for a forced-air system to be effective. Based upon CFM design, a ¾-in. to 1-in. gap beneath bedroom doors should allow for sufficient return airflow.

SUPPLY REGISTERS AND RETURN-AIR GRILLES

Warm air registers are almost always located along exterior walls, beneath windows, to moderate cooler air sheeting (descending) from glass, which conducts cold. In forced-air heating systems, there will also be one or more return ducts, centrally located so that the air returning to the furnace ducting will not be all that cold.

Registers may be located on the floors, walls, or ceilings. The location is not as critical with forced-air furnaces as with gravity. Look for debris in the ducting below floor-mounted registers. You will almost certainly find dust and perhaps construction debris, and in some older systems, asbestos tape used to seal duct and furnace joints. Air flowing over asbestos in a heat register may circulate fibers throughout the house. If you see asbestos tape when inspecting furnace plenums and ducts, and suspect it in supply registers, recommend that any asbestos in the airflow be abated (removed, wrapped, painted) by a qualified contractor.

Note on your report if any supply registers contain dark soot deposits or have a lingering smell of unburned fuel, which may indicate a cracked heat exchanger or faulty draft. Last, note the force of heated air rising from each supply register when the blower is running. Homeowners can adjust dampers in branch ducts to increase or decrease flow to individual rooms, but rebalancing the whole system should be done by an HVAC contractor.

HUMIDIFIERS

AS HOUSEHOLD AIR IS RECIRCULATED BY forced-air heating systems, it becomes increasingly dry, which can be uncomfortable for inhabitants during cold winter months. Humidifiers increase the moisture in the air, which is also helpful to the heating system itself. Because moist air feels warmer, homeowners can use lower temperature settings and reduce fuel use.

When inspecting an older HVAC system, examine the humidifier reservoir to make sure that it is not leaking onto the heat exchanger, which could cause it to rust and fail prematurely. Also note mineral build-up, mold, or bacteria, which can grow in always-wet drum humidifiers. (The water in the reservoir will look scummy and may smell bad.) The humidifier should be drained and cleaned periodically or replaced with an atomizer humidifier, which injects moisture into furnace airflow.

Homes that have been remodeled often have supply registers that become filled with sawdust and other debris. They should be checked and vacuumed clean as needed.

WHAT TO LOOK FOR

- Are all furnace plenums and ducting at least 4 in. above the ground? Note ducts that have holes or gaps, or sagging or insufficient support.

- If the furnace is installed in an area that floods periodically, scrutinize the bottom for stains or rust.

- Ducts must be airtight. Joints should be sealed with metallic tape, mastic, or gaskets but not fabric duct tape.

- Do you see dark stains on ducts wrapped with fiberglass insulation? Those stains indicate air leaks.

- Note sagging ducts. Rigid ducting needs support every 6 ft.; flexible ducting, every 4 ft.

- Do bedrooms have return-air grilles or gaps beneath doors to allow return airflow?

- Does the HVAC system have a humidifier? If it has a drum humidifier, does it look as though it has been maintained or is the water scummy and foul smelling?

- Remove a floor-mounted register and look down into the boot. Is it full of dust and debris? If so, all registers should be vacuumed. Fraying white or gray tape inside is probably asbestos.

Venting

Venting is the system of flue pipes, connectors, and other components that convey combustion gases safely out of a house. Furnaces and boilers vary greatly, so vent assemblies must follow manufacturer specifications. For example, flue gases from conventional furnaces can exceed 500°F, whereas high-efficiency condensing furnace flue gases may be only 100°F. Obviously, their vent pipes can be very different. A general inspector is not an HVAC expert but if you have a working knowledge of furnace types (see p. 181), you will have a better idea of what type of venting each requires.

COMMON FAILURE POINTS

Combustion produces water vapor and toxic gases. A toxic gas such as carbon monoxide can poison people and animals, so clearly it needs to be vented, but water vapor can also do great harm by corroding heat exchangers, rusting vent pipes, and otherwise shortening the life of a heating system and reducing its efficiency. So water must also be vented or drained.

Inspecting vent pipes is primarily a search for corrosion, especially in older systems. Corrosion may be caused by restricted vent air flow, a flue that is too long, inadequately sloped piping, flue pipes with an improper vertical-to-horizontal ratio, or flue gases that cool too rapidly and so condense in the flue piping and cause corrosion. This moisture can also enter heat exchangers causing corrosion and heat exchanger failure.

Inspectors must also keep an eye out for flue pipes that are a fire hazard because they pass too close to combustible surfaces such as wood framing. The symptoms are obvious: charred or scorched wood, discolored siding, melted pipe insulation, and make-

A forced-hot water system, seen from above. The object that looks like an inverted pail (*right*) is a draft diverter. The red cylinder to its left is a circulating pump. The large black piping that rises out of the top of the boiler is insulated supply piping.

Water from gas-fired appliance flue gases can rust out a poorly sloped metal connector in a few years. A properly installed Type B connector would be less likely to corrode or rust.

Vent flues can get very hot and are a potential fire hazard. This pipe cap should terminate at least 1 ft. above the dormer roof at left.

shift insulators or heat deflectors installed by someone who realized there was a problem. Flue pipes that are wrong for the system or were installed improperly are fire hazards.

VENTING METHODS

There are several ways to vent heating appliances:

1. Terra cotta–lined masonry flues (chimneys) or rigid cement asbestos flues (Transite™).
2. Type B vents, typically double-wall metal vent piping that requires a minimal 1-in. clearance to combustibles surfaces.
3. Type BW vents, oval-shaped Type B vents designed to be installed above wall furnaces.
4. Type L vents for fuel oil–fired appliances.
5. Plastic PVC pipe vents for high-efficiency, condensing appliances (see p. 185).
6. Integral vent assemblies for direct-vent wall furnaces (see p. 202) and exterior appliances.

   NOTE: Single-wall metal vent connectors between the appliance and the vent require a 6-in. clearance to combustibles.

OUTDATED VENTING

Various materials have been used in the past to vent gas heating appliances. The earliest were brick or masonry chimneys built onsite. These were followed by factory-made, tile-lined, sheet-metal flues called patent flues or cement asbestos flues, or the brand name Transite.

These materials heat up slowly and the low temperature may restrict the upward flow of flue gases. For this reason many manufacturers specify that only listed galvanized sheet-metal vents that terminate above the roofline be used on their equipment. (Type B, double-wall galvanized-steel vent piping is most often specified.)

NOTE: Ungalvanized blue-metal and aluminum clothes-dryer vent piping are *not* approved materials and should be replaced with proper galvanized steel piping.

Most jurisdictions will allow some furnaces and water heaters to reuse the older outdated vertical flues as long as their installation does not violate the equipment manufacturer's specifications.

VENT RISE

The general rule is that the vertical portion of an older style metal or masonry vent system should be at least one-third longer than the horizontal portion. Vent pipes that slope above 45° are considered vertical. The longer vertical portion is necessary to provide sufficient upward movement in the gases to prevent flue-gas spilling at the appliance. Actual vent and flue design should be determined by a qualified heating contractor after a review of the manufacturer's specifications.

INSTALLATION RULES OF THUMB

- Single-wall vents and connectors (where allowed) require 6-in. clearance to combustible surfaces; Type B, double-wall vents and connectors require 1-in. clearance to combustibles.
- All unused openings in a venting system must be closed or capped.
- A vent or vent connector should not penetrate or enter an air duct or plenum.
- Vent piping in occupied spaces should be enclosed to avoid personal contact.
- Furnaces and water heaters shall not vent into a fireplace or fireplace chimney.

VENT DAMPERS

Vent dampers, which are electrically or mechanically operated, may be installed to prevent heat loss up the vent when the appliance is not in operation. Vent dampers must be designed to prevent the burner from firing up when the damper is in a closed position.

FLUE-GAS SPILLAGE

The flues or vent connectors are connected to a draft hood at the furnace. The draft hood provides an opening for air to flow into the flue above and improves the upward flow of flue gases. A draft hood that is rusted or discolored may indicate flue-gas spillage, in which unburned gases spill from the hood. Spillage can be a life-threatening condition and requires immediate correction.

Flue-gas spillage can be caused by inadequate venting, improper configuration, or damaged vent piping, such as a rain cap that has been mashed down at the top of a vent pipe. After the furnace has been operating for 3 minutes to 5 minutes, place your hand or your inspection mirror at the furnace draft hood. You will be able to feel dampness or observe fogging on the mirror if flue gases are spilling from the venting system.

WHAT TO LOOK FOR

- Single-wall vents and connectors (where allowed) require a 6-in. clearance to combustible surfaces; Type B, double-wall vents and connectors require a 1-in. clearance to combustibles. If you see charred or scorched wood, or melted pipe insulation, these clearances were ignored.
- What type of vent piping and connectors have been used? Note unapproved materials being used for venting, such as ungalvanized blue-metal and aluminum clothes-dryer piping.
- Is the vent pipe sufficiently sloped to carry off flue gases safely?
- Inspecting vent pipes is primarily a search for corrosion, especially in older systems. Do you see pipe connectors and sections of vent pipe with little (or negative) slope? They frequently rust out first.
- Use a mirror or a bare hand to detect the moist, warm air of flue spillage near a furnace draft diverter.

Hot Water and Steam Heating Systems

Hot water and steam systems are frequently called hydronic heating systems because both use some form of water to transfer heat throughout a house.

The oldest form of hydronic heating is a single-pipe steam system, in which steam rises in large (3-in.) supply pipes, heats cast-iron room radiators, condenses, and then flows downward along the bottom of the supply pipes, back to the boiler, to be

Backdrafting is a reverse flow of air down a vent or flue pipe or chimney. Instead of rising, combustion gases spill out into living spaces. By holding a mirror next to the draft hood, you can detect spillage: Water vapor will fog the mirror. In time, the draft hood will rust.

Old-style hot water boilers like this were often originally coal or oil fired, and many have since been converted to natural gas. Typically gravity fed, they operate very quietly but are relatively inefficient compared to systems with circulating pumps.

reheated. Though we will briefly discuss inspecting steam systems, they are increasingly rare and have not been installed in new construction for decades. Though steam systems are reliable, they are not very energy-efficient and their heat is slow to arrive. Two-pipe steam systems have a second pipe for the return water or condensate, but that change only modestly improved performance.

Gravity hot water systems followed steam. This system's pipes are filled with water, which expands as it is heated in a boiler, rises to radiators, where it displaces cooler water, which returns to the boiler to be reheated. That is, the water in this system circulates on its own, without mechanical devices such as pumps. Gravity hot water is also considered an outdated technology. Like steam, it requires 3-in. pipes, is slow to heat, and is not very energy-efficient.

Forced–hot water heating systems use circulating pumps to deliver hot water to radiators and return cooled water to the boiler. Far more efficient than gravity hot water or steam, forced–hot water systems use ½-in. to 1-in. distribution piping and a boiler that is much smaller. Because forced–hot water systems are the most common type of hydronic heating, most of this section will explain how to inspect them.

STEAM SYSTEMS

A steam boiler is readily distinguishable from a hot water boiler by the presence of a sight glass, or a level gauge, which shows the water level inside the boiler. The upper water edge (or meniscus) should be in the upper part of the sight glass when the boiler is cold and in the lower half when the system is producing steam. If the gauge is empty, there's not enough water in the boiler; if the gauge is completely full, there's too much water in the system.

Steam systems typically have an automatic water valve (float valve) that replenishes boiler water when it drops below a preset level. (The sight glass reveals that the float valve is working.) If the water drops below the safe level, a low-water cutoff will shut off fuel to the burner.

The sight glass of this steam boiler will tell you if the float valve (automatic water fill valve) is functioning properly. Old steam boilers with chronic leaks should be replaced.

The pressure control (pressuretrol) valve is usually set to restart the boiler when pressure drops to between 0.5 psi and 1 psi. To check the pressure valve, run the system through a heating cycle or adjust the set point to a lower temperature to see if the burner turns off. If the burner fails to shut down, the valve is defective—a potentially hazardous condition.

When the system is full, the steam pressure increases until it reaches the set point, usually between 2 psi and 3 psi. Low-pressure steam systems should never exceed 5 psi. There should be a pressure-relief valve to discharge excessive pressure should the other regulators fail. Relief valves are typically set between 12 psi and 15 psi. A leaking safety release valve is an indication of system or control malfunction.

Some systems have a combination pressuretrol/pressure-relief valve, which will trip if a high pressure level is exceeded. The boiler will not fire until a service person or a homeowner pushes the valve's reset button. In addition to making sure gauges and valves work, an inspector should survey control equipment for corrosion and damage.

Banging radiator noise is usually caused by steam blocked by water ponding in the pipes. Shimming the radiator to slope downward toward the inlet pipe usually drains the water and stops the noise.

GRAVITY HOT WATER SYSTEMS

In gravity hot water systems, there is no circulating pump. Water heated by the boiler rises to radiators by convection and returns by gravity, so these systems are quite simple. Because gravity-fed hot water systems are older, their boilers were often cast-iron or heavy-gauge steel and extremely durable. Inspectors report finding 50-year old boilers that still work fine.

All gravity hot water systems use an expansion tank located in the attic. Such tanks can become waterlogged and should be checked annually as part of routine servicing. The most common symptom of a waterlogged expansion tank is a system that short cycles, or turns on and off in very short intervals. Gravity hot water systems should also have a relief valve mounted on the boiler.

WHAT TO LOOK FOR

- What kind of hydronic system does the house have? Try to determine the age of the unit, researching information on the boiler nameplate if necessary.
- If the boiler has a sight glass, which shows the water level inside, it is a steam system.
- If the sight glass is empty, there's not enough water in the boiler and the automatic water valve is probably not functioning and should be replaced.
- Check the pressure control valve by running the system through a heating cycle to see if the burner turns off.
- Is there a pressure-relief valve mounted on the boiler? Is there water below the relief valve's discharge pipe? (Relief valves should not be discharging, so if it is, have it checked.)
- Does the heating system short cycle (start and stop on very short intervals)? If so, the expansion tank may be waterlogged.

FORCED-HOT WATER SYSTEMS

When inspecting a forced-hot water system, start with the big stuff: the condition of the boiler. Whereas older boilers were made of cast iron and lasted decades, newer steel boilers typically have 20-year warranties and are lucky to make it to 25 years. The repeated expansion and contraction as boilers heat and cool leads to corrosion, splits, and leaks.

Water dripping into the firebox is an early sign of boiler failure and should be checked by an HVAC contractor. If you see rusted metal and water pooling around the base of the boiler housing, the boiler is almost certainly shot and needs to be replaced. Extensive leaks on a relatively new boiler in the Snow Belt may have been caused by frozen water piping due to a fuel line that got clogged or a fuel tank that didn't get refilled. Once the burst pipes are repaired, the system should function normally.

WATER PRESSURE. Forced-hot water systems typically operate at pressures between 12 psi and 25 psi, so the unit's pressure gauge should read somewhere in that range. When the pressure drops

This is a gas-fired, hydronic hot water boiler that has at least two zones, each with a separate pump to distribute hot water to different portions of the house. There may also be multiple thermostats located in the heated areas.

EXPANSION TANKS

WATER EXPANDS WHEN IT IS HEATED, SO ALL closed (self-contained) hydronic systems need an expansion tank to store the additional volume of water that has been heated. As water flows in and out of the tank as it is heated and cooled, equilibrium in the system is maintained. Without an expansion tank to relieve the additional pressure (and volume) of heated water, heating system pipes could rupture.

In forced-hot water systems the expansion tank is usually near the boiler. There are two types of expansion tanks: air cushion and diaphragm. Because water cannot be compressed but air can, the air serves as a cushion that compresses as water enters and expands as water leaves. In time, however, air-cushion tanks become waterlogged so that when a boiler heats water, there is no room for its increased volume in the expansion tank and the relief valve blows. Water-logged expansion tanks must be flushed periodically so the air cushion can be reestablished.

Diaphragm expansion tanks have flexible diaphragms (rubberized membranes) that isolate the air in the tank so it can't become waterlogged. Diaphragms work well, but in time may wear out or become less flexible or, more commonly, the tank will rust out first.

below 12 psi, an automatic water-fill valve lets water in. If system pressure exceeds 25 psi, a pressure-relief valve should open to let water out. The boiler also has a pressure-relief regulator to drain water at the high pressure limit, typically 30 psi; this is a safety device and should not activate during normal operation. Any condition that causes a relief valve to discharge is serious: It must be identified by an HVAC specialist and corrected.

WATER TEMPERATURE. The boiler water temperature is measured by an aquastat, which turns the fuel to the burners on or off, depending on the temperature setting. The normal operating temperature is 175° to 185°F. Temperatures above 190°F may indicate insufficient radiators, an undersize boiler, or improperly adjusted controls.

Altitude is the internal boiler pressure indicated by a pressure/temperature gauge mounted on the boiler. The red needle in the gauge is typically fixed at 30 psi, the maximum safe pressure. Burners should shut off if the boiler pressure exceeds 30 psi. Excessive boiler pressure may be caused by a stuck fill valve, a leak in a domestic hot water exchanger coil, a ruptured expansion tank diaphragm, or a waterlogged expansion tank.

OPERATING NOISES. Water movement in the piping and boiler should be silent. Noise typically indicates that air has entered the system as a result of turbulence, defective valves, or leaking fittings. However, some squeaking is normal when the unit turns on and water pipes expand.

CIRCULATING PUMPS move water to radiators and distribution pipes. Ideally, the circulator should be installed on the distribution return pipe just before it connects to the boiler. Older circulators need to be oiled regularly.

Because pumps are the most actively moving part of the system, they wear out, particularly at the coupler between the pump and its motor. When that happens, the motor turns but the pump doesn't, so heated water won't circulate. Feel a distribution pipe to see if a pump is working: the pipe should heat up quickly. Further, you can check for leaks around the pump, usually caused by a failed gasket between pump and motor.

Pumps or motors that whine or clank are inadequately lubricated or perhaps have worn bearings that need replacing. If you smell smoke or burning rubber when a pump is operating, shut down the system and have an HVAC contractor inspect and repair it.

HEATING ZONES. For greater efficiency, forced–hot water systems can be divided into zones, each with its own thermostat and zone control valve. This enables temperatures that are appropriate to each

room's use. Each zone can have its own circulating pump or a single pump can serve the whole system. When the temperature in a zone drops to the lower setpoint, the thermostat opens the zone valve, the boiler fires up, and the pump moves hot water to the zone. If there's a single circulating pump and the boiler is on, signals from other zone thermostats simply open their respective valves to admit heated water.

When inspecting zoned heating systems, examine each zone valve for leaks and mineral buildup, which can cause valves to stick open or shut. Leaking valves should be replaced.

RADIANT HEATING SYSTEMS, in which heat piping is encased in a concrete slab that acts as a radiator, are almost always divided into multiple zones, each with a separate thermostat and zone control valve. Radiant heating is reliable, but inspectors should have piping pressure tested if the house is about to be sold. Houses from the 1950s through the 1970s with radiant heating typically employed copper tubing in the slabs, which could be compromised by improperly poured slabs that have shifted or cracked. Many older systems used steel piping, much of which has rusted out by now. Frequently, modern in-slab systems use PEX or other plastic tubing. Always try to identify the type of in-slab piping. Replacing a radiant system is a big expense, so it's best to know about it beforehand.

WHAT TO LOOK FOR

- What is the age and general condition of the boiler? Use the information on the boiler nameplate to research the manufacturer and boiler model.
- Water dripping into a firebox is an early sign of boiler failure. Is the bottom of the boiler rusty and is there water leaking around the base? If so, it's probably time to replace it.
- Read the boiler pressure gauge: 12 psi to 25 psi is a normal range. If the pressure drops below 12 psi, an automatic water-fill valve should open.
- Is a pressure-relief valve mounted to the boiler? If there is water beneath the relief valve discharge pipe, have an HVAC specialist inspect the boiler.

This radiant heating system has two pumps—one for each heating zone—to circulate hot water through piping in slab floors. As the pumps run, listen for unusual sounds.

- The boiler altitude gauge is typically fixed at 30 psi, the maximum safe pressure. Burners should shut off if the boiler pressure exceeds 30 psi.
- Does the water circulate quietly in boilers and piping? Noisy operation is usually caused by air in the system, defective valves, or leaking fittings.
- Does the pump motor turn but pipes don't heat up? If so, a gasket has probably failed. Frequently, there will also be a leak below the pump.
- Pumps or motors that whine or bang are insufficiently lubricated or have a bad bearing.
- If the house had radiant heating installed before the 1970s, have piping pressure tested to check for leaks.

Room Heaters

Room heaters, such as baseboard units, floor and wall furnaces, and direct-vent wall units, are usually electric or gas-fired and heat only the rooms in which they are installed.

ELECTRIC ROOM HEATERS

Stationary electric heaters include baseboard heaters and wall panels. Electric heat is a popular retrofit option for many homeowners because heaters are relatively inexpensive and easy to install. Long term, they can be a costly solution because electric heat tends to cost more than gas- or oil-fired systems.

Baseboard heaters with integral thermostats are perhaps the easiest to install because they don't require a separate switch leg to a thermostat higher on the wall. Their shortcoming is that a thermostat near the floor doesn't give an accurate read of ambient room temperature.

Electric wall heaters are surface mounted or recessed into a wall, with a fan to project heat out into the room. Older exposed electric-coil wall heaters can burn someone or become fire hazards, especially in bathrooms where towels are sometimes left to hang in front of them.

Portable electric heaters are sometimes used in unheated rooms. A 30-amp or 60-amp main electrical service may not be adequate to support multiple

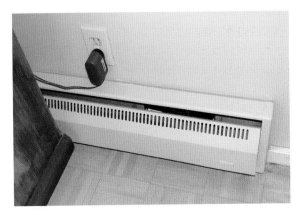

Electric receptacles should not be located above baseboard heaters because appliance cord insulation will become brittle. Avoid placing furniture in front of baseboard heaters; it denies access to controls and blocks air flow.

Older electric heaters common in bathrooms have exposed heating elements that are fire and burn hazards. Such heaters should be disconnected and/or replaced.

electric heaters, so it may be necessary to upgrade either the main electrical capacity or the heating system.

FLOOR FURNACES

Floor furnaces, common in older homes in moderate climates, are typically gas fired. Examine furnaces above and below the floor. Their vent connectors often have insufficient clearance, upslope, or vertical length and should be checked carefully for rust and corrosion. The draft hood (draft diverter) between the vent and the furnace is often damaged. When the furnace is not venting properly, there will be a lot of

Floor furnaces are hazardous and are not permitted in some areas. Their hot surfaces can burn bare feet in an instant, and their heat exchangers can scorch nearby wood framing.

Stains and rusting at the top of wall furnace covers are usually caused by flue-gas spillage, in which moist flue gases don't exit the flue pipe, usually because it is too short.

moist air and window condensation during winter because water vapor–laden combustion gases are escaping into living spaces.

Check floor framing for charred or burned wood. Because floor furnace grilles get very hot, they can burn anyone who comes in contact with them, especially children. It is best to replace an old or damaged floor furnace with central heating.

There should be an access opening large enough to remove the floor furnace: minimally, 30 in. by 30 in. The furnace burner opening should not be farther than 20 ft. from the access door. Floor furnaces should be supported on a concrete slab at least 3 in. above the ground or else suspended from the floor framing with at least 6 in. clearance to ground.

If excavation is necessary for suspended floor furnaces, adequate clearance should be provided at all sides. If the excavation is deeper than 12 in., a concrete or masonry lining extending 4 in. above the adjoining ground level is required. Always check subgrade areas for indications of previous flooding or standing water, which can rust out heating units.

GAS-FIRED WALL FURNACES

Gas-fired wall furnaces usually use radiation to transfer heat but some have fans, too. Back-to-back wall furnaces are common between living rooms and hallways in apartments. Wood doors and other combustibles must be kept away from these units. It is important to keep wall furnaces clear of dust to provide adequate combustion airflow. Inspectors should remove the cover on wall furnaces to inspect heat exchangers and vent hoods.

Wall furnaces typically vent vertically through the roof using an oval-shaped Type BW vent or flue. A gas-fired appliance vent should extend at least 2 ft. above the roof and at least 2 ft. higher than any portion of the building within 8 ft. When vents are too short above flat roofs, draft will be poor and wall furnaces are likely to spill fumes from their draft hood, leaving smoke or rust stains on the upper part of the furnace cover.

DIRECT-VENT WALL UNITS

Direct-vent wall furnaces have special double vents that run through the wall directly behind the unit: They vent horizontally. The double vent provides both combustion air intake and exhaust discharge. The end of a gas-fired appliance flue should terminate at least 4 ft. below or 4 ft. horizontally from and at least 1 ft. above a doorway or operable window.

These units are safer than other heaters because they are sealed; there is no direct air connection between the living space and the combustion chamber. They can be installed on almost any outside wall and do not require a vent pipe that extends above the roof.

Direct vent gas-fired wall heaters get quite hot, so residents must be careful to avoid placing combustible furniture and materials too near. The furniture here is too close to the heater.

But the vent caps can create a burn or fire hazard if they are located too close to a walking surface or plantings.

WHAT TO LOOK FOR

- Are there electrical cords, towels, and other things hanging in front of electric heaters? Note them.
- Check floor furnace connectors for rust and corrosion. The draft hood between the vent and the furnace is frequently rusted through and sending combustion gases into living spaces.
- Is there a bad smell when the floor furnace heats up? (Floor furnaces collect large amounts of dust and pet hair.)
- Is the floor framing scorched or charred near a floor furnace? If any vent piping is single-wall metal, it must be at least 6 in. from combustible surfaces.
- Are there smoke or rust stains on the upper part of a wall furnace cover? This indicates insufficient draft and flue-gas spillage into living spaces.
- Make sure that direct-vent wall furnaces are not blocked by doors, furniture, and the like.
- Go outside to inspect direct-vent flues, which should terminate at least 4 ft. below or 4 ft. horizontally from and at least 1 ft. above a doorway or operable window.

Central Air-Conditioning

Central air-conditioning systems typically use ducting to distribute cooled air to more than one room. Other systems use piping to distribute chilled water to the various rooms. Some rooms not connected to a central system may have individual exterior wall-mounted A/C units plugged into electrical outlets.

Typically, home air-conditioning is installed in a split system configuration with the condenser at the building exterior and the evaporator adjacent to the interior furnace equipment. Before operating an air-conditioning system, always be sure that the electrical power to the unit has been turned on for at least 24 hours before the inspection. Many air-conditioners are equipped with electric heaters wired to the power supply that keep the lubricating oil from absorbing refrigerant and losing its effectiveness.

INSPECTING AN A/C SYSTEM

The outside ambient temperature should be at least 65°F to operate the equipment. Look for a disconnect switch that should be visible from the exterior equipment. Disconnect the power at the exterior compressor unit before turning on the system at the inside thermostat. By closing the switch near the condenser, you can note any unusual vibration or noise that may occur as the compressor begins operating.

In a short time, the large suction line will feel cold and the small liquid line will feel warm. Do not grab these lines: lightly touch them with your fingertips. The warm air emerging from the condenser fan should be 20°F to 25°F warmer than the outside air. Observe the equipment carefully for excessive vibration or noise. Check the piping at the evaporator or compressor for any oil stains or drips indicating refrigerant leakage.

Some inspectors will use an ammeter to check the running load amps (RLAs). The equipment ID plate will specify the normal RLAs. This rating should not be exceeded, and a reading of 60% to 90% is considered normal. A defective compressor or low refrigerant will create a low reading. A low current draw of the RLAs will usually correspond to a smaller

Exterior A/C coils eventually deteriorate. Especially when exposed to salt air. This coil probably cannot be saved and will likely need to be replaced.

temperature differential at the evaporator. A reading higher than 90% of the RLAs may indicate a defective compressor or a refrigerant overcharge.

Check for adequate clearance at the sides and top of the equipment. Follow installation instructions for clearance—typically, 12 in. at sides and 4 ft. to 5 ft. above the unit for air flow. Note the general condition of the exterior equipment. The condenser should be on a level platform at least 4 in. above grade. Vines, plants, and other vegetation should be cleared away from the unit. Look for damage in the compressor fins caused by pets or physical contact. Note excessive plant debris or dirt inside or beneath the unit.

Note the condition of the insulation on the refrigerant lines. Frost or ice on the large suction line, or at the interior evaporator coils, indicates insufficient airflow. This condition is possibly caused by a dirty filter, dirty evaporator coil, or defective metering device.

In each room, measure the temperature differences between the cold air return and the air flowing from the registers while the air-conditioner is operating. The difference in temperature should be 14°F to 22°F (some inspectors use 15°F and 20°F). If the difference is too great (the cooled air is too cold), there may be restricted air flow that does not allow the evaporator to cool properly. This can result in ice formation in the evaporator coils. A difference of less than 14°F indicates a system that is not working correctly, usually because of compressor malfunction or insufficient refrigerant.

An important function of air-conditioning is dehumidifying. Cooler air holds less moisture. Air that has reached its maximum moisture content at a given temperature has a relative humidity of 100%, or has reached the dew point. The normal relative humidity at a room interior at 70°F is between 20% and 40%.

CONDENSATE PIPING

Air-cooling coils and evaporative coolers should be provided with condensate piping that is not smaller than ¾ in. in diameter and installed with a slope of ¼ in. per foot, which discharges to an approved plumbing fixture or disposal area. Condensate may be discharged into a laundry tub or plumbing standpipe if a proper air break is maintained. Condensate drain lines should not be connected directly to waste or vent piping.

Note the location of the condensate drain outflow. Substantial cold air emerging from the condensate drain line may indicate the absence of a trap in the condensate drain piping. A trap is suggested to reduce cold air loss. Check the condensate drain piping between the interior and exterior equipment for sagging or improper sloping.

If the furnace or evaporator unit is installed in an attic or above a finished ceiling, a secondary condensate drain line is necessary to prevent potential leaks should the primary condensate line become clogged. The secondary pan should have a separate ¾-in. minimum drainpipe whose discharge is visible. Water flowing from this drain indicates that service is needed immediately to clear the primary condensate drain. Many modern systems are now equipped with water sensor alarms attached to the condensate overflow drain, or placed in the pan below the unit, that will shut down the A/C when water floods the evaporator coil.

If the furnace air-conditioning system is located in a basement, a condensate lift pump is typically required to deliver the condensate to the building exterior. In rooftop installations the condensate drain piping should be directed to a downspout opening. Historically, PVC piping was not to be used for condensate

Condensate pipes that don't empty into an approved drain or outlet can do a lot of damage. This condensate pipe has dripped onto the stucco siding for months, causing the siding to detach from the sheathing and soaking the wall framing.

Evaporator coils should be located on the down-flow side of the system heat exchanger. Check the ducting next to the evaporator for excessive dampness, rust, or frost.

drains in areas exposed to the sun. While copper is a better material, in recent years much copper piping has been stolen from rooftops and other areas, so many users are returning to PVC, which can last for many years in areas exposed to the sun, especially if it is painted.

A/C DUCTING

To detect air leaks, place your hands around pipe fittings and connections at the evaporator and furnace equipment while the air-conditioning is operating. (Keep hands away from moving parts, however.) Note duct damage or separation.

Evaporator coils should be located on the down-flow side of the system heat exchanger. Damp air coming off the coils can lead to heat exchanger rusting. Check the ducting next to the evaporator for indications of excessive dampness, rust, or frost.

Cool air is substantially heavier than warm air. If the older ducting is too small to support the heavier cool air (4-in. round ducts were once common), they should be replaced with larger ducts. Check the volume of cold air at the registers. If you suspect that the A/C system has been added to an existing heating system without upgrading the blower or duct capacity, have an HVAC contractor assess the system.

ANNUAL SERVICING

If you see signs that the system has not been properly or recently serviced, recommend that a qualified contractor do a full service soon. Air-conditioning equipment is complicated and can fail if not properly maintained; it should be serviced at least annually.

WHAT TO LOOK FOR

- Before inspecting an A/C system, be sure that its power has been on for at least 24 hours and the temperature outside is at least 65°F.
- While the equipment is running, observe it carefully for excessive vibration or noise.
- Are there any oil stains or drips indicating refrigerant leakage in the piping at the evaporator or compressor?
- Outside, look for damaged compressor fins, excessive plant debris, and dirt inside the unit.
- What's the condition of refrigerant lines? Frost or ice on the suction lines or interior evaporator coils indicates insufficient airflow, often because of a dirty filter.
- Do air-cooling coils and evaporative coolers have condensate piping at least $3/4$ in. dia. with a slope of $1/4$ in. per foot? Where does the condensate line discharge?
- If the furnace or evaporator unit is installed in an attic, is there a metal pan beneath it and a secondary condensate line to prevent leaks?

- Is there a water sensor alarm at the A/C condensate overflow or in the pan beneath the unit?

- If the furnace A/C system is located in a basement, is there a condensate lift pump? Rust stains and dampness at the furnace or below the cooling coil suggest there is not one.

- Has the A/C system been recently serviced?

Heat Pumps

Simply put, a heat pump is like an air conditioner that extracts heat from exterior air and moves it inside or extracts heat from inside air and transfers it to the outside. Basically, there are two types of heat pumps: air to air and water to air (or geothermal). Air-to-air types are most commonly installed in homes. Geothermal heat pumps, which rely on the constant temperature (55°F) of well water, are more efficient and more expensive.

The main difference between a heat pump and an air conditioner is a reversing valve that changes the direction of the refrigerant's flow. A heat pump also has an accumulator to keep liquid refrigerant from entering the compressor. Metering devices, also found in A/C systems, control the amount of refrigerant that flows to the coils to absorb heat.

If the system fails to provide heat, an emergency backup may be operated manually to activate the supplemental heating system.

Outside condensers should be mounted on a level pad well above the ground, unlike what is shown here. In heat pump systems this equipment is typically referred to as the "outside unit," which operates as a condenser only in the cooling mode.

INSPECTING A HEAT-PUMP SYSTEM

To inspect a heat-pump system, use the thermostat control only. Operate the system only in the mode it is set at when you first see it. Do not change to heating or cooling mode as this could damage the system. The system should be energized for at least 24 hours before you operate it. This allows the sump heater to heat the lubricant to an effective temperature. Do not operate a system that has been turned off at a breaker or fuse.

Do not run the unit in the heating mode when the temperature is over 65°F or in the cooling mode when it is less than 60°F. If it operates in one mode, it will also operate in the other mode unless the reversing valve is defective, and these are relatively inexpensive to repair.

In the cooling mode, the discharge air from the outside compressor should be 14°F to 22°F warmer than the ambient air. The discharge air from the air registers should be 14°F to 22°F cooler than the air at the return duct. The large suction line should be cold to the touch.

In the heating mode the discharge air from the outside coil is cooler than the ambient air, the air at the registers should be between 90°F and 105°F, and the suction line should be warm to the touch. Hotter air at the registers will indicate that the unit is operating on supplemental heat.

Home inspectors don't usually assess the adequacy of heating and cooling systems. Heat pumps are typically sized for the cooling load. If heat-pump capacity is too large, the unit will short cycle and not remove enough humidity to prevent condensation indoors during the summer. If its capacity is too small the house will be cold in winter and too warm in summer.

WHAT TO LOOK FOR

- When inspecting a heat-pump system, operate it only in the mode in which it is set. Changing its mode immediately before testing could damage it.

- Outside, make sure there are no branches within 5 ft. of the unit or bushes within 1 ft.

- In heating mode, the air at registers should be between 90°F and 105°F.

- In cooling mode, discharge air at the registers should be 14°F to 22°F warmer than the return air.

CHAPTER 9

CHIMNEYS *and* FIREPLACES

BRICK CHIMNEYS AND FIREPLACES are romantic hold-overs from a time when they were often the only way to heat a house or get hot gases safely out of it. These days fireplaces are not particularly cost-effective to build or energy-efficient to operate. But if a house already has a brick chimney and fireplace in decent repair, then we try to live with their shortcomings.

A WELL-CONSTRUCTED CHIMNEY

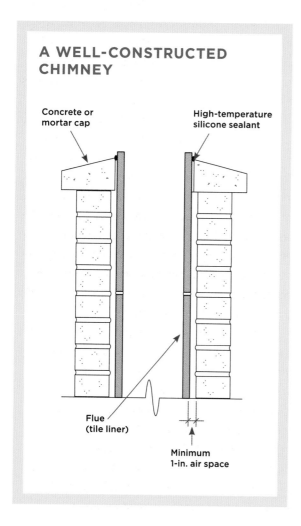

Concrete or mortar cap

High-temperature silicone sealant

Flue (tile liner)

Minimum 1-in. air space

Chimneys

Chimneys are inspected in several stages, the first being part of the roof inspection and the exterior walk-around, then, later, in the basement or crawl space where the chimney footing rests, and perhaps in intervening floors if there is a fireplace or wood-stove venting into it.

At each stage, the inspector's concerns may be a little different. On the roof, the primary concern is how skillfully the chimney is flashed into the roofing membrane—in other words, how leak-free and weather-tight junctures are. Exterior inspections focus on the chimney's mortar joints and structural soundness. The basement look-see typically focuses on the chimney pad (footing), on settlement (if any), and on structure. If there's a fireplace, the flue and firebox safety are big issues. We'll discuss each of these topics at length.

STRUCTURAL CONDITION

The visual regularity of brick chimneys, with alternating patterns of brick and mortar, makes irregularities easy to spot. An inspector's first task is to scan exposed portions of brickwork and note missing bricks, eroded mortar, obviously patched areas, cracked caps, and the like.

Masonry chimneys are usually freestanding—that is, they are supported by a footing that is independent of the house foundation. Consequently, if the footing and the foundation settle at different rates, gaps may develop between the chimney and, say, house siding. Uneven settlement is not necessarily a problem, though gaps should be sealed with a durable caulk to keep water from entering behind the siding. Elastomeric caulks are a good choice because they stay flexible and accommodate seasonal expansion and contraction of materials.

If the footing is failing, however, the chimney may begin to lean, which is serious. Severe leaning is often accompanied by cracking along mortar lines and, in some cases, cracks that run across brick faces. Chimney-siding gaps with several applications of caulk indicate longstanding settlement that

Chimneys are usually supported by a footing that is independent of the house foundation. When uneven settlement occurs, a gap like the one here can open between the chimney and the house.

Heavy-duty bracing like this can help stabilize a masonry chimney, but complete removal and/or replacement with a metal flue is likely to be much safer.

may be growing worse. Undersize chimney pads in older houses may lack reinforcing steel or be made of inferior concrete that is now crumbling. If visible deterioration is widespread, the chimney should be replaced because exterior cracking is almost always accompanied by flue-tile cracking, which is a fire hazard.

Bracing is sometimes prescribed as a cure for leaning chimneys, especially in earthquake-prone regions, but it may be ill-advised. Bracing may limit the amount of sway above a roof but will do nothing to alleviate racking (twisting) forces on a rigid, rather fragile masonry structure. Bracing certainly won't remedy inadequate footings or weak mortar joints.

MORTAR JOINTS

Even materials as durable as brick and mortar break down in time, frequently near the top of a wall or chimney, where masonry is most exposed to the elements or near the ground where water wicks up from dampness in area soils. Often, the chimney wasn't capped or flashed correctly. Loose bricks at the top of a chimney will have to be removed until the repairer reaches bricks that are solidly attached, usually at the roofline.

If brick courses or mortar joints are eroded but bricks remain firmly attached, the mortar joints will need to be repointed by partially cutting back joints, applying new mortar into the joints, and shaping the new mortar. Shaping mortar joints is especially important in regions with freezing temperatures because shaping compresses the mortar, helps it shed water, and improves its weatherability.

Brickwork in direct contact with the ground frequently has damaged mortar joints because sustained dampness leeches out minerals and weakens the cement. Efflorescence, a powdery white mineral surface deposit, is also caused by masonry absorbing water, but its presence does not necessarily mean the structure is failing. A lot of efflorescence near the top of an old chimney is noteworthy because it suggests that water has been running down the inside of the chimney for many years, usually because a chimney's mortar cap (discussed later) has failed.

If vertical or diagonal cracks run through several courses, there may be underlying structural problems, which must be corrected before repointing. When they can safely access the roof, inspectors sometimes give a chimney a gentle push to check for looseness; you can do the same to chimney sections next to the ground. Take it easy: the point is not to push it over, but to assess its condition. Any chimney that does move, however imperceptibly, should be replaced. A final test of mortar joints is scraping

Sustained contact with moist soil has hastened the erosion of this chimney's mortar joints. It may be possible to replace loose bricks and repoint tired mortar, but it needs to be done soon.

them gently with a screwdriver. If the mortar is sandy, crumbling, or easily dislodged, the chimney should probably be removed.

WHAT TO LOOK FOR

- Scan the chimney for missing bricks, eroded mortar joints, and obvious patches.
- Are there gaps between the chimney and house siding? Have the gaps been caulked before?
- Does the chimney lean? Has rooftop chimney bracing been installed?
- Is there cracking along mortar lines or cracks that run across brick faces?
- Can you see loose bricks or a cracked mortar cap atop the chimney?
- What is the condition of mortar joints? Scrape joints gently with a screwdriver to see if they are sound or crumbling.
- If chimney surfaces show efflorescence, how widespread is it?
- If the chimney is accessible, *gently* push test it for loose bricks or sway.

CHIMNEY HEIGHT AND DRAFT

Chimney draft affects how well heating appliances vent flue gases or whether a fireplace smokes. However, creating a chimney with a strong draft is an inexact science of variables, such as chimney volume, fireplace proportions, negative pressurization in airtight houses, prevailing winds, and topography, many of which a homeowner can do little or nothing about. Chimney height, though, is one variable that strongly affects draft and is somewhat remediable.

Old-timers hold that the top of a chimney should be higher than the roof ridge to prevent downdrafts, but that's not always practicable. Most building codes specify that the top of a chimney must be at least 3 ft. above the roof on the chimney's upslope face. In addition, the top of the chimney must be at least 2 ft. higher than any other part of the roof within 10 ft., measured horizontally. If the chimney is a little shy of those heights, adding a concrete cap or a rotating wind cap usually gains 8 in. to 12 in. and can use prevailing breezes to help venting.

MORTAR CAPS, RAIN CAPS, AND SPARK ARRESTORS

Speaking of caps, mortar is typically applied at the top of masonry chimneys as a transition between the flue liner and the surrounding brickwork (see "A Well-Constructed Chimney" on p. 208). The mortar cap is designed to shed rain and prevent water entry into the brickwork at the top. Cracks often form in this mortar and should be caulked or patched with mortar. Loose or damaged mortar should be replaced.

SEPARATE VENTS FOR FIREPLACE AND FURNACE!

DO NOT VENT A FIREPLACE AND A furnace (or any heating appliance) into the same chimney flue. Carbon monoxide from the furnace could enter living spaces from the fireplace or the furnace vent draft could be compromised. A furnace should vent to a separate flue.

A mortar or concrete cap on a chimney helps prevent rainwater from entering the brickwork. In snow country such caps are typically much larger and can be effective in keeping the melting snow away from the bricks below. This cracked cap should be replaced.

Modern metal chimney caps often have two screens: one that keeps any sparks inside and a lower one that keeps rooftop creatures out of the wood framed chimney enclosure below.

In areas that get heavy winter rains or snow, homeowners often install a peaked rain cap (wash cap) above the mortar cap to keep creosote and other combustion residue from running down the inside of the flue liner. If there is enough water washing down the inside of a flue, creosote can run all the way down to metal flue pipes, where it leaks out of joints. Sticky and black-brown, creosote is unsightly, smells awful, and is a fire hazard.

Local codes may require that the chimneys venting woodstoves or fireplaces have a tight-fitting spark arrestor on top. This requirement is common in fire zones, to prevent airborne embers from starting brush or forest fires. Local codes will specify the size of the arrestor's screen mesh, though the mesh is typically 19-gauge galvanized wire with openings between ⅜ in. and ½ in. Screen mesh must be small enough to stop sparks, yet large enough for unimpeded airflow and draft. As a bonus, screened spark arrestors keep critters from entering or nesting in a chimney.

NOTE: Most home centers sell combination rain cap/spark arrestors.

If the flue damper inside the fireplace is damaged (see p. 215), you may see a spring-loaded damper mounted to the top of the chimney. Most chimney-top dampers are opened and closed by pulling a stainless-steel cable that hangs down the flue into the

STRESS AT THE TOP

THIS OLD BRICK CHIMNEY HAS FOUR STRIKES against it: crumbling mortar, failed base flashing, no flue lining, and a wind-buffeted TV antenna that stresses mortar joints further. Strapping antennae, satellite dishes, and other paraphernalia to chimneys is a terrible idea.

fireplace. As part of your fireplace inspection, pull the cable open and shut to make sure the damper is working.

WHAT TO LOOK FOR

- Check the height of the chimney. It should be at least 3 ft. above the part of the roof it passes through and at least 2 ft. above any other part of the roof within 10 ft.
- Do the fireplace and furnace (or any heating appliance) vent to separate flues?
- Are cracks visible in the mortar cap? Does the chimney have a rain cap?
- Does the chimney have a spark arrester?
- If the fireplace damper doesn't function, is there a spring-loaded damper atop the chimney?
- If a TV antenna, satellite dish, or other object is strapped to the chimney, write it up and recommend removal.

FLUE LINERS

To restate an important point: a flue is a liner inside a chimney that vents combustion gases from a fireplace, woodstove, or heating appliance to the outside.

Sometimes an inspector can actually look down inside a fireplace chimney or furnace flue and discover that it was never properly lined. Unlined flues like this are a fire hazard and could also allow flue gases to escape into living spaces. The best solution is to add a metal liner or completely replace the chimney.

Because such gases are very hot (450°F to 500°F from conventional gas furnaces), a flue liner must be continuous and airtight, from the heat source to the outside air. Simply put, the purpose of a flue liner is to contain a potential chimney fire.

Modern brick or concrete block chimneys are lined with clay tile or concrete sections that are mortared together. Liners and the mortar that joins them will eventually deteriorate with age and use, reducing their effectiveness. Chimney fires can reach 2000°F, and if mortar joints are not intact, those superheated gases can escape from the flue liner ("breech the chimney") and set fire to wood framing.

PRE–WORLD WAR II CHIMNEYS ARE OFTEN UNLINED. Unlined chimneys should not be used for venting fireplaces or furnaces even if the masonry seems structurally sound. Even a small crack can allow superheated gases to escape and ignite wood framing. Moreover, given the corrosiveness of combustion gases, it's unlikely that an old chimney will be 100% intact. It may be possible to retrofit a metal flue liner or to pour a cementitious one (by first inflating a balloon-like form inside the chimney), but retrofits are expensive. If a metal flue liner has been inserted into a masonry chimney, examine the metal for corrosion and rust.

Flue liners are not typically accessible to visual examination, beyond a short section you can see down the top of a chimney or up from a fireplace. Some chimney contractors will lower a video camera down the length of a chimney, which could probably detect large cracks or sections of failed mortar but more likely all one would see is a more or less continuous surface of dull black or shiny black buildup. Better to spend the money on an annual chimney cleaning.

It's impossible to overstate the importance of cleaning a chimney before each heating season. In addition to creosote, which may harden to the consistency of glass, incomplete combustion produces tar, ammonia, methane, carbon monoxide, toluene, phenol, benzene, and eventually, turpentine, acetone, and methyl alcohol. All, need we add, quite flammable.

This flue and mortar cap were cracked by a chimney fire in a flue that was overdue for a cleaning.

If you see signs of a chimney fire, the chimney should be professionally inspected. Those signs include creosote flakes on the roof or the ground, scorched or cracked flue liners or chimney crowns, warped dampers, or charred studs or joists near a chimney. Many local codes require inspections before homeowners fire up new wood-burning appliances.

WHAT TO LOOK FOR

- Has the chimney been professionally cleaned in the past year?
- Does the chimney have a tile flue liner? Are visible parts of the liner in good condition?
- If the flue is metal, is it in good condition or rusted through?
- If the chimney is unlined, what is its general condition? Is its construction in solid enough condition to retrofit a flue liner?
- Are there signs of previous chimney fires, such as creosote flakes on the roof or ground, or scorched or cracked flue liners?

CHIMNEY FLASHING AND CRICKETS

Because chimneys have the potential to dam up water running down a sloping roof, chimney–roof joints must be counterflashed to prevent leaks. The upper pieces of counterflashing (see "Chimney Flashing" on p. 70) are usually tucked into chimney mortar joints and made to overhang various pieces of base flashing, which are nailed to the roof deck.

Counterflashing and base pieces overlap but aren't physically joined, so they can move independently and still repel water. (This independence is necessary because house foundations and chimney footings often settle at different rates, causing single-piece flashing to tear and leak.)

Diverting water around the upslope side of the chimney is particularly tricky, so if the chimney is more than 2 ft. wide, a cricket is sometimes installed. Crickets look somewhat like a tiny roof with two sloping planes. The upper flanges of a cricket are overlapped by shingles above. The guiding principle of flashing is that upper overlaps lower so that water flows downhill unimpeded, till it is carried away by gutters and downspouts.

As you can see, flashing can get complicated, so it is often done incorrectly and leaks occur or materials wear out. If you can get close enough to inspect the base of the chimney at the roof, see if counterflashing is tucked tightly into chimney mortar joints and if base flashing is free from nail holes and rust damage. Once leaks develop, many homeowners slather asphalt roofing cement around the base of the chimney, as shown in the bottom photo on p. 69. Roofing cement patches are unsightly but generally effective, though they need to be touched up periodically when the cement dries up and cracks.

WHAT TO LOOK FOR

- Is roofing cement smeared around the base of the chimney? If so, look for corresponding water damage when you inspect the attic and upper floors.
- Is the chimney correctly flashed with counterflashing or do single flashing pieces attach to both chimney and roof deck (incorrect)?
- Is base flashing free from nail holes and rust holes that could leak? Is counterflashing securely tucked into mortar joints?
- Was a cricket installed above the chimney (on the upslope side of the roof) to divert runoff?
- Do pieces of flashing and shingles overlap roofing elements downhill?

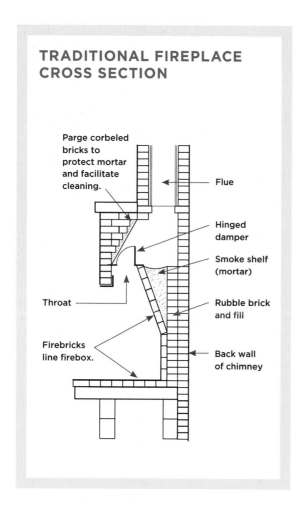

TRADITIONAL FIREPLACE CROSS SECTION

Parge corbeled bricks to protect mortar and facilitate cleaning.

Flue

Hinged damper

Smoke shelf (mortar)

Throat

Rubble brick and fill

Firebricks line firebox.

Back wall of chimney

Smoke stains above a fireplace may indicate a chimney with a poor draft or that someone left the damper closed when a fire was burning.

Fireplaces

Fireplaces need maintenance and occasional repairs, but as long as the flue and the firebox are intact, repairs tend to be modest and inexpensive. For many homeowners, the bigger question may be the cost of having a fireplace, given its energy inefficiency. When a fire is blazing, less than 15% of its heat radiates out into the room and when a fire is starting up or dying out, fireplaces are net energy losers as conditioned air escapes up the chimney.

GENERAL CONDITION

Start by noting the fireplace's general condition and assessing what elements are present or missing. Are there smoke stains on the fireplace surround (the area just outside the firebox)? Is there a damper? Is the firebox intact or are there gaps and missing

bricks? Is the hearth intact? Is the chimney lined? You might want to don coveralls for this part of the inspection.

SMOKING FIREPLACES, as we've noted, can have complex causes. Apart from the possible fixes discussed earlier, here are a few more to consider.

Installing a smoke hood, a narrow metal strip across the top of a fireplace opening, may be helpful when a fire first starts and is smokiest. But if the chimney draft is poor, smoke will leak out from under the hood sooner or later.

Inserting fireplace doors is another smoke-containing strategy that works best when the unit has air vents along the bottom to give the fire enough combustion air.

Installing convection ducts near the base of the firebox improves draft by increasing airflow, but because it typically involves rebuilding part of the firebox, it's an expensive fix.

Parging the fireplace throat and smoke shelf to reduce air turbulence and improve draft can be accomplished in a day or two if the mason is experienced. The key to success for this method is cleaning sooty inside bricks well enough for the parging mortar to stick.

Creosote is a highly combustible substance that can accumulate and eventually cause a chimney fire that could reach 2000°F. Regular cleanings can prevent excess creosote buildup.

Dampers prevent heat loss when a fireplace is not being used. Old dampers that don't work can be replaced with a spring-loaded damper atop the chimney, whose pull chain hangs down into the firebox, as shown here.

Burning dry wood. Burning wet or green (unseasoned) firewood creates a steamy, smoky fire whose low heat output doesn't create much of an updraft and promotes creosote buildup.

Cleaning the fireplace and chimney annually reduces air turbulence and increases safety.

Rebuilding the firebox with Rumford proportions is a viable strategy if the firebox needs to be rebuilt anyhow and the opening is large enough to accommodate a new firebox that is taller and shallower than a standard fireplace. Rumford fireplaces smoke less and radiate more heat into living spaces. When you research Rumford fireplaces on the Internet, read up on Count Rumford, a contemporary of Benjamin Franklin's and perhaps as ingenious. Despite a number of his inventions that survive to this day, Rumford is not much known in the United States because he bet on the British and left in a hurry after his side lost the Revolutionary War.

BACKDRAFTING

Another cause of smoking fireplaces, especially in newer, relatively airtight houses, is backdrafting, in which air being vented by bath fans, kitchen hoods, and draft-inducing fans creates negative pressurization inside the house. Thus when a fireplace damper is opened, air rushes *down* the chimney so that smoke rises listlessly or even billows back into the room.

Opening a window to admit more air should reduce fireplace smoking somewhat, but if backdrafting exists, it needs to be investigated as part of a whole-house energy audit (see p. 83). Backdrafting also affects the performance of fuel- and gas-fired water heaters, furnaces, and boilers and can suck combustion gases back into living spaces—a dangerous condition.

DAMPERS

When shut, dampers prevent conditioned air from escaping up the chimney or cold air from coming down it. And, of course, the damper must be opened when you use a fireplace or the house will fill with smoke. So see if the damper works or if there's one at all. A damper that sticks can usually be cleaned to get it operable but if it's bent or becomes dislodged, perhaps the most cost-effective remedy is removing it and installing a spring-loaded damper atop the chimney. Typically, the top of a chimney is much more accessible than the narrow brick throat above a fireplace.

IS THERE A FLUE?

While you're on your knees peering up at the chimney, use your flashlight to see if the chimney has a flue liner. Wear eye protection and a dust mask because you're likely to dislodge soot while positioning yourself for a better look.

You may not see much, beyond a lot of powdery black soot, especially if the brick chimney is slightly offset. Happily, soot can be easily brushed out. But if you see shiny black creosote coating the surfaces, write it up because thick creosote often indicates that the chimney has not been cleaned regularly, thus increasing the chance of a chimney fire.

FIREBOX

A firebox is typically a three-walled, freestanding structure, which is independent of the back wall of the chimney, as shown in "Traditional Fireplace Cross Section" on p. 214. Thus a firebox can usually be rebuilt without disturbing the chimney mass, if the chimney is sound. Firebricks, which are made of special fire clay, are bigger and softer than conventional facing bricks and less likely to expand and contract (or crack) from heat. Yet because they are soft, firebricks can be damaged when logs are thrown against them.

If the back wall of a firebox has loose bricks, they should be removed and remortared, and the back wall rebuilt.

If you see crumbling, missing, or broken firebricks, or missing mortar, the firebox needs to be rebuilt. The back wall of a firebox often needs rebuilding because it suffers the highest temperatures (reflected heat) and the most physical abuse. Firebrick sidewalls can often be left in place. If firebox mortar joints seem thin, that's normal. It doesn't take much refractory mortar to hold firebricks together. In fact, some masons pride themselves on cutting and fitting firebricks so exactly that they don't need mortar.

While examining the firebox, inspect floor bricks for damage, too. Surprisingly, floor bricks rarely need replacing. Most fireplaces have andirons or grates that elevate burning logs and because heat rises, floor bricks have a relatively cool time of it. If the floor has a trap door that opens to an ash chute and a cleanout below, see if it opens. Also check to be sure it can be closed easily so hot ashes do not escape to the subfloor area or building exterior creating a fire hazard. (Sweeping ashes down chutes has fallen out of favor because people forget to clean them for years.)

FIREPLACE SURROUNDS AND HEARTH EXTENSIONS

Ideally, the surround that runs around a fireplace opening and the hearth extension that extends into the room should be made of noncombustible materials. Surrounds are often made of wood but, per code, no combustible material is allowed within 6 in. of the fireplace opening. So surrounds should be tile, stone, metal, or anything else that won't burn.

Because embers frequently fly out of fireplaces, hearth extensions must be a noncombustible material to a distance of at least 20 in. and preferably more. Fine-mesh screens or fire-rated glass doors are also recommended to contain sparks.

As you inspect surrounds and hearth extensions, note gaps or cracks through which hot gases or sparks could pass. Older hearth extensions were commonly supported by wood framing, which may be visible in the subarea (below the floor). This construction method was discontinued in the 1950s,

The wood surrounds of this fireplace, being combustible, violate the fire code. The gap between the firebox floor and the hearth extension is worrisome because hot coals could fall into it, possibly igniting subflooring or framing underneath.

NO FLEX CONNECTORS IN FIREBOXES!

FLEXIBLE GAS CONNECTORS MAY BE EASILY damaged by impact or the high heat of burning wood in a firebox. They may be used only in decorative fireplaces that have only gas fires. Because decorative fireplaces are sometimes converted back to wood-burning uses, home inspectors sometimes find flex connectors where they shouldn't be. All fireplace conversions must be code compliant and inspected by a fireplace specialist before use.

NOTE: Where log lighters are permitted within a fire pit, only hard gas-supply pipe may be used.

but many wood-supported extensions still exist. Framing could ignite if hot coals or ashes were allowed to spill onto the hearth extension or if wood supports extend to the area under the firebox. Because removing wood supports could cause the hearth extension to crack or fall, a qualified fireplace contractor should be contacted to determine how best to support the hearth extension.

GAS FIREPLACES

Gas fireplaces are intended to burn only natural gas or propane; there are both vented and unvented types. It's unsafe to burn anything other than gas in such a fireplace or to operate it other than as specified in the installation manual. This may sound like legal boilerplate, but an inspector should check a fireplace's use against those specs, especially venting provisions.

VENTED GAS FIREPLACES are similar to direct-vent wall furnaces, described on p. 202. Vented gas fireplaces typically employ concentric vent piping whose outer pipe draws in outside air for combustion, while its inner pipe vents combustion gases directly outside or up a chimney. To forestall a buildup of carbon monoxide inside living spaces, local codes may require that the chimney damper be fixed in the open position.

UNVENTED GAS FIREPLACES are not allowed in many locales, but when allowed, they employ thermal sensors and oxygen depletion sensors to protect inhabitants. These safety devices keep fireplace temperatures from getting too high or shut off the unit before carbon monoxide levels became too high indoors. There is some controversy around unvented gas fireplaces so get familiar with local requirements.

Whether a gas fireplace is vented or unvented, there should be a carbon monoxide detector installed in the room.

WHAT TO LOOK FOR

- Ask the residents if the fireplace smokes. Are there smoke stains on the fireplace surround? Has a smoke hood been installed?
- Check to see if there is an operable damper.
- Can you see a flue liner when looking up the chimney?

- Does the fireplace and area above it look like it has been cleaned regularly or are some surfaces shiny with built-up creosote?
- Are there crumbling, missing, or broken fire-bricks, or missing mortar in the firebox?
- In the floor of the firebox, is there a trap door that opens to an ash chute with a cleanout at the bottom? Has the chute been emptied recently or is it clogged with ashes?
- Are fireplace surrounds and the hearth extension made of noncombustible materials? Does the hearth extension extend out of the fireplace at least 20 in.? Are there cracks or gaps present?
- If you see a gas flex connector in the firebox, write it up. It shouldn't be there.
- If there is a gas fireplace, is it vented or unvented?
- Is there a carbon monoxide detector in the room where the fireplace is located?

INSERT STOVES

An insert is a wood-burning stove installed inside a fireplace. A common problem with such installations is the absence of a metal liner inside the masonry flue. The colder masonry flue may cause an accumulation of soot or creosote at the insert connection, creating a potential fire risk. In a correct installation, a metal flue pipe is installed inside the existing chimney, extending to a termination above the roof. To achieve this continuity, it is usually necessary to remove the fireplace damper and portions of firebox. This also applies to metal stoves installed at the front of fireplaces. Inserts and stove flues should be checked annually by a qualified chimneysweep or fireplace contractor.

Wood Stoves

The safety issues relevant to wood-burning fireplaces also pertain to wood stoves. Wood stoves and stovepipe should be cleaned at least once a year to keep creosote and other combustion byproducts from accumulating inside the stove, stovepipe, and chimney.

If you see a dark liquid leaking from stovepipe joints, that's liquid creosote, and it's probably running out of pipe joints because an installer incorrectly oriented crimped male pipe ends toward the chimney thimble rather than the wood stove collar (takeoff). Over time, creosote dries and hardens, becoming a shiny, tarlike substance that is hard to remove and extremely flammable. When it ignites, a chimney fire results that could burn the house down.

STOVE AGE AND EFFICIENCY

Repeated expansion and contraction as a wood stove heats up and cools down fatigues metal. Heavier cast-iron wood stoves will last longer than those built of rolled steel, but even heavier stoves should be replaced if gaps develop along seams. Above all, a wood stove must be airtight. So when stove doors no longer fit tight and seams between panels start to separate, it's time to retire the stove. Gaps could leak combustion gases into living spaces.

If a wood stove seems new, remind homeowners that it should be inspected by a local authority, such as the building department or fire department, before it is used. If possible, determine the age of the wood stove. Wood stoves manufactured before 1990 are, on average, one-third less efficient that those built after, when the EPA implemented stricter efficiency requirements.

New stoves are also cleaner. To quote Martin Holladay of www.greenbuildingadvisor.com: "EPA-certified stoves are also less polluting than pre-1990 stoves. The smoke emission limit for an EPA-certified stove is 7.5 grams of smoke per hour for non-catalytic stoves and 4.1 grams of smoke per hour for catalytic stoves. Pre-1990 stoves were much dirtier; they released between 15 and 30 grams of smoke per hour."

Wood stoves may be no closer than 36 in. to unprotected combustible surfaces, so this old Franklin stove is surrounded by violations, including the basket of burnables leaning against it.

REQUIRED CLEARANCES

A wood stove should be no closer than 36 in. to an unprotected combustible surface, including stud walls covered with plaster or drywall. By installing metal heat shields on the walls behind the stove you can reduce that clearance to 12 in, provided that the shield has a 1-in. air gap between it and the wall. (In rural areas, installers often use the porcelain insulators sold for electric fences to space head shields 1 in. away from walls.) Metal heat shields also need a 1-in. air gap at the bottom, so air can circulate between the shield and the wall.

Floors must be protected a minimum of 18 in. beyond the stove on all sides. (*Protected* means a noncombustible surface.) A good circulation of air under a wood stove is essential, so wood stove legs are typically 2 in. to 6 in. long. Floor protection beneath a stove must be at least 2 in. thick if stove legs are longer than 6 in.; if stove legs are 2 in. to 6 in. long, the floor protection must be at least 4 in. thick.

STOVEPIPE (CONNECTOR) is the pipe that connects the wood stove to a metal or a masonry chimney, so stovepipe lengths should be as short as possible, typically only 3 ft. or 4 ft. Stovepipe, which is single walled, is not the same as metal chimney, which is double walled and fire rated for use as a chimney. Single-wall stovepipe must be kept at least 18 in. away from combustible surfaces and may *not* pass through walls.

Stovepipe must also maintain a minimum ¼ in. in 1 ft. upward slope from the wood stove collar to the chimney. Any corrosion, rust, or separations in stovepipe are unacceptable and unsafe, so note them on your report. Stovepipe is inexpensive, so it should be replaced at the first sign of damage or deterioration.

WHAT TO LOOK FOR

- Has the wood stove been cleaned annually?
- Are there any signs of liquid creosote leaking from stovepipe joints or hard creosote buildup inside the wood stove, stovepipe, or chimney?
- How old is the wood stove? If built before 1990 EPA standards, it is inefficient and possibly unsafe.
- Measure to ascertain minimum clearances to combustible surfaces.
- Is the stovepipe correctly sloped and free from rust, corrosion, and gaps? Does the stovepipe terminate in an approved metal or masonry chimney?

CHAPTER 10

INTERIORS

AS YOU INSPECT INTERIOR SURFACES, be methodical. It doesn't matter whether you start in the attic and work down or start in the basement and work up, but examine every room and every closet, open and close every cabinet door or drawer, step on every stair tread, and note every detail you pass as you walk through the house. For the most part, the condition of interior surfaces—peeling paint, scuffed floors, abraded countertops—will be largely cosmetic, not too costly to repair or replace and thus no great cause for concern.

But occasionally, cracked plaster, extensive mold, or tilting trim boards echo a larger pattern of neglect or failure that is serious. An observant inspector will recall troubling conditions seen in other parts of the house and start to see patterns.

Some elements of a house interior are sufficiently complicated that they warrant their own chapters, so they are only mentioned in passing here: doors and windows (Chapter 11), kitchen and bathrooms (Chapter 12), electrical wiring (Chapter 6), plumbing (Chapter 7), and hazardous materials (Chapter 14).

Finish Surfaces

People have used plaster in buildings since prehistoric times. Drywall, the other material commonly used to cover walls and ceilings, is a relative newcomer that became widespread after World War II. Installing drywall is radically different from applying plaster, but drywall's core material is gypsum rock, the same material used since ancient times to make plaster.

Plaster and drywall are so widely used as interior surfaces because both are hard and durable. They are also relatively inflexible and hence brittle; they crack when the framing they are attached to moves. And all buildings move to a degree because of the seasonal expansion and contraction of building materials (or soil), or because of foundation settlement.

It's worth repeating that most hairline cracks, surface pocks, and dings can be repaired easily with patching plaster, joint compound, or spackle and then painted.

DRYWALL

Sometimes called Sheetrock® after a popular brand, drywall typically consists of 4-ft.-wide panels that are screwed or nailed to ceiling joists and wall studs. Sandwiched between layers of paper, drywall's gypsum core is almost as hard and durable as plaster, though it requires much less skill to install. Appropriately, the term *drywall* distinguishes these panels from plaster, which is applied wet and may take weeks to dry thoroughly.

NOTE: A special paperless drywall is manufactured to use in mold-prone areas such as basements and bathrooms.

Panel joints are concealed with tape and usually three coats of joint compound that render surfaces smooth. Each panel's two long edges are slightly

Interiors are mostly about surfaces: floors, walls, ceilings, steps; openings: mostly doors and windows; and fixtures: bathrooms, kitchens, and fireplaces. Inspecting interiors is a bit like seeing through walls to see what has happened before you arrived.

beveled, providing a depression to be filled by joint tape and compound. Each layer of joint compound must be allowed to dry thoroughly before sanding smooth and applying the next coat.

IS IT DRYWALL? Most homes built after the 1950s have drywall surfaces, except for high-end homes whose owners could afford plaster. Run your hand over the surface. Drywall surfaces tend to be smooth, whereas even slick plaster surfaces have a slightly gritty feel. Look across a drywall surface into the light and you can almost always see a faint panel joint, even when expertly done. But perhaps the best test is rapping a knuckle across a panel: Drywall sounds hollow till you cross a stud, at which point the sound becomes higher and less hollow.

NAIL AND SCREW PULL-THROUGHS AND POPS. The most common cause of nail or screw pops is an installer driving them too deep or not using enough of them. After new nails or screws are driven near popped ones, holes can be filled with joint compound, sanded, and painted.

If nail or screw pops are widespread in a new house and are accompanied by gaps at the top and bottom of walls, green lumber was used to frame the house rather than kiln-dried lumber, which shrinks less. The framing must be allowed to finish shrinking before repairs are made.

Isolated bulges in walls indicate that individual studs have twisted, again, because green lumber was used.

Widespread nail or screw pops in a ceiling may be due to attic joist flexion—in other words, when joists are not sized large enough to support items stored in the attic or the live loads of someone walking across attic joists.

READING DRYWALL CRACKS. Hairline cracks are rarely a problem and can usually be ignored.

Cracking along panel seams and joint tape pulling free from drywall occurs when an installer didn't use enough joint compound beneath and over the tape. Loose tape should be removed and replaced with new compound and tape.

Vertical cracks at door and window corners are telegraphing drywall joints that were (incorrectly) aligned with framing around the opening; headers shrank and drywall cracked. Cracks can be patched.

Water damage on the ceiling and this high on the walls may have multiple causes, including excessive interior moisture, inadequate attic ventilation, missing or un-maintained gutters, and perhaps a leaky roof.

If the roof is framed with trusses, cracking along wall–ceiling joints on exterior walls is not uncommon. Because these cracks are in response to seasonal fluctuations they will recur. It's best to seal cracks with an elastomeric caulk that will flex, or hide them with trim.

Large cracks that run diagonally from door or window corners (see the right photo on p. 224) are often caused by structural movement. Loads concentrate on headers, so diagonal cracks indicate that one end of the header is sinking. It may be necessary to have a structural engineer assess the foundation.

Similarly, large cracks at the top or bottom of a wall and flooring that slopes toward the base of the wall are typically caused by inadequate support beneath the wall. Floor joists may need to be bolstered or perhaps a girder added; a structural engineer may be needed to design a long-term solution.

WATER STAINS AND MOLD. Excessive condensation on and water stains around windows is often caused by excess interior moisture or from insufficient ventilation in the attic. Adding roof vents (see p. 80) and making sure that existing bath and kitchen fans vent to the outside should help. A cracked heat exchanger (see p. 185) and leaking furnace ducts can also dump water vapor (a byproduct of combustion) into living spaces.

Water stains on exterior walls, especially above windows, may be caused by missing flashing above the window, gaps between exterior trim and siding, and roof and gutter leaks.

Mold needs three things to grow: water, a temperature range between 40°F and 100°F, and organic matter, such as lumber or paper, to feed on. When inspecting damp-prone areas such as finished basements, be sure to pull furniture away from sub-area walls to look for mold.

Minor surface mold on walls, especially in kitchens and baths is typically caused by excess moisture and insufficient ventilation. Minor mold can often be wiped or scrubbed off. Adding or upsizing ventilation fans will probably keep mold from returning.

Extensive surface mold and crumbling drywall indicates sustained/severe exterior leaks or excess interior moisture. In such cases, there's probably extensive mold growing inside the walls, too. After the source(s) of the moisture are identified and corrected, a mold-remediation contractor will need to remove and replace the moldy drywall and perhaps the studs, too.

WHAT TO LOOK FOR

- Determine what the walls and ceilings are covered with—drywall or plaster.

- Are any surfaces cracked? Is cracking isolated or widespread? Are they mostly hairline cracks or are some deeper? Are cracks active or inactive?

- If surfaces are drywall, note instances where there's cracking along panel joints or lifted joint tape. If it's widespread, the installer may have been inexpert.

- Take special note of cracks that run diagonally from window or door trim corners.

- Is there water damage on any surfaces? If so, try to explain it by possible leak sources you've seen elsewhere during your inspection.

- Are any surfaces moldy? How isolated or widespread is the mold?

- What is the most likely explanation of where mold-related moisture is coming from?

PLASTER

Traditional plastering is installed in several steps. After wood or metal lath is nailed to the framing, the plasterer trowels on a scratch coat (base coat) of wet plaster that oozes through the gaps in the lath and becomes a mechanical key when it hardens. When the scratch coat has dried sufficiently, a brown coat is troweled on and then roughened after it has set slightly. The finish coat (white coat) is the final surface, typically smooth though sometimes textured to conform with an architectural style.

Before the twentieth century, plasterers often mixed animal hair into scratch and brown coats to help them stick. The finish coat was usually a mixture of gauging plaster and lime, for uniformity. Scratch

coats and brown coats were left rough and were often scratched with a plasterer's comb before they set completely, so the next coat would have grooves to adhere to. Finish coats are quite thin (1/16 in.) and very hard.

IS IT PLASTER? Once it has dried, a plaster-and-lath assembly is considerably thicker and harder than drywall. When you rap across a plaster surface, the sound is uniform whether you rap over a stud or between studs. Plaster is also slightly gritty (cementitious) to the touch. If the attic is unfinished, you should be able to see the backside of the plaster lath.

READING PLASTER CRACKS. Because plaster is harder and more brittle than drywall, hairline cracks are common and usually cosmetic. Gently pressing along both sides of a crack will help determine if the plaster has detached from its lath; soundly attached plaster won't move.

Cracks that expand and shrink seasonally are common in older homes whose lot has a high clay content. Soil beneath the foundation swells during the wet season, lifting the house; during the dry season, the house settles downward. Using flexible mesh tape and sealing cracks with flexible elastomeric caulk may make cracks less obvious.

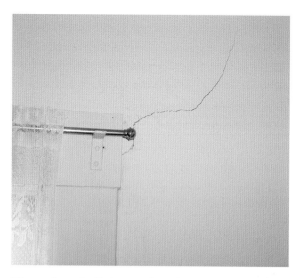

The plaster that oozes through lath is called a "key"; when keys break, plaster may crack or even fall off. Extensive plaster cracking is difficult to repair so it's frequently replaced or covered over with drywall panels.

Diagonal cracks that extend out from the corner of a window or doorway may be a sign of periodic movement or even structural failure. Headers over doors and windows carry considerable loads and when they aren't supported adequately, one side of the header drops and finish surfaces crack.

Large cracks that run diagonally from door or window corners, as shown in the right photo above, are typically caused by structural movement. Because loads concentrate on headers, diagonal cracks indicate that one end of the header is sinking because the bottom of a stud has rotted or some part of the foundation has failed. A structural engineer should assess the foundation.

Cracked ceilings and damaged ornamental plaster molding or medallions are common in older homes: plaster keys break and gravity does the rest. If cracking is limited, it may be possible to rescrew the plaster to the lath, using washered screws. Another strategy is covering cracked ceilings with a layer of drywall screwed to ceiling joists. If attic joists are undersize, storing personal effects on them will increase flexion and ceiling cracking.

WATER STAINS AND MOLD. Water stains on plaster are caused by most of the conditions that stain drywall (discussed earlier), including absent window flashing, leaking roofs, inadequate ventilation, and excess interior moisture. Finding and correcting the source of the water is the first step in any remediation. In older homes, a leaky tub, shower,

or toilet may be the source of the leak, or perhaps old pipes are leaking. If the wet wall of a bathroom has an access panel, open it to see what condition the pipes are in.

Mold is less common on plaster because plaster, unlike paper-faced drywall, is inorganic. Any mold that does form on plaster usually forms on soap residue or dirt that has adhered to the plaster surface. Minor mold should scrub off easily. But extensive

LOW CEILINGS

ROOMS WITH CEILINGS LESS THAN 7 ft. 6 in. high may not be considered habitable by local building departments. Such rooms should not be counted as bedrooms in a real-estate listing, though there are exceptions to the general rule that allow for sloping ceilings and low beams.

mold and detached or crumbling plaster suggest a sustained moisture problem and probable mold damage inside the walls. A mold-remediation contractor should be hired to assess and correct the problem.

WHAT TO LOOK FOR

- Is any of the plaster water stained? What is the most likely source of the moisture?
- Is the plaster solidly attached or are there areas where it is cracking or bulging?
- Are cracks mostly hairline cracks or are some larger, with crumbling edges?
- Do any of the larger plaster cracks suggest structural movement?
- What is the condition of plaster ceilings? Do any ceilings sag or crack excessively?
- Is mold present on any plaster surfaces? Is it widespread or isolated?

MISCELLANEOUS SURFACES

You may also find walls covered with wood paneling or wallpaper; report on their condition.

WALLPAPER WITH PURPLE-PINK BLOTCHES bleeding through probably has mold growing on it and the wallpaper adhesive. The wallpaper will probably also be lumpy. Mold loves wallpaper, especially when there's excess moisture present. Have a mold-abatement specialist assess the condition and make recommendations.

BLISTERING VINYL WALLPAPER is common in humid regions. When vinyl wallpaper is installed on exterior walls, moisture can get trapped behind it and mold will flourish. The wallpaper should be stripped and walls scrubbed to remove mold, if any. If mold is extensive, a mold-abatement specialist should remove a section of drywall to see if mold is inside the walls, too.

WOOD PANELING can be left alone if it's in decent condition. Press it with the palms of your hands to see if it flexes excessively and then rap your knuckle across its surfaces. An even, dull sound suggests that it may be installed directly over plaster or drywall, perhaps because the original wall surface

ACOUSTIC TILE CEILINGS

IF HOUSE WALLS ARE PLASTER BUT CEILINGS are covered with acoustic tiles, the tiles are probably covering up plaster ceilings in bad condition. Note stained or sagging sections of tile, because they may indicate that other sections are about to fail. If the tiles hang from a metal support grid, you may be able to remove (push up) a few tiles to get a better idea of what's going on above. Wear a dust mask and eye protection if you do so.

NOTE: Pre-1979 acoustic ceilings with a "cottage-cheese" texture may contain asbestos to deaden sound and retard the spread of fire. If you come across such a ceiling texture, call in a certified asbestos-abatement inspector to assess its condition and advise homeowners.

Spray acoustic ceilings allow builders to finish ceilings quickly and cheaply because the material is sprayed directly on the drywall. Acoustic ceilings installed before the late 1970s often contain asbestos.

was in bad condition. If the paneling flexes when you press it and knuckle-rapping produces a high, booming sound, the paneling may be attached directly to studs, a common technique in the 1950s and early 1960s. Mid-century wood paneling can be pretty thin (¼ in. thick or less, also called doorskin), so it may flex and crack if its only supports are studs 16 in. or 24 in. on-center.

Some jurisdictions are concerned about wood paneling installed directly over open wood framing, as these structures burn down very quickly if a fire should start. Paneling over drywall or plaster is much more fire resistant.

WHAT TO LOOK FOR

- If walls are covered with wallpaper, what is its general condition? Are any seams lifting?
- Scrutinize wallpaper at the tops of walls and near windows and doors for water stains.
- Is any of the wallpaper lumpy, with purple-pink blotches? It's probably moldy.
- Vinyl wallpaper is a bad choice for moisture-prone regions. It should be stripped.
- If any walls are paneled, are panels attached directly to studs or have they been installed over plaster or drywall?
- Is any wood paneling abraded, delaminating, or water-stained?

Paint and Clear Finishes

The state of house paint and clear finishes is a surface matter, but it's not superficial because it reflects the level of house maintenance and care.

This tip from a pro: "Check the closets. When houses are gussied up for sale, they often get re-planted and landscaped, painted inside and out, and staged to the max. But in the rush to get a house to market, homeowners usually run out of steam and time and so ignore closets. Thus closets may show water stains, cracks, and lead paint that was painted over elsewhere."

COMMON PAINT CONCERNS

Because many homeowners paint a house just before putting it up for sale, inspectors sometimes find paint-related issues that would be unnoticeable if the paint weren't fresh.

PAINT THAT CONTINUES TO SMELL weeks or even months after it has been applied probably had upper coats applied over a first coat that was not fully dry. As paint dries, it outgases (gives off gases),

releasing water vapor or mineral spirits and additives into the air.

The warmer the room and the better the ventilation, the sooner smells will dissipate. In a room that is 60°F or warmer, acrylic latexes typically will be dry enough to recoat in 2 hours to 4 hours. Oil-based paints require at least 24 hours. In cooler or more humid conditions, odors may linger because paints need longer to cure: up to 10 days for latex, up to 30 days for oil-based paints.

NEW PAINT THAT DOESN'T ADHERE WELL or fully hide paint beneath probably wasn't adequately prepped or applied; poor-quality paint doesn't cover well. Surfaces will probably need to be washed and sanded before a new coat of good-quality paint can be applied.

IF OLD WATER STAINS OR WOOD KNOTS BLEED THROUGH newer paint, the stains were never sufficiently primed with a sealer such as white pigmented shellac. It's also important that the source of the water leak be located and repaired before repainting.

IF PAINT AT THE TOP OF A WALL IS MOLDY, there is excessive interior moisture, gaps in exterior siding or flashing, a leaky roof, or some other condition that needs attention before painting.

IF FLAT PAINT ON TRIM IS GRIMY, worn, or difficult to clean, it should be sanded and painted over with semigloss or gloss paint. Trim gets a lot of wear, especially from children.

IF PAINT SAMPLES TEST POSITIVE FOR LEAD but paint surfaces are intact—not peeling or flaking—there is little chance of ingestion or inhalation as long as the paint is not disturbed. (Lead paint typically becomes airborne if it is sanded, stripped, or abraded.) In other words, painting over existing lead paint with nonlead paint is a reasonable short-term solution. For more information about lead-related questions, see Chapters 2 and 14 or contact the National Lead Information Center at www2.epa.gov/lead/forms/lead-hotline-national-lead-information-center.

Lead paint, which was banned in 1978, is usually not a health hazard if it is sealed by newer paint in good condition. The old enamel lead paint on this threshold, however, has abraded badly and could be inhaled or ingested; it should be removed by a lead-abatement specialist.

WHAT'S THAT CLEAR FINISH?

Clear finishes include polyurethane, varnish, lacquer, and shellac. Polyurethane is the most durable of the clear finishes and thus the most suitable for heavy-traffic surfaces, such as trim and stair parts. Although poly and varnish resist moisture, they may become cloudy with sustained exposure to wet conditions. Shellac also clouds up near water. Spar varnish—originally used on boats—has a hard finish that stands up well to water, if well maintained.

Home inspectors aren't expected to identify what clear finish was used, but your clients might appreciate knowing the simple sequence of identifying finishes that follows. If homeowners know what finish is presently on woodwork, stairs, or floors, they will have a better chance of finding a compatible material with which to refinish or touch up what's there.

To identify a finish, rub on a small amount of the test solvents given in this list, starting at the top of the list (the most benign) and working down till you've got your answer. When applying solvents, wear rubber gloves, open the windows, and wear a respirator.

OIL. If a few drops of boiled linseed oil soak into the woodwork, you have an oil finish: tung oil, linseed, Watco®, or the like. If the oil beads up on the surface, the woodwork has a hard finish, such as lacquer, varnish, or shellac. Keep investigating.

DENATURED ALCOHOL. If the finish quickly gets gummy after applying denatured alcohol, congratulations! It's shellac, which will readily accept a new coat of shellac after a modest sanding with an abrasive nylon pad or 220-grit sandpaper. Older woodwork with an orange tinge is often shellac-coated.

MINERAL SPIRITS (PAINT THINNER). Mineral spirits will dissolve wax immediately. Dampen a rag and wipe once. If there's a yellowish or light brown residue on the rag, it's definitely wax. If your woodwork finish has an unevenly shiny, runny appearance, suspect spray-on wax.

LACQUER THINNER. Because lacquer thinner dissolves both varnish and shellac, try denatured alcohol first. If alcohol doesn't dissolve the finish but lacquer thinner does, it's varnish.

ACETONE. Acetone will dissolve varnish, too, in about 30 seconds. But if acetone doesn't affect the finish, it's probably polyurethane.

WHAT TO LOOK FOR

- Does new paint still smell? How recently were rooms painted? Find out from homeowners if the paint was latex or oil based.
- If a home has been newly painted, check closets for evidence of earlier, lead-based paint.
- Home centers sell inexpensive DIY kits for testing the presence of lead paints. If suspect paint is abraded, worn, or detaching, it should be tested.
- Scan painted surfaces for bleed-through water stains or knots on wood trim. Such blemishes suggest surfaces that were not adequately prepped before painting.
- If any painted surface is moldy, try to determine the source of the moisture that is promoting mold growth.

Interior Trim

Interior trim is often called casing or molding. Trim helps establish the character of a room by accenting or embellishing features, like a picture frame. Trim is also functional, concealing gaps and rough edges where walls meet floors, ceilings, doors, and windows. It may seem merely decorative, but trim can signal potential structural problems if you know how to read it.

COMMON TRIM CONCERNS

GAPS AT CORNERS where trim pieces meet are common as the wood shrinks. If the trim is painted, gaps can be filled and painted.

PAINTED TRIM SPLIT by nailing too close to the edges can be filled and painted over. If the trim has a clear finish, try to match the original wood color with wood filler before refinishing.

GAPS UNDER BASEBOARD TRIM are common. In fact, baseboard trim should float above wood flooring so that flooring can expand and contract seasonally.

TILTING TRIM AND OUT-OF-SQUARE DOOR CASING are common and usually cosmetic in older homes. These conditions are usually caused by cumulative settlement over many years, especially if the foundation is undersize or unreinforced. But when trim tilts downward in one direction and is

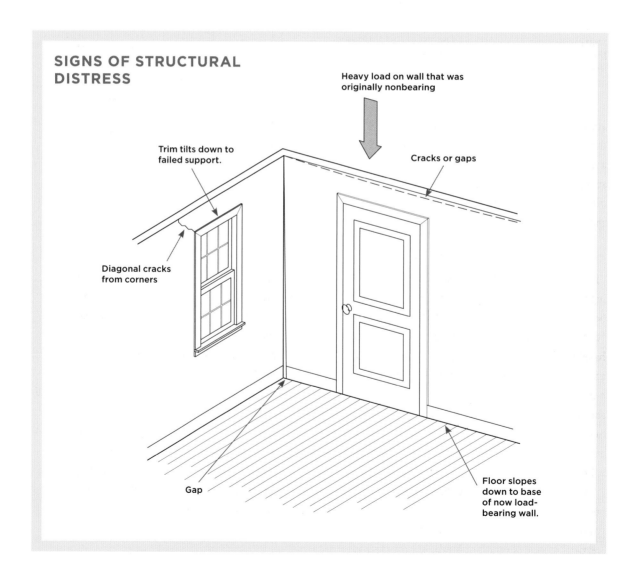

SIGNS OF STRUCTURAL DISTRESS

Trim tilts down to failed support.

Diagonal cracks from corners

Gap

Heavy load on wall that was originally nonbearing

Cracks or gaps

Floor slopes down to base of now load-bearing wall.

This wooden baseboard below a window has suffered water damage for many years, as has the flooring that abuts it. The baseboard should be removed so that the framing behind it can be checked for water damage and decay.

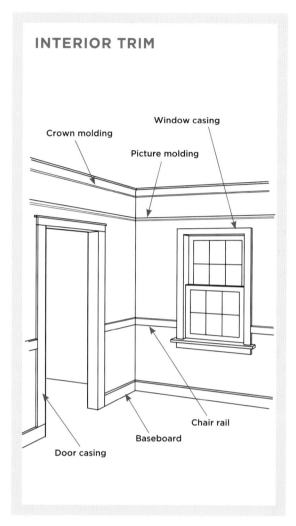

INTERIOR TRIM

Crown molding

Window casing

Picture molding

Chair rail

Baseboard

Door casing

accompanied by diagonal cracking at door and window corners, there may be structural distress, such as a rotted support post or a sinking pad, a failed or absent girder, or a section of foundation that is failing, often because inadequate drainage has undermined the footing.

THE CASE FOR NOT LEVELING TRIM

The older a house, the less likely its floors and ceilings will be level. If homeowners ask you what can be done about unlevel trim, give them this advice: "Leave it. Don't make yourself crazy trying to level baseboards or crown molding. You won't succeed, and trim that's level next to a surface that isn't will only emphasize the discrepancy. Horizontal trim should be roughly parallel to a floor or a ceiling." As master carpenter Joseph Beals puts it, "Baseboard is effectively floor trim, and the floor plane is the critical reference, level or not."

Mid-wall elements such as chair rails, picture rails, and wainscoting require yet more fudging. Ideally, chair rails should be level and wainscoting stiles (vertical pieces) should be plumb, but those ideals

may clash with existing trim that's neither. A good carpenter will split the difference, raising or lowering one end of a trim board until the eye accepts the compromise.

Trim can also help give the illusion of a level ceiling—helpful, when upper kitchen cabinets must be set level even if the ceiling isn't. After leveling and securing upper cabinets, a smart installer will use a strip of molding to cover any gaps above. If you know what to look for, you may see an uneven strip of molding between the cabinets and the ceiling. But if the cover trim matches the cabinet finish, chances are nobody else will notice the difference.

WHAT TO LOOK FOR

- Small gaps where trim boards in a corner meet are common. Gaps under baseboard trim are also common.
- Trim split by nails or screws too close to the edge can be filled and refinished.
- Tilting window or door trim and diagonal cracking at corners may indicate failed structural supports. Did you see likely causes in the basement or crawl space inspection?

Floors

Flooring and base molding are usually the last building materials to be installed and flooring is the first to show its age, as it is crushed by footsteps, swollen by moisture, and abraded by dirt. Today's crop of flooring and floor finishes is far more durable and varied than was available a generation ago. Some types of engineered flooring are so sophisticated that they are hard to distinguish from solid wood. Frequently, an inspector's first task is determining what type of flooring is present.

Flooring is only the top layer of a system that usually includes underlayment and subflooring as well as structural members, such as joists and girders. If finish floors are to be solid and long lasting, all parts of the flooring system must be sized and spaced correctly for the loads they will carry. Excessive flexion degrades all types of flooring. Also, although some flooring materials can withstand moisture better than others, all will degrade in time if installed in chronically damp locations.

DETERMINING WOOD FLOORING TYPE AND THICKNESS

The type of flooring is usually obvious just by looking at it but some types of engineered wood flooring are hard to distinguish from conventional solid-strip

FLOORING CHOICES

CHARACTERISTIC	SOLID WOOD	ENGINEERED WOOD	LAMINATE	RESILIENT FLOORING	BAMBOO	PALM	CORK	TILE AND STONE	CONCRETE
DURABILITY	Good	Very good	Excellent	Excellent	Very good	Very good	Good*	Excellent	Excellent
REQUIRED MAINTENANCE	Sweep regularly	Sweep regularly	Damp mop	Damp mop	Sweep regularly	Sweep regularly	Sweep or damp-mop	Wet mop	Wet mop
WATER RESISTANCE†	Poor	Fair	Good	Good to excellent	Poor to fair	Poor to fair	Poor	Excellent	Excellent
COMFORT UNDERFOOT	Flexes	Flexes	Flexes	Soft	Flexes	Flexes	Soft	Hard	Hard
GREEN CREDS	Yes	Mixed	No	Linoleum, yes vinyl, no‡	Yes	Yes	Yes	Yes	Mixed
COST§	$-$$$	$-$$	$	$	$-$$	$$	$$-$$$	$$-$$$	$-$$

*Durable but deforms if furniture sits on same spot for too long.
†Correct persistent moisture problems before converting any areas to living space.
‡Linoleum and recycled rubber are considered green; vinyl is not.
§Costs do not reflect installation charges.

flooring, except by noting engineered board ends, which are the width of three pieces of conventional strip flooring. To ascertain the thickness of wood flooring and subflooring, remove a forced-hot air register and look at the exposed cross-section of flooring.

If that's not possible, you can pull up a doorway threshold or remove baseboard trim and bore a small hole to expose a cross section of flooring. Or drill in a closet where no one will see the hole. If floors are covered with carpet, pull up a corner to expose plywood or OSB subflooring, whose thickness is usually stamped on each panel. If the underside of the subflooring is visible in the basement, look for answers there. Knowing the thickness of subflooring is useful if you are trying to determine why floors are springy or if, say, you plan to install new flooring that requires subflooring of a certain thickness. Resilient flooring, for example, is thin and so depends on a relatively thick subfloor and an underlayment that's smooth, thick, and flat. The grout between floor tiles will crack if subflooring that's too thin flexes.

COMMON FLOOR CONCERNS

The most common flooring complaint is squeaking, which is caused by movement: floorboards rubbing together or subflooring rubbing against a nail shank that no longer holds the subfloor to a joist. It's usually hard to eliminate floor squeaks completely.

FLOORS THAT ARE NOT LEVEL are common in older homes in which shrinking floor joists or foundation settlement has occurred. If floors are otherwise sound, homeowners should enjoy their charm and learn to live with them.

SQUEAKING BENEATH CARPETS is usually caused by subflooring that was not adequately nailed or glued in newer homes. Carpet must be removed to access and renail the subflooring. If carpet has been newly installed over wood flooring, an inspector should ask homeowners to verify (in writing) that the wood flooring underneath is in good condition; too often, new carpet is hiding wood flooring that was trashed (or soaked) by an unruly pet.

THICK ENOUGH TO SAND?

YOU CAN SAND ONLY THE TOP VENEER LAYER of engineered wood flooring, which is typically $5/32$ in. thick. Solid-wood, tongue-and-groove (T&G) strip flooring is typically ¾ in. thick, but you can sand down only to the top of the tongue at one edge of each board. If you sand lower, you'll hit flooring nails. T&G nail heads should be driven in at an angle through the top of the tongue and then set flush.

These hardwood floors are cupped. The raised edges suggest moisture came from below, perhaps from damp subflooring and/or poor ventilation.

HARDWOOD FLOORING THAT CUPS has usually absorbed moisture through its underside. Because the underside of each board expands in relation to its drier top side, top edges are pushed up. If cupping is slight, it may be possible (if unlikely) to sand down high spots. Otherwise, cupped flooring should be removed and the moisture corrected before replacing the flooring.

DAMAGED FLOORING NEAR EXTERIOR DOORS is usually caused by water: excess condensation in cold weather, driving rains or drifting snow, insufficient weather stripping, a failed threshold or absent floor pan, a deck or patio that is too high or inadequately flashed, an exterior door unprotected by a porch roof, poor maintenance (not refinishing worn floorboards), and so on.

FLOORING THAT BOWS in the center of a room may have been installed without a gap around its perimeter to allow for expansion. As flooring expands, it has nowhere to go but up. Bowed flooring may be removed, cut down to create a gap around the perimeter, and reinstalled.

LOCALIZED SPRINGINESS or low spots in flooring are probably caused by an undersize footing pad or by a deteriorated or absent post beneath a girder. If you find wet rot or insect damage at the base of the post, that situation will need to be corrected before anything else can be done.

WIDESPREAD SPRINGINESS in floors and joists sagging in mid-span are caused by joists that are too small for a span or by a failed or absent girder. If the girder seems sound, adding posts or new pads may fix the problem. Otherwise, add a girder to reduce the distance that joists span.

FLOORING THAT CROWNS ABOVE A GIRDER, sloping downward toward the outside walls, can often be explained by the failure of all or part of a perimeter foundation, as can doors and windows that are difficult to open and cracking at the corners of openings.

LOOSE CERAMIC FLOOR TILES and cracked grout joints are caused by adhesive that was insufficiently thick or inexpertly applied or by excessive flexion because of subflooring that was too thin.

LARGE PAVER TILES (12 in. sq.) with cracks across their faces were set in a mortar bed that was not thick enough to support the pavers, which can be irregular.

LOOSE OR DETERIORATED LINOLEUM near a toilet or tub may be hiding a persistent leak or, possibly, rotted subflooring. Existing flooring may need to be removed so the subflooring can be examined and, if necessary, replaced. The leak source must also be corrected.

LINOLEUM OR VINYL TILES that are stained or lumpy were probably installed over a slab that is wicking moisture from below. Repairs may be extensive. At the very least, the slab should be sealed with a moisture-resistant coating before new flooring can be installed. Unglazed ceramic tiles are often best for below grade or basement concrete floors as the moisture from below can flow through the tiles and dry on the surface.

RESILIENT TILES THAT CONTAIN ASBESTOS are generally not a health concern unless they have become abraded or have deteriorated because of sustained contact with moisture. If they are flat and

These cracked ceramic tile floors may indicate water entry and decay in the supporting subflooring. Areas beneath should be checked, if accessible, and repaired as needed.

Sometimes it's possible to pull up a carpet at a corner and find water stains, rusted nails, and decay. This condition is common in basements or on other below-grade concrete slabs.

well attached, it may be possible to cover them with new flooring; if not, they should be removed by an asbestos-abatement contractor.

CARPET IN BASEMENTS is often suspect because of persistent dampness and inadequate ventilation in subgrade areas. Carpet installed over slab is particularly problematic because moisture can wick through concrete.

WHAT TO LOOK FOR

- What kind of flooring is present? What is its general condition and how is it wearing where it abuts exterior doors and other high-wear areas? Any water-related damage?

- Are floors solid or springy? If springy, try to find out why, such as too-thin subflooring or joists spaced too far apart.

- Does flooring squeak? Try to determine why.

- If there's wood flooring, remove floor registers to see a cross section of the flooring and subflooring. Is the top layer of the wood flooring thick enough to be sanded?

- Do any portions of wood flooring cup, bow, or perhaps crown over a girder?

- If there are ceramic tile floors, are tiles solidly attached? Is grout intact or cracked?

- Is resilient flooring water stained, lifting, or damaged where it abuts cabinet bottoms, along tubs or showers, or along the base of toilets? If the floor seems springy, the subfloor or floor joists may be water damaged. Check further.

- What is the condition of resilient flooring in a basement or other subgrade area? If the flooring was installed over a concrete slab, look for lifting or moisture-related damage.

- Carpet installed in subgrade or moisture-prone areas warrants a closer look. Ask the homeowner if you can lift a corner.

Staircases

Staircases are complex structures and diagnosing problems can be tricky. It may be possible to repair squeaky treads with glue and a few screws; but if, say, stairs tilt to one side and there's a gap along a stair-

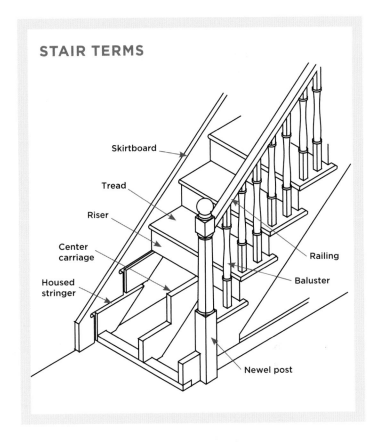

STAIR TERMS

Skirtboard

Tread

Riser

Center carriage

Housed stringer

Railing

Baluster

Newel post

well wall, the carriages beneath the staircase may be failing. In that case, an experienced carpenter should expose the substructure (the framing that supports the stairs) to better diagnose the situation.

RISERS AND TREADS

Each step consists of a riser, the vertical part that determines its height, and a tread, the horizontal part you step on. Stair dimensions must be consistent within each flight. Varying riser height between one step and the next will disrupt a stair-user's rhythm, which could cause him or her to trip and fall.

Tread widths sometimes vary on the bottom two or three steps of a main staircase, for dramatic effect. Widths also vary on portions of winder stairs, in which a narrow turning radius requires that some treads be pie shaped. But riser height must *never* vary more than 3/8 in. in a single run. If you find uneven steps, emphasize them in your report because they

Step height must not vary in a flight of stairs; steps of uneven height can disrupt a stair-user's rhythm and cause a fall. Here, a smaller top step could put someone on an unsafe footing.

are a safety hazard; uneven steps should be reframed or rebuilt so that step heights are consistent.

LOW HEADROOM AND DOORS THAT SWING OUT over downward staircases are safety hazards that are not allowed in new construction, but are often permitted under grandfather clauses (long-established prior use) in older houses. If there is

a major remodel, however, homeowners may be required to rebuild such structures so that they conform to current building codes.

TREADS CRACK because they aren't supported adequately or they weren't made from thick enough stock, which is typically 1 in. thick after milling. Removing damaged treads requires prying or cutting them out. But installing replacements gets tricky because tread edges are often rabbeted to risers or tread ends must be housed in (let into) stringers.

A FEW SQUEAKY STEPS may be fixable without removing finish materials around the staircase. If stairs are painted or carpeted, try caulking squeaky joints with subflooring adhesive, which stays somewhat flexible after it has cured. Don't use nails; they will work loose or split the tread. It's better to countersink screws, but they won't hold for long if stairs are springy.

SOLID BUT EXCESSIVELY SQUEAKY STEPS have probably worked loose. When new they are tightly wedged into housed stringers, but wedges work loose. Or treads flex excessively because the

Low stair headroom is typically permitted in older homes but not in new construction. Here, homeowners have alerted users to the hazard and provided a solid vertical grip-rail to aid descent.

This staircase has two strikes against it: a door that swings out over a downward run and the upper end of a railing that projects out and could catch a stair user's clothing, causing a fall.

staircase's center carriage slips down and now no longer supports them. To drive in wedges or bolster a failing center carriage, the repairer will need access to the underside of the staircase.

STEPS THAT ARE EXCESSIVELY SPRINGY or sag in the middle need the same cure: accessing the underside of the staircase to bolster the center carriage.

RAILINGS, BALUSTERS, AND NEWEL POSTS

Railings, balusters, and newel posts make up the staircase superstructure and are usually repaired after the substructure has been fixed. But because loose newel posts are common in any home with kids, newels often need tightening even if the staircase is fine otherwise.

STAIRS WITHOUT HANDRAILS must be written up as a fall danger. Handrails must be installed at a height of 34 in. to 38 in. above three or more stair treads. (Guardrail openings must be less than 4 in. wide to prevent a child from falling through.)

LOOSE RAILINGS should be tightened at both ends. The upper end of a railing often dead-ends into a wall above, where it is anchored to a bracket underneath. Make sure the bracket is tight. The lower end of a railing often attaches to a newel post, typically by a star nut on the underside of the railing (see "Inside a Newel Post" on p. 236). Remove the access plug and tighten the star nut.

LOOSE BALUSTERS ARE COMMON. Balusters can usually be accessed by removing the nosing (nose molding) at the end of each step; reshimming and regluing balusters usually works.

IF THE NEWEL POST WOBBLES, a carpenter can try shimming underneath its base or screwing the post down with 3-in. screws. If that fix doesn't suffice, the post's internal hardware probably needs tightening. Newel posts often are hollow, with a long, threaded rod inside, as shown in "Inside a Newel Post." To tighten the upper end of this rod, concealed by the post cap, turn a nut against a restraining plate. If the bottom end of the threaded

STAIRCASE SAFETY AND CODE

MODERN BUILDING STANDARDS CALL FOR railings at least 36 in. high for any deck, stair, or landing more than 30 in. above an adjacent surface. Openings between balusters or between rails and steps must be less than 4 in. wide. Large railing openings that could allow a child to fall through should be modified for safety. Staircases with four or more steps should have handrails that are between 1½ in. and 2 in. wide. Handrails should be placed and shaped so they can be readily grasped for safety. Handrails should be 34 in. to 38 in. above the leading edge of the stair treads. Handrails must return to the railing or post or to the ground; they may not end in a projection that could be hooked by clothing.

The openings in this guardrail (here, the distance between balusters) are too large; a small child could slip through them. Guardrail openings must be less than a ball 4 in. in diameter.

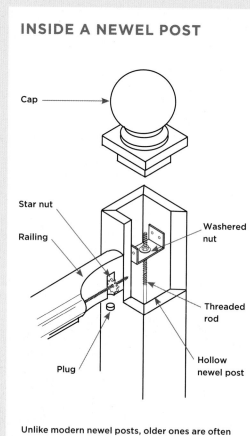

INSIDE A NEWEL POST

Cap

Star nut

Railing

Washered nut

Threaded rod

Plug

Hollow newel post

Unlike modern newel posts, older ones are often hollow and attach to railings in various ways. One common way is a star nut centered in the end of a railing, which is accessed by removing a plug on the underside. The bottom of the post may be screwed to a stringer or held fast by an adjustable rod-and-plate assembly running down the middle of the post.

rod emerges on the underside of the subflooring, it can be tightened as well.

SUBSTRUCTURE REPAIRS

If stairs tilt to one side, the carriage on the low side is having difficulty—that is, nails or bolts holding it to wall studs may be pulling out, the framing may be rotting or splitting, or the carriage may be separating from a stringer. Sagging on the open side of a staircase is common because there are no wall studs to bolt carriages to.

If there are large cracks or gaps at the top and bottom of the stairs, you are seeing symptoms of a falling carriage. When such failure occurs, the center carriage has often pulled free from the doubled header at the bottom of the stairwell opening.

To determine exactly what is going on, finish surfaces on the underside of the staircase will have to be removed. Not surprisingly, rebuilding a staircase can be disruptive and costly.

WHAT TO LOOK FOR

- Do stair treads squeak? How widespread is the problem? Are any treads split?

- Stair heights must never vary within a flight of stairs. If you see steps of uneven height within a flight, note it prominently in your report. It is a fall hazard.

- Do staircases flex noticeably when someone walks on them? Stair carriages (supports underneath) may be undersize or failing.

- Write up any staircases without handrails, they are a fall hazard. Handrails must be installed at a height of 34 in. to 38 in. above stair treads.

- Note loose railings or railings that end in a projection that could catch clothing and cause a fall. Railings should end in a return, or attach to a post or to a wall.

- Are all openings in guardrails less than 4 in. to prevent a child's falling through?

- Does the newel post wobble? It should be tightened so its wobble does not increase.

- If a staircase tilts to one side, its structural supports on the low side may be failing.

- Large cracks or gaps at the top and/or bottom of the stairs may indicate a falling carriage.

CHAPTER 11

DOORS *and* WINDOWS

DOORS AND WINDOWS MUST WITHSTAND extreme weather shifts, UV damage from the sun, cycles of soaking and drying, and impatient inhabitants trying to force them open when they are swollen or painted shut. Doors and windows must be durable yet movable, let in light yet keep out rain, and admit views and guests but deny drafts. Mediators of outside and in, they play a critical role in how comfortable, healthful, and energy-efficient a home is.

Doors should never open over a descending staircase, which could lead to a serious fall. Solutions include reversing the swing of the door or removing the door from the frame.

The crack above this door frame could be telegraphing a header that is sinking because a foundation support—a post, a pad, or a footing—has failed.

Doors

Historically, most doors have been made from wood, though that is changing, partly because wood is a bit too affected by the natural forces just listed. (We'll look at other door materials in a bit.) Even small variations in temperature and moisture cause wood doors to expand and contract. Meanwhile, the house in which the doors are installed is also moving. Mostly built of wood, a house expands and contracts, but it also shifts due to seasonal or seismic soil movement. (Houses must also withstand lateral loads—side loads—such as wind or soil pushing against walls and the live loads of the people inside, but that's enough structure for now.)

Given all that movement and the close fit of doors to frames (⅛-in. gap is common), sooner or later something's got to give. How long a door fits in its frame and how long it opens and closes without binding or scraping depends on the quality of its wood and its manufacture, how well it was prepped and sealed, and how skillfully it was installed. And, indirectly, how skillfully the house around it was framed. Let's look at the whole assembly.

DOORS, DOOR FRAMES, AND ROUGH OPENINGS

A ROUGH OPENING is a framed opening in a wall, roof, or floor platform. This opening will remain stable despite all the loads and movement around it. Headers (lintels) are bearing beams that carry loads across the opening. Supporting a header on each side of the opening is the job of a king stud (full length) and a shortened jack stud. Short cripple studs transfer loads from the wall's top plate to the header, though sometimes oversize headers big enough to reach the top plate are installed instead. Top and bottom (sole) plates further distribute loads.

DOOR FRAMES consist of several pieces: two side pieces (or side jambs) and a head jamb (or frame head) running across the top; exterior doors also have a sill spanning the bottom. (The sill may also have a threshold, but more about that later.) Jambs are further distinguished by the hardware they bear: The jamb on which the door is hung is the hinge jamb; the jamb that receives the latch is the latch jamb (also called strike jamb or lock jamb).

DOOR ELEMENTS. On a common frame-and-panel door, the thicker vertical elements are called

DOOR, DOOR FRAME, AND ROUGH OPENING

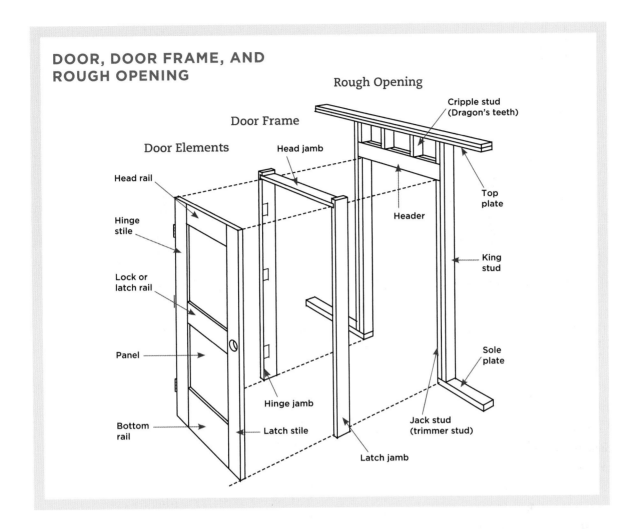

stiles, hence hinge stile and latch (or strike) stile. Horizontal elements are called rails. Individual rail names are also defined by their location, hence head rail (top rail), lock or latch rail, and bottom rail.

DOOR SPECS

Building codes usually specify minimum door sizes for entry and interior doors between rooms. Clients may find it helpful to know if house doors are standard size or must be ordered specially, which costs more.

INTERIOR VS. EXTERIOR. Exterior doors are generally thicker (1¾ in. vs. 1⅜ in.), more expensive, more weather resistant, and more secure than interior doors. Exterior doors may have water- or UV-resistant finishes and often are insulated and

weather stripped. If you see interior doors used as exterior doors, note that in your inspection report; they won't last.

WIDTH. Standard interior doors are 2 ft. 6 in. and 2 ft. 8 in. wide. For doors leading to busy hallways, or if extra room is needed for a wheelchair or walker, architects often specify 2 ft. 10 in. or 3 ft. Narrow doors (2 ft. to 2 ft. 4 in.) are available for half-baths and closets, and even narrower ones (1 ft. 4 in. to 1 ft. 10 in.) for linen closets and such.

Standard exterior doors are 3 ft. wide, though side doors are sometimes 2 ft. 8 in. or 2 ft. 10 in. wide. Extrawide 42-in. exterior doors can be special ordered but their greater weight and width requires larger hinges and a greater area of free space when they swing open.

If you suspect that a door height is substandard, always measure. Interior and exterior doors must be at least 6 ft. 8 in. high.

HEIGHT. Standard door height on newer houses is 6 ft. 8 in., for both interior and exterior doors. Older houses (1940s and earlier) sometimes had doors 7 ft. high, so that size is still widely available. Of late, 8-ft.-high French doors are in vogue because they allow light to penetrate far into living spaces. Of course, you can special-order a door of virtually any size if price is no object. Salvage yards are also excellent sources of odd-size doors.

HARDWARE. Hollow-core or solid-wood interior doors up to 1⅜ in. thick can be supported by two 3½-in. by 3½ -in. (opened size) hinges; whereas 1¾-in.-thick exterior doors usually require three 4-in. by 4-in. hinges. Extraheavy exterior doors may need even bigger hinges or hinges with ball bearings or grease fittings. Door hardware is not typically part of a home inspection, but if you see a door whose hinges are obviously too small, write it up.

Exterior locksets are most often cylinder locks, which require a 2⅛-in. hole drilled through the face of the door, or a mortise lock, which is housed in a rectangular mortise cut into the latch edge of the door. Mortise locks are more expensive and difficult to install, so they are most often used only on entry doors. For added security, exterior door locksets can be supplemented with a dead bolt and a reinforced strike plate.

Interior locksets are almost always some kind of cylinder lock: passage locks or latch sets on doors that don't need to be locked and privacy locks or locksets on doors that do need locking, such as bedroom doors. Bathroom locks are specialized locksets with a bathroom-facing knob in a metal or color to match plumbing fixtures.

TYPES OF DOORS

Inspecting doors is largely limited to whether they work or not. Here are types you may find.

HINGED SINGLE DOORS are what typically come to mind when we think of doors, and they are by far the most common type, but their biggest drawback is that they need room to operate.

FRENCH DOORS are a pair of hinged doors that meet at a common mullion (vertical divider); both doors may open or one door may be fixed. French doors are largely glass, so they are usually installed overlooking a patio or a deck, though they are sometimes installed between rooms to maximize natural light inside. French doors require an opening that's twice the size of a single door, so the header must be considerably larger and greater carpentry skills are required to make both doors fit the frame exactly. Consequently, French door installations often need periodic fine-tuning.

SLIDING DOORS are a smart choice when space is tight and a hinged door's swing would eat up too much interior or exterior living space. Most sliding door sets (one door slides, one is fixed) glide on roller-wheels confined by an integral channel. Here again, sizing the header correctly is essential because the rough opening is so wide. If the header is not large enough and adequately supported, it will sag and bind the doors. Similarly, the bottom channel must be as flat as possible if the wheels are to roll freely. The channel must also be cleaned periodically of debris, ice, and anything else that would impede the wheels.

OVERHANG SLIDING DOORS are high rollers: their wheels glide along a track mounted across the top of an opening. The rolling mechanism is usually called barn door hardware because it was first widely used on barns and farm outbuildings. Ironically, most barn door hardware used in residences is now used to hang interior doors because overhang sliding doors don't offer much of a seal against weather. (Those models that do are very expensive.)

POCKET DOORS slide into interior wall cavities specially framed to receive them; such walls are typically 6 in. thick. Older pocket doors typically had wheels above, which rolled along a track mounted to the underside of a header. Other pocket doors had both overhang wheels and floor channels. Early pocket doors worked fine till the house shifted enough to bind them, after which their faces became scuffed each time they rubbed against wall cavities. If the binding worsened, homeowners either had to rebuild the wall to free the doors or stop using them. Modern pocket doors tend to be hollow, much lighter, and less likely to bind.

BIFOLD DOORS (accordion doors) have multiple hinged-folds, so they can span wide distances while needing little room to operate. Because bifolds are rather lightweight, however, they are limited mostly to utility uses indoors, such as hiding a washer and dryer, covering a storage area, or temporarily dividing living spaces for visual privacy.

The horizontal slats in these bifold doors allow closet ventilation. Louvers (slats) should slope downward so closet contents are not readily visible; these doors were installed upside down.

TROUBLESHOOTING HINGED DOORS

An inspector is obligated to note only if a door works or doesn't. But, should a client ask, here are a few concise explanations about the causes of common door problems.

DOOR BINDS AGAINST TOP OF THE LATCH JAMB or scrapes the floor. Most likely, the top hinge is loose, allowing the door to sag into the opening. Replace top hinge screws with longer ones.

DOOR BINDS ALONG THE LATCH JAMB but hinges are screwed tightly. The hinge is probably bent; hinge-leaf "knuckles" (that receive hinge pins) should be bent back into the original position.

BIG GAPS ALONG THE HINGE JAMB while the door binds on the latch jamb; hinges are screwed down tightly. Hinge leaves are not mortised deeply enough into the frame and/or door.

DOOR BINDS ALONG THE HINGE JAMB. Hinge leaves are set too deep. The hinges should be removed, shimmed up, and reattached.

FLOOR IS ABRADED UNDER THE DOOR. This is usually caused by seasonal shifting. As expansive clay soil dries and subsides, undersize footings subside with it, leaving a girder and the flooring over it higher than surrounding supports. The door scrapes on this high point.

As houses settle or shift, portions of the flooring may lift relative to door framing, causing the door to scrape on the floor.

Hollow-core interior doors should never be used as exterior doors. They aren't insulated and simply can't take the weathering.

DOOR BINDS BECAUSE FRAME IS RACKED (out of square). This situation is caused by seasonal shifting or a settling foundation and there may be no easy fix. It is possible to trim the door to fit the skewed opening, but if the racking is seasonal, the frame may return to square and the trimmed door won't fit. Alternately, one can replace the old frame with a new prehung door.

DOOR SHUTS BUT WON'T LATCH. The strike plate is misaligned and needs to be raised or lowered.

TROUBLESHOOTING SLIDING DOORS

The following explanations should hold true for most sliding and pocket doors.

DOOR SLIDES ROUGHLY. Dirt buildup on the floor needs to be vacuumed periodically.

FLOOR IS ABRADED UNDER THE DOOR. The top track is sagging or (more likely) the top-mounted rolling mechanism needs some adjustment.

DOOR DOES NOT SLIDE AT ALL or is very hard to operate. The door has come off its track. If it is a bottom track, lift the door back onto it. If a top track, trim may need to be removed to gain access and set tracking wheels back onto the overhead track.

DOOR DRAGS, BALKING REPEATEDLY, wheels squeal. Most likely, the wheels are not turning freely; they may be rusty or the track is bent or broken.

DOOR FACE IS ABRADED, door is difficult to operate. Either the door has fallen off the track or, due to structural shifting, a stud has bowed into the pocket. If lifting the door onto the track doesn't solve the problem, it may be necessary to plane down or replace the errant stud.

WHAT TO LOOK FOR

- Survey the house for doors that do not operate correctly. Note any that are difficult to operate, that don't shut fully, that scrape floors, or that don't move at all.

- Note door damage such as delamination, dents, water damage, and abraded faces and missing or broken elements such as door handles, glass panes, and trim pieces.

- Note obviously substandard conditions, such as interior doors used as exterior doors.

- Note any doors whose width or height do not meet modern building code. Doors should be at least 6 ft. 8 in. high and exterior doors should be at least 36 in. wide.

- Are all door faces and edges sealed? Use a small mirror to examine bottom door edges.

- Do all doors shut solidly in their frames or can they be rattled? Do all lock mechanisms work, whether a door is interior or exterior?

Exterior Doors

Because exterior doors must withstand extreme fluctuations of moisture and temperature, two factors are critical to determine how well a door will function and how long it will last.

The first factor is whether the door is protected by a porch roof or eaves. As a rule of thumb, an overhang should project out from the house an amount equal to at least half the distance from the doorsill to the underside of a porch roof or eaves. So as you inspect each exterior door, take note of the overhang protecting it, if any. That degree of protection determines what material the door should be made of—the second factor.

If an overhang projection obeys the rule of thumb, a wood exterior door beneath it can survive the insults of a harsh climate. If the depth of the overhang is less than that, or if there is no overhang, a fiberglass or steel door may be a more durable choice for that location.

ENTRY DOOR ESSENTIALS

To assess the condition of an entry door, a home inspector should know a little about its construction. Any entry door is a trade-off of durability, maintenance, energy efficiency, and price. Ironically, a cheap, leaky entry door will cost homeowners the most in the long run.

WOOD. Quality wood doors feature panel-and-frame construction, with mortise-and-tenon joints at the corners for greater durability. Traditionally, panels have floated free within the frame to allow for expansion and contraction; today's energy-efficient models add elastic sealants around the perimeter of the panel to cut air leaks and moisture penetration. To minimize warping, many panel doors have engineered wood cores. Wood doors can be clear finished, stained, or painted, but a factory finish with an exterior grade, oil-based varnish or polyurethane with UV protection will be most durable. Whatever the finish, however, wood doors should be refinished every 1 year to 3 years. Whether sealing a wood door for the first time or refinishing it later on, *all* edges must be sealed to forestall water absorption.

Newly installed doors are sometimes left unpainted along the edges. This is a common omission when houses are remodeled or fixed up for resale.

Energy profile: Not great. On average, wood doors have an R-2 value, though more efficient ones achieve R-5. Interestingly, doors with low-emissivity (low-e) glass have higher R-values than wood doors without glazing.

FIBERGLASS. Spurred by energy efficiency, fiberglass doors have been gaining market share for the last decade. Typically, fiberglass skins are applied to a wood composite, LVL, or steel frame to lend rigidity; the core of the door is then filled with insulating foam. Fiberglass doors are dimensionally stable and surprisingly sturdy. Once painted, they are almost indistinguishable from wood, and several manufacturers offer unfinished fiberglass doors that can be stained. As with wood, though, the most durable coatings are factory finished.

Energy profile: Among the best for doors, R-8 or higher. As fiberglass expands and contracts at the same rate as glass, glazing seals are especially stable in such doors.

STEEL. Economical but unexciting, steel entry doors are nonetheless durable, energy-efficient, and easy to maintain. Most residential steel doors are made from 24-gauge steel skins over an engineered-wood or steel frame; internal cavities are filled with expanding foam, usually polyurethane. Steel doors are sometimes required by code for multifamily houses, where there's a shared wall between living space and an active garage, or where houses are located in a fire zone. In those cases, codes also will specify the core insulation, the thickness of the steel skin, and so on. Steel doors need repainting less often—every 3 years to 5 years—and if the steel skin begins to rust, it can go fast.

Energy profile: Not quite as good as fiberglass, but close. Some models hit R-5 or R-6.

FLASHING AND CAULKING DOOR TRIM

This section summarizes the lengthy discussion in Chapter 2 because its importance can't be overstated. Correctly flashing door units (doors and frames) and sealing gaps where siding meets trim are essential to keep out water and minimize air infiltration.

In new construction, water-resistive barriers are usually installed before window and door units have been inserted into rough openings. Windows and doors are then installed and their perimeters weather-proofed with flexible flashing strips. As shown in "Flashing Details" on p. 30, the uppermost WRB layer overlays rigid cap flashing. Cap flashing, also called head flashing, redirects water that might otherwise dam up behind door or window head casing, leading to stains and mold on interior surfaces, swollen sashes, peeling paint, and rot. All flashing is important, but flashing the head of a window or door is *the* critical detail to get right.

This sliding exterior door opens directly onto a deck unprotected by an overhang. Splashback from the deck, failed seals, and a lack of maintenance have resulted in a rotted threshold and damaged wood flooring.

In older houses, gaps frequently develop between door trim and wood siding because of normal shrinkage and wear. Inspectors should note such gaps and recommend that they be filled with an elastomeric caulk and then painted to prolong the life of the caulk.

WEATHER STRIPPING AND THRESHOLDS

Quality door systems will have integral weather stripping, which fits into a kerf (slot) milled into the door frame. Integral systems have close tolerances, tight fits, and nylon-jacketed foam stripping that can be compressed repeatedly without deforming or losing its resilience. This type of weather stripping is often called Q-LON®, after a popular brand. In general, weather seals held in place by an adhesive aren't as durable and can migrate out of position.

Weather stripping at the bottom of a door must create a tight seal and be durable; elements that attach to door bottoms are called shoes or sweeps. Though primarily intended to reduce drafts, they also must resist water seeping or blowing in under the door. Sweep gaskets seal the bottom of a door, typically with a compressible neoprene gasket in a metal channel. The sweep also may be mated to a gasketed

A WATER-RETURN THRESHOLD

IN REGIONS THAT GET A LOT of precipitation, especially driving rains, homeowners are well advised to retrofit a water-return threshold, which includes a sill cover, a drain pain, and a threshold with weep holes. The assembly is sloped to send water back outside, hence its name, water return. (The sill cover needs to slope only ⅛ in. to shed water effectively.) In addition to protecting the door bottom and the doorsill, the unit goes a long way toward protecting interior flooring, too.

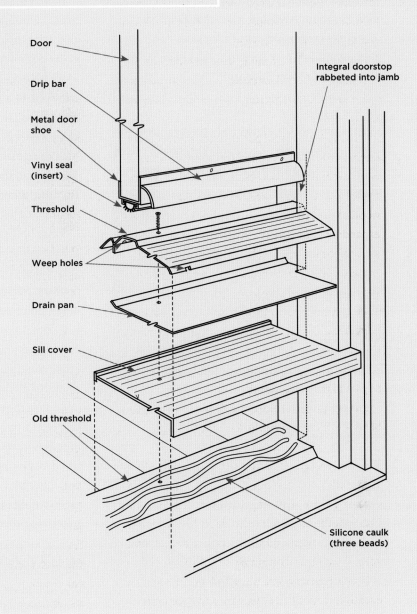

channel in a threshold. Better-quality sweeps are adjustable and have replaceable gaskets because they become abraded in time. In general, avoid bristle-type sweeps—they don't block air or water well and aren't durable.

In addition to door shoes and sweeps, there are also thresholds, specialized weather-stripping pieces

that seal the doorsill. Thresholds may attach directly to an existing sill or it may be part of a sill–threshold combination. If a sill is badly water damaged, a home inspector might suggest replacing it with a sill–threshold combination. If the sill is nonstandard, homeowners can take photos to show to the supplier at their home center. How much rain an area gets is also a key consideration. The sill–threshold combination shown in "A Water-Return Threshold" on p. 245 fits over an existing sill, includes a sill cover and a drain pan, and can withstand just about anything short of Noah's flood.

ENTRY DOOR HARDWARE

Apart from finishes, styles, and other aesthetic considerations, entry door hardware choices can be boiled down to a few essential differences between hinges and lock assemblies.

HINGES. Prehung doors from a reputable supplier should have hinges matched to the weight and width of the door; width is a lesser consideration but wider doors do exert more torque on hinges as they swing. Modestly priced exterior doors usually come with standard 4-in. by 4-in. butt hinges. If an entry door is oversize or wood (which tends to be heavier than fiberglass or steel doors), 4½-in. or 5-in. ball-bearing hinges provide an extra margin of strength. A home-owner can also specify adjustable hinges, which are mortised into the edge of the door and can accommodate vertical and horizontal adjustments—rather like the German hinges used in good-quality cabinets. Adjustable hinges seem like a good idea for houses subject to seasonal shifting, such as those built on adobe soil.

LOCK ASSEMBLIES. Most exterior doors sport a single-point lock that lodges into a plate on the latch side of the door frame. For a modest bump in price, homeowners can add a dead bolt and a reinforced strike plate, which can't be dislodged by a kick—the preferred method of entry by B&E men. Beyond that, one enters the world of multipoint locking systems that secure two more sides of the entry door to the door frame; some designs seem inspired by the mechanisms used to lock bank vaults. With multipoint locking systems priced at $2,000 and up—way up—owning a bank might be a prerequisite for purchasing them.

WHAT TO LOOK FOR

- Is every exterior door protected by a porch or by overhanging eaves?
- What material is each exterior door made of: wood, fiberglass, or steel? What is each door's general condition? Note any that are badly weathered or damaged.
- Scanning the perimeter of the door when shut, can you see any daylight between the door and the frame? Running your hand around the perimeter, can you feel drafts?
- Open exterior doors and look for weather stripping around door frames. Is there weather stripping on the bottom of exterior doors or across doorsills?

INSIDE KEY LOCKS

DEADBOLTS AND OTHER LOCKS WITH removable inside keys could prevent escape in a fire emergency should the key be elsewhere. Thus inside key locks are prohibited in many locales. Always leave inside keys in the locks when the building is occupied. Consider replacing inside key locks with thumb latches, which are safer.

Installing an inside key deadbolt won't make you safer; it will just shatter the jamb when a burglar kicks in the door. This flimsy lock should be replaced with a 3-in. deadbolt and strike-plate reinforcement that will keep the door frame intact.

- Are any door frames obviously out of square? Do their doors bind?

- Note water damage to the doorsill or finish floors near the doorway. Is the damage superficial or is the wood splitting?

- Can you see water stains on interior surfaces around the door? The door's cap flashing may be damaged (or missing), or there may be gaps between siding and exterior door trim.

- Are there any signs of condensation or water damage around metal sliding doors?

- Are any of the exterior door frames racked because of structural movement or settling? If frames seem out of square, look for signs of the door binding, door glass cracking, and so on.

- Do all doors swing freely, regardless of their width or weight?

- Do door locks align with strike plates on the latch side of the frame? Do all door locks turn freely or do any stick?

- Note any doors that have key locks on the inside; recommend that they be replaced so that occupants can always escape easily in an emergency.

- Do all exterior doors have companion storm doors or storm insets for combination screen–storm units?

Windows

Unlike doors, windows rarely have overhangs to protect them (beyond eaves), so they are exposed more and sooner damaged, especially on south-facing walls. There, the quality of a window, the skill of its installation, and the regularity of its maintenance are revealed dramatically.

WINDOW STYLES

An inspector's chief concern is that a window be in good, operable condition, free from damage or decay, with all glazing and seals intact. Seals that have failed will admit moisture between double- or triple-pane units, and look cloudy. Any of the window styles in the following list may have single, double, or triple glazing.

DOUBLE-HUNG windows are the traditional choice, with two sashes that slide up and down; if the top sash is fixed, it's a single-hung.

Pros: The widest choice of sash patterns, from single pane to tiny four-over-four arrays separated by delicate frame muntins. Snap-in muntins enable affordable double-glazing and easier cleaning, but they won't fool an experienced eye.

Cons: Sliding sashes are tough to weatherproof well and old sashes rattle and leak air; if sash ropes break, windows cease to function reliably. Meeting

Windows take a lot of abuse. Swollen, weather-worn sashes of double-hung windows frequently separate at the corners when homeowners try to force windows open.

WINDOW STYLES

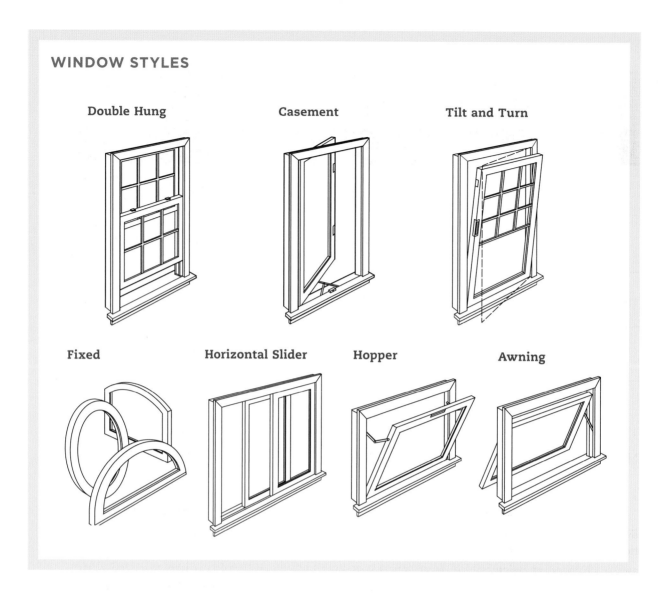

Double Hung

Casement

Tilt and Turn

Fixed

Horizontal Slider

Hopper

Awning

rails between the sashes have two faces exposed to outside air, which hastens heat loss, convection, and condensation. And only half the window area offers ventilation.

CASEMENT windows are side hinged and swing outward, usually operated by a crank.

Pros: A single large pane of glass maximizes solar gain, a tight compression seal minimizes air leaks, and the whole area ventilates when open. Excellent choice for egress.

Cons: A casement opening onto a deck or walkway is hazardous to those walking by.

AWNING windows are hinged at the top, the bottom swings outward.

Children can fall out of open casement windows positioned too low. A restraining bar or chain that keeps the opening less than 4 in. wide is a good safety precaution.

WINDOW FRAME MATERIALS

FRAME MATERIAL	DURABILITY	INSULATING LEVEL	MAINTENANCE	COST	COLORS	COMMENTS
ALUMINUM	Good	Poor	Low	$	Limited	Most conductive of cold, but OK in mild climates
WOOD	Fair	Good	High	$$–$$$	Paintable	Need painting every 10 years, cleaning
CLAD	Good	Best	Low	$$$$	Custom colors cost extra	As attractive as wood, but easy to maintain; choice of claddings
VINYL	Fair	Fair to good	Low	$	Limited	Vinyl degrades if overheated; otherwise, it's durable
FIBERGLASS	Good	Good	Low	$$$	Paintable	Least conductive, can also be insulated with foam*

* Fiberglass's rate of expansion and contraction is virtually the same as that of glass, which helps glazing seals last longer.

Pros: A single large pane of glass maximizes solar gain, and you can leave the window open for ventilation even when it's raining; the window acts as an awning. Tight compression seal like a casement.

Cons: A sash that swings onto a deck or walkway is hazardous; the screen is on the inside.

HOPPER windows, which tilt from the bottom, are like upside-down awning windows.

Pros: Same energy profile and compression seal as casement and awning windows.

Cons: Hazardous if it swings down at head height, poor choice for egress.

TILT-AND-TURN windows are hybrids that swing like a casement or bottom-tilt like a hopper.

Pros: Easy to clean, good choice for an egress, tight compression seal, good energy profile.

Cons: Two moving parts mean two things that can break or jam. Roller shades and curtains can interfere with the window's operation.

HORIZONTAL SLIDE windows are like miniature patio doors, sashes slide in tracks.

Pros: Great choice for egress and because there are no muntins, good solar gain.

Cons: Sliding sashes are tough to weather strip, crud collecting in tracks can impede operation, and only half of a window's area offers ventilation.

FIXED windows don't open.

Pros: Can't be beat for being airtight, less expensive than operable window of same design. With acoustic glazing, best choice to reduce outside noise.

Cons: No ventilation, no egress, can't wash outside from inside.

WINDOW FRAMES

"Window Frame Materials," above, is intended to aid home inspectors when discussing replacement options with clients. Windows are expensive and would-be buyers or homeowners who must replace many units are looking at a major expense.

In the last few decades, there have been so many improvements in insulated glass that the R-value of the glazing generally exceeds that of the frames.

In other words, windows with a larger percentage of glass (and a smaller percentage of frame) are better energy performers. In response, window makers are hustling to make window frames less conductive (of heat and cold), more airtight, and more durable. To do so, they have developed frames with a wide range of core materials, cladding, finishes, and in some cases, insulation.

The chart on p. 249 will give buyers an overview of how different frame materials perform but, to be honest, the best way to select a window is to choose a frame style that fits the house, calculate the energy performance the window must deliver (hence the type of glazing, etc.), and then talk to builders and building-supply staffers about which window brands they favor. Try opening and shutting display models to see how tightly they fit, how smoothly they operate, and how sturdy they feel. Frame corners, glazing seals, and weather-stripping gaskets deserve close scrutiny, for that's where windows fail first.

"You get what you pay for" is especially true when buying windows. Even frames fabricated from less expensive materials, such as vinyl, offer options such as chambers filled with foam insulation, which raise performance and cost.

WINDOW GLAZING

Glazing is best thought of as a system of glass panes, seals, gases that insulate between panes, specialty coatings to enhance or reduce solar gains, and so forth. Of course, the inspector must focus on what is observable: the condition of frames, panes, and seals.

NOTE CRACKED OR BROKEN GLASS on your report, but if glass cracking is widespread, consider what might be causing it and why it appears where it does. If structural shifting or foundation failure is the cause, window frames and trim will likely be out of square and tilting. Single-pane windows are typically glazed with putty, which dries out if not kept painted, allowing panes to rattle in their frames and leak air.

CONDENSATION BETWEEN PANES occurs when seals have worn out and moisture enters. Seals failing after 15 years to 20 years is common, although it can occur after 2 years or 3 years if window manufacture is faulty. Because most of a house's windows typically come from one supplier, when seals do fail, they tend to do so on many windows in a short period of time. It is generally not possible to repair windows whose seals have failed; they must be replaced.

METAL WINDOWS

METAL IS A SUPERB CONDUCTOR OF HEAT AND cold but a lousy insulator, so windows with metal frames have the lowest R-values. Ambient moisture condenses on cold metal frames, resulting in chronic water stains and, in time, compromised drywall surfaces under windows. Aluminum also corrodes. Insulated, clad-steel windows are a better choice for those who must have the narrow profile of metal windows, but the windows' performance is only marginally better, considering the expense. Metal windows, even insulated, don't offer much of a thermal break to reduce conductive heat loss.

Metal-frame windows conduct cold, which leads to condensation, water stains, crumbling drywall, and damaged flooring.

Failed glazing putty on wood-framed windows is common in older houses. Putty needs to be repaired as necessary and kept painted.

Windows at the bottom of staircases must contain tempered glass, because someone falling down the stairs could land against the window.

Because of failed seals, moist air has seeped between the doubled panes of this sash, fogging it up. It's not possible to repair seals, the sash needs to be replaced.

TEMPERED GLASS (safety glass) is required in new construction when a window is less than 18 in. from the floor (and larger than 9 sq. ft.), adjacent to a door, or in a door. Low windows by walkways should also have tempered glass and so should windows at the bottoms of stairways, a common location for trips and falls.

While few codes require changing existing glass, tempered glass is required when panes are replaced in such areas. Until tempered glass is installed, homeowners can reduce risk by moving furniture to direct traffic away from nontempered glass windows and by applying decals to sliding glass doors and large windows to prevent people from walking through them. Special plastic films can be applied to the glass to reduce the likelihood of injury should the glass break.

WHAT TO LOOK FOR

- What style(s) of windows are presently on the house? Note the overall condition of each unit and try to determine the frame material of each window.

- Can all windows be opened and shut easily? Note missing hardware or operating mechanisms (such as casement cranks) that are balky or do not work at all.

- When closed, do all window sashes fit tightly to their frames?

- Note the location and condition of any metal-frame windows. Is there condensation, water stains, or water-related damage on the trim or wall surfaces around those windows?

- Note cracked or broken panes, and panes whose putty is worn or dislodged.

- Is there condensation or cloudiness between any double- or triple-pane units? If so, their seals have failed and the units will have to be replaced.

- Do windows within 18 in. of the floor, adjacent to doors, along walkways, or at the bottom of staircases contain tempered glass?

- Are egress windows large enough for an inhabitant to exit or a firefighter to enter (net-clear opening of 5.7 sq. ft.), and low enough to climb out of (maximum 44 in. above the floor)?

DOUBLE-HUNG WINDOWS

Double-hungs are by far the most common style of window, especially on older homes, but wood sashes sliding in a wood frame is a pretty archaic technology, especially when vinyl, fiberglass, and clad sashes are available. Wood absorbs water—it's what trees are designed to do—so, consequently wood sashes swell in their frames. That wood-against-wood contact absorbs yet more water, and forcing swollen sashes to move soon takes its toll on sash frames; corner joints go first. When inspecting wood double-hungs, scrutinize sash corners and, above all, the bottom sash–windowsill juncture, which is where rot usually starts.

Even when they slide freely in their frames, double-hung sashes are pretty heavy and require sash weights to counterbalance the weight of the sash. But sash cords break, people don't replace them, and sashes are used less and less. Then, at some point they get painted shut. A sitting sash (wood on wood again) often rots, so note on your report both broken sash cords and windows painted shut. If there's not a rot problem now, there soon will be.

THE MOST COMMON REMEDIAL STRATEGY for homeowners with a houseful of weary wooden double-hungs is removing old sashes, cleaning up and perhaps insulating around the frame, inserting new channels (vinyl jamb liners) in the frame, then

Sash cords often come loose or break, making a weighty sash difficult to raise. It is usually necessary to remove jamb trim and the sash itself to reattach cords to sash weights.

WINDOW EGRESS

TO ENABLE OCCUPANTS TO EXIT QUICKLY IN case of a fire, building codes require a method of escape—egress—for sleeping rooms on every level of the house, including the basement. Because egress windows must also be large enough to allow a fully equipped firefighter to enter, codes specify the size of the egress—typically, at least 20 in. wide and at least 24 in. tall, with a combined net-clear opening of 5.7 sq. ft. To make it possible to climb out of an egress window, codes generally specify a maximum sill height of 44 in. above the floor,

If an egress window has security bars, they must have a release mechanism that is operable from the inside without a key or special tool. Interior release mechanisms should be tested periodically to be sure they are functional.

The moving parts of hinged windows need occasional maintenance. Here, recurrent condensation has rusted a casement window's cranking mechanism and damaged the wooden windowsill.

installing new replacement sashes. Window trim inside and out stays put, drafts are reduced, and sashes slide nicely.

HINGED WINDOWS

Hinged windows include casement, awning, hopper, louvered, and tilt-and-turn styles. Because hinged windows are generally newer than double-hungs, they are less likely to be wood on wood and thus less likely to swell shut in their frames. Operate them to be sure they work.

When inspecting hinged windows, be on the lookout for crank mechanisms that are corroded because of condensation collecting along the sill, defective or missing latches, sashes that do not fit snugly in the frame, and missing seals or weather stripping around the frame.

WHAT TO LOOK FOR

- Are double-hung windows operable or painted shut? If they are operable, are sash cords connected to sash weights. (Sashes that are propped up usually have broken sash cords.)
- Survey double-hung windows for rot where the bottom rails of lower sashes rest on windowsills, where upper and lower sashes meet, and along frame channels.
- Note windows with replacement sashes: Do they operate freely or do they bind?
- Do hinged windows fit tight to frames? Is all hardware present and operable?
- Does every window have a storm sash or panel? Are window screens intact?
- If an egress window has security bars, is there an interior release mechanism that can be opened without a key or special tool? Test the release mechanism to see if it opens.

CHAPTER 12

KITCHENS, BATHROOMS, and LAUNDRY

KITCHENS AND BATHROOMS ARE THE ROOMS where it all converges: electrical and plumbing, heating outlets and pipes, fixtures and finish surfaces of all kinds. In addition, there's lots of water and water vapor generated by the people using these rooms, so adequate ventilation is a must for anyone who wants to forestall mold and enjoy a healthier indoors.

To protect a household from electrical shocks, all bathroom and kitchen receptacles within 4 ft. of a sink must be ground fault circuit interrupters, or whatever the local building code requires. Finally, maintenance is crucial to keep water at bay: keeping tub, sink, and lavatory joints caulked; replacing tile grout if it gets crumbly; and attending to leaking fixtures immediately. The same rules hold true for laundry setups.

Kitchens

Because safety is always top of mind for a home inspector, let's start with an encapsulation of electrical safety in the kitchen.

A SUMMARY OF NEC REQUIREMENTS

GFCIs are sensitive devices that can detect very small current leaks and shut off power almost instantaneously. The NEC requires that all kitchen outlets be GFCI protected. Kitchen appliances are heavy power users, so their circuits must be sized accordingly. There must be at least two 20-amp small-appliance circuits in the kitchen serving kitchen countertops. No point along a kitchen countertop may be more than 2 ft. from an outlet; in other words, countertop receptacles should be spaced at least every 4 ft. Every counter at least 12 in. wide must have a receptacle.

All critical-use and fixed appliances should, and in most cases must, have their own dedicated (separate) circuits. These fixed appliances include freezer, refrigerator, oven, cooktop, microwave, water pump, water heater, furnace and/or whole-house air-conditioning unit, and window air conditioners. A bathroom heater requires a dedicated circuit, whether it

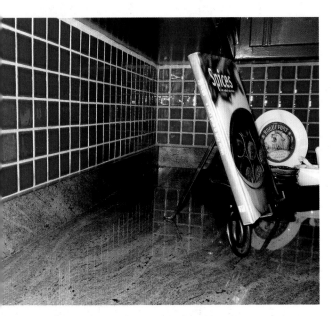

What's missing here? Along counters, there should be an electrical outlet at least every 4 ft.

is a separate unit or part of a light/fan. Laundry room receptacles must be on a dedicated circuit; so must an electric clothes dryer.

NOTE: Major appliances on dedicated circuits, such as refrigerators and freezers, should not be plugged into a GFCI receptacle. Appliances with large motors may cause nuisance tripping of GFCIs because those motors typically have large starting loads.

WHAT TO LOOK FOR

- The bottom of wall cabinets should be at least 30 in. above ranges and cooktops and at least 18 in. above noncooking portions of countertops. Measure to be sure.
- Check the breaker panel (or fuse panel) to ascertain that there at least two 20-amp small-appliance circuits serving kitchen countertops.
- Are countertop receptacles spaced at least every 4 ft., and does every countertop at least 2 ft. wide have a receptacle?
- Do lights dim or flicker when a refrigerator, washing machine, or a microwave starts?

RANGES, OVENS, AND COOKTOPS

First, a few definitions: The enclosed cooking area in which one roasts a turkey is an *oven*; pots and frying pans sit on *cooktop burners*. A *range* has both an oven and a cooktop.

IN OLDER HOMES WHERE THE WIRING HAS not been upgraded, kitchen lights may flicker or dim when a refrigerator or washing machine motor starts up, or a fuse may blow. Such circuits should be re-wired because flickering lights indicate an overloaded circuit. Each critical-use and fixed appliance should be on its own dedicated circuit.

This built-in oven is coming loose from the cabinet and should be properly secured. Freestanding ranges should also have anti-tip brackets. Unsecured, they can fall if the door is left open and a large pot of stew or other heavy object is placed on them.

Cooking appliances, whether gas or electric, should be professionally installed. The heating elements of ranges, ovens, and cooktops generally require 240 volts, but today's smart appliances come with a plethora of timers, clocks, sensors, buzzers, and other gizmos that use 120 volts. For this reason, many units require 120-volt/240-volt wiring, with two hot wires, an insulated neutral, and an equipment ground wire. Fixed appliances, as noted earlier, should be on dedicated circuits and circuit wiring should be matched to the appliance's amperage rating.

Appliances must also be securely mounted. Built-in ovens, for example, must be secured to the cabinet

in which they are housed. Otherwise, if an oven door were left open and a heavy pot of stew placed on the door, the built-in oven could pitch forward and fall, probably ripping out wiring connections and possibly injuring someone. Similarly, floor-mounted ranges must be provided with anti-tip brackets to keep them from falling over. During your inspection, ascertain that ovens and ranges are securely mounted.

REFRIGERATORS AND FREEZERS

Refrigerators and freezers are both critical-use and fixed appliances, so each should be on a dedicated circuit, whose wiring is appropriately sized to the appliance's amperage rating.

These appliances rarely fail, though they require occasional maintenance such as vacuuming to dust off condenser coils to run optimally. Refrigerators that can be rolled out for cleaning should have outlets situated high enough so that the unit does not run over its appliance cord.

Refrigerators with integral ice makers sometimes leak if the ¼-in. flexible water supply line for the ice maker is inexpertly connected or becomes crushed. Because these connections are typically on the back of the refrigerator, there is little an inspector can do

ESSENTIAL GROUNDS

ALL ELECTRICAL APPLIANCES MUST HAVE AN equipment-grounding conductor that connects to both the appliance frame (or housing) and to the metal outlet box for the safe discharge of fault currents. Use a circuit analyzer (see p. 146) to test each circuit for ground and to make sure it is correctly wired. Never assume an outlet is grounded just because it has three-hole receptacles.

This disposer's faulty wiring—with no protective clamp and exposed wire connections—is a shock hazard to anyone who inadvertently pulls on or touches the wire.

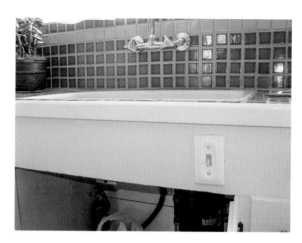

Locating a disposer switch on a cabinet face is extremely hazardous. If someone clearing out the disposer with his hand accidentally hits the switch, the disposer could turn on.

to inspect hookups or to anticipate problems. However, if during an inspection you observe wet spots near the base of the refrigerator or kitchen flooring damaged by unexplained wetness, a leaking ice maker connection may be the cause. Over time, small leaks can have devastating effects.

DISHWASHERS AND DISPOSERS

Dishwashers and disposers are both 120-volt, 20-amp appliances, supplied by 12 AWG cable. Ideally, a garbage disposer will have a flexible cord that plugs into a receptacle. Appliances that vibrate should be provided with flexible multistrand cords. Hard-wiring them with Romex or BX creates a potential hazard.

WARNING: A disposer switch should never be located on a cabinet face, as shown in the top right photo, because someone cleaning out the disposer with his or her hand could accidentally operate the switch, turning the disposer on.

Because they slide out for installation and maintenance, dishwashers are also installed with a cord and plug. Most of the time, the dishwasher junction box is located in the front of the unit, just behind the kick panel. When not pulled out for maintenance, a dishwasher must be secured to the countertop above so the appliance does not fall forward when its door is lowered.

Some dishwashers drain through an air gap located above the sink. When gaps get clogged they spray water on the counter when the appliance drains. Air gaps are outmoded in many jurisdictions. New dishwashers typically have built-in antibackflow or air-gap devices.

Older dishwashers often vent through an air gap located above the sink; the gap is typically covered by a chrome cap. When air gaps become clogged, water may spill or squirt out of the chrome cap onto the counter when the dishwasher drains. This nuisance can be avoided by removing blockages or kinks from the dishwasher drain hose that leads to the air gap or by upgrading to a new dishwasher with a built-in antisyphon valve that prevents the backflow of waste water into a clean dishwasher.

Exposed wood cabinets should be 30 in. above heat sources such as cooktops or range burners. A 24-in. vertical distance is considered adequate for metal or insulating millboard-covered wood. Follow range-hood manufacturer's recommendations for height above the cooking surface.

RANGE HOODS

All cooktops and stoves should be vented by a range hood. In addition to sucking up the smoke of a charred steak, range hoods exhaust airborne grease that might otherwise migrate to cool corners and feed mold. Range hoods vary but basically each has a hood to collect smells and smoke, a fan to expel them, and ducts to carry exhausts out.

Range hoods are most often wall-mounted directly over a range. Alternatively, there are downdraft and side-draft vents that pop up from a counter area to suck away fumes. Over island and peninsula ranges, chimney-type vents are commonly installed.

Ideally, a range hood should be slightly wider than the range, say, 3 in. wider on each end, and mounted 30 in. above the range. More powerful hoods can be installed higher. Each hood should have a good-quality filter that can withstand regular washing with soap and water. Most filters are aluminum mesh, better ones are stainless steel, and many can be popped into a dishwasher. Report clogged filters: They force fans to draw less, run longer, and fail sooner.

Range-hood fans have filter screens to collect grease from frying food below. This hood and screen are so clogged they have become a fire hazard and should be replaced.

THE KITCHEN SINK

When inspecting a kitchen sink, keep an eye out for drips, damage, and durability. Drips or leaks from the bottom of a sink faucet handle or lever are easy to fix yet, unattended, can lead to delaminating countertops or rotted base cabinets (see p. 270). So, as you manipulate each faucet handle or lever to turn water off and on, note water running from its base because of a worn washer. Are faucets worn or loose, or are hot and cold pipes reversed? (An amateur likely installed them.) Look under the sink for water damage and, while there, note the condition of the sink

Penny wise and pound foolish. Here, a good-quality enameled cast-iron sink has been paired with a cheaply made single-lever faucet whose washer has failed.

drain: Is it leaking or made of an improper material such as corrugated plastic? Does the floor below the sink cabinet look worn or water damaged?

Damage to the sink itself includes surface chips, cracks, rust, and dull finishes that should have been scrubbed with a nonabrasive cleanser, but weren't. Durability is largely a matter of sink materials—enameled cast iron is especially durable—and maintenance.

WHAT TO LOOK FOR

- Ascertain that built-in ovens and dishwashers are securely mounted to cabinets and cannot fall forward when their doors are opened.

- Is the disposer switch safely located so that it cannot be inadvertently switched on?

- Does water spill or squirt out of an air gap onto the counter when the dishwasher drains?

- Check the range-hood filter to be sure it is cleaned and not clogged with grease.

- Are faucets loose or leaking? Examine the base cabinet under the sink for water damage.

- Note countertop and sink chips, cracks, dents, rust, or abrasions.

Bathrooms

Water reigns in the bathroom. Inspecting this complicated space is an exploration of what materials were chosen and how well they were installed. It's also important to consider safety. Is there enough light and ventilation and are all electrical outlets GFCI-protected? As important, has the bathroom been well maintained, with small leaks fixed before they became big problems?

ELECTRICAL AND LIGHTING REQUIREMENTS

BATHROOM RECEPTACLES. GFCIs are sensitive devices that can detect very small current leaks and shut off power almost instantaneously. All bathroom receptacles must be supplied by a 20-amp GFCI-protected circuit. The NEC allows the 20-amp circuit to supply the receptacles of more than one bathroom or to supply the receptacles, lights, and fans (excluding heating fans) in one bathroom. Receptacles in bathrooms must be GFCI protected, either by GFCI receptacles or by a GFCI breaker.

In addition to being GFCI-protected, bathroom receptacles (and switches) need to be located safely. Receptacles and switches should be placed beyond the reach of water that could spray or splash on them from a shower or a sink, as a rule of thumb, at least 3 ft. away.

BATHROOM LIGHTING. It is important to illuminate the face evenly in mirrors. Common practice is to place good-quality light sources either above the vanity mirror or on either side of it. Recessed light cans over the vanity provide adequate light but can be problematic because they can cast shadows across the face. Many jurisdictions also have energy-efficiency requirements for lighting in bathrooms, including lighting and occupancy sensors.

Bathroom light fixtures with outlets in their bases are not permitted in new construction. In fact, any fixture outlets should be disconnected and replaced with code-approved, three-hole GFCI-protected outlets.

If bathroom lights dim when a hair dryer is used on a bathroom outlet, the circuit is inadequate for modern usage. A bathroom needs at least one 20-amp circuit, with no lighting on it, for heavy users such as hair dryers.

Metal light fixtures within a shower area are potential shock hazards and are ideally protected by a GFCI-protected circuit. Because such fixtures in older homes are not adequately protected, the wise course would be to remove them all.

VENTILATION

New or remodeled bathrooms must have an exhaust vent fan. Because fans usually need to continue venting after someone leaves the room, an electronic switch with an integral timer will keep the fan running after the light has been turned off. The fan can be connected to a humidistat, a moisture sensor that will turn off the fan when a preset moisture level is reached.

By reducing ambient moisture, vent fans should reduce the incidence of mold. If the bath fan draws well but mold persists along the ceiling, suspect a fan whose duct ends in an unheated attic above. This installation defect is surprisingly common. Fan ducts should extend through a wall or roof to outside air. Insulating fan ducts in unheated attics will reduce condensation inside the duct. If a bath fan is rusted, condensation may be part of the problem.

If a bath fan continues to run but mirrors remain clouded, the fan may be too small or its ducting may be blocked. A contractor should disconnect ducting to check for blockage. If there is no blockage, the fan should be replaced with a more powerful unit.

TESTING GFCI RECEPTACLES

INSPECT ALL GFCI-PROTECTED RECEPTACLES.
GFCI receptacles have a test button on their face. To test receptacles protected by a GFCI receptacle upstream, many inspectors insert a three-prong, ground-fault receptacle tester and circuit analyzer. To test a GFCI breaker, look in the breaker panel; the breaker will have a test button.

NOTE: The only UL-sanctioned test is to use the test button built into the device, be it a GFCI outlet, breaker, or blank-face type.

Holding a tissue near a bathroom fan is a simple way to test its draw. The fan is supposed to draw moist air upward into a venting system.

Ouch! In this space-starved bathroom, a glass shower door makes contact with the corner of a lavatory. Both items could be damaged if the door is opened too far, too fast.

ROOM TO MOVE SAFELY

Bathroom space isn't efficient if there isn't enough room to use the fixtures easily and safely.

Local building codes specify minimum distances between fixtures and walls, shower stalls, cabinets, and the like. "Bath Fixture Clearances" at right reflects those minimum distances, measured from typical drainpipe and supply pipe centers for each fixture.

From an inspection standpoint, this is all common sense. If you see a toilet so close to a tub that someone would have to sit side-saddle to use it, a shower door that broke when it hit a sink, a lavatory that cannot be used when a bathroom door is open, or a shower door that swings inward, which would trap a shower user who fell against the door, write it up.

WHAT TO LOOK FOR

- Are all bathroom receptacles GFCI protected?
- Are light switches and receptacles located well away from splash or spray zones?
- Can a light switch be easily reached by someone in a shower or tub? This could greatly increase the risk of electrocution.
- Note any light fixtures that have outlets in their base; they should be replaced.
- Do bathroom lights dim when a hair dryer plugged into a bathroom outlet is used?

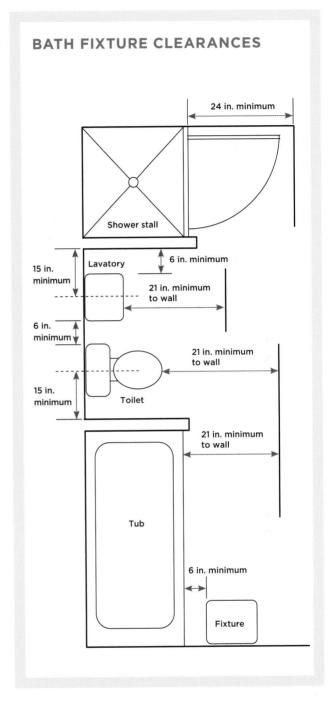

BATH FIXTURE CLEARANCES

- Does the bathroom have a vent fan to expel moisture? Do bathroom mirrors remain cloudy even after the fan has run for a while?
- If the bath fan is rusty or if the ceiling is moldy, see if the fan duct terminates in the attic.
- Is there enough room to use all bathroom fixtures comfortably and safely?

The midline of a toilet should be 15 in. away from a wall or a fixture on both sides. Almost touching the tub, this toilet would be awkward to use.

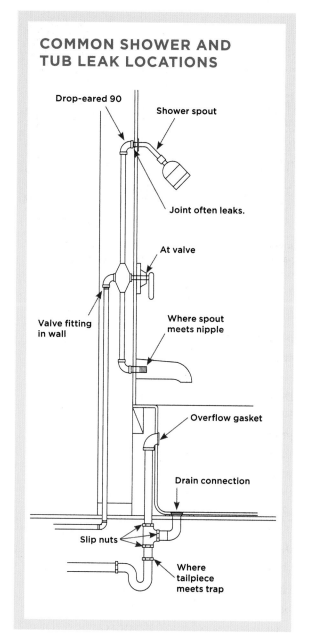

COMMON SHOWER AND TUB LEAK LOCATIONS

Drop-eared 90

Shower spout

Joint often leaks.

At valve

Valve fitting in wall

Where spout meets nipple

Overflow gasket

Drain connection

Slip nuts

Where tailpiece meets trap

TUBS AND SHOWERS

When inspecting tubs and shower surrounds, pay close attention to hardware penetrations in walls (see "Common Shower and Tub Leak Locations" at right), where walls adjoin a tub or shower pan, and all supply pipe and drainpipe connections. That's where leaks are most likely to occur.

A CRITICAL JOINT. The joint where walls meet the tub is prone to leak if not properly caulked. Because tub shoulders are flat, water collects on them. Moreover, filled tubs are heavy, so each filling causes the tub to sink imperceptibly in relation to the framing and finish surfaces around it. And, of course, people using the tub or shower cause slight shifts as well.

If the tub is separate from the walls (that is, not a molded one-piece unit), there should be a ¼-in. gap between the bottoms of surrounding walls and tub shoulders. And the gap should be sealed with an elastomeric caulk such as silicone or flexible polyurethane to seal out water. Sealing this joint and maintaining the seal is critical to keeping the framing around and the subfloor beneath the tub

dry. In inexpert installations, wall tiles or their grout joints may come in contact with the tub. Note it in your report: Even if that juncture is not cracked now, it will likely crack before too long as the tub moves slightly. Moreover, there is not enough room for an elastomeric seal.

TILED WALLS. Tile can be very beautiful and, if installed by a skilled artisan over a stable substrate, very durable. Tile installed over a mud (mortar) bed

Always check ceramic tile shower walls for loose tiles. Periodic recaulking can protect critical joints where pipes and valve stems penetrate walls, but these bulging tiles suggest a failed substrate.

The supply pipes and drain assembly of this old clawfoot tub are a hodgepodge of brass, chrome, galvanized steel, and copper pipes, some of which are corroded and leaking.

or a cementitious backer board can last for decades and be virtually maintenance-free.

Tile installed over drywall is another story. Drywall's gypsum core is relatively soft, and as the bumps of daily usage add up, the core compresses, grout cracks, tiles loosen, moisture gets behind finish surfaces, the drywall substrate crumbles, and mold blooms. If the bath fan isn't properly vented, or there isn't a fan at all, things can deteriorate pretty quickly.

This is not an inevitable process. Some tile-over-drywall installations last for years and look great. But if an inspector sees the symptoms of a failed installation, he or she should note that walls will need to be stripped to the studs and the failed substrate will need to be replaced before the area can be retiled or replaced with another, more durable wall material.

TUB AND SHOWER HARDWARE. Every time a pipe nipple or hardware stem penetrates a tub or shower surround, there's the potential for leakage. Ideally, the workers installing wall panels over roughed-in plumbing will keep wall openings small, caulk openings well, and install trim hardware (trim plates, escutcheons, etc.) to cover the hole.

In addition, before tub/shower walls are closed in, supply pipes and drainpipes must be joined tightly to supply stems, tub drain, and overflow openings

TUBS A-POPPIN'

A POPPING NOISE WHEN SOMEONE STEPS INTO a fiberglass or lightweight steel tub or shower stall is a symptom of inadequate support. The material is flexing under the added weight. Initially, this condition is more of an annoyance than a problem, but in time it can lead to separating joints and leaks. In the short term, caulking tub or shower-stall perimeters may keep water damage at bay. Long term, it may be necessary to expose the framing and replace the failed shower pan, to inject expanding spray foam, or to place a mortar bed beneath the tub to support it.

and checked to be sure they are watertight. If the tub/shower's wet wall (the wall in which pipes run) has an access door, those connections and suspected leaks can be checked or repaired later on with minimal fuss. But if there is no access door, leaks can persist for a long time before they are discovered.

When inspecting a tub/shower, examine hardware penetrations as best you can, lifting trim pieces or escutcheons if you can do so easily and without break-

This diverter valve is probably also leaking behind the shower wall. The faucets and valve are old and worn and should be repaired or replaced.

The resilient flooring around the base of this toilet is deteriorating and starting to lift because of prolonged exposure to moisture. The subflooring may be water damaged, too.

ing seals (trim is sometimes bedded in caulk). Operate faucet handles and diverter valves and note any leaks around them. If there are leaks or if shutting a valve does not fully stop water flowing out of the tub spout or showerhead, valve washers may be worn and need replacing. Are faucet handles loose? Also note if hot and cold supply pipes are reversed (the hot should be on the left), as this mixup indicates an inexpert installation.

NOTE TOO IF THE TUB SPOUT OR THE SHOWERHEAD moves, which may be a sign that fixture spouts are not securely anchored to blocking in the wall. Short term, spout penetrations should be caulked so water doesn't get into the wall. Long term, movement is not a good thing because it can stress pipe connections and cause leaks; if other evidence of leaking emerges, the walls may need to be opened to re-anchor pipes to framing.

DETERIORATED FLOORING along the base of a tub, toilet, or shower enclosure usually indicates leaking. The edges of resilient flooring often darken, lift, and fray, whereas ceramic tile floors may have crumbling grout and cracked or loose tiles. Water-stained subflooring may even be visible. If the underside of bathroom subflooring and framing are visible in an unfinished basement below, scan them for discoloration and rot.

WATER DRIPPING FROM A CEILING BELOW after someone takes a shower is usually caused by a failed shower pan, eroded grout along tub–wall joints, worn or missing caulk, valve stem/shower-spout leaks, or leaking tub drainpipe connections. By the way, if a tub drains slowly or gurgles as it does, it either has blocked drains or venting that is inadequate or missing.

GLASS SHOWER ENCLOSURES whose doors leak are usually missing a plastic gasket that runs along the bottom and edge of the door; door manufacturers have replacements. Clear plastic shower panels that have become cloudy were probably cleaned with an abrasive cleanser or an ammoniated one that interacted chemically with the plastic; cloudy panels can be replaced.

Tempered safety glass has been required in shower enclosures and doors since the 1960s; untempered glass could shatter into sharp pieces if a shower user fell against it. Look for a label on the glass that says tempered or safety glass; if you don't see one, assume the glass is not tempered. Cracked glass panels are probably not tempered; in any case, cracked glass should be replaced.

Because of a failed gasket, this glass shower door has leaked and rotted the tackless strips holding the carpet. (Carpet is a poor choice for moisture-prone areas such as bathrooms.)

WHAT TO LOOK FOR

- Is there a shower only, tub only, one-piece tub and shower unit, or separate tub and shower? What is it (are they) made of?

- Are any surfaces cracked or abraded? If tub walls are tiled, are grout joints intact? Does the tub flex when someone steps into it? Does the tub hold water?

- Are tub–wall joints sealed with a bathroom-grade caulk? Is there any deterioration along joints?

- Are all wall penetrations sealed with caulk? Do trim pieces such as escutcheons fit tightly?

- Is there leaking around faucet handles or diverter valves? Does water continue to dribble out of the showerhead or tub spout even though faucet handles are shut tight?

- Note deteriorated or springy flooring along the base of tubs or shower stalls.

- Do glass shower doors leak? Are any panels cracked or abraded?

- Note weak shower pressure, which may be caused by clogged showerhead filters.

- Do shower users get scalded or frozen when someone uses another fixture? Supply pipes are most often galvanized steel pipes that are constricted with mineral deposits.

LAVATORIES

Lavatories (bathroom sinks) come in many shapes and sizes. Wall-hung lavatories make good use of space and budget, but their pipes are exposed, and there's no place to store supplies underneath. Pedestal sinks are typically screwed to wall framing and supported by a pedestal that hides the drainpipes. Counter-mounted lavatories are the most diverse and may be mounted over or under or may be fused to a countertop.

Lavatory materials should be easy to clean, stain resistant, and tough enough to withstand daily use and the occasional dropped item. The most durable lavatories are enameled cast iron. Vitreous china (porcelain) lavatories have a hard, glossy finish that's easy to clean and durable, but it's not as durable as enameled cast iron; it can chip and crack. Solid-surface lavatories are usually bonded to the underside of a countertop of a similar material.

MOUNTING CONCERNS. A lavatory's mounting is rarely a problem unless some unusual stress is put on it, such as an adult sitting on or a child climbing onto it. Wall-mounted units are perhaps the most easily abused: in time, the brackets or screws holding them to a wall can pull out and the lavatory will tilt forward, showing a gap between the lavatory and the wall. Missing lavatory legs also stress brackets and

The hardest thing to see during a home inspection is something that isn't there. This lavatory is missing a leg, making it precarious. Though partly supported by wall brackets, the lavatory could tear loose and fall if someone leaned too hard on its unsupported corner.

holding screws. In addition to the danger of a lavatory falling over altogether, plumbing connections are strained.

Lavatories mounted to a cabinet are very stable, although top-mounted lavatories tend to collect crud around the lip of the sink and standing water can leak under the lip if it is not caulked. Undermounted lavatories are usually held to the underside of a countertop via clips; if clips slip or caulking fails between the sink lip and the countertop, leaks can occur.

CRACKS AND CHIPS are not a leak problem as long as they are superficial; they can be filled or re-enameled in some cases. But if the crack extends all the way across the bowl, and especially through a drain opening, it should be monitored for leaks. Enameled steel or enameled cast-iron lavatories may rust if their metal substrate is exposed; the lavatory's underside is the portion most likely to rust. Again, rust may not affect a lavatory's ability to hold water.

WORN VALVES AND FAUCETS are perhaps the most common failing of lavatories. Water dripping from a spigot after valves are shut tight is a sign of worn washers. (If the washer is ceramic, the valve stem must be replaced.) Water leaks from the base of a faucet indicate a valve stem that is not seating correctly. (The valve stem or the faucet needs replac-

ing.) If a faucet chatters or vibrates as it is operated, it has worn, loose valves. (Replace stems or faucet.) A faucet spout that terminates below the level of a filled sink must be replaced because waste water in the sink could reverse-syphon into drinking water, contaminating it. (There should be a 1-in. air gap between the bottom of a spout and the top of a filled sink.)

NONAPPROVED SUPPLY PIPES OR DRAINS usually occur when an amateur plumber gets creative to save money. Occasionally an inspector will see flexible plastic tubing or connector as supply lines; this tubing tends to swell with time and some eventually leak or actually burst, causing water damage. Such connections should be replaced with metal sheathed burst-proof-type flexible connectors. Corrugated drainage connectors are often installed as drain traps or fixture tailpieces. These materials lack smooth interior walls so they collect sludge, blocking the line. They should be replaced with conventional drainage fittings and materials.

Sinks that drain slowly may have clogged drains or traps, or their drains may not be sloped enough. (They should slope ¼ in. per 1 ft.) Bathroom sinks that gurgle loudly as they drain or that have lingering sewage smells have faulty venting. Most likely, when the toilet flushes it is sucking water from the sink

COMMON SINK AND LAVATORY LEAK LOCATIONS

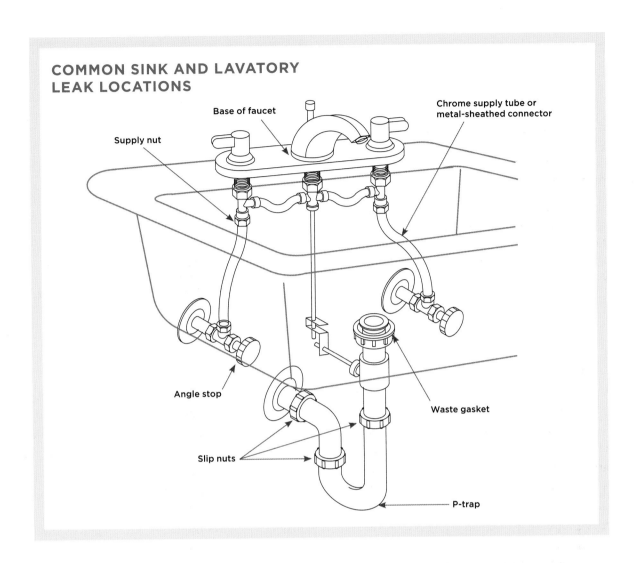

Base of faucet

Chrome supply tube or metal-sheathed connector

Supply nut

Angle stop

Waste gasket

Slip nuts

P-trap

Porcelain or ceramic lavatories with through-cracks such as this should be replaced.

Sink drains should slope down, not up, and this type of corrugated drain is not approved for sink drains by most jurisdictions. It can become easily clogged.

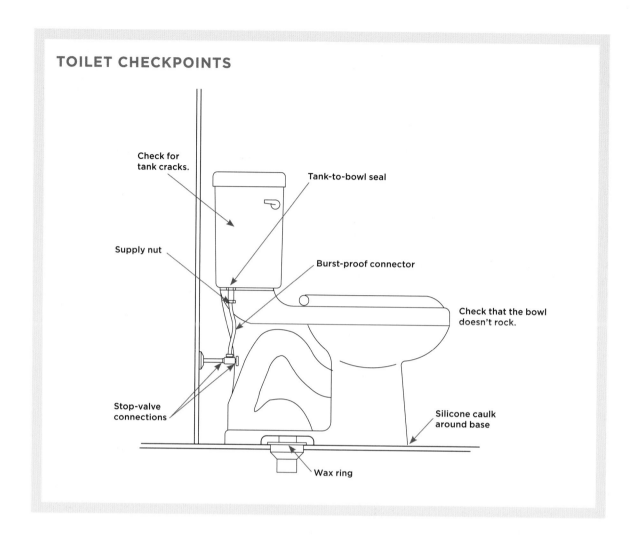

TOILET CHECKPOINTS

Check for tank cracks.

Tank-to-bowl seal

Supply nut

Burst-proof connector

Check that the bowl doesn't rock.

Stop-valve connections

Silicone caulk around base

Wax ring

---

trap; or an old S-trap beneath the sink is allowing all the water in the trap to exit. Replacing the S-trap with a P-trap or upgrading bathroom venting is a job for a licensed plumber.

TOILETS AND BIDETS

Toilets and bidets are almost always vitreous china and are distinguished primarily by their type and flushing mechanism. Almost all toilets are one of three types: traditional two-piece units, with a separate tank and bowl; one-piece toilets; and wall-hung toilets. Wash-down toilets are cheap, inclined to clog, and banned by some codes. Reverse-trap toilets are quieter and less likely to clog than wash-downs. The quietest and most expensive models are typically siphon-jet or siphon-vortex (rim jet) toilets.

SURVEYING ITS CONDITION. As you start inspecting a toilet or bidet, scan the bowl and tank for cracks. Surface cracks are not a problem, but leaking stress cracks are a reason to replace the unit. To check for leaks, examine the tank-to-bowl seal on two-piece toilets, the water-supply fitting on the underside of the tank, and the stop-valve fittings. Dripping at these connections can usually be fixed by installing a new washer or bushing. If the toilet has flexible plastic supply lines that are swollen, they should be replaced with burst-proof metal-sheathed connectors. If water drips from the outside of the toilet tank in warm weather, that is probably just moist air condensing on the tank filled with cool water, a normal condition that can be mitigated by installing

Broken toilet lids are common. Sometimes it is difficult to locate a matching replacement and it becomes necessary to replace the toilet with a new one.

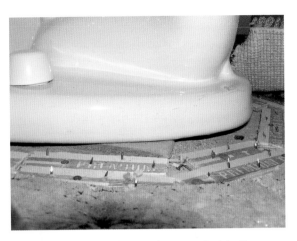

This toilet base is inadequately supported. In time it will move, breaking the wax ring seal between the underside of the toilet and the drain, allowing leaks and sewage gas to enter living spaces. A basic rule is that the toilet perimeter should be sealed to water-resistant flooring with silicone or other caulking.

an expanded polystyrene "sweat stopper" insulator inside the tank.

ROCKING THE LOO. Put your hands on both sides of the bowl and try to rock the toilet (gently) from side to side. Stand over the toilet, with one leg on each side and give it a light shove. The toilet should not rock. If the rocking is slight, tightening the nuts on the base of the toilet may be all that's needed. If the toilet rocks and wetness or sewage smells are present, the nuts have worked loose, the wax ring on the underside of the bowl may have failed, and sewage gases from the drainpipe are escaping. The toilet should be drained, removed, the wax ring replaced, and the toilet reset and bolted tight. If the toilet wobbles (rocks badly), there's wetness, and the flooring has deteriorated or seems springy, sustained leakage may have rotted the subflooring and possibly the framing underneath. In addition to removing the toilet and replacing the wax ring, flooring and framing may need to be repaired or replaced.

NOTE: Whenever a toilet is pulled (removed), the underside of its base should be caulked with a bathroom-grade sealant before the toilet is reset.

CHECKING ITS OPERATION. If a toilet overflows, there's blockage. Using a plunger usually clears it but if it persists, there may be a cracked soil pipe that tree roots have entered. If a toilet runs continuously after flushing, the tank may be leaking or a tired fill valve (ballcock valve) is not working, which should be replaced. When you lift the lid of the tank, you may see the fill valve submerged. The fill valve should be above the water level of the tank to prevent potential siphoning and cross connections. Many unapproved valves are available that are designed to be submerged, but they don't meet code and should be replaced.

WHAT TO LOOK FOR

- Identify the type and material of each lavatory and examine each for cracks and chips.
- Look for water dripping from a spigot after valves are shut tight and leaks around the base of faucet handles (typically caused by worn washers).
- Look inside bathroom cabinets for water stains, active leaks, and deterioration.
- Look for nonstandard supply pipe and drainpipe materials, such as flexible plastic.
- Do lavatories gurgle when they empty or is there a lingering sewage smell?
- Scan toilets and bidets for cracks and leakage around their bases.
- Look for leaks around tank-to-bowl seals, water-supply fittings, and stop-valve fittings.

- Does the toilet rock when you exert gentle side-to-side pressure?
- If a toilet rocks or wobbles, are there sewage smells, wetness, or springy flooring nearby?

COUNTERTOPS AND CABINETS

The diversity of countertop and cabinet materials (and hardware) makes it difficult to generalize about how long kitchen and bathroom cabinets will last. As with other house systems, maintenance is critical, especially repairing leaks quickly, caulking joints where water collects, and monitoring cabinet interiors for signs of water damage.

COUNTERTOP MATERIALS

The most critical areas of a counter, where it is most likely to be damaged, are where the counter meets the back wall; where there are cutouts for sinks, cooktops, and the like; and along counter edges.

Maintaining counter edges is mostly about limiting impact. Installing backsplashes—and keeping them caulked—is the best way to protect the joint where a counter meets a back wall. Sealing the perimeters of sinks, lavatories, and cooktops with a quality caulk, and keeping it sealed, is the surest way to keep water from leaking under these objects and damaging the cabinets underneath. So as you inspect countertops, you will, of course, look for chips, cracks, scratches, and scorch marks. But focus on the critical areas.

BASE CABINETS

Kitchen and bathroom cabinets today are basically boxes of plywood, particleboard, or MDF panels that are glued and screwed together. Side panels, bottoms, and partitions are typically $5/8$ in. thick; back panels are usually $1/4$ in. thick.

MOVEMENT. Base cabinets rarely move because they are screwed to wall studs, toe-nailed to toe kicks and subfloors, weighed down by countertops, and screwed to other base cabinets. But should you note gaps between cabinets and between cabinets and walls, apply gentle pressure to see if you can tilt or move them in any way. Base cabinets that do move

This inexpensive laminate counter and base cabinet are badly worn and should be replaced. Standing water, abraded surfaces, handles wired shut, and a disposer switch on the cabinet face (see p. 257) make this setup unsightly and unsafe.

could break caulking seals, possibly crack countertops and, in very unlikely instances, fall over.

NOTE: The one exception to these observations is a moveable island, a base cabinet that rolls freely; it is not fixed. Rolling cabinets are particularly dangerous to small children because they can tip over if a child tries to climb up one. Consequently, many local codes ban them. If you come across a moveable island, red-flag it in your report.

DOORS. Cabinet doors get banged and scuffed a lot, which is mostly cosmetic damage that a coat of paint or a refinishing will fix. Doors that don't align to frames or other doors need to have their hinges adjusted or reset. In time, hinge screws can pull out. Note missing door hardware, including hinges, pulls, and knobs. If doors have glass panels, note cracked ones.

DRAWERS. Fully loaded drawers, especially those holding pots and pans, can weigh 50 lb. or more, so it's not surprising that their gliding mechanisms jam or fail. Misaligned, sticking drawers aren't just inconvenient. As impatient humans continue to yank on them, stuck drawers can pull apart, with the face

The faces of these base cabinets are badly worn, though it may be possible to refinish them. Most likely, the doors were wiped with an abrasive pad, when a damp sponge would have been adequate.

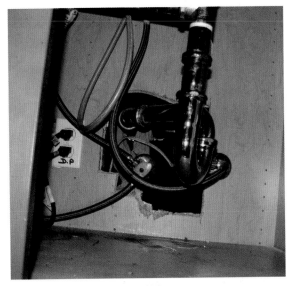

Remodeled kitchens often have large openings in the cabinet wall below the sink. A new back panel closely fitted to pipe sizes should be installed to keep rodents and other critters out.

panels usually pulling off first. So note drawers that do not pull out easily, those whose faces do not align to other drawers or cabinet frames, and drawers that are falling apart. Drawers that stick are frequently missing pulls and knobs.

UPPER CABINETS

Upper cabinets have most of the failings of base cabinets, including scuffed, damaged, and misaligned doors; hinges that need adjusting or replacing; and missing door pulls and knobs. Perhaps the most serious concern is that upper cabinets be securely mounted to wall studs because a lot of weight—fully loaded shelves may bear hundreds of pounds—rests on relatively few attachment points. Fortunately, upper cabinets rarely fall, but keep an eye out for gaps between upper cabinets and walls behind them, sagging shelves, and cabinet bodies or shelves that tilt forward away from the walls they are anchored to.

WHAT TO LOOK FOR

- What material are countertops made of? What is their general condition?
- Scrutinize the back of each countertop, where it meets the wall. Is there a backsplash? Is the joint well caulked, especially behind the sink and faucets?
- Are counter edges intact, or are they worn, cracked, or delaminating?
- Are both upper and base cabinets well secured? Do shelves in upper cabinets sag or do the cabinets tilt away from the wall they are attached to? Are there gaps behind upper cabinets?
- Is there a moveable island in the kitchen? Note its danger to children in your report.
- Note the condition of cabinet doors, both their surfaces and whether doors line up with cabinet frames and other doors. Do hinges need adjustment?
- Do cabinet drawers move freely? If drawers stick, examine their hardware rollers for worn wheels or bent tracks.
- Are any doors or drawers missing pulls, hinges, or handles?

These two receptacles behind a washer and dryer are extremely unsafe and should be replaced immediately by a licensed electrician. Neither is securely mounted and their exposed conductors could short out against an appliance's metal housing.

Laundry

Home inspectors are likely to find laundry setups almost anywhere in a house, including the garage, kitchen, basement, or a second-floor closet off the master bedroom.

So start your report by noting the laundry location and the type and condition of the flooring. If the flooring or subflooring is water damaged, try to determine the cause.

Place a short level atop the washer and dryer to see if they are level. If they are stacked units, check that they are securely attached. Then run each briefly—the spin cycle is sufficient for the washer—to see if they vibrate excessively. From time to time, wash loads get imbalanced and machines that vibrate or "walk" can stress electrical and plumbing connections and make a terrific racket. Washers and dryers need stable footing, leveling adjustments, and, for stacked units, secure attachment to stack-racks or support frames.

WIRING REQUIREMENTS FOR LAUNDRY SETUPS

Clothes washers and dryers are often wired with two surface-mounted receptacles. Dryers typically require 120-volt/240-volt wiring because, in addition to their 240-volt heating elements, dryers have components that use 120 volts, such as drum motors, timers, and buzzers. Therefore, dryer circuits include two hot

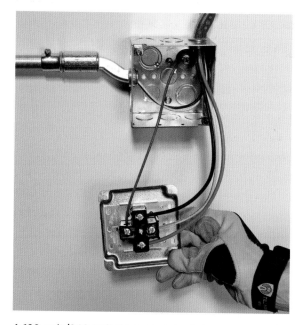

A 120-volt/240-volt dryer receptacle has screw terminals for two hot wires (red and black), a neutral wire (white), and a ground wire or pigtail (green).

wires, a neutral wire, and an equipment ground wire. Equipment grounds on washers and dryers connect to appliance housings to provide a safe route for fault current should a short circuit occur.

Gas valves that are not in use should have a safety cap installed to prevent gas escape should someone become curious and open the valve.

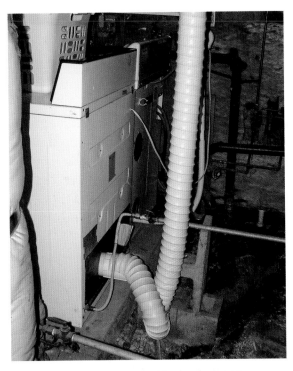

Flexible vinyl exhaust piping is not approved for clothes dryers because it can constrict airflow or, worse, could melt from high temperatures.

THE IMPORTANCE OF FOUR-POLE, FOUR-WIRE DRYER RECEPTACLES

In many older homes, 120-volt/240-volt, three-pole, three-wire, nongrounded receptacles for appliances such as dryers and ranges are common. Older dryers were configured so that the neutral also served as the equipment ground; thus the circuit serving such a dryer had two hots and one neutral conductor.

The shift from nongrounding-type receptacles to grounded receptacles and appliances was made to improve safety and was required by the NEC in the early 1970s. Newer dryers had cords and plugs with four wires: hot, hot, neutral, and ground.

Code allows a nongrounded receptacle to be replaced with another nongrounding receptacle but also requires a grounded receptacle (120-volt/240-volt, four-pole, four-wire) if there is some way to bring an equipment-grounding conductor in the outlet box. The code also requires a grounded four-pole, four-wire receptacle for all new installations.

GAS HOOKUP FOR DRYER

Approved gas piping and connectors are discussed at greater length in Chapter 8, particularly on p. 182. The following is an encapsulation.

GAS PIPING. Approved gas piping includes rigid galvanized steel, rigid black steel, and CSST flexible gas tubing; some types of plastic piping are approved if used underground or outside. Unapproved piping includes cast iron, copper, brass, and aluminum, though some exceptions are made for copper and brass tubing for natural gas with low amounts of hydrogen sulfide. Gas piping must be properly supported, typically every 6 ft.

GAS CONNECTORS. A gas connector is the flexible tubing that connects a gas-fueled appliance such as a furnace to rigid gas supply piping. Modern connectors are typically corrugated and have a shiny gray plastic coating. Flexible stainless-steel or bright yellow connectors are also found on some new equipment.

DRYER VENTING

It's imperative that dryer lint filters be changed after each load, and vent ducts be regularly checked and cleaned as necessary. Clogged ducts slow drying, waste energy, and their contents can cause fire. Make sure the dryer vent terminates outside and is capped by a weather hood that keeps out precipitation and critters. Too often, dryer vents terminate in an attic or a crawl space, which dumps warm, moist air inside the house and thus promotes mold.

The following are some common venting problems.

FLEXIBLE DRYER VENT PIPING. Only smooth-wall metal vent piping is approved for attic or crawl space use. Flexible clothes dryer vent piping should be used only between the dryer and the wall or floor connection. The rough interior surface of flexible venting can collect lint, and if the vent bends too sharply or collapses, it can obstruct air flow.

VERTICAL DRYER VENT. Dryer vent piping that runs straight up is more likely to accumulate lint and clog. Ideally, most of the vent should have only a slight upslope.

VENT TOO LONG. Dryer venting that is too long may reduce efficiency, accumulate lint, and create a fire hazard. The general rule is that dryer vent piping should be no longer than 14 ft. with a maximum of two 90° bends. For each extra 90° bend, the total vent length should be reduced by 2 ft. The manufacturer's instructions should be followed.

SUPPLY LINES

To allow washing machines to be slid out without disconnecting water supply and to accommodate a certain amount of vibration during operation, washing machines have flexible supply lines that screw onto threaded hose bibs. Standard supply lines are reinforced rubber, whereas more durable ones are braided stainless steel over polymer cores. Inspect supply-line connections for wear and leaks.

CATCH PANS. Washers over wood flooring or on the second floor may leak and cause substantial

This dryer vent correctly terminates outside in a weather hood, but the hood has become clogged. Hoods should be checked periodically for blockage and cleaned as needed.

damage before the leak is detected. Washers in such locations should have a catch pan underneath whose drainpipe runs to an approved drain or discharge area.

DRAINPIPES

Washing machine drainpipes should be 2 in. diameter of any approved material. In older houses, drains are often cast iron; ABS plastic drains are most common in new construction. Flexible piping may not be used as drains. Inspect drainpipes to see if they are free of cracks and connections are tight, if pipes are securely anchored so they cannot move, if the drain has a P-trap (never an S-trap), and if any leakage or sewage smells are present.

Nonstandard constructions may include the following.

A 1½-IN. DRAIN. Older clothes washer drain lines are often 1½ in. dia., which can discharge only 9 gal. per minute, maximum. Some new washers discharge up to 13 gal. per minute. If a new washer is installed, it may be necessary to install a 2-in. drain line, which has a 15-gal.-per-minute capacity. Determining drainpipe adequacy is beyond the scope of most inspections.

Water supply connectors may wear out and fail over time. Rubber hoses like these are susceptible to failure and should be replaced with metal sheathed washer connectors.

This washer drainpipe runs straight through the floor and does not have the required U-shaped trap located above the floor.

IMPROPER DRAIN PIPING. Washing machine drains should have a trap located above the floor level. The vertical standpipe should be between 18 in. and 30 in. long, and there should be a vent connection on the waste pipe past the trap. The trap and vent piping are often not accessible to inspection. If pipes gurgle as water drains, venting may be inadequate or absent.

WHAT TO LOOK FOR

- Where is the laundry located? What kind of flooring does it have and what condition is it in?

- Are both washer and dryer tops level? If it's a stacking unit, are both machines securely attached? Do you observe excessive vibration or walking when machines are running?

- Is the dryer gas or electric? If gas, are gas piping and connectors an approved type? If electric, is the dryer receptacle three-hole or four-hole?

- Remove the dryer lint filter and examine the cavity in which it sits: Is it clogged with lint?

- Is the dryer vent flexible plastic or smooth metal? If flexible, are any sections collapsed or crimped enough to impede air flow?

- Where does dryer venting terminate? If venting terminates outside (as it should), does it have a weather hood?

- Are dryer vent ducts mostly horizontal with a slight upslope or vertical?

- What are washer supply lines made of? Are they in good condition? Are connections tight?

- Is there a catch pan beneath washers on wood floors or those located on a second floor?

- What is the size and composition of the washer drainpipe? Does it have a trap?

CHAPTER 13

ATTACHED STRUCTURES

ONCE YOU'VE INSPECTED THE MAIN HOUSE, apply what you've learned to porches, decks, garages, and other attached structures. All need solid footings or foundations, good weatherproofing, effective drainage, and correct flashing where they join the house. Attached garages that share a common wall with the house raise important safety issues such as carbon monoxide from vehicles and fire hazards from fuel fumes or spills. Building codes are strict about safety violations, so be sure to note them in your report.

At first glance it can be difficult to determine how a porch is constructed. This porch is most likely concrete supported by wood framing, which can be durable and low maintenance, but the weight of the materials makes it subject to settlement, cracking, moisture entry, and wood rot.

Porches

Porches are intermediate structures that intercept the weather, keeping it off people as they fish for their keys or wait for someone to answer the door. Porch construction varies greatly, ranging from a roofed overhang barely large enough to shelter someone carrying grocery bags to a sprawling verandah with a full complement of wicker furniture. Almost all porches are open to the elements to some degree, so maintenance is critical for their structural health.

PORCH FOUNDATIONS

Porch foundations vary greatly, though most start with a wood-framed floor platform of posts and joists, with a girder supporting the joist loads of larger platforms. Floor platforms may rest on a low concrete perimeter wall or, more likely in older houses, on an array of concrete or concrete block piers. Whatever the foundation, its footing must be below the frost level in colder climates or the foundation will settle unevenly, tilting the porch above it.

Speaking of tilt, porch floors exposed to the weather typically slope slightly down (say, ⅛ in. per foot), away from the house, so that rain runs off rather than

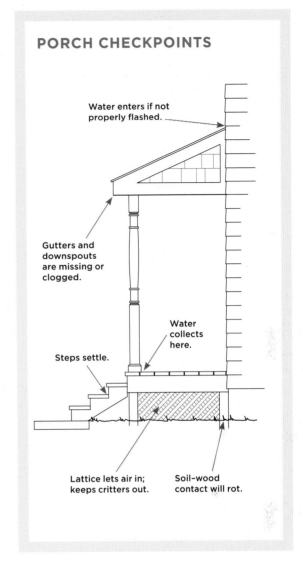

PORCH CHECKPOINTS

Water enters if not properly flashed.

Gutters and downspouts are missing or clogged.

Water collects here.

Steps settle.

Lattice lets air in; keeps critters out.

Soil-wood contact will rot.

pools next to the house. However, if there are gaps between porch decking (floorboards) that water can drain through, it's acceptable to build a level porch. Gaps must be kept open, or decking may rot.

Wood framing should be at least 6 in. or 8 in. (depending on local requirements) above the soil to minimize wood rot and insect infestation. To forestall rot, pressure-treated lumber is typically used to frame the porch substructure, with metal, building felt, or sill seal placed between wood and concrete.

Even with these preventative measures, however, porch framing will be exposed to a lot of moisture and metal connectors frequently rust. It is important,

Though difficult to access, the underside of these porch steps shows a new stair stringer bolted to an old section of decayed sheathing. The new stringer is not rot resistant. The damaged wood should be repaired or replaced. The framing should be treated with a good-quality preservative and the connections above sealed as needed to prevent future water entry.

PORCH DWELLERS

RACCOONS AND OPOSSUMS DENNING UNDER A porch or deck may not be a problem to some people, but such creatures can be aggressive when disturbed and a real danger to house pets not smart enough to leave them alone. Sealing the area under the porch with wire mesh or lattice porch skirts may keep them out, but seal only after you are sure there are no babies still in the den.

therefore, that there be adequate drainage and ventilation, especially if porch skirts (the area between the floor and the ground) are clad with siding. Traditionally, skirts are covered with lattice that allows good airflow yet keeps critters out.

SUBSTRUCTURE. Inspecting the condition of a porch substructure can be challenging in two respects. First, it may be close to the ground: Typically codes allow the undersides of joists to be as low as 18 in. above grade. Second, if porch skirts are covered with stucco or wood siding, you may have to access the subporch area by crawling under the house, if there is any access door, or you can pop a ventilator screen and shine your flashlight into the area.

Before you crawl under a porch scan its upper parts for obvious problems such as cracked siding or sinking porch posts. Underneath the porch, look for concrete piers that are clearly too small or without footings, posts that are tilting or not secured to piers, wood–soil contact, termite infestations, or a ledger that is incorrectly flashed and/or pulling free from the house.

LEDGER. A ledger is a board fastened to the house to support one side of a deck. The ledger–house connection is usually flashed with sheet metal to prevent water entry. If water leaks behind this juncture, it can rot house studs, and if leaves and other debris accumulate above the ledger, they will retain moisture and hasten rot inside and out. So if you can reach the ledger, probe it to see if it's rotted or loose.

Learn what you can about the condition of the framing that supports the porch stairs. The lower ends of stair supports (called stringers) will be almost impossible to reach because the bottom tread is only inches above the ground. But inspect it as best you can for soil contact, fungus, rot, and insect infestation. Probe, too, the underside of stair treads and risers, then turn off your flashlight and look for daylight coming through gaps and cracks.

PORCH STAIRS AND RAILINGS

Determine what the stairs are made of. Porch stairs, landings, and decking are finished in many materials, such as concrete, brick, tile, stucco, and wood, but almost all of these surfaces are supported by wood framing underneath. A water-resistant membrane is often placed over the framing to prevent moisture entry and damage, but membranes wear out in time. Any cracks or openings in surface materials should be caulked or filled to prevent water entry.

Next, assess the condition of the stairs and railings. Use the stairs and grasp the railing firmly to see if it moves as you ascend and descend. Railings

As steps settle they can leave large gaps at the house-to-wall connection. Caulking the gap will lessen water entry, but rebuilding the stairs is the only lasting solution.

Uneven steps are inherently hazardous. Painting the bottom step or walkway a different color will help warn stair users, but these stairs should be rebuilt as soon as possible.

should be solidly attached, with minimal sway when tugged on, with no splits or rot visible. Do the stairs seem springy, and are any steps cracked, cupped, or rotted? Does the staircase tilt to one side (supports on one side may have failed), or are there gaps between either end of the steps and the stairwell casing? Is the top of the staircase pulling free from the porch deck? Note on your report if stairs are painted because painted steps can be slippery when wet.

Be sure to keep the following issues in mind as you inspect exterior stairs.

UNEVEN STEPS. Individual steps in staircases should have a consistent height and depth for safe use. The difference between one step and any other step in the same staircase should not be more than ⅜ in. Uneven steps are a potential trip hazard and should be corrected.

GUARDRAILS. Modern building standards call for railings at least 36 in. high for any porch, deck, stair, or landing more than 30 in. above an adjacent surface and for openings in the rail to be less than 4 in. wide. Railing openings large enough for a child to fall through should be modified for safety. This standard was recently changed from 6 in. to 4 in. after it was found that small children can slip through a 6-in.-wide opening.

This railing has the correct shape, but it could catch someone's clothing as they descend, possibly causing a fall. Railings must terminate against a wall or a post.

HANDRAILS. Staircases with three or more steps should have handrails that are between 1½ in. and 2 in. wide. As with handrails inside the house, porch rails should be placed and shaped so they can be readily grasped for safety and should be 34 in. to 38 in. above the leading edge of the stairway treads. They should return to the railing, post, or ground and should not end in a projection that could be hooked by clothing.

WHAT TO LOOK FOR

- If possible, examine the porch framing and determine which finish materials have been used on its surfaces.

- Do screened openings allow ventilation under the porch or is the area closed off?

- Scan the porch for obvious signs of distress? Are any parts of the porch sinking or badly tilted? Is the porch floor–house joint flashed? Is there standing water or rot along that joint?

- Beneath the porch, are concrete piers too small or without footings? Are there posts that are tilting or not secured to piers? Is there wood–soil contact or insect infestations?

- Do wooden stair stringers rest directly on soil?

- What is the general condition of stairs and railings: solid or shaky?

- Do stairs tilt to one side? Are there gaps, cracking, or other signs of deterioration?

- Are all steps the same height and depth or are they uneven, which is a fall hazard?

- Are there guardrails along the stairs? Are openings between guardrails 4 in. or less?

- Are handrails the correct size and the correct height above steps? Do they return so that clothing will not hook on them?

PORCH DECKING

If floorboards are snug against each other, porch floors should slope slightly down away from the house to clear water. If boards have slight spaces between them that water can run through, porch floors can be level. Look for fungus and minor decay where water has been allowed to stand, particularly where porch floors abut house walls. That juncture should be flashed, but if it is not and debris has accumulated, you may find rot. Rotted decking should be replaced.

Floorboards that sag between supports are probably too thin to span the distance between joists. If the sagging decking has some rot, it's probably wise to replace it with thicker boards. However, if the decking is in good condition, the remedy may be crawling under the porch and adding joists between existing ones to shorten the distance decking must span.

Moisture collects and rot often occurs at the base of wood posts that support the porch roof, especially if wood posts rest directly on wood decking. Ideally, there should be a piece of metal flashing under the post. Fixing post rot can be a complicated job that requires temporary shoring to support the roof load while the wood post is repaired or replaced. In some cases, a wood post or column is hollow, with a weight-bearing metal post inside.

If porch stairs and decking are painted, you may wish to spray them with a garden hose to see how slippery they are when wet. If they are slick, self-adhering strips or nonslip paint should be applied to provide safer walking surfaces.

PORCH SUPERSTRUCTURE

The superstructure of the porch includes all the elements above the decking, including posts, railings, braces or brackets, porch roof framing, and all trim and finish materials.

POSTS OR COLUMNS should be rot-free top and bottom and more or less plumb. Because wood is strong in compression, posts rarely fail, but they can be weakened if they rot, split, or are forced out of plumb by settling or failed footings. Decorative

Wooden porch posts that sit directly on wood or masonry decking will wick moisture and rot. One solution here would to replace the wood post with wrought iron. The brick mortar has deteriorated allowing gaps for water entry. New brickwork and flashings will be needed.

brackets often serve a structural function, as do diagonal braces that help keep posts plumb.

THE PORCH HEADER may be seen instead of a roof rim joist, depending on how the porch roof is framed. In either case, its function is to support the rafter ends overhanging the porch and transfer their loads, down through the posts, to the foundation. Porch headers should not sag; if they do, they are undersize for the loads they carry and the distance they span. The simplest remedy for a sagging header is adding posts. If the header is cracked or rotted, however, it should probably be replaced.

FLASHING THE PORCH ROOF to the house is a critical detail to get right and is explained on p. 72. Flashing details will vary depending on how the roof is framed (shed or peaked), what kind of siding is on the house, and what type of roofing is used. The general rule is that upper overlaps lower. So the upper leg of the porch-to-house flashing slides up under the house siding, whereas the flashing's lower leg goes over the top course of porch roofing.

GUTTERS, DOWNSPOUTS, AND DRAINS. Even a small porch roof concentrates a lot of runoff, which should not be dumped next to house or porch foundations. Just like a main roof, a porch roof requires a system of gutters to catch runoff at the eaves, feed it to downspouts, and direct it away from the house by an assembly of drainpipes (see p. 73).

WHAT TO LOOK FOR

- If porch floorboards (decking) are placed snugly together, does the porch floor slope down away from the house so that rain water can run off?

- If the porch floor is level, are there ¼-in. gaps between floorboards so water can clear? Are any gaps filled with debris? Is there any rot because of standing water?

- If floorboards sag between joists, the boards are too thin; if the whole porch platform sags, the joists are too small for the distance they span.

- Is there rot along the base of wooden posts?

- If porch decking is painted, is the surface slippery when wet?

- Scan the porch header (roof rim joist) for cracking or sagging.

- Is the porch roof correctly flashed where it abuts the house wall?

- Are there rain gutters along the porch eaves and downspouts and drainpipes to carry runoff away from the porch and the house?

Decks

Decks are like porches without roofs, thus they are more exposed to weather and more prone to rot. Decks, however, frequently host social gatherings and the accumulated live loads of dozens of people make deck foundations, framing supports, and bracing crucial to get right, especially if a deck is high above the ground. Though decks are traditionally simple structures, many local codes now require that they be engineered.

Inadequately sized and footed, this deck's unbraced supports could fail. Many decks like this one fail each year when overloaded for barbecues or parties.

DECK FOUNDATION AND FRAMING

Most decks are wood-framed floor platforms with joists typically supported by girders running below for support. Often, rim joists (joists that run around a deck's perimeter) are doubled up. An array of posts is positioned under the rim joists and girder(s), with each post resting on a concrete pier whose footing is below the frost line. This is essential in cold climes because footings that merely sit on the ground will move. Even if the ground doesn't freeze, footings should be set 12 in. into undisturbed ground.

If the deck is close to the ground, its support posts will be short and generally not need diagonal bracing, though all deck joints should be reinforced with steel framing connectors such as joist hangers, standoff post bases, post-to-beam connectors, and the like. When a deck is well above the ground—say, at a second floor or on a sloping lot—its taller posts should be braced diagonally to resist lateral movement and shifting live loads on the deck.

The top of concrete piers and other foundation elements should be at least 6 in. to 8 in. above grade to prevent wood–soil contact and minimize insect infestation. Pressure-treated lumber is commonly used to frame the porch substructure, with metal between wood and concrete (or any masonry surface) to prevent moisture wicking up and rotting wood posts.

NOTE: Some pressure-treating chemicals are incompatible with metal and will corrode it.

INSPECTING UNDER A DECK will be challenging if it is built close to the ground. As with porch framing, many codes allow the undersides of deck joists to be as low as 18 in. above grade. Look for piers that are sunken or tilted and thus not fully supporting posts, posts that lean or can be moved by hand, and posts that lack steel framing connectors. Note connectors that are badly rusted. Use a screwdriver to probe post ends for rot and to probe under footings that you suspect are sitting only on the ground, to see how deep they are.

Note any wood–soil contact or insect infestation to wood framing. Particularly note the bottoms of stairs or stair carriages: They too should rest on footings at least 6 in. to 8 in. above grade, but often they rest directly on the ground and are rotted. Note any wood connections that are pulling apart, such as stair treads to carriages or joists to rim joists.

Support posts and beams need strong connections, typically large bolted metal brackets. These connections are only minimally nailed.

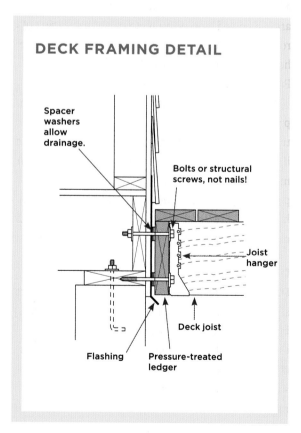

DECK FRAMING DETAIL

Spacer washers allow drainage.

Bolts or structural screws, not nails!

Joist hanger

Deck joist

Flashing

Pressure-treated ledger

Metal deck connectors frequently corrode when they come in contact with the chemicals used to pressure-treat lumber. A peel-and-stick membrane such as Vycor® is a good way to isolate pressure-treated wood from metal connectors.

Modern composite deck materials made of wood fiber and recycled plastic are largely rot resistant and typically last longer than wood decking, but they do require some maintenance.

Again, all joints should be reinforced with steel framing connectors.

DECK RIM JOIST/LEDGER. If the deck is not freestanding, often the deck rim joist that runs along the house is bolted to house framing or supported by a ledger beneath that is bolted to the house. Decks are rained and snowed on (without the protection of a roof), and a gap between the rim joist/ledger and the house can allow water to drain, as shown in "Deck Framing Detail" on the facing page.

The ledger–house connection should be flashed to prevent water entry. If water leaks behind this juncture, it can rot house framing as well as decking. And if leaves accumulate above the ledger, they can retain moisture and hasten rot. As you inspect the ledger, probe it to see if it has rot or is pulling free from the house. If the ledger is only nailed, it should be bolted or attached with code-approved structural screws.

DECKING

Decking (floorboards) on a deck is spaced ¼ in. apart so that water can drain through; for that reason, it's important that debris between boards be regularly removed. Decks whose boards are snug against each other or that are covered with synthetic coatings should be designed to drain freely. (More about that in a bit.)

In addition to looking for rot, inspect decking for cracking, cupping, discoloration, and splitting. Cupping typically occurs when there is standing water, caused by boards that have been installed too close together or by debris that has lodged between them. Discoloration has similar causes; dark stains may be the first stages of mold. Splitting is usually caused by sun damage, which periodic recoating with a good wood preservative can often prevent. Badly worn decking should be power-washed and recoated.

Walk the deck. Decking that sags between supports may be too thin to span the distance or the joists may be too far apart. The basic rule is that 2× decking will span 24 in. and 1× decking needs joists every 16 in.

MODERN MATERIALS. There have been great advances in decking materials, connectors, and fasteners. To solve the persistent problem of deck nails popping up and deck boards lifting, many installers now use special deck screws or, to prevent nail splits, hidden decking clips.

Composite lumber made of recycled plastic and wood fiber is now widely used for decking, handrails, and trim, though it should *not* be used for structural purposes. Composite decking is largely impervious to water and insect damage, but it must be maintained.

This deck's guardrails are extremely hazardous to kids. Openings exceed the 4-in. maximum required by safety codes and a small child could easily climb the horizontal rails.

Handrails need to be gripable; a 2× board on edge doesn't qualify.

STAIRS, GUARDRAILS, AND HANDRAILS

As you go up and down stairs to a deck, note if any treads are cracked, cupped, separating from their carriages, or excessively springy. They should be solid afoot and securely attached at top and bottom, with the bottom cleat resting on a footing at least 6 in. to 8 in. above grade. It bears repeating that the vertical distance between stair treads should be even—of equal height—so the stair user's rhythm is not interrupted, causing him or her to trip and fall.

GUARDRAILS. For decks more than 30 in. above an adjacent surface, building codes require railings at least 36 in. high. As with other guardrails, openings in guardrails must be less than 4 in. wide (see p. 279).

HANDRAILS. If the deck is accessed by three or more steps, handrails are needed. The requirements for size, shape, and height are the same as for porch handrails (see p. 279). In addition, it's important that all railings be soundly attached as well as the posts supporting them. Support posts should be *bolted* to deck framing, not merely nailed, because in time nails work loose. If posts or rails wobble, write them up. Special steel connectors that tie railing posts to framing can usually correct wobble if the post and framing are sound.

SECOND-STORY DECKS AND BALCONIES

The structural concerns for decks just discussed are even more compelling for second-story decks and balconies because of the greater height of such structures. These concerns include extending foot-

Insufficiently braced stairways to a porch or a deck can be very dangerous for someone trying to move a heavy object such as a refrigerator to the upper floor. These stairs should be replaced.

Metal drip-edge flashing should extend beyond the edge of the stucco below. Burying this flashing's edge in stucco has created water stains and, possibly, water entry and rot.

ings well below the frost level, adequately sizing and bracing support posts, using metal connectors to reinforce critical joints, securely attaching deck and balcony platforms to house framing, correctly flashing junctures to prevent rot, and fastidiously monitoring and maintaining surfaces and structures. All take on increased importance when one considers the potentially catastrophic consequences of a balcony or second-story deck collapse.

Keep in mind the following components, especially when inspecting second-story decks and balconies.

ADEQUATE SUPPORTS. Correctly sized, footed, and braced deck-support posts are essential. In addition to bearing the dead weight of deck materials, supports may need to be engineered to support live loads that can shift as people on the deck move, exerting considerable lateral force.

STRONG CONNECTIONS. Support posts and beams need strong connections, typically large bolted metal brackets. Metal rusts and corrodes, however. One persistent problem is corrosion due to metal connectors' incompatibility with chemically

treated, decay-resistant lumber. Replacing corroded brackets, screws, and nails with stainless-steel materials is one solution, but may be an expensive one. Painting connectors showing minor rust with a rust-inhibiting coating may extend the life of corroded connectors but is not a permanent solution.

Some contractors will wrap the framing with a waterproof tape before adding the metal connector. This approach will work as long as there is no direct wood to metal contact. The screws that secure the connectors may need to be stainless or have a special coating.

FASTIDIOUS FLASHING. Flashing a deck ledger to the main-house framing (see p. 282) must be done properly to keep water from getting behind siding and rotting the house framing. As the right photo above shows, metal drip-edge flashing must extend beyond the edge of the siding to avoid water intrusion, staining, and extensive rot damage.

MULTIPLE DRAINS. Balconies are often constructed over portions of the building below. It's best to have at least two surface-mounted drains in case one becomes clogged. Wall-mounted overflow drains should be located low on the wall, at least lower than any door threshold.

A surface drain with a nearby overflow, as shown here, is ideal. If the drain becomes clogged, water can exit out the overflow rather than flooding the adjacent rooms.

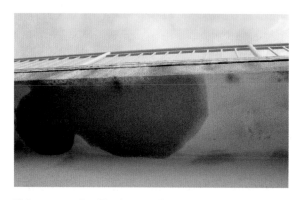

This unvented soffit shows substantial water staining. It is water stained because the deck membrane has failed and its drain is clogged. After those problems are corrected, screened openings on the underside would allow trapped moisture to escape.

FLAWLESS SKIN. Balconies frequently have professionally applied, high-tech coatings that must be durable and as flawlessly waterproof as is humanly possible. Undetected, even small leaks can cause extensive water damage to framing and finish surfaces. It's important to know the name of the waterproofing, the company that applied it and, if the coating has a warranty, if the warranty is transferrable to new owners.

VENTILATION. Balconies that extend out from a building often have stucco undersides called soffits. Soffits should have screened vent openings to allow any moisture that enters from above to drain, thereby reducing the potential for moisture-related damage or decay.

WHAT TO LOOK FOR

- Do all deck footings extend below the frost level or, in frost-free areas, at least 12 in. below grade? Are the tops of all footings at least 6 in. to 8 in. above grade?
- Under the deck, look for wood–soil contact and rot. Do the bottom of stairs rest on footings at least 6 in. to 8 in. above grade?
- Have steel framing connectors been used to secure posts to footings and to joists, joists to girders and rim joists, and stair stringers to framing? Are any connectors corroded or rusted?
- Are support posts diagonally braced to resist lateral movement?
- Is a house–side rim joist or ledger securely bolted to the house framing? Is it flashed to prevent water entry? Is there a gap between the ledger and the house to allow water to drain?
- Are there ¼-in. spaces between deck boards so that water can drain? Does debris block any of those spaces? Is rot present between deck boards?
- Is decking in good condition and solid under foot? Or is it sagging and excessively springy?
- If decking is covered with a synthetic coating, is it intact?
- If the deck is at least 30 in. above adjacent surfaces, is there a railing 36 in. high?
- Are guardrail openings less than 4 in.? Are the railings easily climbable by a curious child?
- Are steps, railings, and support posts solid, with minimal sway?
- Do you feel any sway on a second-story deck when you grip a railing and repeatedly push on it with some force or jump up and down on the deck?
- Does second-story deck or balcony flashing extend beyond siding so water can drip free?
- Do balconies with perimeter walls have at least two surface-mounted drains?
- Are balcony coatings intact and free of rips, tears, or cracks?
- If there are finished (closed) soffits on the underside of balconies, are they vented?

This garage wall leans significantly and the stucco appears to have been patched several times. The foundation should be replaced by a qualified contractor.

Garages

Garages vary widely in configuration and construction. Some are detached from the main house and some are attached, which has big implications for safety. Garages also range from simple wood-framed shells whose mudsills sit directly on the earth, all the way up to two- or three-story structures with sophisticated in-law apartments.

SAFETY CONCERNS

It's not something we think about much driving down the road, but most automobiles are powered by a series of controlled explosions involving highly flammable materials. Because the primary function of a garage is storing this mobile explosion maker, the primary safety concerns of attached garages involve confining flammable gasoline fumes, oil leaks, and exhaust gases (such as carbon monoxide) to the garage and out of the main house.

Fuel-fired appliances located in garages should be mounted on a platform at least 18 in. above the garage floor and protected from being struck by a car, which could cause an explosion.

GARAGES LOWER THAN LIVING SPACES.

Gasoline, auto exhaust, and many chemical vapors are heavier than air and tend to collect on the garage floor. Most modern attached garages have a concrete slab floor located below the floor of the room next to the garage. Ideally, there should be at least one step up to house living spaces from the garage, so that chemical vapors stay largely in the garage when the door between those spaces is opened.

A garage on the same level as house living spaces might be considered a health and fire hazard because, in addition to being flammable, many auto-related fumes are toxic. Houses with garages in unpartitioned basements are particularly hazardous, especially if the basement areas are poorly ventilated and create a location where flammable vapors could collect.

FUEL-FIRED APPLIANCES IN GARAGES. Any fuel-fired appliance located in a garage, such as a gas- and oil-fired furnace, boiler, older water heater, or clothes dryer should be situated on a stable platform at least 18 in. above floor level. This height puts the appliance's ignition source (pilot light or burner) sufficiently above any flammable vapors that might collect on the garage floor.

Here, fire-resistant drywall panels create a 1-hour fire-rated firewall. The smoke seals on the bottoms of each metal-clad fire door would also help confine fire and smoke to the garage.

Many newer water heaters are now equipped with flammable vapor ignition resistance (FVIR) systems with flame-arrestor plates that allow them to be installed directly on garage floors.

Other strategies for minimizing risk include building a low, continuous wall around the appliance and isolating the appliance in a room with a tightly sealed door. A tightly sealed enclosure will also need its own source of fresh combustion air, as explained on p. 179.

In addition, fuel-fired appliances, gas lines, and gas meters must be protected from accidental impact from a car. This protection could be a low masonry wall or a bollard—typically, a concrete filled steel post. Either structure must be stout enough to stop a car. Judging from the number of cracked studs inspectors find in garage back walls, inattentive drivers misjudge distance (and speed) all the time.

INCIDENTAL HAZARDS. Note that firewood should never be stored in a garage: in addition to being fuel to burn, it's often home to wood-destroying insects. Household goods stored in a garage may be innocuous from a safety standpoint, but they will limit your inspection, could add fuel to a fire, and may impede a resident's escape in an emergency.

FIREWALLS AND FIRE DOORS

To limit the spread of fire from an attached garage to house living spaces, building codes require that the firewall (the shared wall between the garage and the house) be constructed of fire-rated materials. Typically, a firewall is a solid wall built of a nonflammable material, such as brick or concrete block, or a stud wall covered, on the garage side, with Type X, fire-resistant ⅝-in. drywall.

A drywall-covered wall is not, of course, perfectly fireproof, so building codes typically specify how long the firewall must contain the fire. Thus code requirements may call for a wall with a 1-hour fire rating, though, again, codes vary. A firewall must extend from the garage floor to the ceiling, including shared attic walls, if any. (Some codes require that firewalls extend from the floor to the underside of the roof.) If there is an attic hatch, it must be covered at all times. If you see an uncovered attic hatch, write it up as a potential fire hazard.

Air-conditioners are not permitted in firewalls. The large opening in the wall could draw fire or smoke into the home. Ducts that penetrate firewalls or ceilings should be at minimum 26-gauge sheet steel or other approved material and should have no

Pull-down stairs allow access to storage space above the garage ceiling. The underside of the access stairs also needs a fire-rated surface, and stairs should be kept shut.

openings into the garage. Flexible ducting should not be installed through a garage firewall unless it has a rated fire damper at the wall connection.

ABS plastic waste piping should not be installed through a fire-rated wall or ceiling.

Multiple-story houses and duplexes in urban areas often have large garages at the first-floor street level. These large open spaces may have a large central beam running from front to rear. Sometimes these are steel I-beams, which are much more susceptible to fire damage than are wooden beams because they will melt and fail long before a wood beam will burn through. Steel beams should be insulated and wrapped with a fire-rated material.

A FIRE DOOR is a fire-resistant interior door at least 1⅜ in. thick, situated on a firewall. A fire door should have smoke seals to prevent the infiltration of smoke, flammable vapors, or superheated gases; it should also be self-closing, though codes vary and some homeowners find this feature inconvenient when they arrive home with a car full of groceries. Fire doors should be free of through-holes of any kind, whether for glazing or pet ports.

Some codes once required that the garage side of a fire door be covered with sheet metal, but metal

Fire-rated doors between the garage and adjacent living areas may not contain openings, such as a pet door.

HOW THICK IS THE FIREWALL?

DURING YOUR INSPECTION, IT MAY not be obvious if a firewall's drywall is thick enough to meet local fire codes. The easiest way to determine its thickness is to remove a switch plate or receptacle cover and look at the cut edge of the drywall. Brick or concrete-block firewalls can be any thickness, as long as they extend from floor to ceiling (or roof).

alone is not sufficient fireproofing because it heats up quickly and can ignite the wood beneath it. Consequently, many modern fire doors have cores filled with gypsum, which is a so-called endothermic fill that absorbs heat. A new fire door should have a label on the hinge side edge stating that it is a fire-rated door.

WHAT TO LOOK FOR

- Is the garage lower than adjacent living spaces?
- If fuel-fired appliances are housed in the garage, are they installed on a stable platform at least 18 in. above the garage floor level?
- Are fuel-fired appliances, gas lines, and gas meters protected from an auto impact?
- If the garage is attached to the house, there must be a floor-to-ceiling (or floor-to-roof) firewall. Is it built of appropriate materials and thick enough to satisfy code fire ratings?
- If there is an attic hatch in the garage, is it covered with a fire-rated surface? Is it closed at the time of your inspection?
- Is there a listed (code-approved) fire-resistant door with a smoke seal? Does it have a self-closing mechanism?
- Are there any improper firewall penetrations?

Driveways that slope down into a garage can concentrate rain runoff onto the garage floor. This broken driveway is in poor condition and should be replaced.

This nicely detailed garage approach has a concrete apron that slopes down to a grated drain. The cracking where the main structure connects to the driveway is superficial.

GARAGE FLOORS, DRIVEWAYS, AND DRAINAGE

Water is by far the most-cited cause of house problems, and garages are no exception. Ideally, the ground should slope down and away from the garage and runoff should be directed away from it, but that doesn't always happen. As noted earlier, garage construction often gets the tail-end of the construction budget.

Start by noting the condition of the roof, how much eaves overhang, the presence or absence of gutters, if gutters are connected to downspouts, and downspouts to drains. Use a garden hose to flush gutters and downspouts and note if the system is clogged or if it carries water away from the garage foundation (however rudimentary). For a more detailed inspection of the garage roof, exteriors, gutters, and downspouts, review Chapters 2 and 3.

GARAGE FLOORS. A garage slab on a wet site is probably going to be damp. If the slab has minimal or no steel reinforcement, the slab may crack if soil is unstable or the ground water pressure is sufficient. Small cracks can be sealed, but larger, through-slab cracks will likely get bigger. Write them up. If there is a floor drain, you may want to use a garden hose to flush it with water and see how it drains. Be careful:

Inserting hoses in drains can cause water damage if the drains are not working properly. If there is a sump pump in the garage floor, check its operation, too.

DIVERTING DRIVEWAY RUNOFF. If a garage is downhill from the road that runs by the property, a lot of water will run down the driveway toward the garage. It may be possible to landscape the lot and create intervening swale drains (see p. 19) to intercept the runoff, but such solutions will be too expensive for most homeowners. More commonly, a small concrete apron in front of the garage opening is used to divert runoff to one side, to be carried off by perimeter drains.

A GRATED DRAIN BOX in front of the garage opening is another common solution. The drain box is typically rectangular in cross section, with its top buried flush to the drive surface. A removable, slotted metal grate (sturdy enough to be driven over) sits atop the box, allowing rain to flow into it; either or both ends of the drain box attach to a gravel-and-perforated-drainpipe system that carries the runoff away. When used in tandem with a concrete apron, the drain box is typically placed before (uphill from) the apron, though the drain box can be useful on either side. It's important that drain grates be cleaned periodically because they fill up with leaves. The box should periodically be flushed with a garden hose to clear any buildup of dirt, gravel, and the like. If drains fill up with debris, they will be useless.

WHAT TO LOOK FOR

- Garages should have overhangs, gutters, downspouts, and drains to direct water away. Use a garden hose to see if gutters and downspouts are clogged or open.
- Is the garage slab in decent shape? Does it have a drain? Flush the drain to see if it works.
- Does the driveway slope downhill to the garage? Is the bottom of garage trim or the garage door water stained or damaged?
- Is there a sloped concrete apron or a grated drain box in front of the garage door to divert runoff away from the garage opening?
- If there is a drain box, is it free of debris? Flush drains to see if to see if they empty quickly.

FOUNDATION AND FRAMING

As with the main house foundation, the top of the garage foundation should be at least 6 in. to 8 in. above grade, but this is more the exception than the rule with garage construction. Far too often, a concrete slab floor is poured on grade and the garage mudsills sit directly atop that. If the mudsill is pressure-treated or a rot-resistant wood such as redwood, it may last decades before it rots out, but in the meantime stud bottoms and attached wood siding will have also rotted out or become infested with wood-destroying insects.

SUBSTRUCTURE AND FRAMING. On your report, note what kind of foundation there is, if any, and its condition. Note the absence or presence of anchor bolts tying sills to the foundation and whether the concrete around such attachments is solid or crumbling. Note the sheathing, studs, plates, and rafters and any observed deficiencies. Note the absence of any needed bracing (including foundation ties), whether let-in wood braces or metal ones.

MOISTURE-RELATED DAMAGE. Walk around the outside of the garage, using a screwdriver to probe mudsills, studs, sheathing, and siding, especially if

Garage framing that sits on concrete slab floors is often damaged. Soil coming through the wall usually indicates a soil level that is too high, exerting pressure against garage walls. Because damage is often obscured by stored items, you may need to move a few items during an inspection.

there is wood–soil contact; and note an absence of gutters, downspouts, and drainage; surfaces that slope toward the garage; splashback, water-stained siding, or discolored framing; or vegetation touching the building. Relatively minor decay or rot can often be treated locally with a preservative, but significant damage typically requires replacing rotted material. Have a qualified structural pest control firm determine if fungus, decay, or other moisture-related organisms are present.

EMBEDDED SIDING/TRIM. The lower edges of wood siding or wood trim are often buried in concrete, masonry, or asphalt when patios, sidewalks, or driveways are installed. There should be a gap between the wood and the surface below, so embedded siding should be cut back and its ends sealed to prevent moisture-related decay or termite damage. In some cases, however, such repair is neither practical nor necessary, such as with garage siding and trim that are well protected by roof overhangs and showing no overt signs of damage.

MASTER PLUMBER AND ELECTRICIAN REX Cauldwell has a simple test to tell how well built a garage is: He slams a side entrance door good and hard. If garage walls shake and garage doors rattle in their tracks, the structure is probably underbuilt, with framing members too small and/or too widely spaced. Remedies will vary and may include placing new studs between existing ones, adding diagonal bracing, or sheathing the inside of the garage to stiffen it. A seasoned contractor can spell out the options.

The basic rule is that any beam that sags is undersize. This sagging beam should be monitored to see if its deflection is increasing or if the beam and its loads have stabilized.

IF IT SAGS, IT'S UNDERSIZE . . . MAYBE.

The wide openings required for auto access require large beams to span and distribute the loads across the openings. An engineer should size such beams. Technically, any beam that sags is by definition undersize and should be monitored and reinforced, or replaced if needed. But as long as the sagging does not impinge on garage door operation, a sagging beam can be checked over time to determine whether its downward deflection is increasing. The beam and load above may have stabilized and not need any reinforcement.

WHAT TO LOOK FOR

- Does the garage foundation rise 6 in. to 8 in. above grade or do mudsills sit directly on a slab floor?
- When you slam a side entrance door, do garage walls shake?
- What is garage framing sheathed with? Is the framing braced? Is the framing tied to the foundation?
- Probe mudsills, stud ends, and the bottom of siding for rot and insect damage.
- Are the lower edges of wood siding or trim buried in concrete, masonry, or asphalt?
- Do beams across garage door openings sag? Does that interfere with door operation?

GARAGE WIRING

Garages are not required to have electricity, but if they are wired they must be wired safely. Electrical wiring in new garages must meet current electrical codes, whereas existing wiring in older garages is frequently something of a gray area. Consult local electrical codes to be sure. To be protected, all general-use receptacles in a garage should be GFCI receptacles.

Garage receptacles have appliance plugs inserted and removed far more often than common household receptacles. So it makes sense to spend a bit more and install good-quality garage receptacles with durable nylon faces and backs reinforced with brass yokes. As you inspect garage receptacles, note any whose plastic faces are cracked, broken, or scorched; they should be replaced immediately.

Your inspection of garage receptacles should include testing each with a circuit analyzer (p. 146) to determine if the receptacle is GFCI protected, to ascertain that its polarity is correct, and to make sure that it is correctly grounded. Stationary appliances such as electric water heaters, tablesaws, freezers, and other large energy users should be on grounded, dedicated circuits.

NOTE: Dedicated outlets do not require GFCI protection.

Garage wiring below 7 ft. should be mechanically protected. Exposed Romex cable, as shown here, could be potentially hazardous should someone hang tools from it (which is a surprisingly common occurrence).

If the garage has more than six circuits, it should have its own electrical panel, a subpanel serviced by four incoming feed wires: hot, hot, neutral, and ground. In a subpanel, neutral and ground wires (and buses) must be physically and electrically isolated from each other. For more about service panel and subpanel wiring, see Chapter 6.

The most common electrical violations you will find in a garage will likely be installations that are not quite complete, such as receptacles without covers, exposed runs of Romex (nonmetallic) cable below 7 ft., wiring runs that aren't stapled to framing at least every 54 in. and within 12 in. of outlet boxes, wiring splices that aren't in a covered box, and ceiling boxes that are not secured to framing. If they aren't done right, write them up.

WHAT TO LOOK FOR

- Would garage wiring pass an electrical inspection or are parts of it incompletely finished?

- Are general-use electrical outlets in the garage GFCI protected?

- Examine all receptacles. Are the plastic faces of any cracked, broken, or scorched?

- Are stationary appliances on dedicated circuits?

- If the garage has more than six circuits, does it have its own electrical panel?

GARAGE DOORS

Note the type, composition, condition, and operation of all garage doors. By far the most common type of garage door is a sectional door that rolls up and out of the way on overhead tracks (see the photo below). When an overhead door is open, it takes up little usable space. One-piece overhead doors tend to be flimsy because they must be light enough to lift. Hinged garage doors are relatively rare and mostly found on older homes; hinged doors require a lot of room to open and nearly level or down-sloping ground in front of them. Much less common are hybrid types that fold and slide off to one side rather than overhead.

Whatever the type, open and shut the garage door repeatedly to see how easy it is to operate, if guide wheels align to tracks, and if parts bind or stick. Write up cracked or broken glass, double-glaze seals that have failed, or clear laminate glazing that has become cloudy. Note squealing wheels, rusted tracks, missing hardware, and door sweeps that don't seal tightly to the garage floor. Most of these problems are relatively minor and can be repaired easily.

Garage doors are made of various materials, primarily wood, metal, or plastic. Look for obvious signs of damage, especially along door bottoms.

MANUAL DOORS. Overhead doors that close manually have tensioned springs on both sides that

Roll-up sectional garage doors are very popular in newer construction. Some newer models have horizontal joints especially designed to reduce finger pinching.

Roll-up door tracks added to older garages may lower the overhead height of the ceiling and create an eye-level hazard. Ideally, overhead clearance should be at least 80 in. above the floor.

Manual door opener switches should be located well away from a tension-spring door-hinge mechanism, unlike in this example, to prevent injury.

help offset the weight of the door. Spring tension is adjustable. Typically, a rod or stranded metal restraining cable (safety retainer) runs through the center of each tensioned spring, to keep the spring from flying off and injuring someone should it break or pull free from its mounting bolts.

As you operate a manual overhead door, note how much effort it takes to raise or lower it, whether guide wheels stick or roll smoothly in tracks, if the door stays up when rolled open, and how fast the door descends when it is lowered. A manual door should never slam down as it closes, which could be hazardous to anyone, especially children, standing beneath it. Most of these failings can be fixed with minor repairs, such as adjusting tension springs so that the door ascends and descends slowly and gently.

When a manual overhead door is closed, its locking bars should slide into slots in the tracks and click shut. If locking bars do not align, they can be adjusted.

AUTOMATIC, MOTOR-DRIVEN DOORS.

Modern garage doors are typically sectional overhead types run by a remotely controlled motor. An important part of this setup is a pair of electric eyes (photoelectric sensors) on both sides of the door. These sensors should be between 4 in. and 6 in. above the floor. The transmitter of the pair shoots a continuous

light beam across the garage-door opening, which is received by the second sensor. If a person, animal, or object interrupts the beam, the door will not roll down, or if it is in the process of closing, it will halt.

It is easy to see if electric eyes are working. Simply put your foot in front of a sensor to interrupt the light beam. If the door is open, click the remote control to see if it will shut or, if the door is closing, to see if the door will stop descending or reverse itself. Automatic doors vary, but almost all have an autoreverse that reverses direction when electric eye beams are blocked or the door meets resistance before it reaches its closed position.

To test the door's autoreverse, slide a small cardboard box or empty plastic bottle into the garage opening, in the path of the descending door. If the door does not reverse, the safety feature is not working correctly and should be inspected by a garage-door specialist. Electric eyes can usually be added to older automatic doors.

Last, all automatic garage doors also have a pull-down cord that enables you to open and close the door manually (very useful when the power goes off and your car is parked in the garage). Yank down on the cord to see if it works. Opening and closing the door may be a bit of work, but it should not be prohibitively difficult.

Most jurisdictions now require electric-eye auto return mechanisms placed 4 in. to 6 in. above the floor. This one is located too high and should be adjusted.

WHAT TO LOOK FOR

■ Note the type, material, and condition of the garage door(s). Is it manual or motor driven?

■ Scrutinize the bottom of the door for water-related damage. Does the sweep on the bottom seal tightly to the garage floor?

■ Note squealing guide wheels, rusted tracks, missing hardware, and broken panes, if any.

■ If it's a manual door, does it open and close easily, without slamming down? Are tensioned springs on both sides intact? Does each spring have a metal restraining cable?

■ If it is an automatic door, does it have an electric eye safety device? When you block the device's light beam, does the door halt or reverse?

■ If the door lacks an electric eye, test the automatic door's autoreverse feature. Does the door halt or reverse before crushing a cardboard box in its path?

■ On an automatic door, verify that its pull-down cord (manual override) works.

■ Is there an in-law unit in or over the garage? Was it built with a permit?

Outbuildings

Outbuildings are typically storage or garden sheds. They are not included in a normal home inspection. But it's a good idea to take a quick look and check

A GRANNY OVER THE GARAGE

BECAUSE GARAGES ARE USUALLY ACCESSIBLE, simply framed, and unfinished, they are among the easiest structures to convert to in-law units—granny flats, as they are commonly known. If the garage has a granny flat, ask homeowners if a permit was pulled and if a structural engineer approved the conversion. Depending on local codes and when the space was converted, the unit may need to meet all code requirements for a residence, such as firewalls (and fire-rated ceilings) between living spaces and the garage.

If the granny flat is over the garage, the space may have been originally intended only for storage, not people, and the existing foundation may not be large enough to support the live loads of someone living upstairs. But if the garage was built with a potential live-in space above it, the foundation may be adequate. A structural engineer should make the call. If the unit's floors are springy, it may be possible to add a girder and support posts underneath to shorten the span of floor joists without affecting the garage's functionality.

Large garage door openings impact structure. An in-law unit over a garage may experience structural failure in an earthquake, particularly if the opening of the garage doors does not line up with other walls of the building. This situation is commonly referred to as a "soft story." A qualified engineer should be consulted about reinforcing this area.

for any improper electrical wiring, stored gasoline, dumped used motor oil, or other potentially hazardous chemicals.

Also, while walking the backyard, check the ground for any lids or covers over possible deep sumps or pits. Some of these covers can be easily removed by a curious child creating a real hazard. On a downsloping lot, walk to the far end and look for failing retaining walls hidden behind shrubs and fences.

CHAPTER 14

ENVIRONMENTAL CONCERNS

IN RECENT YEARS, BUILDING SCIENTISTS have greatly increased our understanding of how hazardous materials, both human made and naturally occurring, can impact our health and that of our environment. The hazardous materials that affect our homes include asbestos, lead paint, mold, radon, and a host of volatile organic compounds (VOCs) such as formaldehyde. Many of these materials are no longer produced, but their side effects linger on, hidden in walls, buried in backyards (leaking oil tanks), or invisibly present in the air we breathe. Hazardous materials and environmental remediation are not typically included in the scope of a general home inspection, but by alerting homeowners to these environmental concerns and informing them of their options, home inspectors can offer a valuable service.

Asbestos

Asbestos is a family of six long-fibered, naturally occurring silicate minerals. Asbestos has been mined and manipulated for millennia. Its tensile strength imparts both durability and flexibility: Asbestos was mixed with clay to make cooking pots that could sit in a fire, and woven into clothing. From the nineteenth century on, it was widely added to building materials because of its ability to retard fire, absorb sound, and resist electrical and chemical damage.

Its endlessly useful, long fibers contained a deadly side effect, however. Inhaling asbestos fibers over a prolonged period can cause serious illnesses such as mesothelioma, lung cancer, and asbestosis (a restrictive lung disease similar to miner's lung). In 1978, textured acoustic ceilings with asbestos were banned in the United States. And in 1989, the EPA issued the Asbestos Ban and Phase Out Rule, which, though later overturned in court, accelerated the movement to remove asbestos from consumer products. (Asbestos has not been banned altogether; it is still found in niche products such as automotive brake shoes.)

Given its wide use and its relatively recent disuse in building materials, asbestos is frequently found by home inspectors. If the asbestos-containing material is intact, generally it isn't a health hazard. However, when it is damaged, disturbed, or begins to deteriorate, its fibers can become friable (easily crumbled) and airborne, which is a hazard. So an inspector's job is to document asbestos occurrence, assess its condition, and recommend appropriate action.

Whenever you might encounter hazardous materials—such as chemically treated wood or rodent infestations in a tight crawl space—dress appropriately.

HEATING SYSTEM COMPONENTS

Because of its fire-retarding and insulating qualities, asbestos can be found on most fuel-oil or gas-fired heating systems installed before 1979. It takes many forms.

Boilers and hot water piping in older homes were frequently covered with a white-gray asbestos swaddling that was applied as fabric strips and parged (troweled on) like plaster. Visually, the texture is rather like a mummy's wrapping. The flexibility of the strips and the plasticity of the parging allowed the material to adhere to irregular shapes. Straight sections of hot water piping were often wrapped with thin corrugated sheets of asbestos, visible when viewed from a pipe end, with asbestos plaster applied to seal joints, elbows, and transitional pieces. The flat, sheet-metal surfaces of forced-hot-air (FHA) plenums and rectangular ducts were usually covered with sheet asbestos.

Asbestos coverings on furnaces and boilers were, for the most part, durable except when a pipe or duct

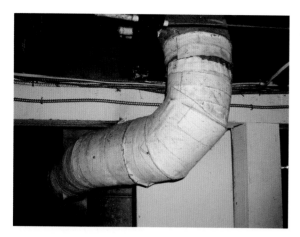

Asbestos is a common wrap on older heating system ducts.

Asbestos was sometimes used inside heat supply ducts at registers, which can contaminate the air in living spaces, especially if the asbestos is friable.

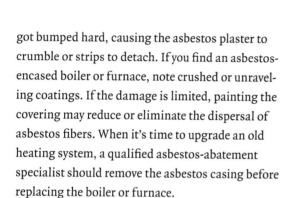

got bumped hard, causing the asbestos plaster to crumble or strips to detach. If you find an asbestos-encased boiler or furnace, note crushed or unraveling coatings. If the damage is limited, painting the covering may reduce or eliminate the dispersal of asbestos fibers. When it's time to upgrade an old heating system, a qualified asbestos-abatement specialist should remove the asbestos casing before replacing the boiler or furnace.

ASBESTOS INSIDE A HEATING SYSTEM is a definite health hazard. Damaged asbestos on the outside of ducts may be drawn into the air supply system, but asbestos *inside* ducts or the fan/blower housing is a potential hazard even if it is intact. Moving air will in time lift and detach asbestos fibers. If you see a flexible white-gray fabric transition between a blower fan box and the main warm-air duct, it may be asbestos, put there primarily to isolate the fan vibration—to keep it from being transmitted to the metal ducting. Have the fabric tested by a qualified laboratory; if it contains asbestos, it should be replaced.

Asbestos was sometimes used inside heat supply ducts at registers. Register covers are frequently removed to vacuum dust out of the supply duct; less frequently, they are removed to sand old flooring or install new. In either case, removing the cover can release asbestos close to living spaces. If there are

Some older furnaces and water heaters have asbestos cement flues. Because the asbestos is usually in a rigid form, it is not normally considered friable. These vents become damaged over time. Ideally, all asbestos cement flues should be scheduled for removal as part of water heater or furnace replacements.

small children crawling around the floors, the danger becomes even more pressing. The asbestos needs to be removed by a specialist.

APPLIANCE FLUE PIPES

Some older furnaces and water heaters have asbestos-cement flue pipes. (Sometimes called Transite pipes after a Johns-Manville brand that no longer contains asbestos.) The asbestos is in rigid form and is not generally considered friable, so the flue piping can be left in place unless it is damaged. If, however, the

Old electrical panel boxes may contain asbestos. The material shown is damaged and friable, so it should be removed by an asbestos-abatement expert.

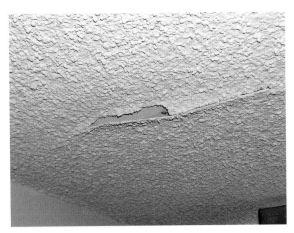

Pre-1979 spray acoustic ceilings often contain asbestos; they should be removed. Damaged fibers can easily become airborne and be inhaled.

appliance is being upgraded, it's advisable to replace the flue pipe with a type specified by the appliance's manufacturer. Many modern tankless water heaters, for example, discharge flue gases so cool that plastic flue pipe is appropriate.

ELECTRICAL PANEL ENCLOSURES

Old electrical panel boxes often contain asbestos, installed because it is fire resistant and impervious to electrical activity. Typically, panel boxes were mounted low on an outside wall. Installed when a 30-amp or 60-amp main was plenty of power, they have seen many years of weathering and wear. The asbestos is usually in sheet form, so its edges become more worn and friable each time the panel box door is opened and closed. Such boxes should be removed. Children playing outside can easily open such an accessible little door, exposing them to asbestos and electrical hazards.

CEILINGS

Textured acoustic ceilings ("popcorn ceilings") brought the asbestos problem home (literally) and prompted the first ban of asbestos products in the United States. To reduce shrinking and cracking, asbestos fibers were mixed into a plaster-like slurry that was sprayed onto ceilings. At the time it seemed like a great idea: fast, economical, and forgiving of sloppy framing and drywalling. It could even hide cracked plaster. And it deadened sound.

Trouble was, the mixture didn't always adhere, either because of inadequate prep work, an inexact blend, or springy ceiling joists overhead. Before long, those asbestos-impregnated ceilings started to crack, crumble, and create respiratory problems for the people below. The bottom fell out of the popcorn-ceiling market, while lawsuits flourished.

Some of the textured acoustic ceilings that did stick are still in place and pose little hazard. If there are living spaces below and undersize ceiling joists overhead, it would be prudent to seal the ceiling with a good coat of paint. Or cover it with a new layer of drywall or, if there is enough headroom, with a suspended ceiling. Ideally, though, they should be removed.

FLOOR TILES

Vinyl asbestos flooring was very popular in the 1950s, both as resilient sheet flooring and as tiles, typically 9 in. sq. The asbestos is embedded in the vinyl, so it is not generally considered to be hazardous unless the flooring is sanded, drilled, or sawn. Asbestos was also an additive in resilient flooring adhesive, which, 60 years later, is a gray-white substance with a texture similar to dried taffy. If homeowners intend to

Vinyl asbestos (VA) tile flooring was very popular in the 1950s. The asbestos is encapsulated in the vinyl and is not generally considered to be hazardous unless it is sanded, drilled, or cut.

remove the flooring or the asbestos adhesive beneath, an asbestos abatement contractor can advise how best to proceed.

MISCELLANEOUS USES

In the 1950s and 1960s, asbestos was in everything short of the cake batter. Occasionally, home inspectors still find it as rope-like door gaskets on vintage kitchen ranges, fire-stop caulking, range hood seals, drywall joint compound, window putty, house drainpipe and sanitary sewer drainpipe, and landscape edging. Asbestos-cement roof tiles and shingle siding have proven durable as long as they are not cracked by falling branches, rocks, and other hard knocks. As long as they are intact, these materials represent almost no hazard. Somewhat more friable are the exposed edges of economy asbestos-cement roof sheets. (Look for frayed edges.) Blown-in asbestos insulation is mostly hidden behind finish walls, where it will probably remain, unseen and unoffending, until some renovator decides to gut the walls.

PROFESSIONAL ABATEMENT

Removing or containing asbestos-laden building materials should be done only by properly trained and equipped professionals. Thus general contrac-

tors and subcontractors in flooring, roofing, heating, plumbing, or electrical trades should anticipate asbestos-abatement costs as they prepare estimates for repairing or remodeling older homes. Asbestos-abatement specialists can help determine the need for remedial action and its cost. Where the presence of asbestos must be determined by laboratory analysis, an asbestos specialist can collect samples and explain results, which is well beyond the scope of a general home inspection.

Lead

Lead is a neurological toxin, particularly damaging to children six and younger, who seem drawn to it because it's slightly sweet. Breathing it, eating it, or drinking water with a high level of lead can cause mental retardation in children. In people of all ages, lead can cause headaches, anemia, lethargy, kidney damage, high blood pressure, and other ailments.

In residences, old paint is the principle source of airborne and ingested lead contamination. Lead solder, old sections of lead supply pipe, and residual lead in some faucets contribute to lead contamination of drinking water.

UNDERSTANDING LEAD PAINT

Lead-based paint adheres to almost any surface and weathers well, so it's not surprising that it can be found in 90 percent of houses built before 1940. However, as lead's health hazards became known in the 1950s, paint manufacturers began to phase it out and it was banned altogether in 1978 by the U.S. government.

Because of its durability, lead paint was commonly used on exteriors, glossy kitchen and bathroom walls, in closets (which rarely get repainted), and as an enamel on interior doors, windows, stair treads, and woodwork. So each time a swollen window or sticking door was forced open, it ground lead paint into flakes and dust. Roof leaks, drainage problems, and inadequate ventilation add to the problem because excessive moisture causes the paint to degrade and detach sooner.

Old wood window sashes frequently contain lead paint, which can become an airborne hazard if the paint is sanded or becomes loose.

In well-maintained older homes, the presence of lead may not be a dire problem if old paint is well adhered. Lead becomes most dangerous when it becomes airborne, especially during sanding or heat-stripping, for then it can be inhaled and easily absorbed into the bloodstream. Anyone considering renovating an old house should postpone demolition or paint removal until the structure has been tested for lead paint and appropriate remediation is planned.

TESTING FOR LEAD PAINT

Testing is the only way to know for sure if an older house contains lead paint. It's easiest to gather paint samples from areas where it's already flaking or peeling, such as on door trim, windowsills, and stair treads. There are a number of test kits available at home centers but at this writing only one satisfies EPA criteria for false positives and false negatives: LeadCheck.

Testing is pretty straightforward. Using a utility knife, cut away a small amount of surface paint to get at earlier layers underneath. Rub the test swab on the exposed area, as shown in the bottom photo on p. 32. The brighter the swabbed area, the greater the concentration of lead. Test several areas, such as

door and window trim and siding. A LeadCheck kit contains 16 swabs and costs less than $50.

If sample areas test negative, it's probably safe to work on the house, though one should of course still wear appropriate respirators and minimize exposure to paint dust. Homeowners planning an extensive renovation would be well served to order a lead-testing kit from an accredited testing lab, take additional samples, and have the lab validate the results gotten from the inexpensive kit. To locate a qualified lab or ask any other lead-related questions, contact The National Lead Information Center at www.epa.gov/lead/nlic.htm.

LIMITING LEAD-PAINT CONTAMINATION

Because lead paint sanded or scraped by home renovators can become airborne, it can contaminate neighboring houses, too. This section gives renovators an overview of how to limit contamination to workers, family members, and neighbors; it is excerpted from *Renovation: 4th Edition* (Taunton Press, 2012).

All lead-contaminated materials must be bagged or wrapped in plastic before they can be disposed of.

COVER UP. Wear a respirator with N100 or P100 HEPA filters and snug-fitting goggles; a full-face respirator is not a bad idea but may be too hot to work in. Disposable coveralls, booties, and gloves are a must; tape shut neck, wrist, and ankle openings. At the end of the day, shed contaminated work clothes at the job site: Wearing them home could endanger your family.

NOTE: You can find disposable respirators for about $10, but a reusable respirator with replaceable filter cartridges is a better buy if the job extends beyond a few days.

CONTAIN THE MESS. Tape all HVAC registers shut and turn off the furnace and A/C so it won't start while you're working in the room. To contain lead-paint dust and debris inside, use 6-mil sheet plastic and painter's tape to isolate and contain the mess. Tape plastic across door openings to seal off work areas from living spaces, and cover walls inside the work area with plastic as well, so they can be wiped down and vacuumed when you're done. Protect floors with rosin paper or heavy cardboard, and cover that with sheet plastic taped to baseboards to keep it in place. When cleanup is complete, roll up and discard the plastic.

PROTECT THE NEIGHBORS. It's impossible to predict the movement of air or neighbors, so containing the mess of an exterior renovation is complicated. Start by taping sheet plastic over doors and windows to keep dust out of the house. Next use 6-mil black plastic to cover the ground to a radius of 10 ft. from any lead-bearing surfaces that will be disturbed. To keep dust, paint chips, and debris inside this 10-ft. containment area, construct a box around it—rather like the sides of a sandbox—using lumber set on-edge. Staple the plastic to the box. Last, create a cordon of rope or plastic warning tape in a 20-ft. radius from lead-bearing surfaces to keep people out of the work area.

MINIMIZE DUST. An essential part of confining lead contamination is minimizing dust. Any sanding, grinding, or scraping tools must be attached to a HEPA-filtered vacuum system. Noxious fumes are equally taboo, so avoid using heat guns, which generate temperatures exceeding 1100°F. Setting dry old wood ablaze is another hazard to avoid. So if strip you must, chemical strippers are safer, especially environmentally friendly ones. Before scraping, stripping, or removing any lead-painted materials, mist the surfaces to suppress dust. During cleanup phases, mist plastic wall and floor coverings too to keep down dust. A gardener's pump sprayer is a good tool for this operation.

DECONSTRUCT, DON'T DEMOLISH. Carefully dismantling materials will release less dust than demolishing them. Scoring along the edges of painted trim, siding, and other building materials will reduce debris when removing them. When you pry such materials, do so gradually along their length to minimize breakage. If it's necessary to cut tainted materials to a more manageable size, use a power saw attached to a HEPA-filtered vacuum system. Remember, *every piece* of contaminated building material must be bagged in extra-strength plastic disposal bags or wrapped in plastic and vacuumed before removing it from the containment area.

CLEAN THOROUGHLY. Outside, after bagging or wrapping everything sizable, use a HEPA-filtered vacuum to capture dust and small debris. Mist the plastic to keep dust down, detach the plastic anywhere you stapled or nailed it to the house exterior or the containment frame, then fold the plastic in on itself to capture remaining residue, and bag the plastic. While still in the containment area, vacuum your coveralls and booties, then remove and discard them.

Inside the house, once you've bagged, wrapped, or removed any interior debris, wipe down the plastic covering the walls. (Wet- and dry-cleaning cloths can be purchased at most home centers.) Then wipe plastic floor tarps. Roll each plastic sheet in on itself to trap remaining debris, then bag it. Vacuum coveralls and booties and discard them. Finish up by wiping down all surfaces with a wet-cleaning cloth; each cloth is good for cleaning about 40 sq. ft.

WHEN TO CALL IN A LEAD-ABATEMENT SPECIALIST

In 2010, the EPA issued the Renovation, Repair, and Painting (RRP) Rule, which required professional contractors working on houses built before 1978 to take extensive precautions to protect their crews and homeowners from the potential presence of lead dust. Though the EPA exempts homeowners working on their own homes, lead poisoning doesn't exempt anyone. Everyone should take it seriously.

The EPA's 2010 RRP Rule is complex, and this brief discussion is no substitute for knowing the law. You can read about it at www2.epa.gov/lead/renovation-repair-and-painting-program.

Broadly stated, the rule is designed to make people aware of the hazards of lead, requires renovation firms to be certified in lead-safe work practices, presents ways to limit potential contamination, and, in effect, directs those doing the work to *capture* lead-contaminated materials, treat them as toxic wastes, and dispose of them safely.

The law is quite specific about how waste is to be captured. Containing the limited amount of debris generated by, say, a kitchen remodel is probably within the capabilities of most contractors or well-prepared homeowners. But if the renovation project involves a sizable modification of an exterior that has tested positive for lead, hire lead-abatement specialists. Complying with particulars of the RRP Rule will be their headache, not yours.

In theory, containing lead-painted debris is straightforward but, in practice, it is a nightmare. Most job sites are a chaotic stream of delivery trucks, subs, inspectors, and crew coming and going. Add to the mix nervous neighbors, thanks to extensive notifications of lead-abatement in progress, posted throughout the neighborhood. If it's windy, containment may also involve erecting scaffolding and a plastic envelope around the house. It can be a huge undertaking.

LEAD PIPES

The deleterious effects of lead have been known for a long time, so finding lead water supply pipes during an inspection is increasingly uncommon. When lead supply pipes are found at all, they are usually as short lengths near the water main's entry into a house or beneath an old, little used utility tub in the basement. Lead pipe is typically a dull gray, which when scraped with a penknife or a screwdriver blade gleams silvery.

Until the late 1980s, the solder used to sweat copper pipe contained a small amount of lead, which dissolved into standing water in pipes, especially if the water was slightly acidic. Copper supply piping is very common, so some amount of dilute lead in drinking water is found in about a third of homes. Homeowners concerned about the presence of lead can draw samples and have them analyzed by a laboratory. EPA lead limits in drinking water are 15 micrograms/deciliter. For more, visit the EPA site at water.epa.gov/drink/index.cfm.

Water samples are typically taken in two draws: The first draw is of water sitting in supply pipes for at least 4 hours; the second draw is taken after the water has been allowed to run for 1 minute. The concentration of lead, if any, will of course be higher in the first draw. However, 80% or 90% of houses whose first draw shows high lead levels show virtually no lead on the second draw. So homeowners who don't have the resources to replace lead-tainted supply piping are well advised to run the tap for 1 minute.

Slightly more common are lead toilet bends or waste pipes, which are often left alone if they are functioning well; they pose little risk because they are not part of the supply water system.

Mold

Mold is a diverse family of fungi that causes natural materials to degrade. Mold spores are microscopic and found pretty much everywhere.

Mold needs three things to grow: water, a temperature range between 40°F and 100°F, and organic matter such as lumber or paper. Short of building houses

Mold often occurs below kitchen and bathroom sinks. If these areas are covered with wood or plaster they can probably be washed and repainted with a mold-inhibiting paint. But if there is moldy drywall, it should be removed, the area behind washed and dried, and new mold-resistant gypsum board installed.

SOURCES OF EXCESSIVE INTERIOR MOISTURE

Common sources of excessive interior moisture are (1) air infiltration (moist outside air leaking in); (2) poorly installed roofing or incorrectly flashed windows and doors; (3) improper surface drainage; (4) unsealed crawl spaces; (5) inadequately vented bathrooms, kitchens, laundry appliances, water heaters, and furnaces; and (6) leaking HVAC ducts.

Because the largest source of interior moisture comes from kitchens and bathrooms, one of the easiest, most cost-effective ways to reduce it is to install exhaust fans.

ASSESSING THE EXTENT OF MOLD

If mold is limited to small areas at the top of a bathroom or exterior wall, it may be surface mold caused by condensation or inadequate ventilation. However, if mold is widespread around windows or doors, bathroom drywall is crumbling, or tiles mounted on drywall are loose, there's probably mold growing in the walls. Start looking at the base of the walls.

General inspections are limited to visible conditions. To better assess the extent of mold, however, a homeowner could turn off power to the area, remove a baseboard, and use a utility knife to cut small holes in the drywall. If there's no mold, holes can be patched and covered with the baseboard. More likely, you'll find discolored or rotted framing and extensive mold colonies.

Moldy lumber and engineered wood products such as plywood, particleboard, and OSB may just have surface mold, so they should be probed with a screwdriver or a pocketknife to see how sound they are. If they are spongy, they will need to be replaced. Engineered wood products are particularly susceptible to rot because they contain adhesives that fungi feed on.

CLEANING UP MOLD

Mold can't grow without moisture, so before removing mold-tainted materials, one must first identify and correct the source(s) of the excess moisture.

out of inorganic materials, the easiest way to thwart the growth of mold is to exhaust excess moisture, sending it outdoors.

Interior moisture generally isn't a problem unless it's excessive and sustained. (Normally, relative humidity indoors should be 35% to 40% during the heating season.) Signs of excessive moisture include condensation on windows, moldy bathrooms or closets, soggy attic insulation, and exterior paint peeling off in large patches.

Mold thrives on the paper and adhesive in drywall, and because drywall is so widely used in houses, there are a lot of places for mold to grow when conditions are right. Toxic molds are rare. But combine mold and excess moisture with a tight house and poor ventilation and people sensitive to mold can develop serious respiratory problems. Fortunately, inspectors have highly specialized equipment—noses—for detecting mold. If your nose gets stuffy, your eyes itch or water, or you start coughing when you enter a room, start looking for mold.

Mold can grow behind vinyl wallpaper and may not be visible unless the paper is pulled away from the wall. Plaster walls can usually be washed and painted, but moldy drywall will have to be replaced, ideally, with mold-resistant gypsum board.

Otherwise, the mold can return. If mold is extensive, homeowners should hire a professional clean-up mold-remediation company. Here are some of the clean-up steps.

SURFACE MOLD should be washed with soap and water and allowed to dry thoroughly. There's no need for caustic bleaches to kill mold spores (and irritate lungs) because washing should remove mold. After the surface has dried, it should be painted with a stain killer such as B-I-N®. If mold has caused the drywall's paper facing to roughen or delaminate, the drywall should be cut back at least 1 ft. beyond the damaged area and replaced.

MOLD IN WALLS. If an inspection reveals mold growing inside wall cavities, the affected area (including heating registers) should be sealed off with sheet plastic. Damaged drywall should be cut back at least to the nearest stud center on both sides; optimally, the whole finish wall should be gutted to expose the framing. Surface mold on framing should be scrubbed and allowed to dry well before new drywall is installed. Removing damaged framing is a job for a licensed contractor, because replacing more than one stud typically requires temporary shoring to support the loads above.

LIMITING EXPOSURE TO MOLD

Workers involved in mold-abatement should limit their exposure to mold spores by wearing respirator masks with N95 filters, rubber gloves, eye protection, and disposable coveralls, which they should discard at the end of each day.

After assessing the mold's extent, workers should determine the shortest way out of the house for contaminated materials to minimize spreading mold spores to clean areas. Surface mold should never be sanded as that will spread spores. To control dust, rent a commercial-grade vacuum with HEPA filters.

REMOVING TAINTED MATERIALS. To contain spore-laden dust, a helper should hold the hose of the commercial-grade HEPA vacuum near the materials being cut. Moldy debris should be wrapped in 6-mil plastic before it is carted away to an appropriate disposal site.

Interior Air Quality

At the same time that houses have become tighter to save energy, sophisticated building materials with chemical components have increased greatly. Though largely benign, these chemicals can cause allergic reactions. So, having looked at airborne irritants such as asbestos and mold, now let's clear the air about this new generation of building products.

FORMALDEHYDE AND OTHER VOCS

VOCs are organic chemical compounds that evaporate (become vapor) under normal indoor conditions. There are many kinds of these human-made and naturally occurring chemicals and they are everywhere. VOCs are present in thousands of building products, including paints, caulks, adhesives, and plywood. To cite just one category, they help paints spread easier, dry faster, and adhere better.

But VOCs' remarkable versatility comes with a price. As they evaporate, they outgas (give off gas) a variety of chemicals that adversely affect air quality, especially if ventilation is poor and concentrations are high. According to the EPA, the agency that regulates VOCs, "Building occupants complain of . . .

headache; eye, nose and throat irritation; dry cough; dry or itchy skin; dizziness and nausea; difficulty in concentrating; fatigue; and sensitivity to odors."

Numerous studies show a correlation between the incidence of some cancers and prolonged exposure to VOCs in indoor environments. *Prolonged* exposure is an important point: Harmful VOCs are typically not acutely toxic, so symptoms and conditions, if any, are slow to emerge. For that reason, research into VOCs and their effects is difficult.

It would take many volumes to discuss these chemicals in a serious manner. So let's take a look at just one VOC, formaldehyde, that's widely used and widely known as a carcinogen.

UFFI INSULATION. In response to the oil shortages and price spikes of the early 1970s, energy conservation became a priority for many homeowners. Insulation products were rushed to market, including urea formaldehyde foam insulation (UFFI), which was sprayed inside the walls of roughly a half million homes in less than a decade.

Almost immediately, complaints of acrid, lingering smells surfaced, followed by reports of respiratory problems; watery, itching eyes; headaches; and nausea. When inexpertly mixed, UFFI outgassed formaldehyde for weeks or months and some homeowners sensitive to the chemical felt that the smell never really went away. Subsequent research suggested a link between prolonged exposure to high concentrations of formaldehyde and cancer rates in lab animals. So UFFI insulation was discontinued. Most of the houses insulated with UFFI still contain it, but the consensus is the foam no longer outgasses to any significant degree.

CONSTRUCTION MATERIALS. Formaldehyde is used to manufacture many building products, including paints, lacquers, paint strippers, caulks, adhesives, pressed wood products such as plywood and OSB panels, and prefabricated cabinets made from such products. Once again, a sizable number of homeowners report lingering smells, respiratory problems, and headaches.

Home inspectors face a quandary in reporting a problem so vaporous. If you detect acrid smells, say so, but note that such smells typically dissipate in time, do your best to assign a cause, such as fresh paint or newly installed plywood cabinets, and suggest that if would-be buyers or homeowners are concerned, they can have the air analyzed by a lab. There are, for example, VOC sensors, electronic devices that can detect (and identify) faint traces of organic compounds based on how they interact with sensor components.

PRACTICAL NEXT STEPS. Whether homeowner, home inspector, or home renovator, read up on VOCs. Do not rely on general information sites such as Wikipedia; instead read the material provided by the EPA, the National Institute for Occupational Safety and Health (NIOSH), and the Occupational Safety and Health Administration (OSHA). Equally useful is surveying a house's cache of unused or under-used paints, solvents, and glues and getting rid of most of it. Adding a workshop, garage, or basement fan (or opening windows) is a good way to increase ventilation and decrease VOC concentrations in the air.

LOW- OR NO-VOC CHOICES. Building-supply manufacturers continue to explore and develop less toxic components. They have, for example, greatly reduced UF resins in structural panels such as CDX plywood, primarily by switching to phenol formaldehyde resins (PFs). Such panels are usually stamped NAUF.

There are formaldehyde-free options for the sheet materials used inside a house—such as molding, paneling, and cabinet frames, doors, and shelves. These low-VOC materials greatly help the quality of indoor air.

Last, there is now a wide selection of solvent-free, low-VOC adhesives that are nontoxic, as well as complete lines of green paints, such as Benjamin Moore® Natura® and AMF Safecoat®, which contain no VOCs. It's a category sure to expand. To help you make your choice, many manufacturers now offer interactive, online product selectors.

Spray polyurethane foam (SPF) is usually a two-part foam whose components travel through separate, heated hoses to mix at the spray gun nozzle. Getting the correct mix takes skill and training, otherwise the foam may not be durable and leaks can occur.

SPRAY FOAM INSULATION

NOTE: Polyurethane is the dominant spray foam today, but the comments in this section hold true for most types of spray foam insulation.

Spray polyurethane foam (SPF) is usually a two-part foam whose components travel through separate, heated hoses to mix at the spray gun nozzle. Sprayed wet onto a surface, the chemicals undergo an exothermic reaction (give off heat), foam, and expand dramatically, then gradually harden as they cure. *Correctly mixed, applied, and cured,* SPF is inert, non-offgassing, and odorless and thus safe in both interior and exterior applications.

A SKILLED INSTALLER IS ESSENTIAL. Sprayed polyurethane foam is a remarkable performer if applied precisely. But if its chemical components are not heated to the correct temperature, mixed in the right ratio, and applied in the prescribed thickness, the foam may not cure correctly and could emit noxious fumes for months. If the substrate being sprayed is too moist or too cold, the installation can fail. A seasoned installer also understands the importance of adequate ventilation during and after the installation.

In response to consumer concerns about lingering smells and potential health problems, information

clearinghouses have emerged. Canadians can find spray-foam insulation contractors whose product meets the National Standard CAN/ULC/S705.1 by visiting www.sprayfoam.com. In the United States, the Air Barrier Association of America (ABAA) lists accredited contractors and describes its on-site quality assurance program at www.airbarrier.org. The ABAA will also recommend third-party auditors.

Proving cause and effect is difficult, even with an army of auditors testing the air in a house. Many building materials are used in a renovation, any one of which could contain chemicals or glues that could offgas for a time. Hard data are hard to come by when pursuing airborne pollutants, smells, and side effects.

COMBUSTION GASES

Combustion produces water vapor and toxic gases (see, for example "Carbon Monoxide Detectors" on p. 187). Heating system components such as heat exchangers or flue pipes that corrode or crack are the principal sources of combustion air escaping into living spaces; though negative pressurization (see p. 215) can also cause flue gases to spill back into living spaces rather than exiting up a chimney or flue.

The faulty cap of this floor furnace is leaking combustion air and friable asbestos fibers into living spaces. The floor furnace is outdated and should be removed; it is also a burn hazard.

Rodents frequently nest in fiberglass insulation. Damaged insulation should be removed and a rodent-abatement (or vector control) specialist hired to prevent a reinfestation.

Vents of this type usually indicate the presence of a buried fuel oil tank. The tank should be tested for leaks, and the ground around it for contamination.

Of course, finding and repairing combustion-air leaks is preferable to after-the-fact alerts from an alarm. As described in Chapter 8, inspecting older heating systems is primarily a search for corrosion. Corrosion may be caused by restricted vent air flow, a flue that is too long, inadequately sloped piping, flue pipes with an improper vertical-to-horizontal ratio, or flue gases that cool too rapidly and so condense in the flue piping and cause corrosion. This condensation can also enter heat exchangers, causing them to fail prematurely.

Flue-gas spillage can be caused by inadequate venting, improper configuration, or damaged vent piping, such as a rain cap that has been mashed down at the top of a vent pipe. See "Flue-Gas Spillage" on p. 196 for how to test for this problem.

RODENT INFESTATIONS

If rodents have nested in a crawl space, basement, or attic, disturbing their nests or breathing contaminated particles may expose one to a number of serious diseases and microorganisms, including hantavirus, which causes hantavirus pulmonary syndrome, for which there is no known vaccine or antivirus. The likelihood of contracting the disease varies according to the extent of the contamination, the lack of ventilation, and other factors, but the danger is real.

Licensed pest-control firms know the safest means of trapping such pests, preventing their reentry, and removing contaminants. Often, they first moisten the affected areas with a 1:10 bleach solution (also a viricide) to minimize dust, while wearing N100 respirators and disposable Tyvek hazmat suits.

Fuel Leaks

When inspecting homes with oil-fired heating systems, an inspector should note active leaks around the furnace (or boiler) and the oil tank, or stains on the basement floor that indicate past leaks. Often, oil tanks are buried so their condition is difficult to assess. Frequently, when homeowners replace an old oil-fired system with a cleaner, more efficient natural gas–fired system, they just shut off the supply lines from the oil tank and abandon the tank to rust away in the ground. Out of sight, out of mind. The only indication that there was or is an oil tank on the property may be small-diameter supply lines that weren't removed or larger tank vent pipes such as those shown in the right photo above.

BURIED TANKS are typically steel and, depending on the presence of ground water and the composition of the soil, tanks may rust and start leaking after 20 years. Many homeowners (and would-be house buyers) are not aware that the owner is responsible for leaking oil tanks and the considerable cost of cleaning up contaminated soil around them. So an inspector should tell them of that obligation and urge them to read up on the local environmental rules concerning oil tanks, abandoned or not.

WHAT TO DO ABOUT UNUSED TANKS is a complicated and potentially expensive decision. A house seller must, of course, disclose the presence of a tank to prospective buyers. Because a buyer would assume the responsibility for the oil tank once ownership was transferred, the buyer could ask the seller to vouchsafe that the tank is not leaking. One party or the other could pay to have the tank tested for leaks. Or the contents of the tank could be pumped out by a qualified service company, contaminated soil could be safely removed, and the tank could be removed or filled. Local codes will specify what must be done.

AUTO OIL LEAKS AND STAINS on a garage floor are unlikely to contaminate surrounding areas, so they are typically not affected by local environmental rules. Nonetheless, because rules change all the time, an inspector should note oil leaks and stains on the inspection report and homeowners who intend to sell should be proactive about cleaning them up.

Other Environmental Hazards

In this section, we'll briefly consider a few environmental hazards that tend to be site or region specific or whose causal links to illnesses are disputed.

RADON GAS

Radon is an odorless, colorless gas produced by the naturally occurring decay of radioactive elements (principally uranium) in the soil. That high concentrations of radon gas can cause cancer is well established. Less clear are the effects of radon concentrations less than the EPA's action level of 4 picocuries per liter of air (4 pC/L). Building scientists have varying opinions of why adjacent houses can have dramatically different concentrations of radon gas and what the best ways to reduce radon gas are.

RADON GAS INTRUSION. It's generally accepted that radon gas migrates up from the soil through dirt

crawl spaces or through cracks in concrete basement floors and seeps out of ground-level openings such as floor drains, sump pits, and cracked mortar joints in concrete-block foundations. The rate of radon gas intrusion depends on a number of factors, including the concentration of uranium in the soil, the construction and condition of the foundation, and variables such as negative pressurization (see p. 215) in the house, barometric pressure, and precipitation. Radon gas can also enter a house via water from a private well, which is released when someone does the dishes or takes a shower.

RADON ZONE MAPS. Homeowners concerned about radon and its risks should first consult maps of radon zones to learn of potential radon levels in their area. One can find such maps by accessing EPA or county environmental authority websites. An Internet search of "radon gas" + "[your county]" will also produce relevant resources.

RADON TESTING. If radon maps or local sites indicate moderate to high potential of radon gas in the area, testing is a logical next step. Home centers sell DIY radon-detection canisters that are placed in specified locations for a short time period, typically a week. Following installation instructions is the best way to get accurate results. Alternatively, homeowners can have a radon-testing service perform long-term (90-day) tests that get more accurate readings. Based on test results, the service will also present a range of remediation options.

PROFESSIONAL REMEDIATION. Reducing radon concentrations needn't break the bank, but remediation is not a DIY task. Typically, an area under a ground-level slab is accessed, a perforated plastic collection pipe is inserted in a trench or pit, and that pipe is connected to a solid plastic vent pipe (commonly 4 in. in diameter) that terminates above the roof. Because an open pipe offers less resistance than a concrete slab, the gas drifts up the pipe and dissipates harmlessly in the air. Homeowners should hire a mitigation contractor who has completed the EPA's Radon Contractor Proficiency Program.

WATER QUALITY

If a house has municipal water, it is almost certainly safe to drink because its quality is regularly tested and must meet EPA standards. Any house whose water comes from a private well should be tested at least annually, when a new resident moves in, and whenever a property is sold. A water-quality analysis should precede a sale.

LEAD CONTAMINATION of water was addressed earlier; the EPA estimates that 35 million to 40 million people in the United States drink water with a measurable amount of lead in it.

EXCESS SODIUM. If a water supply is hard (has high mineral content) and requires water softening, treated water may then have excessive sodium, which occurs when the softening agent replaces excess calcium in the water. Excessive sodium can be a problem to people with high-blood pressure or who are otherwise on a low-salt diet. In that case, a separate cold-water branch line should bypass the water softener and run directly to a kitchen tap.

FRACKING has been much in the news lately. It involves pumping pressurized, chemical-laden water underground to fracture rock and extract natural gas. Critics contend that the process has fouled aquifers from which communities get their drinking water, and is responsible for a wide range of health problems. Opinions are heated on both sides of the controversy, so we urge readers to research the topic and form their own opinions. Fracking is widespread, so house buyers should consult local water-quality agencies to see if the procedure is allowed and presently impacting local wells.

OTHER CONTAMINATION. Potable water from private wells should be regularly tested for bacterial pathogens such as coliform, which could result from faulty septic systems on the property or neighboring properties. Shallow wells are particularly susceptible to such pollution. Water tests will also show the presence of pesticides, chemical spills, and leaking oil tanks. County water-quality agencies should also have records of recent spills that might have affected the property's water.

ELECTROMAGNETIC FIELDS (EMF)

Virtually any electrical transmission line, utility pole transformer, house wiring, and appliance (including computers) generates electrical and magnetic fields. The greater the voltage, the greater the EMF emissions.

Limited epidemiological studies have established statistical correlations between exposure to low-frequency EMFs around power lines and some types of cancer, including leukemia. The potential effects of EMFs vary according to the proximity, intensity, frequency, and period of exposure; NIOSH has cautioned the public of potential health risks while noting the inconclusiveness of the evidence thus far.

Homeowners and prospective buyers concerned about a property's potential exposure can have EMF intensity tested but, again, there are few guidelines on what degree of exposure is normal or excessive, and few authoritative recommendations on what action to take.

Fire and Carbon Monoxide Safety

Although we discussed both smoke and CO alarms earlier, their use is vital enough to warrant a summary of their regulations here.

We strongly urge residents to test smoke alarms by pressing the test button as soon as they move into a new property and again each month. Most standard batteries should be changed sometime between every 6 months and 12 months; batteries with a 10-year life span are now available.

Smoke alarms should be installed in all living areas, including basements and garages. They should be kept at least 20 ft. from appliances such as furnaces and ovens, which produce combustion particles; at least 10 ft. from high humidity areas such as showers and laundry rooms; and at least 3 ft. from heat/cooling registers to reduce nuisance alarms.

As we mentioned, most batteries should be changed once or twice a year. This is easy to remember if you change batteries at the same time as you adjust your clocks for daylight savings time semi-annually. Smoke detectors should be installed on every floor, including basements, and in hallways near sleeping areas. Most jurisdictions now require that smoke detectors be installed in each bedroom in new construction, at changes in ceiling height of 24 in. or more, or when modifications exceeding $1,000 in value are made. Direct-wired smoke detectors should also have backup batteries so they will function in a power outage.

Fire extinguishers should be provided in kitchens and garages for emergency use. We also suggest carbon monoxide detectors be installed in buildings with gas-fired heating systems.

The media (see www.theworldfiresafetyfoundation .org/sfc) report that qualified fire protection experts now believe that ionization-type smoke alarms are *not* reliable and that their failures have resulted in many home-fire-related deaths. We understand that over 90% of all home-installed smoke alarms are the potentially hazardous type. Photoelectric-type smoke alarms are considered much safer and we strongly recommend each alarm device be checked and replaced as needed.

Ionization-type smoke alarms often have a label showing the letter I or the radiation symbol. Photoelectric alarms are typically labeled with the letter P. It may be necessary to dismantle alarms to identify which type each is. Home inspectors typically do not test or dismantle smoke alarms during an inspection. We do not believe that combination alarms with both detection systems are safer because the ionization feature tends to be activated by cooking activities and many have been disconnected as nuisances.

CARBON MONOXIDE ALARMS are now required in dwelling units with fossil-fuel or gas-burning heaters or appliances, fireplaces, and in attached garages. A CO alarm should be centrally located outside of each separate sleeping area in the immediate vicinity of the bedrooms and at least 6 in. from exterior walls and at least 3 ft. from furnace supply or return vents. CO alarms should be replaced every 4 years or at intervals established by the manufacturer. Battery-powered combination carbon monoxide and smoke alarms are now available.

Smoke and CO alarms are typically required in hallways outside bedrooms and on each floor of a residence.

Many areas now require residential fire sprinkler systems be installed in new construction, especially in high fire risk locations. Such systems should be checked by a qualified professional once a year.

Introduction
All photos are by Michael Litchfield except for the bottom photo p. 15 by Brian Cogley.

Chapter 2
p. 32 (bottom): Photo by Rob Wotzak, courtesy of Fine Homebuilding © The Taunton Press, Inc.
p. 40 (top): Photo by Michael Litchfield
p. 43 (right): Photo by Roe A. Osborn, courtesy of Fine Homebuilding © The Taunton Press, Inc.

Chapter 3
p. 54: Photo by Michael Litchfield
p. 67: Photo by Paul Fisette, courtesy of Fine Homebuilding © The Taunton Press, Inc.

Chapter 4
p. 77: Photo by Michael Litchfield

Chapter 6
p. 117: Photo by Michael Litchfield
p. 118: Photo by Michael Litchfield
p. 119: Photo by Michael Litchfield
p. 120 (top): Photos by Michael Litchfield
p. 123: Photo by Michael Litchfield
p. 126 (right): Photo by Michael Litchfield
p. 128: Photo by Brian Pontolilo, courtesy of Fine Homebuilding © The Taunton Press, Inc.
p. 130: Photo by Michael Litchfield
p. 138: Photos by Michael Litchfield
p. 146 (top right): Photo by Michael Litchfield
p. 148 (top left): Photo by Michael Litchfield

Chapter 7
p. 161 (left): Photo by Michael Litchfield
p. 167: Photo by Michael Litchfield

Chapter 8
p. 178 (right): Photo by Michael Litchfield
p. 186: Photo by Michael Litchfield

Chapter 12
p. 272 (bottom): Photo by Michael Litchfield

Chapter 14
p. 297: Photo by Michael Litchfield
p. 301 (bottom): Photo by Rob Wotzak, courtesy of Fine Homebuilding © The Taunton Press, Inc.
p. 307 (top): Photo by Michael Litchfield

If you like this book, you'll love *Fine Homebuilding*.

Read *Fine Homebuilding* Magazine:

Get eight issues, including our two annual design issues, *Houses* and *Kitchens & Baths*, plus FREE tablet editions. Packed with expert advice and skill-building techniques, every issue provides the latest information on quality building and remodeling.

Subscribe today at:
FineHomebuilding.com/4Sub

Discover our *Fine Homebuilding* Online Store:

It's your destination for premium resources from America's best builders: how-to and design books, DVDs, videos, special interest publications, and more.

Visit today at:
FineHomebuilding.com/4More

Get our FREE *Fine Homebuilding* eNewsletter:

Keep up with the current best practices, the newest tools, and the latest materials, plus free tips and advice from *Fine Homebuilding* editors.

Sign up, it's free:
FineHomebuilding.com/4Newsletter

Become a FineHomebuilding.com member:

Join to enjoy unlimited access to premium content and exclusive benefits, including: 1,400+ articles; 350 tip, tool, and technique videos; our how-to video project series; over 1,600 field-tested tips; monthly giveaways; tablet editions; contests; special offers; and more.

Discover more information online:
FineHomebuilding.com/4Join